HISTORICAL DICTIONARIES OF INTELLIGENCE AND COUNTERINTELLIGENCE
Jon Woronoff, Series Editor

1. *British Intelligence*, by Nigel West, 2005.
2. *United States Intelligence*, by Michael A. Turner, 2006.
3. *Israeli Intelligence*, by Ephraim Kahana, 2006.
4. *International Intelligence*, by Nigel West, 2006.
5. *Russian and Soviet Intelligence*, by Robert W. Pringle, 2006.
6. *Cold War Counterintelligence*, by Nigel West, 2007.
7. *World War II Intelligence*, by Nigel West, 2008.

Historical Dictionary of World War II Intelligence

Nigel West

Historical Dictionaries of
Intelligence and Counterintelligence, No. 7

The Scarecrow Press, Inc.
Lanham, Maryland • Toronto • Plymouth, UK
2008

SCARECROW PRESS, INC.

Published in the United States of America
by Scarecrow Press, Inc.
A wholly owned subsidiary of
The Rowman & Littlefield Publishing Group, Inc.
4501 Forbes Boulevard, Suite 200, Lanham, Maryland 20706
www.scarecrowpress.com

Estover Road
Plymouth PL6 7PY
United Kingdom

British Library Cataloguing in Publication Information Available

Library of Congress Cataloging-in-Publication Data

West, Nigel.
  Historical dictionary of World War II intelligence / Nigel West.
    p. cm. — (Historical dictionaries of intelligence and counterintelligence ;
No.7)
  Includes bibliographical references and index.
  ISBN-13: 978-0-8108-5822-0 (hardcover : alk. paper)
  ISBN-10: 0-8108-5822-3 (hardcover : alk. paper)
  1. World War, 1939–1945—Secret service—History—Dictionaries. 2.
Intelligence service—History—Dictionaries. 3. Military intelligence—History—
Dictionaries. 4. Espionage—History—Dictionaries. I. Title. 010a 2007026510

D810.S7W385 2008
940.54'8503—dc22

                                                            2007026526

⊗™ The paper used in this publication meets the minimum requirements of
American National Standard for Information Sciences—Permanence of Paper
for Printed Library Materials, ANSI/NISO Z39.48-1992.
Manufactured in the United States of America.

Der Nachrichtendienst ist ein Herrendienst
(Intelligence is a gentleman's job)
—Admiral Wilhelm Canaris

Contents

Editor's Foreword

Espionage and counterespionage are a dangerous game at any time, but never more so than in time of war, and that is when the skills honed over years and decades are most decisive. No war has experienced a more bitter and pitiless undercover struggle than World War II, and never were the stakes higher. This explains why the main players—Great Britain, the United States, and the Soviet Union on one side, Nazi Germany, Fascist Italy, and Imperial Japan on the other—but smaller ones as well, such as Franco's Spain and Salazar's Portugal and even neutral Sweden and Switzerland, were so deeply involved. But this conflict is notoriously difficult to follow, given the secrecy (and also confusion) involved, some of it coincidental and some intentional. And it has taken more than half a century to bring to light some of the operations of Britain's MI5 and MI6, America's FBI, the Soviet Union's GRU, Germany's SD, Italy's OVRA, Japan's Kempe'tai, and others. So, now that the archives are opening, it is a particularly opportune moment to look back and survey this period.

This is done in its own way by *Historical Dictionary of World War II Intelligence*. To begin with, there is a substantial chronology that lists events year by year and month by month. Next, the intelligence war is set in the context of the broader real war in the introduction. Then, in the dictionary section, several hundred entries describe the main intelligence organizations; the major and many minor operations; both active and imaginary tricks of deception; numerous agents, double agents, and even triple agents, and the people who ran them; and those at the top who had the last word, even if they were unaware of precisely what was going on. Because so many of the operations and personnel are known better under their code names than their real ones, these entries can be decisive in making sense of events. And the dictionary section not only is interesting and informative in its own right but can also help readers make more sense of the rest of the literature, which is presented in a useful bibliography. Not to be forgotten is a list of acronyms and abbreviations, essential in this field, where most organizations are known not by their full name but their initials or code.

This latest volume in the Historical Dictionaries of Intelligence and Counterintelligence series was written by Nigel West, who was voted the Expert's Expert by a panel of spy writers and more recently was awarded the U.S. Association of Former Intelligence Officers' first Lifetime Literature Achievement Award. He has been publishing books on this highly specialized and recondite field for nearly three decades, most of them concentrating on World War II. Among them are *Unreliable Witness: Espionage Myths of the Second World War* and *MI5: British Security Service Operations, 1909–1945*. Three belong to this series, namely, *Historical Dictionary of British Intelligence*, *Historical Dictionary of International Intelligence*, and *Historical Dictionary of Cold War Counterintelligence*. In addition to writing, West teaches the history of postwar intelligence to the current intelligence community at the Center for Counterintelligence and Security Studies in Alexandria, Virginia. It would be hard to find a more experienced and knowledgeable guide.

Jon Woronoff
Series Editor

Acronyms and Abbreviations

AIB	Allied Intelligence Bureau
BCRA	Bureau Central de Renseignements et d'Action (Free French intelligence service)
B-Dienst	Beobachtungdienst (Kriegsmarine radio monitoring service)
BSC	British Security Coordination
CBME	Combined Bureau Middle East
CIA	Central Intelligence Agency
CICI	Combined Intelligence Centre Iraq
CIFE	Combined Intelligence Far East
CoI	Coordinator of Information
CPGB	Communist Party of Great Britain
CPSU	Communist Party of the Soviet Union
CPUSA	Communist Party of the United States of America
CSDIC	Combined Services Detailed Interrogation Centre
DGII	Dirección General de Información e Inteligencia (Chile)
DGS	Dirección General de Seguridad (Spain)
DGSS	Direction Générale des Services Spéciaux
DIB	Delhi Intelligence Bureau
DMI	Director of Military Intelligence
DNI	Director of Naval Intelligence
DOPS	Direção da Ordem Política e Social (Brazil)
DSM	Direction des Services des Renseignements et des Services de Securité Militaire
FBI	Federal Bureau of Investigation
FECB	Far East Combined Bureau
FHO	Fremde Heere Ost
FRA	Försvarsväsendets Radioanstalt (Sweden)
FUSAG	First United States Army Group
GC&CS	Government Code and Cypher School

GCHQ	Government Communications Headquarters
GRU	Glavnoye Razvedyvatel'noe Upravlenie (Soviet military intelligence service)
IIC	Interdepartmental Intelligence Conference
IPI	Indian Political Intelligence Bureau
ISLD	Inter-Services Liaison Department
JIC	Joint Intelligence Committee
KO	Kriegsorganization
KPD	Kommunistische Partei Deutschlands (German Communist Party)
KPO	Kommunistische Partei Österreichs (Austrian Communist Party)
LATI	Linee Aeree Transcontinentali Italiane
MEIC	Middle East Intelligence Centre
MEW	Ministry of Economic Warfare
MI5	Security Service (Great Britain)
MI6	Secret Intelligence Service (Great Britain)
NID	Naval Intelligence Division
NKVD	Narodni Kommisariat Vnutrennikh Del (Soviet Intelligence Service)
OB	Ossewa Brandwag (South Africa)
OIC	Operational Intelligence Centre
ONI	Office of Naval Intelligence
OP-20G	U.S. Navy cryptographic staff
OSS	Office of Strategic Services
OTP	One-Time Pad
OVRA	Opera Volontaria di Repressione dell'Antifascismo (Italy)
POW	Prisoner of War
PVDE	Polícia do Vigilância e Defesa do Estado (Portugal)
PWE	Political Warfare Executive
RAF	Royal Air Force
RCMP	Royal Canadian Mounted Police
RDF	Radio Direction-Finding
RHSA	Reichssicherheitshauptamt
RID	Radio Intelligence Division
RSS	Radio Security Service
RVPS	Royal Victoria Patriotic School
SCI	Special Counter-Intelligence unit

SCU	Special Communications Unit
SD	Sicherheitsdienst (Nazi security service)
SHAEF	Supreme Headquarters Allied Expeditionary Force
SIA	Servizio di Informazioni Aeronautiche (Italy)
SIB	Special Intelligence Bureau (Australia)
SIG	Special Interrogation Group
SIM	Servicio de Inteligencia Militar (Spain)
SIM	Servizio di Informazione Militare (Italy)
SIME	Security Intelligence Middle East
SIS	Servizio di Informazione Segrete (Italy)
SIS	Signals Intelligence Service (U.S.)
SIS	Special Intelligence Service (U.S.)
Smersh	Smert Shpionam
SOE	Special Operations Executive
SR	Service de Renseignements (French intelligence service)
TR	Travaux Ruraux
YCL	Young Communist League

Chronology

1939 **September:** War commences with bogus attack on Gleiwitz. SNOW exchanges radio messages with the Abwehr. **October:** G.W. recruited by the Abwehr. Hans Oster warns Col. Gijsbertis Sas of an imminent Nazi invasion of Holland. **November:** Venlo incident occurs. Adm. Hugh Sinclair dies and is replaced by Col. Stewart Menzies. **December:** *Admiral Graf Spee* scuttled in Montevideo. Mathilde Krafft interned in London.

1940 **January:** Maj. Hellmuth Reinberger detained at Mechelen. Kriegsmarine divers recover Royal Navy ciphers from three submarines. **February:** RAINBOW starts sending letters containing secret writing. **March:** Lord Hankey conducts review of MI5 and MI6 with John Cairncross as his secretary. **April:** RAINBOW recruited by MI5. HMS *Hardy*'s ciphers compromised. **May:** Tyler Kent, Anna Wolkoff, and Christabel Nicholson arrested. William Rolph commits suicide. Dismissal of Vernon Kell and Eric Holt-Wilson. **June:** France surrenders. Anthony Blunt joins MI5. British Security Coordination (BSC) opens in New York. Henry Anthell killed over the Baltic. **July:** The *Arandora Star* sunk by U-47. **August:** Luftwaffe bombs radar stations on England's south coast. **September:** SUMMER and TATE arrested in Cambridgeshire. José Waldburg, Carl Meier, Sjord Pons, and Charles Van Den Kieboom arrested in Kent. Robert Petter, Karl Drücke, and Vera von Schalburg arrested in Scotland. GIRAFFE volunteers to MI5. **October:** GANDER arrested. Japanese introduce the JN-25B cipher. **November:** German prisoner of war reveals imminent Luftwaffe raid on Coventry or Birmingham. **December:** TRICYCLE arrives in London.

1941 **January:** First meeting of the Twenty Committee. CELERY visits Lisbon. Ursula Kuczynski arrives in Oxford. **February:** Josef

Jakobs arrested in Huntingdonshire. George Armstrong arrested in Boston. **March:** SNOW interned at Dartmoor. DRAGONFLY writes to the Abwehr. Sir David Petrie appointed MI5's director-general. An Enigma captured aboard the *Krebs*. **April:** MUTT and JEFF land in Scotland. The body of Jan Ter Braak found in Cambridge. **May:** Karel Richter arrested in Hertfordshire. BALLOON begins writing to the Abwehr. GELATINE writes to the Abwehr. The *München*'s Enigma keys recovered. U-110's Enigma seized. **June:** FATHER reaches Great Britain. The *Lauenberg*'s Enigma captured. Robey Liebbrandt lands in South Africa. **July:** THE SNARK recruited by MI5. **August:** TRICYCLE flies to New York. SWEET WILLIAM penetrates the Spanish embassy in London. **September:** Alphons Timmerman arrested in Glasgow. Kim Philby joins MI6. **October:** Richard Sorge and Max Klausen arrested in Tokyo. **November:** U.S. Navy cryptographers start to read the Japanese JN-25B code. ISOS traffic reveals a German spy at work in the British embassy in Ankara. Operation GUY FAWKES completed. **December:** Japanese attack Pearl Harbor. PEPPERMINT penetrates the Spanish embassy in London.

1942   **January:** USS *Gudgeon* sinks the I-73. Abwehr office in Lisbon burgled. **February:** Luis Calvo interned. José Estella arrested in Gibraltar. The Kriegsmarine introduces SHARK and prevents U-boat traffic from being read for 10 months. **March:** Paul Thümmel arrested in Prague. **April:** Reinhard Gehlen appointed chief of Fremde Heere Ost. GARBO arrives in Bristol. **May:** Japanese fleet defeated at the Battle of the Coral Sea. Johannes Dronkers arrested at Harwich. **June:** Operation PASTORIUS fails in the United States. Office of Strategic Services (OSS) created. American military attaché Black Code is replaced. Japanese fleet defeated at the Battle of Midway. **July:** Franciscus Winter arrested at Gourock. **August:** Duncan Scott-Ford arrested in Salford. **September:** Adm. John Godfrey dismissed as director of naval intelligence. Germans recover Royal Navy codes from HMS *Sikh*. **October:** Capt. Edmund Rushbrooke appointed director of naval intelligence. BRONX begins writing to the Abwehr. BRUTUS recruited by MI5. A Free French courier, Lt. Clamorgan, killed in Spain. U-559 boarded and her Enigma recovered. **November:** Germany occupies Vichy France. Sicherheitsdienst plans LONG JUMP. **December:** ZIGZAG lands in East Anglia. SHARK Enigma key broken.

1943 **January:** Ernst Kaltenbrunner appointed head of Sicherheitsdienst. Joint Security Control established. **February:** Hans Bernd Gisevius volunteers to spy for Allen Dulles in Bern. Schnorkels introduced into U-boats. **March:** GARBO establishes radio contact with Madrid. TANGERINE recruited by MI5. SHARK resists cryptographic attack for much of the month. **April:** METEOR recruited by MI5. PUPPET makes contact with the Abwehr. Adm. Isomotu Yamamoto shot down over Bougainville Island in the Pacific. **May:** Joseph Vanhove arrested in Leuchars. Operation MINCEMEAT completed. **June:** Luis Cordon-Cuenca arrested in Gibraltar. Douglas Springhall, Olive Sheehan, and Ormond Uren arrested in London. Fritz Kolbe volunteers to spy for Dulles in Bern. **July:** José Munoz arrested in Gibraltar. FIDO reaches Great Britain. GUINEA sells secrets to the Germans in Tangier. **August:** Operation BUNBURY completed. TREASURE reaches London. **September:** Benito Mussolini rescued by Otto Skorzeny. Ray Milne suspected of being a Soviet spy in MI6. **October:** Adm. Wilhelm Canaris visits Juan Vigon in Spain. **November:** Crossbow Committee appointed. Oswald Job arrested in London. SNIPER contacts the Abwehr. JUNIOR defects in Lisbon. **December:** Defection of Erich Vermehren in Istanbul. FREAK reaches London.

1944 **January:** Convoy JW 56A compromised by spies in Iceland. COLOSSUS installed at Bletchley Park. **February:** Pierre Neukermans arrested in London. The Abwehr absorbed into the Reichssicherheitshauptamt. **March:** CICERO resigns as valet to the British ambassador in Ankara. Oswald Job executed. **April:** Gen. Karl-Heinrich Kreipe abducted in Crete. HAT TRICK lands on the Malabar coast. **May:** Operation COPPERHEAD completed in Gibraltar. ARTIST abducted in Lisbon and returned to Germany. **June:** ZIGZAG lands in East Anglia for the second time. Rudolf Rössler arrested by the Bundespolizei. **July:** The latest radar-equipped Ju-88G night fighter lands at Woodbridge by accident. **August:** The 212 Committee formed by 21st Army Group. Emile Kliemann arrested in Paris and interrogated in London. **September:** Capture of German intelligence archive in Brussels. P. G. Wodehouse arrested in Paris. FATHER arrives in London. **October:** Mathilde Carré charged in Paris with collaboration. Alfred Langbein gives himself up in Canada. Japanese defeated at the Battle of Leyte Gulf. **November:** KING KONG arrested and confesses. COSSACK arrested near Lille.

December: Panzerbrigade 150 infiltrates American lines during Ardennes offensive.

1945   **January:** TATE reports on notional British minefields in the Channel. Alan Foote and Leopold Trepper reach Moscow. **February:** Alger Hiss advises President Franklin D. Roosevelt at Yalta conference. ASPIRIN and ANTHONY reach the United States. **March:** Allied search for Nazi Werewolf organization. Seventy German prisoners escape from camp at Bridgend, Wales. **April:** Canaris executed at Flossenburg. Nordhausen underground V-2 factory captured by U.S. Army. **May:** Germany surrenders. German rocket experts surrender in the Tyrol. Twenty Committee closes down. Japanese cruiser *Hugaro* sunk. **June:** Carré deported to Paris. **July:** Allied zones of occupation established in Berlin. **August:** Atom bombs dropped on Hiroshima and Nagasaki. Japan surrenders and war ends.

Introduction

Few would have expected all the secrets of World War II to be revealed within the first decade or two following the end of the conflict, but not many might have imagined that important documents shedding new light on covert activities conducted by all the protagonists would continue to emerge some 60 years later.

In the immediate postwar era, information was disclosed, usually from the participants in what has been termed the "shadow war," of the existence of hitherto secret agencies. In Germany, it was the Abwehr and the Sicherheitsdienst; in Britain MI5, the Secret Intelligence Service (MI6), and Special Operations Executive (SOE); in the United States, the Office of Strategic Services (OSS) and the Special Intelligence Service of the Federal Bureau of Investigation (FBI); in Japan, the Kempet'ai; in Italy, the Servizio di Informazione Militare. In addition, all the governments in exile maintained covert organizations, with the Norwegians, Dutch, French, Poles, Czechs, and Belgians running their military intelligence operations from London. Indeed, secret operations were also conducted by ostensibly neutral countries, with the Spanish, Swedes, Argentines, Chileans, Brazilians, and Portuguese possessing intelligence agencies that were especially active. Even the Swiss military intelligence service and Bundespolizei played a significant, if hitherto unpublicized, role in the conflict.

Some of these organizations, such as SOE and the OSS, did not survive long into the peace, and successive British governments maintained the convenient fiction that MI6 had been a purely wartime expedient. A few authors published accounts of their adventures, but it was not until Prof. M. R. D. Foot was commissioned to write an official history, *SOE in France*, in 1961 that the public was allowed to glimpse the extent of the secret world. Then Kermit Roosevelt's two-volume study

of the OSS was released, and thereafter there were many more significant disclosures that changed how the war would be seen by subsequent
generations, and even by some participants. The "need-to-know" prin-
ciple that had been applied so rigorously during hostilities gave way to
a new inquisitiveness, and previously closed areas of research were
opened up by the acknowledgment in 1972 that MI5 had exercised almost total control over the enemy's very extensive espionage networks
in Britain, and the admission in 1974 that codebreakers based at Bletchley Park had succeeded in decrypting a large, war-shortening part of the
Axis communications.

Changes in American, British, and even Soviet official attitudes to
declassification in the 1980s allowed thousands of secret documents to
be made available for public examination, and the result was extensive
revisionism of the conventional histories of the conflict, which previously had excluded references to secret intelligence sources. Since
many of the histories had been written by those with a firsthand knowledge of these sources and methods, this self-censorship had the effect of
creating an image that was missing a vital dimension. Numerous historians, Winston Churchill included, deliberately omitted crucial aspects
of their chosen subjects so as to avoid compromising the techniques
that, in the early part of the Cold War, looked as though they might have
another operational relevance. In fact, of course, Moscow had been all
too well aware of the most highly classified achievements of the war's
secret warriors, largely through the wholesale penetration by moles and
Communist sympathizers of the agencies concerned. Thus, when the
Soviet bloc collapsed in 1991, there was no longer any good reason to
staunch the flow of declassified material into the public domain, and the
old Russian archives themselves were encouraged to make their contribution to the process.

At long last, it can now be claimed that there are few, if any, wartime
intelligence mysteries left to be solved. The double agents were revealed in 1972, and the ULTRA secret exposed two years later. Official
histories have been published of SOE's organization and its operations,
MI5, the OSS, the Political Warfare Executive, British Security Coordination in New York, Camp 020, and strategic deception, as well as *The
Guy Liddell Diaries*. From Moscow, the Russian foreign intelligence
service has published an official account of the Great Patriotic War, and
most recently, a volume on Anglo-Polish intelligence cooperation was

released jointly in Warsaw and London. We now have official confirmation of the relationship between a beautiful MI6 agent, Halina Szymanska, and Adm. Wilhelm Canaris, the enigmatic chief of the Abwehr. We have learned the truth about the Nazi spy code-named CICERO who, most notoriously, penetrated the British embassy in Ankara, and the documents charting the incompetence that allowed the Germans to manipulate the Dutch resistance have been released.

Along the way, many myths have been dispelled. Coventry was not sacrificed to protect ULTRA. Kriegsmarine U-boats were never refueled at secret bases on Ireland's west coast. President Franklin D. Roosevelt did not have advance knowledge of the Japanese attack on Pearl Harbor. Bletchley Park did not leak intercepts to Moscow through the Rote Drei in Switzerland. The true authorship of the Oslo Report has been established. No undetected Nazi agent compromised the planning of D-Day. Operation MINCEMEAT, made famous by the book and movie *The Man Who Never Was*, did not fool the Germans. Kim Philby did not intervene to prevent separate peace negotiations with Hitler's opponents. J. Edgar Hoover never ignored crucial strategic warnings from a British double agent, and the Nazis were not denied an atomic weapon because of a daring sabotage raid on Vermork in Norway.

On the other hand, we learned some astonishing new secrets, now established as fact, such as the extent to which Erwin Rommel relied on information supplied unwittingly by an American military attaché's daily dispatches when he planned his Afrika Korps campaign in the first half of 1942. There is now confirmation, in the form of declassified files, of the real reasons behind the crushing Japanese defeat at Midway.

The extraordinary picture that emerges of the war's covert operations from the published literature is a mixture of fact and fiction, with authors often working in an information vacuum to explain some astonishingly bizarre events and achievements. However, without access to the original files, some journalists and historians bridged the lacunae with supposition presented, at best, as informed conjecture. Very often, though, it was sheer fabrication, and served only to muddy the already opaque waters even further. Who would have believed that the Nazis planned to destroy the Allied economies with counterfeit currency, that the British would send an alcoholic actor to the Mediterranean to masquerade as the teetotaler Gen. Bernard Montgomery, or that the Americans would place a valuable cryptographic source in jeopardy for the opportunity to kill Adm. Isoroku Yamamoto? Very often, the truth was much, much stranger than anything a novelist could invent, which may be why Dennis Wheatley proved such a success as a deception planner for the War Cabinet, Graham Greene was productive for MI6 in Freetown, Kenneth Benton represented Section V in Madrid, J. C. Masterman and Jack Bingham handled MI5's double agents, and Ian Fleming positively thrived in the Naval Intelligence Division. All would turn their imaginations postwar to writing espionage thrillers set in wartime. Even a minister, Duff Cooper, was inspired to turn his hand, in *Operation Heartbreak*, to a plot he had first encountered in classified files while overseeing MI5 in the War Cabinet.

As the bigger picture emerged, the role played by intelligence during World War II came into sharper focus. The revelations concerning the extent to which double agents were manipulated to mislead the enemy prompted a reassessment of the influence of strategic deception, and the great gamble of D-Day began to make more sense, especially as the German analysts were naturally predisposed to believe that the Pas-de-Calais was the obvious invasion site and that the landings in Normandy probably were a diversionary feint, as claimed by GARBO, TATE, BRUTUS, and BRONX. Their achievement was extraordinary, but we now have details of equally imaginative double agents run by the FBI, the Royal Canadian Mounted Police, and other Allied agencies in the Near and Far East.

In the scientific field, the research into proximity fuzes, magnetic mines, snorkels, air navigation systems, and Hitler's vengeance weapons was heavily reliant on agent reports, prisoner interrogation, signals intelligence, aerial reconnaissance, "special means," and other secret sources.

Similarly, as the breakthroughs achieved at Bletchley Park became public knowledge, the triumphs accomplished against the Afrika Korps and the U-boat wolfpacks in the North Atlantic became more explicable. Yet, even after the codebreakers had acknowledged their hitherto secret contribution, certain aspects of their work remained off-limits. Any open discussion of the methods used to read the German Foreign Ministry's one-time pad ciphers was thought to have the potential for compromising similar projects undertaken later against supposedly unbreakable cryptosystems, and no mention was ever allowed of that most fascinating but illicit source code-named TRIPLEX.

The attack on Soviet encrypted communications was also omitted from the growing catalog of Anglo-American intelligence successes, and that particular source went unmentioned even after the declassification in July 1995 of the VENONA messages. Thus some of the intelligence operations of World War II would have a lasting impact on the remainder of the century. But how did this come about?

One explanation might be the very nature of the conflict itself, and the time in which it was fought. From an intelligence perspective, World War II was, as we have seen, a time of great technological innovation, fought by leaders who may have had a grasp of wireless communications but little knowledge of aerodynamics, atomic power, or missile technology. Churchill had fought in the Boer War, Hitler on the Marne, but neither Stalin nor Roosevelt had any significant personal experience of combat. Stalin's injured arm, crushed by a runaway phaeton in an accident while he was a student in Gori, had excluded him from serving in the tsar's army on medical grounds, while Roosevelt merely visited the front briefly in 1918 on an inspection visit. Nevertheless, all four leaders clearly appreciated the age-old need for good intelligence, and each in their different ways came, to a greater or lesser extent, to depend on their secret sources. Churchill had long nurtured a deep appreciation for intercepts and covert warfare; Hitler gambled on sophisticated secret weapons that he believed would turn the tide in his favor; and Roosevelt was brought into the war by a terrible intelligence failure and authorized the establishment of the first unified American intelligence agency, the OSS. As for Stalin, he saw the NKVD, the Communist Party's sword and shield, as the indispensable backbone of his power.

For each, intelligence played a vital role in influencing the way they prosecuted the hostilities, and not surprisingly the war was fought, from the very first opening salvos at Gleiwitz, by clandestine operators. Hitler's pretext for the Nazi invasion of Poland was an intelligence operation, a bogus attack on a German radio station on the border carried out by his own Sicherheitsdienst, which distributed dead bodies on the scene (actually concentration camp victims dressed for the part) to provide the evidence of a deliberate provocation. Thereafter, as the conflict spread across the globe, each country opted for the Axis or the Allies, leaving covert warfare to be conducted by those that declared themselves neutral. Whereas World War I had left much of the world untouched, there was scarcely a territory anywhere, however remote, that was not affected by the hostilities, with South America and even the Caribbean drawn into the war. Buenos Aires, Santiago, and Rio de Janeiro became important centers of German espionage, while Trinidad and Bermuda were transformed into British intelligence bases, with searches conducted from Jamaica for secret U-boat fuel dumps. The neutral capitals became hotbeds of intrigue, and some of the most remarkable secret operations were conducted in Lisbon, Madrid, Ankara, Bern, and Stockholm.

Any military historian will confirm that intelligence has always played a significant role in every conflict, but whereas clandestine operations were conducted in World War I and to some extent in the Spanish Civil War and the Abyssinian campaign, it was the period between 1939 and 1945 that really shaped what are recognized today as the separate disciplines of covert activities, signals interception, the management of agent networks, escape lines, and all the other operations now associated with secret intelligence.

Of course, a distinction has to be drawn between intelligence operations, which are the subject of this historical dictionary, and what became known as "special operations"—the paramilitary, guerrilla, partisan, and resistance work undertaken in enemy-occupied territory. Although commonly mixed together, or confused, special operations and secret intelligence are two very different disciplines, often with mutually exclusive objectives.

Special operations developed from the tactics adopted by Irish republicans during "the Troubles," unorthodox warfare that enabled a small group of well-organized nationalists to pin down a large part of the British Army until their political goals had been achieved. This was accomplished by sabotage, hit-and-run ambushes, sniping incidents, assassinations, and the deployment of armed irregulars choosing their own methods of engaging the enemy, instead of fighting the set-piece battles their opponents had been trained for, thereby preventing them from bringing their vastly superior forces to bear. Now referred to in modern jargon as "asymmetric warfare," the doctrine developed during World War II exploited the natural inflexibility of the uniformed battalions and took full advantage of well-armed militias selecting their targets, undertaking daring raids, and then effectively disappearing by melting away into the local population. Such tactics adopted against the Axis led to ruthless reprisals, the seizure of hostages, mass executions, and other atrocities that often only served to harden the occupied against their oppressors.

The separation between operations and intelligence can be illustrated in the case of a strategically located road bridge behind enemy lines. An intelligence agent might be infiltrated and concealed specifically to watch enemy movements and report intelligence, whereas a special operations saboteur might be sent to destroy the bridge. If the latter carries out his mission, it will attract troops into the area who may endanger the intelligence agent, whose mission anyway has become redundant. With the risk of such counterproductive overlapping operations being high, the need for close coordination becomes essential, and by 1944 the Allies had grown adept at mounting special operations in support of intelligence objectives, a good example being the concentration of attacks on telegraph poles and telephone exchanges in an effort to force the Germans to rely on wireless communications instead of the landlines that could not so easily be intercepted.

The objectives of the British and American intelligence agencies were hugely ambitious. They sought, after the OSS's creation, not just to collect information about their Axis adversaries but actually to control and manipulate them. This was a tremendous departure from intelligence orthodoxy and yet proved largely successful. MI5 ran a double-cross system of labyrinthine complexity and, with MI6, took the concept of strategic deception to new heights, effectively managing the input available to the German High Command's intelligence analysts. Whereas other agencies had rather less elevated goals, the Allies developed an integrated, coordinated structure that encouraged cross-fertilization. Messages written for controlled enemy agents provided the texts for cryptographic exploitation. Overlapping channels gave the enemy the necessary pieces of the jigsaw for them to draw the intended, but wholly erroneous, conclusions.

The French, in contrast, saw their myriad competing intelligence agencies as instruments dedicated to restoring political power once the occupier had been removed, and little of their effort was dedicated to collecting information about the enemy. In contrast, the Norwegian, Czech, and Dutch services concentrated on finding new ways of harrying the Nazis, their priority being liberation from a hated oppressor.

Nevertheless, there are just a few remaining mysteries. For example, where did the Soviet spy ring in Switzerland known as the Rote Drei acquire its accurate information about German strategic intentions? Until the Swiss Bundespolizei files are declassified, the full story of that particular episode will continue to puzzle historians and the wider international intelligence community. In the meantime, most of the rest of the story of World War II intelligence can now be told comprehensively.

The Dictionary

– A –

A-3. A radiotelephone scrambler developed by Bell Laboratories in 1939. The A-3 was intended to prevent the interception and decryption of sensitive transatlantic conversations conducted between the White House and 10 Downing Street by inverting the wavelengths and jumping frequencies. The objective, to distort the voices beyond recognition, failed on 7 September 1941 when the Deutsche Reichspost succeeded in monitoring the traffic from a dedicated intercept station built at Eindhoven in Holland. The cabling in the United States was routed to the American Telegraph & Telephone exchange in Walker Street, New York, and in London the equipment was installed in the basement of the Selfridges department store in Oxford Street.

The German decryption process, supervised by the **Sicherheitsdienst**, became fully operational in March 1942 but was compromised because the decrypts were communicated to Berlin by a Geheimschreiber channel that itself had been compromised.

ABWEHR. The principal **German intelligence** service before and during World War II until it was absorbed into the **Reichssicherheitshauptamt** in February 1944, the Abwehr was a decentralized organization headed in Berlin by Adm. **Wilhelm Canaris** at a headquarters located in a Prussian Junker villa at 74/76 Tirpitzuffer, overlooking the Tiergarten, with operations overseas handled by *Abstellen* (Ast) located in 21 individual German military districts. Each *Abstelle* supervised operations abroad, with Ast Hamburg running agents in Great Britain and the United States. The Abwehr was staffed by military personnel, many of them committed anti-Nazis like Canaris's deputy, a cavalry officer, Col. **Hans Oster**, and Gen. **Erwin von Lahousen**, the head of Abteilung II, the sabotage branch. The Abwehr also drew on a paramilitary branch, the **Brandenburger Regiment**, for volunteers to undertake missions abroad.

The Abwehr's structure consisted of three numbered branches, of which the first, Abteilung I, headed by Col. Hans Pieckenbrock (later succeeded by Georg Hansen), was responsible for the collection of intelligence for the Wehrmacht, Luftwaffe, and Kriegsmarine. The headquarters organization was mirrored overseas by *Kriegsorganizations* (KO) attached to diplomatic missions in neutral capitals, concentrating on **Ankara**, **Madrid**, **Lisbon**, and **Stockholm**, and in Axis countries, including Bulgaria, Italy, and Hungary. Each KO included a representative of the various individual military branches. Subordinate to the KOs were *Nebenstellen*, consisting of substations, usually under consular or commercial cover, reporting to the center.

As an intelligence agency collecting foreign intelligence, the Abwehr performed badly, failing to predict Allied landings on Madagascar in September 1942 and in North Africa in November 1942 and unable to give any advance notice of the January 1943 Casablanca Conference. The Abwehr's limited analytical resources found it hard to discriminate between reliable and poor information regarding the opening of a second front and were misled over **D-Day**. On the occasions the Abwehr acquired accurate intelligence—from agents in Lisbon and Melilla regarding an imminent landing on Sicily—the news reached Berlin too late. The organization's bad performance may in part be explained by a lack of enthusiasm among senior personnel, who were largely anti-Nazi, and the fact that its communications had been compromised at the outset of the war.

ACCOST. British code name for a six-man mission of Annamese dropped into Vietnam in July 1945 but captured by the Japanese. A plan to maintain contact with them for **deception** purposes was abandoned when Tokyo surrendered.

ADDICT. A Hungarian living in Rome who was a stay-behind agent working under Allied control and passed false information to his German controllers from June 1944 until the end of the war.

ADMIRAL GRAF SPEE. The famous pocket battleship *Admiral Graf Spee* was scuttled on Adolf Hitler's direct order in December 1939 after she had been disabled in the first major naval engagement of the conflict, despite having inflicted heavy losses on HMS *Exeter*, *Ajax*, and *Achilles*. Under international convention, the *Graf Spee* was allowed 72 hours of sanctuary in harbor, but when the time came to put to sea and face what were believed mistakenly to be superior forces of up to nine enemy ships, Capt. Hans Langsdorff set off explosives on her and then shot himself a few days later. The hulk burned for a week before finally sinking, and the British then bought the salvage rights to examine her radar equipment.

The British had transmitted bogus signals to give the impression that the enemy force included a battleship and an aircraft carrier, and Langsdorff, having intercepted the dummy wireless traffic, was convinced that any further fighting would be futile. Recognizing that any future change in Uruguay's neutral status might risk an interned *Graf Spee* falling into Allied hands intact, and accepting that it was impossible to reach Buenos Aires without venturing out beyond the shallows, the captain was given permission to blow up his own ship.

The *Graf Spee* turned out to be the **Special Intelligence Service**'s longest case in **Argentina**, where the entire crew of 1,150 was supposed to have been interned. Thirty-six were killed in the naval engagement off the River Plate and 850 were repatriated in February 1946, but the remaining 264 disappeared, and there were only six officers left to make the voyage home.

The Germans had pulled off something of a coup by arranging for their men to be landed in Argentina rather than Uruguay, and they achieved this by transferring them covertly from the *Graf Spee* onto another German ship, the *Tacoma*, a blockaded Hamburg-America Line merchantman that had been moored in the harbor and had accompanied the warship on her final short voyage out into the estuary. Instead of returning the crew to Montevideo, as anticipated, the *Tacoma* unexpectedly transferred them onto smaller vessels and dispatched them to Buenos Aires. Between 30 and 40 of the crew had been released from internment on parole and had disappeared in an operation masterminded by Capt. Dietrich Niebuhr, previously the head of the **Abwehr**'s naval branch. Niebuhr organized an escape route run by his assistant attachés, Lt. Franz Mammen and Lt. Johannes Muller, and assigned to himself the *Graf Spee*'s only Spanish-speaking officer, Korvetkapitän Robert Höpfner, for liaison purposes.

Niebuhr's group of subordinates included several who ran their own spy rings, and among them was Rudolf Hepe of the Antonio Delfino Company, a subsidiary of the Hamburg-South America Line. Hepe had supplied the lighter ships and tugs that carried the *Graf Spee*'s crew to Argentina even before the Argentine government had agreed to accept them.

Mammen and Muller liaised with the internment camps and passed the evaders on to a local travel agent, Wilhelm von Seidlitz, who arranged for them to be escorted over the Andes. Once the *Graf Spee* men had crossed into **Chile**, they were escorted by Eugenio Knoll, code-named FLORES, and delivered to Friedrich von Schulz-Hausmann, the Norddeutscher Lloyd Line's agent in Valparaiso, who had been enrolled into the Abwehr during a visit to Hamburg in the summer of 1938. Code-named CASERO, he supervised the travel of about 50 *Graf Spee* crewmen on ships bound for Vladivostok, who completed their long journey home on the Trans-Siberian Express. The only losses were four officers who were arrested by Chilean police as they attempted to board a Japanese freighter in early October 1940 carrying false passports.

In the three years from January 1940, an estimated 200 men made their way back to Germany, most of them officers or technicians with skills in much demand in the Kriegsmarine. Among them were Korvetkapitän Jürgen Wattenberg, the *Graf Spee*'s chief navigating officer, and Oberleutnant Kurt Diggins, and their successful return to Germany, and their active role in the war, was later to be used by the Allies to tremendous effect.

When the Type IXC U-162 was sunk in September 1942 off **Trinidad** by the destroyers HMS *Pathfinder*, *Vimy*, and *Quentin*, Wattenberg was identified as the captain. On his previous patrol, he had sunk nine ships, including the **Brazilian** merchantman *Parbahyba*—a move that played into Allied hands because it infuriated the Brazilian government. Wattenberg's capture, and his transfer to a POW camp in Phoenix, Arizona (where he made several bids to escape), was eloquent proof of Argentine complacency, if not complicity. Under interrogation by U.S. **Office of Naval Intelligence** officers, Wattenberg revealed that he had escaped from Buenos Aires in April 1940 and had made his way on foot to Santiago with several others, and then home by civilian airlines via Bolivia, Pernambuco, Africa, Spain, and Italy before being assigned to the Second U-Boat Flotilla. During his three patrols from France, he had sunk a total of 14 ships.

Much the same happened with Diggins of the U-458, a new Type VII submarine that survived being caught on the surface by a Canadian Hudson aircraft off Halifax after it had attacked a British tanker, the *Arletta*, at the end of July 1942. Diggins had been Capt. Langsdorff's flag lieutenant and had landed in Uruguay with five *Graf Spee* Merchant Marine reserve officers who were intended to be posted to German embassies in South America, until the Allies lodged an objection. Diggins was required to report to the Montevideo police only once a week, so he was able to stow away on the nightly river steamer to Buenos Aires, where he was supplied with false papers and was able to make his way back to Germany. He was then assigned to the U-751, and in 1942 he was transferred to the U-458, which was sunk off Malta in 1943 by a destroyer, HMS *Easton*. Taken prisoner, Diggins, who was of English ancestry, was accommodated at POW camps in Malta, **Algiers**, and **Canada** before he was finally released in England in 1947. The fact that Diggins and Wattenberg had evaded their internment and returned to play such prominent roles in the sea war served to highlight the need to keep an eye on the internees and, when possible, to disrupt the enemy's escape organization.

Under pressure from the British, the Argentines agreed to move the officers and petty officers to a naval base on the island of Martín Garcia and disperse the rest of the crew, in groups of 100 each, to the provincial towns of Florencio Varela, Rosario, San Juan, Cordoba, Mendoza, and Santa Fe, but when this plan was announced, it prompted a wave of escapes. One of those to get clean away was the *Graf Spee*'s Panzerschiff (artillery technical officer), Friedrich-Wilhelm Rasenack, who escaped in March 1940 with a dozen others. In August, a further 17 escaped from the island, 30 miles up the estuary of the River Plate, which was only three miles from the Uruguay shore.

In 1944, after protests about the unhealthy conditions on Martín Garcia, the crew was moved to a hotel in the resort of Sierra de la

Ventana, where they remained even after their status changed in March 1945, when Argentina declared war on Germany and they became POWs rather than internees.

By January 1943, when U.S. pressure brought the Abwehr's escape operation to a conclusion, von Seidlitz and his collaborator, Eugen Langer, had smuggled 150 *Graf Spee* crewmen onto neutral ships in Argentina, and altogether a total of 90 Kriegsmarine officers or skilled technicians had made their way home to Germany.

"A" FORCE. The cover title of a British **deception** unit in the Middle East, headed by Dudley Clarke, which specialized in the development and management of usually **notional double agents** employed to convey false information to the Axis.

AKHMEDOV, ISMAIL. A **GRU defector**, Ismail Akhmedov failed to return from his mission in Turkey in May 1942 and remained there until after the end of hostilities, supplying the Turkish security service with a comprehensive insight into Soviet activities in the country. At the end of hostilities, the Turks revealed Akhmedov to the Allies, and he was interviewed in 1945 by a representative of the **Secret Intelligence Service**, **Kim Philby**.

ALARIC. The **Abwehr** code name for **Juan Pujol**.

ALCAZAR DE VELASCO, ANGEL. The press attaché at the Spanish embassy in London, Angel Alcazar de Velasco was an **Abwehr** spy whose sources were mainly **MI5 double agents**.

ALGIERS. A center of international espionage throughout the war, Algiers was the western Mediterranean headquarters of the **Secret Intelligence Service**, the local station headed by Col. A. G. Trevor Wilson, among whose subordinates was Malcolm Muggeridge. Their French counterparts were **Louis Rivet** and **Paul Paillole**, who established themselves in the city, in competition with the Free French, following their withdrawal from France in November 1942.

ALLIANCE. Created by a newspaper editor and controversial former French army officer, Georges Loustounou-Lacau, ALLIANCE was a resistance organization created in 1940 and based in Vichy. In November 1940 Loustounou-Lacau, code-named NAVARRE, sent Jacques Bridou to London to make contact with the Free French, but, reluctant to support Charles de Gaulle, was enrolled by the **Secret Intelligence Service**'s **(MI6)** French country section. Bridou was parachuted into unoccupied territory near Clermond-Ferrand in November, having arranged for Loustounou-Lacau to meet MI6's Kenneth Cohen in **Madrid**. At the rendezvous, Cohen entrusted NAVARRE with a transmitter, which was installed in Pau with the call sign KVL, the first of 30 radios that would be delivered to the ALLIANCE network. By the time it was closed down in July 1943 when 150 arrests were made, ALLIANCE had expanded to 3,000 agents.

ALLIED INTELLIGENCE BUREAU (AIB). Following the appointment of Gen. Douglas MacArthur as Supreme Allied Commander in the Pacific in 1942, the AIB was established in Melbourne to coordinate American, British, Dutch, and Australian intelligence operations in the theater.

AMICOL. *See* JADE.

ANDERSON. The location outside Colombo, Ceylon, for the Allied cryptographic center established in September 1943 to handle intercepted Japanese naval wireless traffic.

ANDROS. British code name for a source inside the Spanish Navy run by Comdr. Alan Hillgarth, the British naval attaché in **Madrid**. When employed to convey **deception** material to his **Sicherheitsdienst** controllers, ANDROS was code-named BLIND.

ANGEL ONE. British code name for the head of a notional spy ring in Thailand in 1943 that received messages daily over All-India Radio. The organization's deputy, based in Bangkok, was code-named FOSSIL, and in 1944 it was expanded by taking over the supervision of DICKENS in Jumbhorn, TROLLOPE in Kanchanburi, and THACKERAY in Chiang Rai.

ANKARA. The capital of neutral Turkey, Ankara became a center of international intrigue and espionage following the Axis occupation of the Balkans. Romanian and Bulgarian anti-Nazis sought refuge in Ankara, where the German embassy accommodated a sizable intelligence apparatus, headed by Ludwig Moyszich of the **Sicherheitsdienst**, and the British embassy included a **Secret Intelligence Service** station headed by Maj. Monty Chidson. Moyzisch achieved considerable success by recruiting two sources inside the British embassy, both domestic servants, one of whom he code-named CICERO. The British, Soviet, and German agencies were able to conduct their activities with minimal interference from the Turkish security apparatus, which was generally pro-Allied and, following the **defection** of the **GRU**'s **Ismail Akhmedov** in May 1942, anti-Soviet.

ANTHELL, HENRY W. Killed on 15 June 1940 when his Estonian airliner was attacked by Soviet fighters while flying from Tallinn to Helsinki, Henry Anthell was a cipher clerk at the U.S. embassy who had previously served in Moscow and Berlin. However, when his apartment was cleared by a State Department colleague, dozens of secret telegrams were found, including letters that suggested that Anthell had acquired a girlfriend in Moscow whom he wanted to bring to **Finland**. Also recovered were details of codes, notes of combination locks, and other sensitive documents. Further material showed that Anthell had been in correspondence with a Soviet official, Alexander Fomin, an alias adopted by Aleksandr S. Feklisov, a well-known **NKVD** handler.

ANTHONY. The **Federal Bureau of Investigation (FBI)** code name for a Russian recruited in **Madrid** by the **Abwehr** and sent to the United States in February 1945 on a mission to collect air intelligence. Run as a **double agent** by the FBI, ANTHONY was known as CAMCASE.

ANVIL. Allied code name for the invasion of southern France in 1944.

APOSTLE. British code name for a **Sicherheitsdienst** stay-behind agent run in Rome.

APPRENTICE. In May 1944 a Russian, the son of a tsarist officer, was parachuted into Italy from Albania and gave himself up to the British authorities, declaring himself to have been recruited by the **Abwehr**. Although he had intended to join the Royal Yugoslav Air Force, he was persuaded to act as a **double agent**, supposedly employed as a linguist teaching Serbian to British personnel. APPRENTICE continued to transmit from Bari until the end of hostilities.

ARABEL. The **Abwehr** code name for the network in Great Britain headed by ALARIC, **Juan Pujol**. *See also* GLEAM.

ARCHER, JANE. A barrister and a prewar **MI5** officer, Jane Archer interviewed **Walter Krivitsky** in February 1940 and subsequently was dismissed for insubordination. She was reemploycd by MI6 as head of the Irish section.

ARCHER, LIAM. Head of Ireland's **G-2** military intelligence service in succession to Dan Bryan.

ARGENTINA. In World War II, Argentina had several intelligence organizations, including the intelligence branches of the army and navy, respectively the Servicio de Inteligencia del Ejército and the Servicio de Inteligencia de la Armada; a federal organization, the Servicio de Inteligencia de la Policìa de la Capital; the coast guard's Sección Inteligencia de la Prefectura Maritima; and the border police's Sección Inteligencia de la Gendarmeria Nacional, formed in 1938. Illicit broadcasts were monitored by the Departamento de Control de Radiodifusion de la Secretaria de Correos y Telecomunicaciones. In the capital, the Organo de Informaciones de la Policia de la Provincia de Buenos Aires acted as a political police, while the Departamento Informaciones del Ministerio de Relaciones Exteriores collected foreign intelligence. In the provinces, then known as the *territorios nacionales*, the Sección Informaciones de la Policia Nacional de Territorios acted undcr the direction of the national government.

The chief of Argentina's military intelligence service, Maj. Emilio Loza, collaborated closely with his Axis counterparts, to the extent that in March 1941 an **Abwehr** agent, Hans Leo Harnisch, was granted official Argentine naval intelligence credentials for a mission to Paraguay. The officer responsible for recommending his appointment to Adm. Fincati in April 1943 was President Ramón Castillo's aide-de-camp, Capt. Eduardo Aumann, a *Volksdeutscher*. Code-named VEIRECK, Harnisch was a German lawyer who had emigrated in 1920 and had been recruited by the Abwehr in June 1941 during a visit to Berlin. According to intercepted Abwehr messages, he was placed on a substantial retainer and granted a generous expense allowance.

Intercepted signals to **Brazil** revealed that there was a parallel Abwehr organization in Buenos Aires but based in Rio de Janeiro, where KING and PRINCE maintained an office overlooking the harbor. KING was Friedrich Kempter, a graduate of Tübingen University who had emigrated in 1923 and been enrolled by the Abwehr in March 1940 by post; PRINCE was his partner, Heriberto Muller, an Austrian businessman whom he had met while advertising in the local German language newspaper, the *Diário Alemão*, for an office manager. In November 1940 Kempter was ordered to Buenos Aires, where he had made contact with OTIS and BERKO, who were Ottomar Muller, an ardent Nazi who broadcast Nazi propaganda regularly on Radio Callao's program *The German Hour*, and Hans Napp, a crooked shipping clerk and former proprietor of the Adlon Tea Room Bar with a criminal past. Both *Reichsdeutschen*, they acted independently of the Abwehr representative in the German embassy and passed their information on to Kempter, who relayed it to Hamburg. Napp later recruited the headwaiter of a restaurant near the docks to submit daily shipping reports and opened an office close to the British embassy. With a monthly retainer of $500, he adopted the role of a wealthy businessman and moved his family out of a rented room in the Hotel Vienna to a large house in the suburb of Martinez.

Argentina's political bias toward the Axis changed in June 1943 when Gen. Pablo Ramirez led a revolution and overthrew the government of Ramon Castillo. Thereafter the position of the German naval attaché, Capt. Dietrich Niebuhr, became precarious. After the war, he was questioned by U.S. interrogators, but it was not until a third series of interviews, conducted in June 1946, that he admitted he had headed the Abwehr's organization in Argentina. Niebuhr had been appointed naval attaché to Argentina, **Chile**, and Brazil in 1936, and by the outbreak of war had developed functioning networks in all three countries. In Buenos Aires, his headquarters consisted of two assistant naval attachés, Lt. Franz Mannen, who restricted himself to code duties, and Lt. Johannes Muller, who acted as an intermediary, running agents as a "cutout." Niebuhr's role as the Abwehr's spymaster was considerably enhanced when Brazil and Germany broke diplomatic relations at the end of January and Kempter, who never realized his wireless link LIR–MAX was being monitored, wisely judged that his mail and cable traffic was no longer secure. By the end of December 1941, Kempter had transmitted more than 400 messages to Hamburg and had received more than 200.

Following a meeting with Niebuhr held at the end of the month, Kempter surrendered control of Napp to the attaché and was taken into custody by the Brazilian **Direção da Ordem Política e Social (DOPS)** two months later. With the roundup of his Chilean organization in July 1942, Niebuhr became increasingly isolated and, according to a plea for more funds sent to Hamburg that month, was down to his last $10,000. The Abwehr responded by rebuking him for not having built a wireless transmitter nor encouraging Napp to do so, but evidently Niebuhr, having learned from the experience of his colleague Hermann Bohny, the naval attaché in Brazil, was reluctant to incriminate himself so obviously in espionage. When President Getúlio Vargas severed diplomatic relations with the Nazis, he sent the German ambassador, Kurt Prüfer, accompanied by Bohny, into virtual house arrest in the city of Petropolis, until they could be sent home, in May 1942, on the Portuguese ship *Serpa Pinto*.

Much was learned about Niebuhr from one of his subordinates, Pablo Longhi, that enabled him to be identified him as a mysterious figure in the Abwehr's traffic code-named DIEGO. Longhi himself, who appeared in the traffic rather transparently as PABLO, was an Argentine who had returned to Buenos Aires from Spain in July 1941 as a fully fledged Abwehr agent, if not a very enthusiastic one. In order to subsidize his extravagant lifestyle, he had offered his services to the U.S. embassy as a **double agent**, but had been rejected as a probable provocation. Instead, Longhi worked for Niebuhr and undertook several missions for him to **Mexico** and elsewhere as a courier toward the end of 1941. However, his principal role was that of Niebuhr's link to a network in Rio de Janeiro headed by Heinz Lorenz, and when that organization was rounded up by DOPS in April 1942, Longhi was among them. He was released soon afterward, but for obvious reasons Niebuhr considered him blown and wanted to put him on ice for a while. Chronically short of money, Longhi made a second offer to spy for the Americans, and this time he was accepted by Bill Doyle of the **Federal Bureau of Investigation**'s **Special Intelligence Service (SIS)**, who debriefed him in August 1942 and thus was able to identify him as PABLO and, more significantly, Niebuhr as DIEGO. Thereafter, Niebuhr and his network became the SIS's number-one target in Argentina.

Although American efforts to monitor Axis espionage were handicapped by the lack of cooperation received from the Argentine police, the SIS was able to recruit individual detectives and exploit rivalries between the different forces. In one case, Rosando Almozara Lombera was detained by the Maritime Police in Buenos Aires in May 1943 as he attempted to disembark the *Cabo de Hornos*, on which he worked as a male nurse. A search revealed 30 microfilms and material for secret ink. When he was questioned, he gave false details of where he was to meet his contact, misleading his interrogators and sending the Buenos Aires police to the wrong café. Nevertheless, an examination of his possessions revealed a mailing address in **Madrid** that he was supposed to pass on to his contact. This information fell into American hands, and it was ascertained that cables to this address had been sent recently by Roberto Delgane Rodrigues, a guest at the Plaza Hotel who had also been a passenger on the *Cabo de Hornos*. As the SIS's relations with the capital police were poor and Delgane would have been tipped off if the SIS had asked for his arrest, the Buenos Aires Provincial Police, with whom SIS maintained good relations, were told that Delgane was linked to Hans Zweigert, another espionage suspect then under investigation. However, the revolution of 4 June introduced martial law, requiring the military authorities to take over the entire case, so the SIS adopted an ingenious expedient, a bogus telegram based on those that Delgane had already received from Madrid, instructing him to attend a rendezvous in a bar in Avallenada, which was just within the jurisdiction of the Provincial Police. When Delgane turned up, he was arrested, and he later confessed that he was on a mission to the United States, where he was to collect military information and then send it to an address in Chile for onward transmission to Germany by radio. *See also ADMIRAL GRAF SPEE.*

ARLINGTON HALL. Headquarters of the Army Security Agency, located in a former girls school just outside Washington, D.C. Arlington Hall accommodated the cryptographers who achieved considerable success against Japanese naval, military, and diplomatic ciphers and later concentrated on Soviet cable traffic encrypted on **one-time pads**, a program code-named BRIDE.

ARMOUR. British code name for an Italian aeronautical expert who penetrated the **Abwehr** for the **Servizio di Informazione Militare** and was recruited as a stay-behind agent in Rome. He had immediately surrendered to the Allies and, with his wife acting as his cipher clerk, transmitted **deception** material to the Germans until the end of hostilities. A high-grade agent, ARMOUR had achieved the Wehrmacht rank of Oberstleutnant and enjoyed access to the top levels of Italian society, including Marshal Badoglio.

ARMSTRONG, GEORGE. At the end of February 1941, 39-year-old British merchant seaman George Armstrong was taken into custody in Cardiff, having been deported from the United States. He had been arrested in Boston the previous October after deserting his ship and traveling to New York, where, motivated by his commitment to Communism, he had offered his services to the Germans because of Josef Stalin's support for the Nazis. Armstrong had been intercepted before his recruitment by the enemy could be completed so, as far as **MI5** was concerned, he had no value or potential as a **double agent**. He was convicted in May 1941 and hanged at Wandsworth in July 1941.

ARTHUR. British code name for a Spanish Jewish financier resident in Oran who was used as a **double agent** between March and October 1943 to convey **deception** material to the Germans. Originally run by the French, he had written letters containing information about the U.S. Fifth Army.

ARTIST. MI5 code name for **Johannes Jebsen**, an **Abwehr** officer based in **Lisbon** who had recruited his university friend **Dusan Popov**. Jebsen was the only Abwehr officer to be an agent of the

British **Secret Intelligence Service (MI6)** and, having been run by MI6's Graham Maingot since September 1943, he was abducted by his colleagues and returned to Germany in May 1944. He was accused of having embezzled Abwehr funds and executed.

ASPIRIN. (1) **Federal Bureau of Investigation** code name for José Maria Aladren, a Spanish journalist recruited in Washington, D.C., in October 1942. A protégé of **Angel Alcazar de Velasco**, Aladren returned to **Madrid** in March 1944 and was given a new mission on behalf of the Japanese, arriving back in the United States in February 1945 as a correspondent for the Spanish News Agency. (2) Electronic countermeasures designed to alter the navigation beams followed by German aircraft. *See also* MOONLIGHT SONATA.

ASTOR, HUGH. MI5 case officer who ran BRONX, among other **double agents**. In 1944 Astor was commissioned to write a report on enemy penetration of **Special Operations Executive**, and he concluded that virtually all its **circuits** had been contaminated.

ATLANTIC, BATTLE OF THE. The conflict between the German U-boat fleet and Allied aircraft and surface vessels, conducted between 1941 and 1943, was quite evenly matched until cryptographic successes achieved at **Bletchley Park**, where Kriegsmarine wireless communications encrypted on **Enigma** cipher machines were decoded in May 1941, giving the submarine hunters a significant advantage. Additional measures were introduced by the Germans in February 1942 to heighten radio security, including the development of an Enigma version with a fourth rotor, code-named SHARK. Nevertheless, a combination of sophisticated direction-finding techniques and breaks into the SHARK messages tipped the balance in favor of the Allies in December 1942. Thereafter, with the exception of a period of weeks in March 1943, much of the U-boat traffic was read within hours of transmission. The relative losses of Kriegsmarine submarines and Allied merchant shipping during these four distinct periods are compelling. Between September 1939 and May 1941, 699 Allied ships were lost with only 32 U-boats sunk. Between June 1941 and February 1943, 885 ships were lost and 13 U-boats sunk. In March 1943, 83 ships were lost and 11 U-boats sunk. Between April

1943 and May 1945, 178 ships were sunk, compared to 286 U-boats. In the months the radio traffic could be read, convoys were diverted away from the wolfpacks, and aircraft were vectored to the known location of enemy submarines. When the codebreakers failed to break the messages, Allied merchant losses escalated exponentially. Adm. Karl Dönitz was suspicious of the scale of attrition and ordered an inquiry, which exonerated the U-boat communications but suggested security leaks at the French submarine bases, where departures could not be hidden from the local population.

AUENRODE, ALBRECHT VON. The senior **Abwehr** officer in **Lisbon**, who adopted the alias "Ludovico von Karstoff." Maj. Albrecht von Auenrode was an Austrian aristocrat and handled the cases of **Dusan Popov** and **Georges Graf**.

AXE. British code name for an Italian radio engineer arrested in Florence in late August 1944 as part of a stay-behind network. Run as a **double agent** against the Germans from October 1944, he was awarded the Iron Cross in January 1945.

– B –

B1(a). **MI5** designation for the B Division subsection responsible for the management of controlled enemy agents, headed by **T. A. Robertson**.

B1(b). **MI5** designation for the B Division subsection responsible for signals analysis of ISK and ISOS, headed by **Herbert Hart**.

B1(c). **MI5** designation for the B Division subsection responsible for countersabotage operations, headed by Victor Rothschild.

B1(d). **MI5** designation for the B Division subsection headed by Ronnie Haylor and responsible for liaison with the **Royal Victoria Patriotic School**.

B1(e). **MI5** designation for the B Division subsection responsible for liaison with **Camp 020**.

B1(f). MI5 designation for the B Division subsection headed by Courtenay Young and responsible for Japanese counterespionage.

B1(g). MI5 designation for the B Division Spanish subsection headed by Dick Brooman-White.

B1(h). MI5 designation for the B Division Irish subsection headed by Cecil Liddell.

BACKHAND. British code name for Mohammed Zahiruddin, a triple agent run in Burma in 1944. Zahiruddin was cashiered from the Indian Army for political campaigning. Later, after a change of heart, he volunteered to penetrate Subhas Chandra Bose's nationalist army and was parachuted into Burma in February 1944. Accepted as genuine by Bose, he was employed broadcasting propaganda and used the opportunity to convey messages to the British. Zahiruddin eventually fell under suspicion and was imprisoned, but was freed when Rangoon was liberated in 1945.

BALKANABTEILUNG. The German cryptographic unit dedicated to attacking Soviet cipher systems. It was based at Hirschberg, near Breslau, until January 1945 when the organization moved to Bergsheidungen, the ancestral home of the Graf von der Schulenbergs. Shortly before the end of hostilities, the entire Balkanabteilung archive fell into American hands and was transferred to **Bletchley Park**.

BALLOON. MI5 code name for a **B1(a) double agent, Dickie Metcalfe**, a former British army officer who resigned his commission over a problem with racehorses and supposedly was recruited as a source by **Dusan Popov** in May 1941. BALLOON continued to supply information, mainly on military materiel, until November 1943.

BARON. GRU code name for an unidentified member of the **X Group** with access to raw **Enigma** intercepts, most probably from **Bletchley Park**. One possible candidate for BARON was Karel Sedlacek, a **Czech intelligence** officer, but the identification was never confirmed. BARON's existence was disclosed in some 1941 VENONA traffic from the London *rezidentura*.

BARONESS. British code name for a Russian businessman in **Istanbul** who had been recruited by the **Abwehr** to undertake missions in Syria, Turkey, and India. He moved to **Argentina** in 1944.

BASKET. Code name for an **MI5 double agent**, Joseph Lenihan, an **Abwehr** agent with convictions for fraud and wanted in Eire for his connections with the **Irish Republican Army**, who parachuted into Ireland in July 1941. After his safe arrival in the Curragh, he had made his way to Ulster, instead of sending weather reports from Sligo, and surrendered to the British authorities who turned him over to MI5 for interrogation at **Camp 020**. He claimed to have been recruited in the Channel Islands, and when released, on condition he did not leave the country, he attempted to join the crew of a fishing boat in Fleetwood, Hampshire, so the case was abandoned in December 1941.

BATES. The **Federal Bureau of Investigation** code name for a pilot, a **notional** source run in Washington, D.C., by PEASANT.

BATS. British code name for a series of spies parachuted into Assam by the Japanese in April 1943. Two, code-named OWL and MARMALADE, were recruited as **double agents**.

BATTLE OF CAPE MATAPAN. *See* CAPE MATAPAN, BATTLE OF.

BATTLE OF KURSK. *See* KURSK, BATTLE OF.

BATTLE OF MIDWAY. *See* MIDWAY, BATTLE OF.

BATTLE OF THE ATLANTIC. *See* ATLANTIC, BATTLE OF THE.

BAZNA, ELYESA. True name of the German spy code-named CICERO by the **Sicherheitsdienst (SD)**. Formerly employed by the German embassy, Bazna was the valet to the British ambassador, Sir Hughe Knatchbull-Hugessen, in 1943. He resigned in March 1944 when new security procedures were introduced and he believed he may have fallen under suspicion. In fact, Bazna was not considered a suspect until after his departure. He was later imprisoned in Turkey for possession of counterfeit currency, having been paid in forged notes by his SD contact, Ludwig Moyszich. He died in Ankara in 1971.

BEETLE. Secret Intelligence Service code name for Petur Thomsen, a **double agent** run in Iceland after he had been landed by a U-boat in September 1943.

BELGIUM. Political differences between the Sûreté de l'État, headed by Baron Fernand Lepage, who was responsible for coordinating the government-in-exile's resistance groups, and the Ministry of National Defense, which worked with **Special Operations Executive (SOE)** to run the military resistance networks of the Legion Belge, handicapped Belgian efforts to undermine the Nazi occupation. The **Secret Intelligence Service**'s **(MI6)** head of station in prewar Brussels, Col. Edward Calthrop, had been confined to a wheelchair and fulfilled a liaison role with the prewar Sûreté. His successor as head of MI6's country section was Maj. F. J. Jempson, and he managed in January 1941 to make contact with CLEVELAND, a local network based upon members of a similar **circuit** known as WHITE LADY that had operated during World War I. CLEVELAND was run by Walthere Dewe, a senior telephone executive who had developed a very efficient escape line for Allied airmen. Another veteran of WHITE LADY was Adrien Marquet, who parachuted home on 12 August 1941, made contact with CLEVELAND and its successor, CLARENCE, and started another intelligence-gathering group, code-named MILL. It was through these circuits that MI6 was able to maintain a direct link with Belgium, while SOE's enforced relationship with exiled Prime Minister Hubert Pierlot's administration virtually precluded it from developing any useful contact for a long period.

The isolation of the émigrés undermined SOE's relationship with the Belgian government-in-exile, which failed to share all of SOE's objectives and took the view that large-scale disruption would not damage the German war effort but might handicap Belgium's postwar economic recovery. So, instead of a strategy of wholesale sabotage, a campaign of minor pinpricks was adopted, albeit reluctantly.

On 20 February 1942 an agreement was reached with Prime Minister Pierlot for SOE to liaise directly with Action, a subsection of the

Deuxieme Direction of the Ministry of Defense headed by Maj. Bernard. This arrangement broke down almost immediately, and it was not until October 1942, when Bernard was replaced by Col. Jean Marissal, that a new treaty of cooperation could be negotiated. Even then, the personalities still jarred, with Philip Johns observing that Marissal "had been too orthodox for him to adapt to this relatively newly constituted SOE."

The new document was signed on 30 October 1942 and heralded a two-phase approach: a preparatory stage, in which arms would be stockpiled and a secret army recruited, followed by a coordinated and disciplined general insurrection after the Allied invasion. This ambitious plan was never fully realized, partly because of political infighting and "the paranoiac suspicion and jealousy which existed between Lepage and his staff on the one hand and Marissal and the Deuxieme Direction on the other. The internecine struggle, though understandable up to a point, was deplorable" (Philip Johns, *Within Two Cloaks*, 142).

As well as running a large number of Belgian collaborators, the Germans also exploited the few links that existed between the compromised Dutch networks and the Belgian escape lines. In one lengthy undercover operation in the spring of 1942, the **Abwehr** actually took control of MI6's circuits, infiltrating its own surrogates into key positions, and rounded up all the related resistance groups, including an extensive one run by Maj. Van Serveyt.

During the course of the war, 250 agents were dispatched to Belgium, of whom 105 were arrested. Only 45 of those taken into German custody survived the experience. Part of the blame for this lies with MI6, which requested Gerard Van Os from the GOLF team that parachuted into German hands on 18/19 February 1943, to contact Gaston Van der Meerssche, the MI6 agent who ran the RINUS network. Van der Meerssche had been parachuted home in 1942 and had built up an important organization, which smuggled intelligence via couriers on coastal freighters to Sweden for onward transmission to London. SOE's disastrous signal to Van Os alerted the Germans for the first time to the existence of RINUS, and they were able, through the use of skilled impersonators, to destroy the network. Van der Meerssche himself initially avoided capture but was later arrested in Paris, en route to Spain.

Enemy manipulation of RINUS was so complete that the German who had infiltrated the network had negotiated with SOE in London to receive N Section agents in Belgium, because the Dutch networks had been so comprehensively penetrated. Fortunately, SOE decided to drop its remaining agents "blind," without the benefit of a reception committee, and on 22 July 1943 Capt. Zembsch Schreve was landed near Mechelen. He was followed two months later by A. J. Cnoops, and on 18 October by a further pair, Hans Gruen and J. D. van Schelle, arrived safely. Of these four, only Gruen was entrapped by the Abwehr, and he survived captivity. Once the bitter truth had sunk in, SOE resumed drops into Holland, and two agents dropped during 1943, Peter Gerbrands and Capt. Tonnet, both operated radios and avoided arrest.

The largest resistance organization fostered by MI6 in Belgium was the Armée Secrete, headed by Col. Jules Bastin, but he too was eventually caught in 1943.

BENTLEY, ELIZABETH. Code-named CLEVER GIRL in the VENONA traffic, Elizabeth Bentley was an **NKVD defector** who supplied information to the **Federal Bureau of Investigation (FBI)** in 1945 about Soviet networks in the United States run, until his death in November 1943, by her lover, Jakob Golos, who had been the NKVD's illegal *rezident*. Bentley helped the FBI pursue leads to more than 80 spies who had been active during World War II, including a large ring in Washington, D.C., headed by Nathan Silvermaster. An attempt by the FBI to run Bentley as a **double agent** against her handler, **Anatoli Gorsky**, failed when he held one meeting with her and then failed to attend another rendezvous.

BEOBACHTUNGDIENST (B-DIENST). The German naval radio interception service that succeeded in breaking the Royal Navy's Cipher No. 3 during the Spanish Civil War was based in the Tirpiz-Ufer in Berlin and employed 8,000 cryptographers, linguists, and analysts. In November 1943, following heavy Allied air raids, the headquarters was evacuated to Eberswalde.

The British cipher was primitive and the security lapses committed by individual wireless operators lamentable, enabling the B-Dienst to read much of the Royal Navy's signals throughout World

War II, especially following the recovery of HMS *Sikh*'s codebooks
from the destroyer after she had been sunk in Tobruk harbor in September 1942. The B-Dienst operated seven intercept stations in the
Baltic and four on the North Sea, with a clandestine site at Lange-
nargen on Lake Constance that monitored Italian traffic.

The German signals intelligence service, based at Lauf-an-der-
Pegnitz, near Nuremberg, gained a considerable advantage from signals analysis, especially from Allied aircrew, even if the message content resisted attack, and procedures such as radio checks shortly before
takeoff gave German air defenses good advance notice of imminent
air raids. After **D-Day**, the rudimentary hand ciphers employed by Allied military police directing traffic at strategic locations to make
evening reports provided an excellent source of accurate intelligence.

In addition, the Wehrmacht operated a network of intercept sites
located at Breslau, Dresden, Munich, Munster, and Stuttgart and in
the training areas of Jüterbor and Königsberg. The **Gestapo** also
maintained a radio monitoring service, the Forschungsamt, to watch
for illicit broadcasts.

BERIA, LAVRENTI. The commissar of state security appointed to
head the **NKVD** by Josef Stalin in September 1936, Lavrenti Beria
was the senior Soviet intelligence officer throughout World War II
and was responsible for recognizing the development of an atomic
bomb as a priority. He masterminded ENORMOZ, a joint NKVD/**GRU**
operation to penetrate the **Manhattan Project** and established **XY**
rezidenturas in key cities to concentrate on the collection of technical intelligence.

Occasionally prone to bouts of paranoia, such as his unfounded belief in early 1940 that **Anatoli Gorsky**'s London *rezidentura* had
been penetrated, Beria transformed an organization decimated by
successive purges into a highly professional intelligence agency with
a global reach, represented by *rezidenturas* in most target countries
with diplomatic representation, and illegals established in the others.
Beria's attempt to seize power after Stalin's death in 1953 resulted in
his arrest and execution.

BERMUDA. One of two British **Imperial Censorship** sites in the
Western Hemisphere (the other being **Trinidad**), the colony of

Bermuda proved a geographically convenient location for the scrutiny of mail exchanged between North America and Europe. All correspondence sent to or from Europe was examined by Imperial Censorship staff based at the Hamilton Princess Hotel, and suspect items were intercepted and photographed. This led to the identification of several German spies, among them George Nicolaus and Joachim Ruge. *See also* MICRODOTS.

BERN. The capital of the Helvetic Confederation, better known as Switzerland, proved to be an important center of international espionage because of the ease of travel over the frontier for some Germans, two of whom, **Hans Bernd Gisevius** and **Fritz Kolbe**, supplied information to the local **Office of Strategic Services** representative, **Allen Dulles**. The British embassy included a **Secret Intelligence Service** station, headed by Count Fanny Vanden Heuvel, a representative of **MI9**, and one from **Section V**, Richard Arnold-Baker.

BERNHARD. German code name for the counterfeiting of Bank of England currency, indistinguishable from authentic notes, in 1941 with the intention of undermining international confidence in sterling while simultaneously financing Nazi intelligence operations across the globe. Initially masterminded by Alfred Naujocks, the paper was manufactured by the Spechtausen Paper Company at Eberswalde, and the notes printed by 140 skilled engravers, all prisoners in Blocks 18 and 19, a high-security building inside the Sachsenhausen concentration camp. In 1942, the operation was taken over by Fritz Schwend and run from his Schloss Labors in the Tyrol. Counterfeit pound and dollar notes were produced at a rate of 400,000 per month, to a face value of £150 million, and some went into circulation, including those paid to CICERO in 1943. In 1944 the printers were transferred from Sachsenhausen to Redl-Zipf, at the Ebensee concentration camp in Austria. At the end of the war, the remaining stocks of £50 notes were dumped in the Toplitzsee, where they were recovered in July 1959. Schwend immigrated to Lima, Peru, and Naujocks remained in Germany.

BERTRAND, GUSTAVE. A key French signals intelligence officer, Gustave Bertrand, as head of Section D, the decryption branch of the

Service de Renseignements, had been the recipient prewar of information about the **Enigma** machine from Hans-Thilo Schmidt, a corrupt German cipher officer employed by the Reichwehr's Chiffrierstelle. Between October 1931 and 1939, they had met 19 times (four times in **Belgium**, once in Copenhagen, 12 times in Switzerland, once in Evian, France, and once in Czechoslovakia), and Schmidt, code-named ASCHÉ, had handed over 303 documents. He also revealed that the Forschungsamt, where he was posted in 1934, had broken the Royal Navy's Naval Intelligence Code 1, the French Navy's BGD 30 code, and the French mobilization code, the Code d'Alert. Schmidt would commit suicide in prison in September 1943, following his arrest by the **Gestapo**.

Bertrand's information was shared with Polish cryptographers at two secret conferences held jointly with the British in 1939, and an agreement was reached on the sharing of information concerning their common target, the German Enigma. In June 1940, after the French collapse, Bertrand's small staff moved into the unoccupied zone, continuing to work on enemy communications at Les Fouzes, near Uzès in Provence, until November 1942 when they fled to **Algiers**. He reached London in October 1943, via **Lisbon**, and thereafter cooperated closely with his British counterparts. In 1968 he published *Enigma*, an account of his wartime escapades.

BEST, SIGISMUND. A former World War I **Secret Intelligence Service (MI6)** officer, Capt. Sigismund Payne Best was the **Z Organisation** operative in the Netherlands who was abducted by the **Sicherheitsdienst** at **Venlo** in November 1939. He and his MI6 companion, Maj. **Richard Stevens**, underwent extensive interrogation and survived the war in Nazi captivity. In 1951, Best published his account of the episode in *The Venlo Incident*.

BEURTON, LEN. A member of the **Communist Party of Great Britain** whose French father had become a naturalized British subject and had been killed on the Western Front in 1914, Len Beurton fought in the Spanish Civil War with the International Brigade and subsequently was recruited by the **GRU** to work in Switzerland. In February 1940 he married **Ursula Kuczynski** so she could obtain a British passport. Although initially a sham to allow Kuczynski to stay on in Switzerland after he had returned to England, the couple remained devoted to each other thereafter.

BISCUIT. **MI5** code name for a **B1(a)** **double agent**, a petty crook named Sam McCarthy, who had been a prewar informant and acted as a recruit for **Arthur Owens**. The case was abandoned in August 1941 when it was suspected that Owens might have compromised him to the **Abwehr**.

BIURO SZYFROW. The Polish cipher bureau of the Polish General Staff's Radio Intelligence Office was headed by Col. Gwido Langer and based at Mokotov-Pyry, deep in the Kabackie Woods south of Warsaw. It was dependent on three intercept stations, located at Starogard, south of Danzig, a suburb of Poznan, and Krzeslawice, to collect German **Enigma** traffic.

Langer's staff, including the head of the German section, Col. Maksymilian Ciezki, had achieved considerable progress on Wehrmacht and **Sicherheitsdienst** traffic and attended a conference called by the **Service de Renseignements** in Paris on 9 January 1939 to exchange information on German cipher systems. It was agreed to install a teleprinter link between the British, French, and Polish participants, and Ciezki revealed that a mechanical device, a *bombe*, had been developed to race through Enigma permutations, and that one of his engineers, Henryk Zygalski, had improvised a series of 26 perforated sheets to identify Wehrmacht Enigma keys. In July 1939 a second conference was held in Warsaw at which the Poles agreed to supply their counterparts with replica Enigma machines fitted with the new plugboard, which was delivered to the **Secret Intelligence Service (MI6)** station in Paris on 16 August.

Following the German invasion, some of the Biuro Szyfrow's staff fled to Romania and, having been refused permission to come to England, were accommodated by **Gustave Bertrand**'s organization at the Château de Vignolles near Gretl-Armainvilliers, code-named Poste de Commandement BRUNO, which enjoyed a direct teleprinter link to England. However, when the Nazis attacked France, the Poles withdrew temporarily to Paris and then were evacuated to Oran, but soon returned to the unoccupied zone and were based at the Château des Fouzes, a fortress code-named CADIX, north of Uzès in Provence.

As well as intercepting German radio traffic, the cryptanalysts had the benefit of SOURCE X, a remote tap on the two main cables linking France to Germany.

From CADIX, the 15 Poles made radio contact with their government in exile at Stanmore and reported further progress in reading some German ciphers, but MI6 ensured that there was no exchange of information or disclosure of what had been achieved at **Bletchley Park**. Finally, in October 1942, the Poles were evacuated to **Algiers**, under the protection and sponsorship of **Paul Paillole**, and those that eventually reached England were accommodated at Boxmoor in Hertfordshire, deliberately isolated from Bletchley Park.

BJ. The British signals intelligence abbreviation for BLACK JUMBO, the designation for material derived from intercepted diplomatic wireless traffic.

BLACKGUARD. Security Intelligence Middle East code name for an Iranian in **Istanbul**, a former broadcaster with Radio Berlin. Employed as a talent-spotter by the **Abwehr** to recruit agents willing to spy in Iran, India, and Egypt, he approached the **defence security officer** in 1943 and was enrolled as a **double agent** after he had denounced KISS.

BLACK RADIO. The **Political Warfare Executive** had responsibility for broadcasting subversive programming and news to the enemy via radio stations purporting to be operating from Nazi-occupied territory. Transmitters located in Sussex filled the airwaves with German-language material prepared on the Woburn Abbey estate in Bedfordshire by teams of skilled linguists and **defectors**, supervised by the former *Daily Express* correspondent in Berlin, Tom Sefton Delmer. These unacknowledged stations were known as "black radio" and included *Soldatensender Calais*, a channel especially popular with the Wehrmacht.

BLENHEIM PALACE. MI5's wartime headquarters at Woodstock in Oxfordshire, the ancestral home of the Dukes of Marlborough.

BLETCHLEY PARK. Known within the **Secret Intelligence Service (MI6)** as Station X and originally intended to be MI6's war station staffed by personnel evacuated from London, this 300-acre Bedford-shire estate was renamed **Government Communications Head-quarters (GCHQ)** and accommodated the cryptographers who worked on intercepted enemy ciphers. They had considerable success, beginning with solutions to **Abwehr** hand ciphers and eventually reading large quantities of **Enigma** and **Geheimschreiber** machine traffic, the summaries of which were circulated first under the code name BONIFACE, and after May 1941 with the classification ULTRA. GCHQ also solved some **one-time pads**, including those used by the German Foreign Ministry.

The Luftwaffe's Enigma keys had succumbed in October 1940, followed by some Wehrmacht keys in May 1941. The Kriegsmarine keys were read almost continuously from December 1942, offering a tremendous advantage to the 12,000 cryptographers, linguists, and analysts who worked on the problem assisted by *bombes*, mechanical devices that raced through the possible key-setting permutations, and COLOSSUS, the first programmable analog computer, which exploited the Geheimschreiber. *See also* FLORADORA.

BLUE BOOT. Code name for a British **deception** scheme intended to convey to the Germans a countermeasure that supposedly had been introduced during the "invasion summer" of 1940 by the Home Guard to identify enemy parachutists dressed in British Army uniforms. Following reports that the Nazis had adopted such tactics during their attack on **Belgium**, Holland, and **Denmark**, the War Office allegedly had responded by ordering all British personnel to paint one boot blue. The objective was to persuade German paratroops to do the same, thereby leaving them vulnerable to the defenders who had been instructed to shoot anyone wearing a blue boot.

BLUN, GEORGES. A French political correspondent based in Zurich, Georges Blun was a Soviet spy who learned his tradecraft from the Deuxieme Bureau and the British **Secret Intelligence Service** during World War I. Despite his contacts with numerous intelligence agencies, including the Polish and the American, his first loyalties were always to the Comintern and the **GRU**, and in 1920 he was expelled from Switzerland for Communist agitation. His return in 1939, following a considerable period as a journalist in Berlin, enabled him to cultivate a wide range of Swiss and German contacts from whom he extracted some very worthwhile intelligence for his controller, **Otto Puenter**.

BLUNT, ANTHONY. Recruited into **MI5** in June 1940, Anthony Blunt was already a Soviet mole, having been recruited by Guy Burgess in 1936. He was appointed personal assistant to **Guy Liddell** and subsequently supervised MI5's TRIPLEX source. He returned to academic life in 1945, having completed an investigation for MI5 into the prewar leakage of information from the British embassy in Rome. Blunt was a member of the Cambridge Five spy ring, **NKVD** spies who had all graduated from that university. Prior to joining MI5, Blunt's principal role had been one of a talent-spotter, identifying candidates, such as his students **John Cairncross**, Michael Straight, and Leo Long, as suitable for approach to join the Soviet espionage network. On the one occasion he risked compromise, having identified an MI5 source inside the **Communist Party of Great Britain** code-named M-8, the blame was taken for him by a secretary, Carola Luke.

BONIFACE. Government Communications Headquarters code name for **Enigma**-based signals intelligence until the introduction of the classification ULTRA in May 1941.

BOOTLE. MI5 code name for a Frenchman recruited as a **double agent**.

BOWSPRIT. The **X-2** code name for Ercole Pugliese, an Italian **Servizio di Informazioni Aeronautiche** officer based in Sicily who surrendered himself and his wireless transmitter to the Allies, after which an unsuccessful attempt was made to run him as a **double agent**.

BRANDENBURGER REGIMENT. A volunteer paramilitary unit of the Wehrmacht that acted as a training unit for the **Abwehr**. The Brandenburger Regiment undertook sabotage operations and supplied personnel for intelligence missions abroad.

BRASS. British code name for a group of three Karen tribesmen dropped into Japanese-occupied territory near Rangoon, Burma, in November 1942. Captured soon after their arrival, the agents were equipped with means of conveying they had fallen under enemy control, and the channel was manipulated by the British until they were liberated in 1945.

BRAZIL. The Brazilian secret police, the **Direção da Ordem Política e Social (DOPS)**, maintained a close watch on the large German *Reichsdeutsch* émigré population in the south of the country and, under pressure from the United States, agreed to intercept and then close down broadcasts made by illicit Nazi wireless stations.

The **Special Intelligence Service (SIS)** in Brazil was headed from May 1941 by Jack West and then by William J. Bradley, who operated under difficult, shifting circumstances, but eventually identified **Josef J. Starziczy** as LUCAS, the organizer of a major Nazi spy ring whose radio transmissions to Hamburg, using the call sign CIT, had been monitored by the Allies. Also caught up in the same organization was **Albrecht Engels**, code-named ALFREDO, who was the director of a Brazilian power company and another key figure in the **Abwehr**'s operations across South America.

Although President Getúlio Vargas and his administration were considered to be pro-Allied and would sever relations with the Axis in January 1942, there was a great deal of activity behind the scenes to outmaneuver the very powerful German and Italian influence. In particular, Rio's chief of police, Filinto Muller, was considered very pro-Nazi and had strong links to some of the SIS's suspects. His ruthless reputation was based on his suppression of the November 1935 Communist revolt, which had been orchestrated by the Comintern. The uprising was quelled with bloody efficiency, and Muller had turned to the **Gestapo** for advice on how to deal with Communist subversion. As a result, DOPS, which owed many of its dubious skills and interrogation techniques to the Gestapo, was known to have remained close to the organization, as Muller certainly had the confidence of the German ambassador, Kurt Prüfer, and his military attaché, Gen. Günter Niedenfuhr. The **Federal Bureau of Investigation's (FBI)** had failed to exercise any influence over DOPS, even though **J. Edgar Hoover** had sent Special Agent Edward J. Thompson to Brazil in January 1938, at Vargas's request, to advise on training the national police.

Among the principal Allied targets in Brazil was the Linee Aeree Transcontinentali Italiane (LATI) air corridor from Rome, which the FBI was anxious to close down since it was an obvious conduit for everything from diplomatic couriers to propaganda films, and LATI's own radio network was thought to pose a danger. This last remaining transatlantic route also represented a significant loophole in the FBI arrangement with **British Security Coordination (BSC)**, cemented in November 1940, to channel all European mail through **Bermuda** so it could be subjected to **Imperial Censorship** and any suspicious letters intercepted and returned to the Bureau. This proved to be a highly efficient procedure, with some 75,000 items subjected to further scrutiny during the first year of operation, but LATI's airmail cargo escaped all inspection. Indeed, it was also suspected that LATI aircrew were taking the opportunity to watch for Allied shipping and maybe even signal their observations to U-boat packs while they flew the Dakar-to-Recife leg of the journey.

Initially the State Department tried to apply pressure on Standard Oil of New Jersey, which supplied LATI's aviation fuel, but the attempts failed—at least until the Standard Oil subsidiary in Rio was placed on the official U.S. blacklist. Even a sabotage mission to destroy LATI's fuel stocks in Recife, carried out by BSC's Ivar Bryce who flew down from New York equipped with time fuses and an incendiary device, failed to stop the flights. Although he succeeded in entering LATI's fuel dump to place his bomb, the resulting blaze did not spread far enough and sufficient barrels were saved to allow LATI to continue flying.

One of President Vargas's daughters was married to LATI's operations director, so the issue was a sensitive one, but the remedy lay in a letter, purporting to come from LATI's chairman, Gen. Aurelio Liotta, containing some highly derogatory comments about Vargas, addressed to LATI's local manager, Commandante Vicenzo Coppola. Actually, the letter had been forged by BSC and then reduced to a **microdot** by microphotography. BSC arranged a burglary at Coppola's home and then had an agent, claiming to have been the thief, approach an Associated Press (AP) reporter with the stolen microdot. Having read the shocking contents, in which Vargas was referred to as "the fat little man," the AP journalist showed it to the U.S. ambassador, Jefferson Caffery, who deliberately had not been briefed. Having consulted the SIS, Caffery concluded the document was authentic and handed it to Vargas, who exploded with rage and announced that LATI's landing rights had been terminated.

An unexpected consequence of this episode was the arrest of Coppola, who was caught at the **Argentine** frontier carrying $1 million in LATI funds. The money was confiscated, and he was sentenced to seven years' imprisonment and fined $85,000 for infringing Brazil's currency regulations. As for the rest of LATI, the airline ceased its transatlantic flights, its assets were seized, and the radio net closed down.

MI6's other major target was Starziczy, who had been sent to Rio de Janeiro to assist the German consul, Maj. Otto Übele. Übele was an immigrant to Brazil at the end of the previous century but had returned to Germany to fight on the Eastern Front. Captured by the Russians, he had escaped from Siberia and, at the end of the war, had returned to Brazil. A prosperous, well-known figure in Santos, he had been appointed the German honorary consul in 1935 and, at age 65, had taken over the role of consul when the incumbent died in February 1941. Of his three sons, one was to be killed in the Wehrmacht, another in the Luftwaffe was posted missing in North Africa, and a third, Uli, code-named MENDES, worked in a car sales business owned by his father and played a key role in his spy ring, as did Heinrich Bleinroth, code-named LEAD, who was the consulate's secretary. While Maj. Übele's commitment to the cause was total, perhaps founded on some experience as an agent code-named KUNTZE in World War I, he was also preoccupied by financial worries, and many of his messages expressed his concern about his company being reimbursed for funding the Abwehr's operations. Until the arrival of Starziczy, the organization had collected economic data and information from the docks, which had been posted to a mail drop in Geneva. Afterward, Uli was taught to operate a transmitter and collated the shipping reports submitted by subagents in Recife, Bahia, Salvador, and Rio. However, under the FBI's pressure, DOPS arrested Starziczy and his entire network.

The arrests silenced the JOH–RND circuit to Brussels and the HTT–ORE link to Cologne. JOH had been intercepted since October 1941 and consisted of messages from GRILLO, later identified as

Maj. Othmar Gamillscheg, a former Austro-Hungarian army officer who had fought in World War I and immigrated to Brazil in 1919. Gamillscheg had returned to Germany with his wife and daughter in May 1935 to join Roechling Steel as a export sales manager and, after being commissioned into the Wehrmacht, had been recruited by the Abwehr in early 1941. His mission, organized from Brussels, was to report on U.S. military activities in northwest Brazil as a subordinate to Gen. Niedenfuhr. When he arrived in Rio traveling alone in August 1941, ostensibly to negotiate postwar air routes and represent German aviation, he was met by Herbert von Heyer and was assigned two of ALFREDO's wireless operators, Heinz Lorenz, code-named LAURA, and Ernst Ramaz, to send his messages to Brussels.

JOH went on the air to RND on 14 October 1941, to be monitored continuously by the **Radio Intelligence Division (RID)**, but Gamillscheg also communicated to Germany via secret writing in letters addressed to his wife in Kitzbühl. Although he was commended for obtaining drawings of the U.S. air bases at Belem, Fortaleza, and Recife, he was reprimanded for continuously pressing for permission for his wife and daughter to join him. Eventually, in March 1942, they arrived on a Portuguese ship, carting a clock containing microdot instructions for himself and several of the new recruits he had cultivated, among them an old friend, Adalberto Wamszer, code-named WERNER. It was Wamszer who, when he was arrested by DOPS in March 1942, named Gamillscheg as his main contact, causing him to be taken into custody, too, and his wireless to be seized from its hiding place, buried on a farm in Campo Grande.

The HTT–ORE transmissions to Cologne, which were picked up first by the RID on 21 August 1941, proved to be one of the SIS's most intriguing investigations, as the entire network turned out to be run not by Germans, but by Hungarians. Adm. Miklos Horthy's regime, of course, had sided with the Axis, but this extraordinary case was to be the only example in the Western Hemisphere of a direct collaboration between the Hungarian intelligence service and the Abwehr. In addition, it was significant because of the diplomatic implications. The head of the network was protected by a diplomatic passport, and the minister in charge of the Hungarian legation, Miklos Horthy, was the regent's son.

The evidence of the HTT radio emerged in August 1941 and continued for just five months when it went off the air, but a study of the traffic, consisting of 60 messages transmitted to ORE, combined with reports of interrogations conducted in Rio by DOPS and in **Trinidad** by the British, revealed an extraordinary story of a spy ring that self-destructed for almost entirely political reasons.

The head of the HTT network was a Hungarian sea captain, Janos Salamon, who arrived in Rio early in July 1941 accompanied by a one-legged assistant, Sandor Mocsan, who used his wooden limb to smuggle cigarettes. Both flew in on a LATI flight from Rome, carrying official diplomatic passports accrediting them to the Hungarian legation. Upon their arrival in Rio, they established an office for the Budapest Free Port Shipping Company in the Avenida Copacabana and set up a transmitter, which they had imported as diplomatic cargo. The traffic shows that Salamon, code-named JOSZI, communicated to HUGH in Cologne, using Mocsan, code-named ALEXANDER, as his radio operator. Salamon appears to have been an assiduous spymaster, traveling to Natal and Recife to report on U.S. air bases, and quick to use the legation's lawyer, Rose de Balas Weisz, as an introduction to other members of the local Hungarian émigré community, among them an electrical engineer, Ellemer Nagy. He also recruited a LATI employee, Maria Tereza Calvacanti, who was already working for the Italian intelligence service, and he drew expenses for three others: PAULO, NELSON, and GUTIERREZ. Although PAULO was supposed to be able to supply information about DOPS, NELSON had good naval connections, and GUTIERREZ often traveled overseas, all later turned out to be entirely fictional, with the wily Salamon submitting extravagant accounts for all three.

While Salamon was expanding his network, Horthy at the legation was becoming increasingly embarrassed by his antics, not the least of which was his temporary detention in October 1941 by DOPS in Recife when he was caught masquerading as an American near an air base and carrying a nondiplomatic Hungarian passport in another name. By December, Horthy's patience had worn out and he ordered Salamon out of the country. By then Mocsan, alarmed by the content of the messages he had been transmitting, which he knew to be false, had slipped aboard the Spanish liner *Cabo de Esperanza Buena*, bound for **Lisbon**, but only reached Trinidad where he was detained by BSC on 22 January 1942. Meanwhile Salamon was arrested again, but released in February 1942 to join the *Cabo de Hornos* for Lisbon. He only reached Port of Spain, where he was detained and, according to **MI5**'s official report, was found in possession of "notebooks containing real evidence relating to radio transmission, meteorological reports, indications that they had established communication with German agents in Mexico and **Chile**, and references to US shipping movements off Brazil."

Salamon and Mocsan were then sent to Halifax where, by mistake, an inexperienced interrogator confronted them with copies of their intercepted traffic. Both men were then moved to MI5's internment center, **Camp 020**, where they were interrogated at length, despite their repeated claims to diplomatic status, and where they remained until October 1945. In their very comprehensive confessions, they described their recruitment in Budapest and identified their Abwehr handler as Capt. Hugo Sebold, code-named HUGH, to whom they had also written in secret ink via mail drops in Rome and Lisbon.

The SIS's task, having eliminated the transmitters, was to piece together the information obtained from the intercepts, match it to the interrogation reports, compare it to what was known from other sources such as **double agents**, wiretaps, and surveillance logs, and ensure that the entire Abwehr organization had been put out of action. The Nazis' reaction to the convictions was to retaliate by deploying U-boats to sink five Brazilian ships, a strategy that resulted in Brazil declaring war in August 1944.

BRIDE. The U.S. Army Security Agency's code name for a project that commenced in 1943 studying encrypted Soviet cable traffic exchanged between Moscow and diplomatic missions in Washington, D.C., New York, and San Francisco. As the volume of messages escalated, the cryptographers compared the ciphers used to list cargo manifests with those messages containing sensitive intelligence data. Some duplication was spotted, and eventually BRIDE developed into a major code-breaking operation that partially solved more than 2,000 texts transmitted between 1940 and 1949, later declassified as VENONA.

BRITISH INTELLIGENCE. The wartime British intelligence establishment consisted of the three intelligence branches of the fighting services: the War Office's military intelligence directorate, headed by the director of military intelligence (Gen. Paddy Beaumont-Nesbitt, then Gen. Francis Davidson and finally Gen. John Sinclair); the Admiralty's Naval Intelligence Division, headed by the **director of naval intelligence** (Adm. **John Godfrey**, then Capt. Edmund Rushbrooke); and the Air Ministry's Air Intelligence Directorate, headed by the director of air intelligence (Air Commodores Archie Boyle, then Charles Medhurst, and finally Frank Inglis). The three principal civilian services were the **Secret Intelligence Service (MI6)**, headed by **Stewart Menzies**; the Security Service (**MI5**), headed by Sir Vernon Kell and then Sir **David Petrie**; and the **Government Code and Cypher School**, subsequently renamed **Government Communications Headquarters (GCHQ)**, headed by Cmmdr. **Alastair Denniston** and then Cmmdr. **Edward Travis**. In addition, the Metropolitan Police's Special Branch, headed by Albert Canning under the supervision of Assistant Commissioner (Crime) Norman Kendal, acted as a link between MI5 and the country's county forces.

Within the War Office's Military Intelligence Directorate were geographical sections (MI2, MI3, and MI4) and military intelligence designations for the **Radio Security Service** (MI8), headed by Lord Sandhurst; the escape and evasion service (**MI9**), headed by Jimmie Langley; the Field Security Police (MI11); the German order-of-battle unit (MI14); and the **Combined Services Detailed Interrogation Centre** (MI19) headed by Col. Rawlinson.

Overseas, the British intelligence structure included MI6's representative organization, the **Inter-Services Liaison Department** in the Middle East, headed in **Cairo** by Cuthbert Bowlby and then John Teague, and in the Far East, headed in Delhi by Wng-Cmmdr. Pile and Colin Tooke; MI5's branch in the Middle East, **Security Intelligence Middle East** in Cairo, headed by Brig. Raymund Maunsell; **Combined Intelligence Far East**, established in 1943 at Kandy, Ceylon, by MI5's Courtenay Young; **Combined Intelligence Centre Iraq** in Baghdad, headed by Sqdn. Ldr. Robert Dawson-Sheppard; GCHQ's regional branches, the **Combined Bureau Middle East** at Heliopolis in Cairo, headed by Col. Freddie Jacob, and the **Wireless Experimental Station** at Anand Parbat outside Delhi, headed by Col. Peter Marr-Johnson; and the **Far East Combined Bureau**, at Singapore until 1942 headed by Capt. F. J. Wiley, and then at Colombo.

Following **D-Day**, the 21st Army Group established its own inter-Allied intelligence service in Paris and then Brussels, as the intelligence division of **Supreme Headquarters Allied Expeditionary Force**, headed by MI5's **Dick White**.

British intelligence liaison with the Allies was maintained in London through the War Office (MI3) and overseas through **British Security Coordination** in New York, a security liaison officer in Ottawa, and via George Hill and Cecil Barclay in Moscow, representing **Special Operations Executive** and MI6, respectively.

BRITISH SECURITY COORDINATION (BSC). The British umbrella organization based on the 36th and 37th floors of Rockefeller Center in New York City, which operated from 1941 to 1945 for the **Secret Intelligence Service (MI6)**, **Political Warfare Executive**, and **Special Operations Executive**. BSC was headed by **William Stephenson**, whose deputy was MI6's **C. H. (Dick) Ellis**, and was intended to liaise with the U.S. and **Canadian** authorities. However, Stephenson was deeply distrusted by the director of the **Federal Bureau of Investigation (FBI)**, **J. Edgar Hoover**, and failed to work closely enough with the Royal Canadian Mounted Police (RCMP). Instead, MI5 established a direct link with the FBI through Arthur Thurston in London, and with the RCMP through Cyril Mills in Ottawa.

Prior to the entry of the United States into the war, BSC ran a successful propaganda campaign to undermine the isolationists and the influence of the German-American Bund. It also provided **defence security officers** across the Caribbean and mounted several successful operations in Latin America to counter Axis subversion in the region.

BROADWAY. The London street in which the headquarters of the British **Secret Intelligence Service** was located at number 54, an anonymous office block identified only as Broadway Buildings and the Government Communications Bureau.

BROMO. British code name for José Laradogoitia, a Basque known to the **Federal Bureau of Investigation (FBI)** as LITTLE JOE. Laradogoitia was recruited in Spain by the **Abwehr** in 1941 after he had been deported from Idaho following his conviction for passing bad checks. He was established in Rio de Janeiro in 1942 but returned to the United States in 1943. Alerted by **MI5**, the FBI arrested Larado-goitia in New York and ran him as a **double agent**. In March 1944 he acquired a transmitter and recruited two **notional** subsources, a military policeman code-named ALBERTO, and LUIS, supposedly a War Production Board official.

BRONX. MI5 code name for Elvira Chaudoir, née de la Fuentes, a **B1(a) double agent** run by **Hugh Astor**. The daughter of the Peruvian ambassador in Vichy, BRONX was well connected in London social circles and communicated with the enemy via secret writing, having been recruited by the **Abwehr** in October 1942. She played a significant role in the **D-Day deception** scheme, intended to draw attention to Bordeaux as a possible site for an Allied landing in 1944, and continued to send letters containing secret writing until the end of hostilities.

BROUWER. **British** code name for a stay-behind **Sicherheitsdienst** agent in Rome equipped with a transmitter and active in 1944.

BRUTUS. MI5 code name for a **B1(a) double agent**, Roman Garby-Czerniawski, a Polish air force officer who had been captured by the **Abwehr** in Paris in 1942. Betrayed by his lover, **Mathilde Carré**, Garby-Czerniawski declared his true role to the British after the **Abwehr** had arranged his escape from Fresnes. His radio operator, code-named CHOPIN, was actually an MI5 technician. After the war, Garby-Czerniawski wrote an account of his participation in the INTERALLIÉ network in Nazi-occupied France, but omitted his subsequent role as a double agent.

BUNDESPOLIZEI (BUPO). The principal Swiss counterintelligence organization, which investigated and arrested members of the Soviet **Rote Drei** spy ring.

BUREAU CENTRAL DE RENSEIGNEMENTS ET D'ACTION (BCRA). The principal Free French intelligence agency. The BCRA was created in London in 1940 and established a headquarters at 10 Duke Street, in St. James's. In November 1943, the organization merged with the **Direction des Services de Renseignements et des Services de Securité Militaire** to form the **Direction Générale des Services Spéciaux.**

– C –

C. The letter traditionally used in Whitehall to indicate the **chief** of the **Secret Intelligence Service**. Until his death in November 1939, the post was held by Adm. Sir **Hugh Sinclair**. His successor was Sir **Stewart Menzies.**

CAIRNCROSS, JOHN. Code-named MOLIÈRE by the **NKVD**, John Cairncross was a Soviet spy recruited while studying French at Cambridge University under **Anthony Blunt**. Cairncross later joined the Foreign Office and in World War II was appointed private secretary in the Cabinet Office to Lord Hankey, the minister then responsible for undertaking a review of Britain's intelligence agencies. Cairncross passed this information to his Soviet contacts and also copied the Maud Report, an assessment of the proposal made by physicists Otto Frisch and Rudolf Peierls to develop an atomic bomb. A brilliant linguist, Cairncross was later transferred to **Bletchley Park**, where he removed flimsies of ULTRA intercepts that would assist the Soviets during the Battle of **Kursk**, and then was posted to the **Secret Intelligence Service** as an analyst concentrating on the German order of battle in the Balkans. At the end of the war, his espionage undetected, Cairncross worked in the Treasury and finally the Ministry of Supply. He was awarded the Order of the Red Banner by Josef Stalin and was compromised by the **defection** of Guy Burgess in May 1951.

CAIRO. The Egyptian capital was the Middle East regional headquarters for **Security Intelligence Middle East (SIME)**, headed by Raymund Maunsell; the **Middle East Intelligence Centre**, headed by Illtyd Clayton; and the **Secret Intelligence Service (MI6)**, operating under **Inter-Services Liaison Department** cover, led by Cuthbert Bowlby. The MI6 station included a small **Section V** office, headed first by Rodney Dennys and then by Sqdn. Ldr. Michael Ionides. In addition, Cairo provided accommodation for the regional **Combined Services Detailed Interrogation Centre**, the **deception** planners of **"A" Force**, and the **Combined Bureau Middle East**, **Bletchley Park**'s local cryptographic branch, accommodated in the King Farouk Museum in Heliopolis.

Cairo was the focus of considerable Axis espionage, although most of the enemy networks actually consisted of entirely **notional double agents**. One successful mission that reached Egypt, only to be arrested soon afterward in September 1942, was the **Abwehr** team code-named KONDOR and led by Johannes Eppler. Pressure to coordinate the roles of the diverse Allied agencies in Cairo led to the formation in March 1943 of the **Thirty Committee**, which supervised five other subcommittees across SIME's region.

CAMILLA. Code name for the first major **deception** operation of World War II in the Middle East conducted in January 1941 by Dudley Clarke. The objective was to divert attention away from Gen. Claude Wavell's intended offensive in Libya by pretending he was planning an attack in Somaliland. Rumors were circulated in **Cairo**, dummy wireless traffic was transmitted between Aden, Nairobi, Pretoria, and Delhi, and bogus maps and pamphlets about the area were distributed to the troops. The deception succeeded too well, because the Italian commander-in-chief, the Duke of Aosta, in the face of what he perceived to be overwhelming odds, withdrew his forces in the area and transferred them to Libya.

CAMOUFLAGE. The British code name for André Schurmann, known as SERRE to the French, who recruited him as a **double agent** in Le Havre in December 1944. Formerly a ship's telegrapher, Schurmann had worked for the **Abwehr** as a recruiter since November 1941.

CAMP, ERIC GARDINER. A Soviet spy and member of the **Communist Party of Great Britain**, Eric Gardiner Camp was convicted of breaches of the Official Secrets Act shortly before the outbreak of hostilities, but was later found in 1940 to be employed in a sensitive munitions factory.

CAMP 020. The **MI5** designation for Latchmere House, the organization's principal interrogation center, located at Ham Common in Richmond and commanded by Col. R. W. G. Stephens. A report completed at the end of 1943 by Helenus Milmo revealed the success achieved there and the extent to which the staff relied upon tips from ISOS: The total number of cases held there grew from 54 on 31 December 1941 to 90 at the end of 1942 and 120 on the same date in 1943. During 1943, 67 were admitted, 18 released, 7 transferred, and 2 prosecuted. Of those admitted in 1943, 54 proved to be spies, and of these, there were 39 cases in which there were identifiable traces on ISOS (an increase from 56 percent in 1942 to 72 percent in 1943). There were 21 cases in which the capture of the agent was attributable to ISOS (an increase from 35 percent in 1942 to 39 percent in 1943), and there were just 15 cases for which there was no identifiable trace on ISOS at all (a decrease from 44 percent to 28 percent). Of the 54 spies brought to Camp 020 in 1943, 30 were captured abroad and 24 in the United Kingdom (compared to 14 and 29, respectively, in the previous year). Out of the total of 24 apprehended in Britain, only 22 were intended to operate there, ISOS showed traces of 16, and 3 were captured on account of ISOS. Sixteen gave themselves up or were **double agents** *ab initio*. Of the three whose capture was attributable to ISOS, **Rogeiro de Menezes** would certainly have been otherwise detected and **Johannes Huysmann** almost certainly so, but **Raymond Lalou**'s fate would have been problematic. Among those who came to Britain, **Georges Graf**, **Oswald Job**, and **Florent Steiner** are really the only three that MI5 can claim to have captured single-handed.

The only fatality at Camp 020 was a German detainee named Bruhns, who was injured by a Luftwaffe bomb during an air raid on 29 November 1940. Three guards were also casualties, but survived.

CAMP 020R. The **MI5** designation for its reserve detention camp, located in Oxfordshire at Huntercombe Place, near Henley, established to accommodate long-term internees who could not be kept in the main system in case they compromised the identities of other prisoners.

CAMP Z. Code name for **Mytchett Place** in Aldershot.

CANADA. Headed by Commissioner Stuart Wood, who understood the need for a counterintelligence capability, the Royal Canadian Mounted Police (RCMP) devoted only limited resources to the investigation of German espionage because **MI5** posted Cyril Mills to Ottawa to act as a security liaison officer. Previously, the RCMP's embryonic intelligence unit, headed by Charles Rivett-Carnac, had concentrated on the identification of Communist subversives, and his successor, Inspector Bavin, had been dismissed by Assistant Commissioner Tate. Under the guidance of Mills, who arrived too late to influence a proposal to establish SPRINGBOK in Canada, the RCMP exploited the capture of **Waldemar Janowsky**, an **Abwehr** agent landed from a U-boat in November 1942.

The RCMP's liaison with the **Federal Bureau of Investigation** was in the hands of Assistant Commissioner Bruce, based in Washington, D.C., but a series of incidents soured relations with **British Security Coordination**, one being a tactless attempt to appoint Inspector Bavin as a liaison officer in Ottawa, which the RCMP rejected.

Canada made a significant contribution to the Allied interception and decryption of Axis signals, and in June 1941 the **Examination Unit** of the National Research Council employed the controversial U.S. cryptographer Herbert O. Yardley to exploit enemy broadcasts that had been monitored by the Royal Canadian Signals Corps at Rockcliffe Barracks in Ottawa. Under Yardley's supervision, the Examination Unit concentrated on Japanese broadcasts. In January 1942, he was replaced by Oliver Strachey, who had broken the Abwehr's hand ciphers at **Bletchley Park**.

CANARIS, WILHELM. Chief of the **Abwehr** since 1 January 1935, in succession to Capt. Conrad Patzig, Adm. Wilhelm Canaris, then 47, concentrated his limited resources against France, where 21 German spies were caught during that year; Poland; and until the arrest of Dr. Hermann Goertz in Harwich in November 1935, Great Britain. However, the disclosure at Goertz's trial in March 1936 that he had been engaged on a clandestine survey of Royal Air Force aerodromes in southern England, an offense for which he received a prison sentence of five years, resulted in a ban imposed by Adolf Hitler on future Abwehr intelligence missions across the Channel.

Hitler's ban on espionage against Britain, apparently to avoid political and diplomatic embarrassment, was lifted in 1937, and during the following year, three Abwehr agents—Mrs. Jessie Jordan, Donald Adams, and an Irishman, Joseph Kelly—were convicted of breaches of the Official Secrets Act, proof that Canaris had resumed operations. With the Abwehr's decentralized structure, responsibility for collecting intelligence in particular countries was delegated to the *Abstellen* in the appropriate German military districts; for example, Hamburg was the principal base for U.S. and British targets, assisted by the port being the headquarters of the Hamburg-America Line and Norddeutscher Lloyd. Both shipping companies provided a ready pool of bilingual personnel making frequent visits to overseas harbors, ready to act as couriers, photographers, and recruiters.

The Abwehr's uneasy relationship with the **Sicherheitsdienst**— friction that had caused the removal of Capt. Patzig—was eased by the improbable friendship between Canaris and **Reinhard Heydrich**, who had been his subordinate in 1925 on the training battleship *Schlesien*, shortly before the violin-playing cadet had been dismissed. Canaris's wife Erika, an accomplished cellist, was also close to Lina Heydrich, and the families lived in the same neighborhood in the Berlin suburb of Schlachtensee.

Canaris tolerated a large number of anti-Nazis in his organization, which was absorbed into the **Reichssicherheitshauptamt** on 12 February 1944 following a series of damaging security lapses, including the **defection** of **Erich Vermehren**. Canaris was arrested in August 1944 and executed at Flossenburg in April 1945.

CAPE MATAPAN, BATTLE OF. On 28 March 1941, the Italian Navy suffered a heavy defeat at Cape Matapan, off southernmost Greece, when the cruisers *Fiume*, *Pola*, and *Zara* were sunk by Adm. Sir Andrew Cunningham's First Battle Squadron. The Italians also lost two destroyers, the *Vincenti Gioberti* and the *Maestrale*, and their flagship *Vittorio Veneto* was damaged by a torpedo. A total of 2,400 Italians lost their lives, while the only British loss was a single Swordfish biplane. The action effectively eliminated the Italian Navy for the remainder of the war.

Cunningham had been alerted to the Italian fleet movement by a few rare Italian **Enigma** and Luftwaffe intercepts, indicating that the

Axis powers were planning a major naval operation in the eastern Mediterranean. Then, at 12:30 p.m. on 27 March, a flying boat based in Malta spotted the warships 75 miles east of Sicily, heading for **Crete**.

Intending to keep his departure from Alexandria on the carrier HMS *Formidable* as secret as possible, Adm. Cunningham visited the clubhouse of the local golf course, knowing that he would be spotted by the Japanese consul-general, who reported all shipping movements in the port. Convinced that the Royal Navy's Mediterranean Fleet was safely at anchor in Egypt, when in fact it had sailed under cover of darkness, the Italians were taken by surprise when a Walrus reconnaissance aircraft launched from the carrier HMS *Warspite* found them at sea.

Although signals intelligence played a role in the discovery of the Italian warships, their location was not compromised by any ciphers betrayed in Washington, D.C., by the naval attaché, Adm. Alberto Lais, a former director of Italian naval intelligence. Lais had become involved with a British agent, Elizabeth Pack, who would later claim to have extracted a codebook from her lover, but as the Matapan engagement had occurred partly as a result of Enigma intercepts, any code compromised by Lais cannot have been relevant.

CAPRICORN. Secret Intelligence Service code name for an agent in the Peloponnese whose radio was detected as having come under enemy control in late 1942. The channel was kept open for **deception** purposes, although his Italian controllers later claimed they had suspected he had been compromised in February 1943.

CARBUNCLE. Code name for a **double agent** run by **Combined Intelligence Far East** in Colombo, Ceylon.

CARELESS. MI5 code name for a Polish airman used as a **double agent** between July 1941 and January 1943.

CAROLI, GÓSTA. The true identity of **MI5**'s **double agent** SUMMER. Caroli, a Swede, had been taken into custody by the British in Cambridgeshire within a few hours of landing and, in return for a promise that he would be treated as a prisoner of war, had quickly told his interrogators all they had wanted to know, including the identity of his Danish friend, **Wulf Schmidt**, who was scheduled to follow by the same route. On 17 September 1940, operating from Aylesbury police station, Caroli used his wireless to transmit a safe-arrival signal and report that he had been living rough since his arrival. In reality, of course, he was in MI5's secret detention center at **Camp 020**. Caroli was then transferred to a secure MI5 safe house at Hinxton, whence he transmitted wireless reports on the area around Birmingham.

Caroli inadvertently let slip that that an earlier, prewar visit to England had been undertaken for the **Abwehr**, a detail that he had omitted from his original statement, so MI5 brought him back to Camp 020 for further interrogation. This led Caroli, who was already suffering from depression, to attempt suicide by slashing his wrists. MI5 then returned Caroli to Hinxton and allowed Schmidt to join him for the Christmas holiday, but instead of raising his spirits, Caroli sank into an even greater depression. Finally, on 13 January 1941, he half-strangled his lone guard and stole a motorcycle. Fortunately, it broke down, and he was recaptured in Ely en route to the east coast.

Obviously Caroli could be trusted no more, and he was transferred to a special detention facility, thereby bringing SUMMER's case to a conclusion. Once again, the question of his future arose. Was he to be kept in detention or was he another "suitable" case and therefore to be turned over to the prosecuting authorities? MI5 expressed the view that neither GANDER nor SUMMER should be put on trial. Both had cooperated after promises had been made, and neither had been a Nazi. Perhaps more importantly, any public disclosure of the circumstances of their capture would be bound to tip off the enemy to MI5's control of their cases, even if it did not actually jeopardize other double agents.

CARRÉ, MATHILDE. Known as THE CAT, Mathilde Carré was a divorced French army nurse who was recruited into the INTERALLIÉ resistance organization in 1940. She was cipher clerk and mistress to INTERALLIÉ's charismatic leader, Roman Garby-Czerniawski (BRUTUS), but she was betrayed to the Germans by another member of the network, Christine Borue. In November 1941, the Paris **Abwehr** arrested almost the entire membership, including Carré, who agreed to cooperate with her captor, Sgt. Hugo Bleicher. Having reported Garby-Czerniawski's arrest to London, she declared herself the leader of the new **circuit** and gave herself the code name VICTOIRE. In the months that followed, four transmitters maintained contact with London, but VICTOIRE confessed her dual role to an early **Special Operations Executive** parachutist, Pierre de Vomécourt, whose own network had been rolled up by the Germans. Together, in February 1942, they arranged a pickup by boat from the French coast. Once in London, Carré was interrogated about her relationship with the Abwehr. Initially she was allowed her freedom, but in July 1942 she was taken into custody because she was considered unreliable, and the decision was made to prevent her from returning to France with de Vomécourt, which had been their plan. She remained in prison, at Aylesbury and Holloway, until June 1945 when she was deported to Paris, where the French authorities arrested her and charged her with collaboration. She was sentenced to death in January 1949, reprieved and sentenced to hard labor for life, and then released in September 1954. Her autobiography, *I Was the Cat*, was published in 1959.

CARROT. MI5 code name for a Luxembourger run as a **double agent** from June to December 1942.

CELERY. MI5 code name for Walter Dicketts, a former Royal Air Force officer who operated as a **double agent** and accompanied **Arthur Owens** to Portugal and Germany in 1941. The case was abandoned in August 1941 after Owens was detained in England.

CENTRAL BUREAU. Established in South Yarra, near Melbourne, Australia, by Gen. Douglas MacArthur in 1942 to study Japanese air, naval, and military wireless traffic, the Central Bureau became his principal source of signals intelligence, staffed by American, British, and Australian cryptographers. Later moved to Brisbane and organized into eight branches, covering "solutions," traffic, translation, and machine procedures, the Central Bureau established a forward base at San Miguel and was fed intercepts by 3,400 wireless operators spread across the Pacific from Biak in New Guinea to the Solomon Islands. Advance information concerning Japanese efforts to reinforce their troops on Leyte in October 1944 led to the sinking of 17 enemy transports and their destroyer escorts, ambushed by 347 American aircraft in the Gulf of Leyte, a battle that was the last major naval engagement of the war.

CHARLIE. MI5 code name for Bernie Kiener, a German photographer born in England who was recruited by the **Abwehr** in 1938. In 1940 he would be put in touch with **Arthur Owens**, but his case was terminated in August 1941 after Owens was taken into custody.

CHEESE. Security Intelligence Middle East (SIME) code name for Renato Levi, an Italian Jew recruited before the war by the **Secret Intelligence Service**. Levi arrived in **Cairo** in February 1941, on a mission for the Italian **Servizio di Informazione Militare**, only to be returned back to Rome for SIME's Special Section, but he was subsequently imprisoned for his black market activities. In his absence, his **notional** radio operator, "Paul Nicossof," purportedly a Syrian of Slavic background, continued to transmit to the **Abwehr** until February 1945, assisted by an equally fictional Greek girlfriend, MISANTHROPE.

CHER BEBÉ. A Spanish mechanic based in Oran, CHER BEBÉ acted as a **double agent** for the French, after serving a year's imprisonment, and from May 1943 conveyed **deception** material.

CHIEF. The title given to the head of the British **Secret Intelligence Service** and held by Adm. Sir **Hugh Sinclair** and his successor, Col. **Stewart Menzies**. It was often abbreviated to **C**.

CHILE. The Chilean intelligence service, the Dirección General de Información e Inteligencia (DGII), headed by Enrique Frias, was generally pro-Allied, although Chile officially was neutral and President Pedro Aguirre Cerda was reluctant to compromise his country's status. Nevertheless, the DGII closed down several **Abwehr** networks after having been tipped off to their existence by the British **Secret Intelligence Service (MI6)**.

Capt. Dietrich Niebuhr, the German naval attaché, scored an early success by arranging for the escape of seven German merchantmen trapped in Chilean ports at the outbreak of hostilities and, through the intervention of Friedrich von Schulz-Hausmann, the agent in Valparaiso for the Norddeutscher Lloyd Line, they all were able to put to sea and reach either Japan or Vladivostok. Under Niebuhr's supervision, Schulz-Hausmann also removed the ship's radio from the *Osorno*, one of the seven trapped ships, and recruited its operator, Hans Blume, code-named FLOR, as a technician to rebuild the transmitter and make contact with Hamburg, 8,000 miles away. Between 17 April 1941 and 15 June 1942 he transmitted 429 messages, enciphered using F. D. Ommanney's *Southern Latitude*, and received 287 messages from call sign REW in Hamburg, based on a cipher drawn from *The Letters of Catherine Mansfield*, edited by J. Middleton Murray. Assisting Blume was another radio specialist, Johannes Szeraws, from the blockaded *Frankfort*, who adopted the code name ESCO and volunteered to remain in Chile and serve the Abwehr when his ship slipped its moorings in March 1941.

The PYL–REW circuit was operational for only 10 days before the **Radio Intelligence Division** picked up its signals at an intercept station at Millis, Massachusetts, and considerable skill was required to copy the traffic because its chosen frequency was extremely close to one allocated to a scrambled transatlantic radiotelephone channel. MI6 had already alerted DGII chief Frias to their suspicions about Schulz-Hausmann in December 1940, but President Cerda had taken no action, fearing that his country's neutrality could be compromised if he appeared to intervene on behalf of the British.

The local representative of the **Federal Bureau of Investigation**'s **Special Intelligence Service** was Robert W. Wall, the legal attaché since August 1941, with Dwight J. Dalbey operating undercover, and together they gathered information about the PYL transmitter, which had begun broadcasting from the Cerro Alegre home of a licensed amateur, Wilhelm Zeller. At Wall's request, the DGII raided Zeller's home twice, but failed to find the transmitter, which had been dismantled. PYL then went off the air until October 1942, when it was traced to a farm outside Quilpue, near Valparaiso, operated by the German air attaché, Maj. Ludwig von Bohlen, code-named BACH, who had been born in Chile but had fought in World War I. By the time Chile severed relations with the Axis in January 1943, PYL had been silenced by a DGII raid in November 1942, prompted by official protests from Washington, but another transmitter, PQZ, continued to operate from Santiago. When von Bohlen returned to Germany in September 1943, he entrusted his organization to a subordinate, Bernardo Timmerman, but sufficient espionage and cipher paraphernalia had been recovered from the PYL site to compromise him, and he was arrested in February 1944. Thereafter there was no evidence of any continuing espionage in Chile conducted by the Nazis. *See also ADMIRAL GRAF SPEE*; ARGENTINA.

CHINA. Generalissimo Chiang Kai-shek relied heavily on intelligence from his Kuomintang (KMT) security apparatus and employed Gen. Cheng K'ai-min as his director of military intelligence. Both understood the advantages of strategic **deception**, and although their sources behind Japanese lines proved unreliable, they maintained a close relationship with **D Division** of the South-East Asia Command.

CHURCHILL, WINSTON. A voracious consumer of intelligence, Winston Churchill took a close interest in the production efforts of, and came to rely very heavily on, ULTRA, which he later referred to discreetly in his magisterial *History of the Second World War* as **"most secret sources."**

CICERO. The **Sicherheitsdienst** code name for **Elyesa Bazna**, valet to Sir Hughe Knatchbull-Hugessen, the British ambassador in **Ankara** in 1943.

CIRCUIT. Networks run in enemy-occupied territory by **Special Operations Executive** were referred to as *circuits* because originally they were all dependent on radio links to Grendon.

CLAYMORE. The true purpose of Operation CLAYMORE, a raid on the Lofoten Islands on 3 March 1941, was to capture one of the three **Enigma** machines known to be there. In the event, none were recovered because Lt. Hans Kupfinger, the commander of an unarmed trawler, the *Krebs*, threw his overboard moments before he was killed. However, the machine's rotors were seized, and so were cipher documents that disclosed the Home Waters keys for February, allowing **Bletchley Park** to retrospectively read the traffic. Other material helped the cryptographers to solve much of the April traffic, compromising signals sent between 1 March and 10 May. The operation was considered so successful that a further attack, on the *München*, was planned for May. That did not yield an Enigma, either, but another raid on an unarmed weather ship, the *Lauenberg*, took place at the end of June when it was judged she would be in possession of the DOLPHIN keys for July. *See also* U-33.

COBWEB. Secret Intelligence Service code name for Ib Riis, a **double agent**. A Dane of Icelandic parentage who landed in Iceland in April 1941, he continued to transmit until the end of hostilities. *See also* LAND SPIDER.

COG. French code name for Michel Lamour, a Frenchman infiltrated into Bordeaux in March 1945 and run as a **double agent** against the Germans.

COLOSSUS. Code name for the world's first programmable analog computer, built in 1943 in just 10 months at the Post Office Research Establishment at Dollis Hill in North London and installed at **Bletchley Park** in January 1944 to assist in solving **Geheimschreiber** ciphers.

COLUMBINE. MI5 code name for a German **defector**, a Schutzstaffel (SS) officer who escaped to **Stockholm** and proved a useful interrogator when he reached England.

COMBINED BUREAU MIDDLE EAST (CBME). The cover name for the regional **Government Code and Cypher School** headquarters in the Middle East. Established by Col. Freddie Jacob in May 1941, it operated out of the King Farouk Museum at Heliopolis.

COMBINED INTELLIGENCE CENTRE IRAQ (CICI). The principal **British intelligence** collection agency in Iraq, based at Habbaniyah and run by a Royal Air Force officer, Robert Dawson-Sheppard. CICI also ran **double agents**, including KISS.

COMBINED INTELLIGENCE FAR EAST (CIFE). MI5's regional organization in the Far East, established at Kandy, Ceylon, in 1943 by Courtenay Young, MI5's only Japanese-speaking officer.

COMBINED SERVICES DETAILED INTERROGATION CENTRE (CSDIC). The British POW interrogation service, designated MI19. CSDIC operated facilities in Great Britain and at regional centers in **Cairo** and Delhi.

COMMUNIST PARTY OF GREAT BRITAIN (CPGB). The conviction of **Douglas Springhall** and **Ormond Uren** of breaches of the Official Secrets Act in June and October 1943, respectively, demonstrated the link between Soviet espionage and the CPGB, as Springhall had been the party's national organizer. **MI5** would eventually learn that another official, Bob Stuart, had acted as a link between the **NKVD** and its networks in Great Britain in 1940 during a period when the *rezidentura* at the Soviet embassy had temporarily suspended operations.

Prior to the Nazi invasion of the Soviet Union in 1941, the CPGB denounced the conflict as a "capitalists' war" and urged its membership to avoid furthering the war effort. After the attack, however, the CPGB reversed its policy and demanded full support for the Allies.

COMMUNIST PARTY OF THE UNITED STATES OF AMERICA (CPUSA). Headed by an **NKVD** agent of long standing, Earl Browder, code-named HELMSMAN, the CPUSA provided Moscow with a convenient pool of sympathizers in which to recruit sources. Even though CPUSA membership inevitably attracted the attention of the **Federal Bureau of Investigation (FBI)** and threatened to jeopardize the fiction that the party was entirely independent of the Kremlin, the NKVD found it expedient to approach individuals for information and then invite them to suspend their formal membership or join an underground cadre. In addition, the NKVD was under instructions to screen candidates for recruitment through the Central Committee in Moscow, which checked with the CPUSA headquarters in New York for their political reliability.

The extent to which the NKVD depended on the CPUSA became evident when the VENONA traffic was analyzed and the Central Committee's archives were examined. Essentially the records and secret messages revealed that Browder's sister Margaret, code-named GIN (and later ANNA), and his wife Kitty Harris, code-named GYPSY, were both experienced NKVD agents recruited separately in 1931, who had worked abroad as couriers and had been trained as radio operators in Moscow.

The prewar Woolwich Arsenal espionage prosecution in London had caused severe embarrassment for the **Communist Party of Great Britain (CPGB)** because one of the spies charged, Percy Glading, had been the party's national organizer. Naturally he had been expelled from the CPGB upon his conviction, and thereafter Moscow Center directed that as far as possible there should be separation between the clandestine networks engaged in intelligence collection and the party. However, when ENORMOZ became a priority, this precaution was abandoned because of the importance given to penetrating the **Manhattan Project**, which was staffed with university graduates, many of them with current party or past Young Communist League memberships. Significantly, the link between the NKVD and the party became apparent to the FBI only when an activist, Steve Nelson, was watched while he met the New York *rezident*, **Vasili Zubilin**, at the end of December 1941 at his home in Oakland, California, and then spotted him conducting a rendezvous with Piotr Ivanov of the Soviet consulate-general in San Francisco, and then with a Berkeley radiation laboratory physicist, Joseph W. Weinberg. Study of the VENONA texts demonstrated that, for example, the head of the CPUSA in California, William Schneiderman, was a source code-named NAT, and plenty of his party subordinates appeared in the traffic, too.

CONTRABAND CONTROL. The British authorities across the empire posted contraband control officers to conduct searches of suspect vessels. In **Bermuda**, **Gibraltar**, and **Trinidad**, the personnel were drawn from the **Secret Intelligence Service** and acted on advice from headquarters. They were empowered to confiscate cargos and detain both passengers and crew.

COORDINATOR OF INFORMATION (CoI). A post created in July 1941 by President Franklin D. Roosevelt, who appointed Gen. **William Donovan** to head a small intelligence agency that in June the following year became the **Office of Strategic Services**.

COPPERHEAD. MI5 code name for a **deception** operation conducted in **Gibraltar** in 1944 intended to persuade the **Abwehr** that Gen.

Bernard Montgomery would be based in the Mediterranean during the imminent Allied invasion of Europe.

COSSACK. British code name for a Turkish radio technician, a stay-behind agent captured near Lille at the end of November 1944 after his transmissions had been monitored by **Special Communications Unit** 10. He was subsequently run by **Special Counter-Intelligence Unit** 104 against his German controllers, who dispatched a courier to Paris to keep him in funds.

COSTAR. MI5 code name for a Portuguese employee of the British legation in **Lisbon**.

COUGHDROP. British code name for a **notional** group of agents infiltrated into Japanese-occupied northern Sumatra in December 1944 who were intended to be the recipients of radio messages indicating that the island was to be the target of an Allied invasion.

COVENTRY RAID. *See* MOONLIGHT SONATA.

CRETE. The German plan to land airborne troops on Crete in May 1941 and seize the strategically important island was fully anticipated by the Allies because much of it had been intercepted and read in **Cairo** and then conveyed to the local Allied commander, Gen. Bernard Freyberg. Nevertheless, in spite of this apparent intelligence advantage, the defenders' lack of air superiority prevented them from resisting the enemy assault, and the island was captured and occupied.

CROSSBOW. Code name for a British War Cabinet subcommittee chaired by Duncan Sandys to collate and assess intelligence concerning Hitler's secret weapons.

CRUDE. The British **Inter-Services Liaison Department (ISLD)** code name for a Turkish businessman in Iraq heading a **notional** spy ring who remained in contact with the **Abwehr** in Syria through secret writing from January 1943. One of his imaginary sources was ALERT, a civilian employed by a military headquarters in Syria who nurtured a grudge against the British because an Australian sergeant-major had raped his mother during World War I. CRUDE was run by ISLD's Michael Ionides.

CRUZ. British code name for a **double agent** employed as a night watchman by the British naval attaché in **Lisbon**, with access to discarded documents.

CUPID. British code name for the beautiful German Jewish owner of a bar in Casablanca who communicated in secret writing once a week to a German cover address in Barcelona. Her channel was used to convey **deception** material between March and June 1943.

CZECH INTELLIGENCE. The Czech military intelligence service, headed by Col. **Frantisek Moravec**, was exfiltrated to London upon the German occupation of Prague in March 1939, and thereafter was allowed to operate in close cooperation with Harold Gibson of the **Secret Intelligence Service (MI6)**. Of great value to MI6 was Moravec's star agent, Paul Thümmel, code-named A-54, an **Abwehr** officer who remained in contact until his arrest in February 1942. Gibson was later succeeded as liaison officer with the Czechs by another senior MI6 officer, Rex Howard. While based in London, Moravec was accommodated by MI6 in Rosendale Road, West Dulwich, with an office in Porchester Gate and a radio station at Funny Neuk in Woldingham.

Moravec's representative offices in **Istanbul** and **Lisbon** experienced hostile penetration, and an MI6 transmitter supplied to an officer code-named ALEXANDRE for use in Paris came under enemy control, although MI6 could not compromise ISOS by explaining to Moravec how MI6 had developed suspicions about ALEXANDRE, whom he dismissed anyway. ALEXANDRE's duplicity was later confirmed in early 1945 by an Abwehr **defector** in Lisbon, Hans Cramer, although this did not prevent him from being hired by the **Office of Strategic Services**.

– D –

DANILOV, ANTON. A **GRU** officer arrested by the **Abwehr** in December 1941 as he operated an illicit transmitter in Brussels, Anton

Danilov's capture gave the Germans a long-awaited breakthrough. Although he himself gave minimal cooperation and was executed two years later, the woman who was the principal tenant in his building, Rita Arnould, immediately turned informer and revealed her role as a courier and wireless operator in a ring headed by **Viktor Gurye-vitch**. Recently widowed, she also disclosed that her lover, a Belgian diamond merchant named Isadore Springer, was an important Soviet agent, a member of the Kommunistische Partei Deutschlands with experience operating in Palestine, in France, and for the International Brigade in Spain. Like Guryevitch, Springer evaded arrest and moved to France where he started a new network in Lyons.

The other occupant in the house, also a member of Guryevitch's cell, was Sofia Posnanska, a Polish Jew whose husband was later to work with Springer in Lyons. She had been one of **Leopold Trepper**'s subordinates in Paris in 1940 and had received cipher training in Moscow before the war. Rather than collaborate with her captors like her friend Arnould, she committed suicide in St. Gilles Prison, Brussels. Meanwhile Arnould betrayed a forger's workshop concealed in her house and, from seized passport photographs, identified Trepper and Guryevitch as the key figures at the center of the Soviet organization.

The Abwehr's investigation, code-named **Rote Kapelle**, stalled temporarily because of the intransigence of Danilov and Posnanska and its inability to put names to the network's two ringleaders who had disappeared. However, a breakthrough came some eight months later, on 30 July 1942, when the Abwehr radio direction-finders closed in on the attic of a house in Laeken. There they found **Johann Wenzel**, a German Communist of long standing from Danzig who had been trained as a wireless operator in Moscow and was in **Belgium** illegally.

DANSEY, CLAUDE. The deputy **chief** of the **Secret Intelligence Service (MI6)**, Claude Dansey had been the architect of the prewar **Z Organisation**. A professional, Dansey had spent his long career in **MI5** and MI6 and gained a reputation for ruthless but skillful management of networks. Having replaced **Dick Ellis** as MI6's chief of production for Europe, Dansey promoted liaison with the **Czech**, **French**, and **Polish** services and placed a high value on long-term quality political information in preference to sabotage operations conducted by networks run by amateurs that were vulnerable to hostile penetration. Always skeptical of the activities of **Special Operations Executive**, he attempted to exercise some control over its organization by insisting on retaining responsibility for its communications, and indeed those of Allied services based in London. His style led to resentment among some critics, but he prevented wholesale compromise of MI6's operations.

DAVIDSON, FRANCIS. Appointed director of military intelligence at the War Office in December 1940, in succession to Paddy Beaumont-Nesbitt, Gen. Francis Davidson held the post until he was replaced by John Sinclair in 1944.

DAVIL. A French intelligence agent recruited by the Germans in **Madrid**, DAVIL was sent with a radio to Casablanca, where in January 1944 he obtained a job at an airfield. Thereafter he was run as a **double agent**, transmitting **deception** material direct to Hamburg.

D-DAY. The code name for the date of the Allied invasion of France in 1944. As the exact timing was not agreed upon until the very last moment, the planners worked on a schedule based on D+ and D– days. The Allied code name for the operation was OVERLORD, with NEPTUNE being the naval component. The task of transporting 150,000 Allied troops across one of the most notorious stretches of water, the English Channel, to a heavily defended beachhead looked so daunting that the planners opted for a high-risk strategy of taking the longer route to Normandy in the hope of catching the enemy unprepared. An elaborate **deception** scheme, code-named FORTITUDE, was created to persuade the enemy that the assault would take place in the Pas-de-Calais, the most obvious route across the Channel and one that would offer the prospect of capturing a large port, allowing maximum air cover over the combat zone, and eliminating the V-1 launch sites in northwest France. Military orthodoxy dictated that the Allied troops would concentrate in southeast England and embark from Dover and Folkestone for the enemy-held coastline. Predisposed to believe the beaches between Boulogne and Calais were the most likely targets, the **Fremde Heere West** analysts accepted intelligence reports from Luftwaffe reconnaissance flights, Abwehr agents, and signals intelligence that a First U.S. Army Group had assembled in East Anglia and was poised to launch a massive amphibious assault a fortnight after a diversionary feint in Normandy had drawn the defenders away from the area. *See also* BRONX; GARBO.

D DIVISION. The Allied organization in the Far East for planning and executing **deception** schemes, headed by **Peter Fleming**. D Division was created in January 1944 through an amalgamation of GSI(d) and its American counterpart, Ormonde Hunter's Special Planning Section. D Division became the theater's principal coordinating body for all Anglo-American intelligence activities.

DECEPTION. Although the principles of strategic deception had been widely understood since the Punic Wars and the Trojan horse, it was not until World War II that the discipline came to be institutionalized and recognized as an essential instrument of war. The Allies proved adept at exploiting a variety of channels, including deliberate leakages, the spreading of rumors, **double agents**, censorship lapses, wireless traffic, camouflage, and dummy vehicles, to convey misleading information to the enemy. In England, John Bevan's London Controlling Section coordinated the planning and execution of deception plans, with **"A" Force** and **D Division** undertaking similar roles in the Middle East and Far East, respectively. None of the Axis intelligence agencies indulged in such sophisticated deception schemes, although the Soviets proved adept at mounting high-risk stratagems on the Russian front. *See also* FORTITUDE.

DE DEEKER, FRANCOIS. Arrested in September 1941 in Scotland after he had landed from a flying boat, de Deeker was tried in June 1941 and hanged at Wandsworth in August 1941.

DEFECTOR. A person with intelligence value who switches sides and is granted asylum by an adversary. During World War II, several German Foreign Ministry, **Abwehr**, and **Sicherheitsdienst** officers defected to the British, among them **Wolfgang zu Putlitz**, **Erich Vermehren**, **Willi Hamburger**, HARLEQUIN, and the **Kleczkowskis**. No Allied intelligence officers defected to the Axis, although Capt. **Sigismund Best** and Maj. **Richard Stevens** were wrongly suspected of having collaborated with the enemy.

DEFENCE SECURITY OFFICER (DSO). MI5 personnel posted overseas to British garrisons and colonies worked under defence security officer cover. DSOs were based in Aden, **Bermuda**, British Honduras, **Cairo**, **Gibraltar**, the Gold Coast, Iraq, Jamaica, Malta, Palestine, and **Trinidad**.

DELHI INTELLIGENCE BUREAU (DIB). The principal security apparatus in India was the Delhi Intelligence Bureau, a successor to the police-led **Indian Political Intelligence Bureau**. Also based in Delhi was the regional **Secret Intelligence Service** headquarters, headed by Wng-Cmmdr. Pile. Just outside the city at Amand Parbat, Col. Peter Marr-Johnson headed the **Wireless Experimental Station**, actually the regional base for **Government Communications Headquarters**.

DENMARK. At the outbreak of the war, Denmark's intelligence apparatus consisted of the Generalstabens Efterretningssektion (the intelligence section of the General Staff) headed by Col. Mygdal Einar Nordentoft, and the Marinestabens Efterretningssektion (the intelligence section of the Naval Staff) headed by Capt. Poul Adam Mørch. Neither organization employed a staff of more than a dozen because of the government's lack of interest in intelligence during the interwar period, but both played a key role in the development of resistance to the Nazi occupation. Communications with Great Britain were channeled through southern Sweden, as the Germans never succeeded in preventing small boats from crossing the short distance between the two countries.

In mid-1941, an agreement was made between the British **Secret Intelligence Service (MI6)** and **Special Operations Executive (SOE)** that henceforth SOE would be responsible for the collection of intelligence in Denmark and for liaison with the local resistance organization, which was based on the army. Accordingly, thereafter MI6 played almost no role in the development of networks in Denmark, although Euan Rabagliati's Dutch country section did make the attempt, in an operation mounted in September 1941, to drop Thomas Sneum and his wireless operator Christoffersen near Brofelde. Sneum was a young officer in the Danish army who had made his escape to England in June 1941 by the rather improbable means of a homemade aircraft that he flew across the North Sea with a friend. It was only after **MI5** had been satisfied that Sneum's odyssey had been authentic that he had been passed to MI6 for recruitment. Upon their return to Denmark, Christoffersen and Sneum both landed safely, and a Danish police inspector, Roland Olsen, was recruited to improve the flow of intelligence. Olsen was able to warn Sneum of his imminent arrest, allowing him to escape to Sweden.

MI6's reluctance to mount more operations in Denmark was in part a reflection of the quality of information being gathered by SOE's Danish Section, which largely came from Ebbe Munck, an explorer and agent of the Danish military intelligence service who operated under journalistic cover as a correspondent for a Copenhagen daily newspaper, the *Berlingske Tidende*. Munck worked in **Stockholm** and maintained close contact with the SOE representative, Ronald Turnbull, claiming to be the link with a fully equipped resistance movement in the Danish army known as "the Princes." Turnbull's arrangement with Munck, which MI6 endorsed, was that intelligence would be traded for a ban on sabotage, which, it was feared, would bring reprisals but very little lasting damage to the German military machine.

This controversial arrangement was accepted by SOE because it had nobody else to deal with in Denmark, and by MI6 because it had no realistic prospect of recruiting new agents. Of course, it also accorded with MI6's philosophy that subversion and espionage were mutually incompatible. Gradually SOE began to suspect that the so-called Princes had exaggerated their own strength just to impress London and had their own motives for discouraging operations. As Gen. Sir Colin Gubbins commented in October 1942, the Danes "wish to keep their country absolutely free of any sabotage or anti-German action until the Germans break up altogether and begin to leave the country and then in point of fact we shall not need them."

Gubbins was proved correct when, in August the following year, the Danish puppet government fell and the Nazis imposed their own administration. This was the opportunity for the Princes to act, but instead they fled. One of the four leading Princes was arrested, but two others escaped to Sweden. The fourth surrendered but was freed, thus allowing him to make his way to Stockholm and reestablish contact with SOE.

DENNISTON, ALASTAIR. The director of the **Government Code and Cypher School** from 1924, and then head of the **Diplomatic Section** from 1944, Alastair Denniston was an administrator.

DEPUTY. British code name for a Belgian **Special Operations Executive** agent, a ship's telegrapher who was infiltrated back into **Belgium** in 1940 from Cuba, supposedly as a deserter. He was subsequently recruited by the **Abwehr** in **Lisbon** and, after undergoing a refresher course on codes in Wiesbaden, was instructed in late August 1944 to operate as a stay-behind agent in Brussels. When the city was liberated, DEPUTY acted as a **double agent**, transmitting **deception** material supplied by DOMINANT to his German controllers.

DEPUTY DIRECTOR-GENERAL (DDG). Sir Eric Holt-Wilson was dismissed from his post as deputy director-general of the Security Service (**MI5**) in June 1940 and was replaced by Brigadier **Jasper Harker**, who remained until his retirement in 1946.

DERRICK. British code name for a hydrographer and **Belgian** Sûreté agent recruited by the Germans as a member of a stay-behind network in Bruges in March 1944. Once liberated, he made radio contact with his controllers in September 1944 and passed them **deception** material, supposedly from an apartment in Ostend, until the end of hostilities. Unusually, all of DERRICK's messages could be monitored through ISOS, which demonstrated that he was highly regarded by the enemy. When he demanded more funds, a courier named Dreuner was sent, and when Dreuner was arrested carrying $1,000 for him, DRAGOMAN was instructed to send DERRICK some cash instead.

DESIRE. Code name for Alfred Gabas, a Frenchman and member of an **Abwehr** stay-behind network in Cherbourg who was arrested when he attempted to make contact with DRAGOMAN. He proved too unreliable to run as a **double agent**, but under interrogation he accidentally compromised DRAGOMAN, who proved far more amenable.

DE VELASCO, ANGEL ALCAZAR. *See* ALCAZAR DE VELASCO, ANGEL.

DICKINSON, VELVALEE. The owner of a shop on Madison Avenue in New York selling expensive dolls, Velvalee Dickinson and her husband, a California stockbroker who died in 1943, acted as spies for Japanese naval intelligence for many years, collecting mainly naval information. In 1935, they moved to New York and, after December 1941, communicated with their Japanese contact through an intermediary with a mail drop in Buenos Aires. The **Federal Bureau of Investigation (FBI)** learned of the problem in August 1942 when the addressee moved and the letters, written in a very rudimentary code ostensibly dealing with the dispatch and delivery of dolls, were returned by the Post Office to bemused women whose names had appeared on the envelopes as the return addresses. All were Dickinson's clients and contacted the FBI, which then requested a watch in **Bermuda** for more of the same letters. In January 1944, having acquired a further four examples of the illicit correspondence, the FBI arrested Dickinson. At the trial, Elizabeth Friedman gave evidence concerning the rather primitive code. Like her husband, William Friedman, Elizabeth was one of the most accomplished cryptographers of the era, and it was her skill that cracked Dickinson's Japanese code. Dickinson was sentenced to 10 years' imprisonment and fined $10,000.

DIPLOMATIC SECTION. The **Government Communications Headquarters** section responsible for the decryption of target diplomatic traffic. The Diplomatic Section was located in Berkeley Street in London's Mayfair and was headed by Comdr. **Alastair Denniston**. It was responsible for producing intercepts, including FLORADORA and PANDORA, based on **one-time pads**, and **BJ**, which encompassed the diplomatic telegrams sent to and from many foreign capitals.

DIREÇÃO DA ORDEM POLÍTICA E SOCIAL (DOPS). The principal **Brazilian** security apparatus, DOPS was headed by Felisberto Teixeira, who readily cracked down on Axis espionage when supplied with evidence from the **Federal Bureau of Investigation**'s **Special Intelligence Service**.

DIRECCIÓN GENERAL DE INFORMACIÓN E INTELIGENCIA (DGII). The principal **Chilean** security apparatus, the DGII was headed by Enrique Frias, who attempted to maintain his country's neutrality by acting on reports of German espionage submitted by British and American intelligence agencies.

DIRECTION DES SERVICES DE RENSEIGNEMENTS ET DES SERVICES DE SECURITÉ MILITAIRE (DSM). Created in 1940 in London under the leadership of **Paul Paillole** as a Free French successor to the Deuxieme Bureau, the DSM was merged in November 1943 with the **Bureau Central de Renseignements et d'Action** to form the **Direction Générale des Services Spéciaux**.

DIRECTION GÉNÉRALE DES SERVICES SPÉCIAUX (DGSS). The Free **French intelligence** agency created in November 1943 following the merger of the **Direction des Services de Renseignements et des Services de Securité Militaire** and the **Bureau Central de Renseignements et d'Action**. The DGSS was subsequently renamed the Direction Générale des Études et Recherches.

DIRECTOR-GENERAL OF THE SECURITY SERVICE. In June 1940 Maj. Gen. Sir Vernon Kell was dismissed from his post as director-general of the Security Service (**MI5**), which he had held since 1909. He was replaced temporarily to **Jasper Harker**, and then by Sir **David Petrie**.

DIRECTOR OF NAVAL INTELLIGENCE (DNI). At the outbreak of war the British DNI was Adm. **John Godfrey**, who held the post until he was dismissed in September 1942 and replaced by Capt. Edmund Rushbrooke.

DIREKTOR. Code name for the head of the **GRU** in Moscow, as referred to in wireless traffic exchanged with spy rings in western Europe.

DOGWOOD. The **Office of Strategic Services (OSS)** code name for a Czech engineer in Turkey who claimed to run a resistance movement in Austria and Hungary code-named CEREUS. Between June 1943 and February 1944, DOGWOOD provided the OSS's Archibald Coleman with 730 messages from 53 agents. However, when **X-2**'s Frank Wisner reached **Istanbul** in October 1943, he immediately became suspicious when, after he demanded to know DOGWOOD's sources so they could be checked against **Section V**'s indixes, he was rebuffed and the local OSS station chief, Lanning Macfarland, overruled him.

In September 1943, the Hungarian military attaché, Col. Otto Hatz, was enrolled into CEREUS under the code name TRILLIUM, and he proposed a plan for Hungary's withdrawal from the Axis and for a handover to the Americans of all Hungarian intelligence assets. When word spread of the scheme, code-named SPARROW, the local **Secret Intelligence Service (MI6)** station commander, Harold Gibson, banned all MI6 personnel from any contact with the OSS. Furthermore, in March 1944 Germany occupied Hungary and much of the CEREUS organization was arrested and executed.

An investigation conducted by X-2's Irving Sherman, after the disappearance of DOGWOOD and TRILLIUM, was unable to decide whether Hatz had been a **Sicherheitsdienst** penetration, as MI6 claimed, or DOGWOOD had been an elaborate **deception**. Either way, the Social Democrats in Budapest were ruthlessly eliminated, leaving only the Communists to provide an organized resistance to seize power at the end of hostilities. The entire OSS station came in for criticism by Sherman, including Macfarland, whose chauffeur turned out to be a Soviet spy, and even Wisner, whose driver was in the pay of the Turkish Sûreté.

DOMINANT. British code name for a Seamans' Union organizer and Communist in Antwerp, **Belgium**, who acted as a source for DEPUTY, supplying false information about V-2 damage in Antwerp. He was an unconscious agent, unaware that DEPUTY was cooperating with **Supreme Headquarters Allied Expeditionary Force**, and he died of accidental gas poisoning in Antwerp at the end of December 1944 before he could learn the truth.

DOMINO. The **Inter-Services Liaison Department (ISLD)** code name for a Turkish agent working as a Wagons-Lits attendant on the Taurus Express between **Istanbul** and Baghdad who had served in the German Army in World War I and was in contact with a German officer in **Turkey**. From November 1942, DOMINO was handed **deception** material to pass on to his contact, but an attempt to run him as a **double agent** against the Japanese failed.

A major in the Turkish Army reserve, DOMINO was run by ISLD's John Bruce-Lochhart who learned that he was simultaneously in touch with the Italian **Servizio di Informazione Militare** and the Hungarians.

DONOVAN, WILLIAM ("WILD BILL"). Appointed head of the **Office of Strategic Services (OSS)**, Gen. "Wild Bill" Donovan ran the organization until it was closed down by President Harry Truman in October 1945. A New York lawyer who had made his military reputation during the Mexican campaign of 1912 and in World War I, Donovan was appointed by President Franklin D. Roosevelt to the new post of **Coordinator of Information** in 1941. Donovan had undertaken a tour of Great Britain between 17 July and 4 August 1940, and another of the Mediterranean in June 1942, before submitting a report to the White House recommending the permanent establishment in April 1943 of an organization to collect, collate, and distribute intelligence.

After the OSS had been disbanded, Donovan was appointed a prosecutor at the Nuremberg war crimes tribunal, and he later returned to his Wall Street law practice. He died in 1959 and has been the subject of three biographies, by Anthony Cave Brown, Corey Ford, and Richard Dunlap.

DORA. Code name for **Alexander Rado**.

DOUBLE AGENTS. An agent working for one organization may be said to have been turned into a "double agent" when he or she accepts recruitment from an adversary and then knowingly supplies the original employer with false information. The manipulation of double agents is an essential component of counterintelligence, and during World War II the British Security Service (**MI5**), the **NKVD**, and the **Abwehr** all proved adept at the technique. The term *double agent* is often misused, and intelligence officers who decide to spy for an enemy should not be categorized as double agents. The extent to which the Abwehr succeeded in deceiving the British **Special Operations Executive** only became widely acknowledged with the publication in 1953 of *London Calling North Pole* by Hermann Giskes. Similarly, in 1972 a sanitized version of Sir **John Masterman**'s *The Double Cross System of the War of 1939–1945* revealed MI5's role in the development of an extensive double agent network that began with **Arthur Owens** in September 1939.

DOUBLE CROSS SYSTEM. The British equivalent of the German **Funkspiel**, the Double Cross System supervised a stable of **double agents**, under the auspices of first the **Wireless Board** and then the **Twenty Committee**, which subsequently spawned similar organizations in other theaters, such as the **Thirty Committee** in **Cairo**.

DRAGOMAN. X-2 code name for Juan Frutos, a Portuguese linguist and dockyard worker in Cherbourg previously employed by Norddeutscher Lloyd and by American Express, and part of a German stay-behind network. Compromised by ISOS and identified as a spy code-named EIKENS, Frutos was arrested by the 31st **Special Counter-Intelligence (SCI)** unit in July 1944 and agreed to operate as a **double agent** while working as an interpreter in the U.S. Army Post Office. Under the SCI's supervision, he established radio contact with **Abwehr** stations in Stuttgart and Wiesbaden, exchanging more than 200 messages in total, and in August 1944 he helped capture another stay-behind agent, Alfred Gabas, code-named DESIRE.

DRAGONFLY. MI5 code name for **double agent** Hans George, born in Great Britain of German parentage. Recruited by the **Abwehr** while on a visit to Holland in 1939, DRAGONFLY reported the approach to MI5 and was enrolled as a double agent, operating a radio until November 1944 when he ran out of money. A delivery of funds intended for him, to be made by British refugee **Oswald Job**, was prevented by the latter's arrest in November 1943.

DRAYTON, S. J. Appointed the head of the **Federal Bureau of Investigation**'s **Special Intelligence Service** in 1943 to replaced **Percy E. Foxworth**, S. J. Drayton was himself succeeded by Frank C. Holloman.

DREADNOUGHT. MI5 code name for **Ivo Popov**.

DRONKERS, JOHANNES. In May 1942, Johannes Dronkers, a 46-year-old Post Office clerk, was one of several Dutch refugees towed into Harwich by an armed Royal Navy trawler. At the **Royal Victoria Patriotic School**, he underwent routine screening but when he was interviewed by Adrianus Vrinten, a private detective who before World War II had worked for the **Secret Intelligence Service** station in The Hague, Dronkers claimed to be a member of the anti-Nazi resistance in the Netherlands. Vrinten recognized him as a leading member of Anton Mussert's National Socialist Party and, when challenged, Dronkers admitted he had been sent to England by the **Abwehr** and revealed his safe-arrival signal, a message to be broadcast on Radio Oranje.

Under interrogation at **Camp 020**, Dronkers confessed that he had been in the pay of the Abwehr since 1938, but claimed that, although he had been given a mission in England at that time, he had not fulfilled it. He was allowed to see one of his other companions on the voyage across the North Sea, a half-Javanese named John Mulder, about whom MI5 had some suspicions, but their conversation proved Mulder's innocence. The microphones picked up Dronkers explaining his true role as a German spy to Mulder, who reacted with undisguised fury. Dronkers was sent for trial in November 1942 and hanged at Wandsworth on New Year's Eve, while Mulder was released in 1943.

DRÜCKE, KARL. An **Abwehr** spy arrested shortly after he rowed ashore at Potgordon in September 1940, Drücke was hanged at Wandsworth in August 1941. *See also* SCHALBURG, VERA VON.

DÜBENDORFER, RACHEL. A key figure in the **GRU**'s **Rote Drei** network in Switzerland, Rachel Dübendorfer, code-named SISSY, was a Polish Jew who had worked for the International Labor Organization in Geneva since 1934. She married Henri Dübendorfer about 1932, apparently for the sole purpose of obtaining Swiss citizenship, for they had separated almost immediately and she lived with a German journalist, Paul Boettcher, who had adopted her surname. A Communist of long standing who had once been minister of finance in Saxony, Boettcher appeared in the Soviet traffic with the code name PAUL. The Dübendorfers operated their own independent network in Geneva, consisting of local Communist Party activists and members of her own family, including her daughter and French son-in-law, until 1941 when a respected Hungarian cartographer, **Alexander Rado**, revealed himself as the leader of another parallel Soviet network also based in Geneva.

DUCK. (1) **MI5** code name for an agent inside the Spanish embassy in London with access to the ambassador's codes. (2) **MI5** code name for a transmitter in India used by FATHER in 1943. (3) The **NKVD** code name for the assassination of Leon Trotsky. *See also* VASILEVSKY, LEV.

DUFF. British code name for **microdots**.

DULLES, ALLEN. The **Office of Strategic Services** representative in **Bern** between 1942 and 1945, Allen Dulles recruited and ran two important sources, **Hans Bernd Gisevius** and **Fritz Kolbe**, who traveled regularly to Berlin. Dulles also played a key role in negotiating the surrender of Nazi troops in northern Italy in 1946, code-named Operation SUNRISE.

DUQUESNE, FREDERICK. Originally from the Cape Colony in South Africa, where allegedly he had spied against the British, Frederick Duquesne claimed in a sensational book published in New York in February 1932, *The Man Who Killed Kitchener: The Life of Fritz Joubert Duquesne*, written by journalist Clement Wood, that he had been responsible for the loss of the cruiser HMS *Hampshire* in the North Sea in June 1916, while carrying the field marshal to Petrograd. Although the British Admiralty had always believed that the cruiser had hit a mine, Wood reported that Duquesne had slipped aboard disguised as a Russian officer, signaled a U-boat waiting to torpedo her, and then made his escape before she sank.

Duquesne lived with his mistress, Evelyn Lewis, a sculptor from a wealthy Southern family, on West 76th Street, calling themselves "Mr. and Mrs. James Dunn," but he also volunteered his services to the **Abwehr** as a professional spy. His offer was accepted, and he established himself in a small, one-room office at 120 Wall Street operating under the name Air Terminal Associates. It was here that he received **William Sebold** and took delivery of his microfilmed questionnaire. His subsequent visits to Sebold's office were filmed by the **Federal Bureau of Investigation**, which used a clock on the wall and a flip-over calendar placed on Sebold's desk to make an accurate, verifiable record of every conversation. The film was shown in court and proved to be damning evidence following Duquesne's arrest in June 1941.

The leads from the Duquesne case covered the entire country and hemisphere, including South America, and resulted in 19 guilty pleas and a total of 32 convictions. It also spawned a Hollywood movie, *The House on 92nd Street*, which won several awards.

The case ended with prison sentences totaling 300 years and fines of $18,000. Duquesne received the longest sentence, of 18 years, while his mistress received a year and a day. One of the ring members, Else Weustenfeld, who had worked as a secretary in the German Consulate's legal branch on Battery Place, was sentenced to five years' imprisonment. A middle-aged divorcée born in Essen who had been a naturalized citizen for 15 years, she had been implicated by Sebold, and it turned out that she was living in New York with the brother of Maj. **Nikolaus Ritter**, a senior Abwehr officer who had recruited Sebold in Hamburg, **Herman Lang** in New York, and many others. Ritter's textile business in America had collapsed in the Depression, so after 10 years in the United States, he had returned to Germany and followed a new career as an intelligence officer with excellent English and a talent for spotting suitable agents.

On the pretext that Weustenfeld had contaminated the consular offices, President Franklin D. Roosevelt announced that all German consulates would have to close. Orders from Berlin required all sensitive documents to be destroyed immediately and the consul-general, Rudolf Borchers, who was not known to be an Abwehr officer, gave the job to his young subordinate, Siegfried Lurtz, who most definitely was. However, the volume of material was so great that Lurtz relied on the janitor, Walter Morrissey, to burn it all. What the Abwehr never suspected was that Morrissey was himself an FBI source; he retained many of the most sensitive files and handed them over intact to his FBI handler. Contained in them were dozens more leads to other potential espionage cases. As for Ritter himself, he was captured by the British at the end of the war and was still bitter about Sebold's duplicity.

DUTCH INTELLIGENCE. The Dutch military intelligence service was headed by Gen. J. W. van Oorschot, an anti-German with close relations to the **Secret Intelligence Service (MI6)**. His organization, based largely on military attachés posted overseas, was ill equipped to provide foreign intelligence, and when Col. Gijsbertis Sas, the attaché in Berlin, reported that he had received a warning from the **Abwehr**'s Col. **Hans Oster** that the Netherlands would be invaded on

12 October 1939, credibility was lost as the report was circulated widely.

When, following the Nazi invasion, Prime Minister Pieter Gerbrandy's government was evacuated to Stratford House in London's Mayfair, a new Dutch intelligence service, the Centrale Inlichtingendienst, was created, and a former MI6 police contact and police commissioner, Francois van t'Sant, was appointed its director. He took up residence in Chester Square, Belgravia, and liaised closely with **MI5** to screen refugees until August 1941 when he was replaced by Capt. Derksema, who would be succeeded by Col. M. R. de Bruyne. Later a second intelligence agency, the Bureau Inlichingen, was created under Maj. Broekman, who resigned in poor health and handed it over to Maj. J. M. Somer. Because of the suspicion of hostile penetration, the Centrale Inlichtingendienst was closed and Gen. van Oorschot was brought out of retirement to run a new organization with two aides, Maj. E. Klijzing and Maj. de Graaf.

DUTEIL, JOSEPH. A member of the pro-Nazi Parti Populaire Francais, Joseph Duteil used the alias "Joseph Doriot" and served on the Russian Front before he was recruited as a German agent and dispatched to North Africa in 1943 to join **André Latham**'s stay-behind network. Under instructions to murder Latham if he suspected he was acting as a **double agent**, Duteil was arrested after he joined the French army and later executed.

– E –

EASTWOOD, CHRISTOPHER. The drunken cook of the SS *Edenvale*, Christopher Eastwood, approached a Portuguese named Granja Tomas in **Lisbon** and asked him to deliver a letter to the German legation. Granja, having a friend in the press division of the British Consulate, took the letter to him instead, and it was opened and photographed and found to contain code. It was then sealed up again and delivered by Granja to the German legation. Under interrogation in Dublin by **G-2**, Eastwood revealed that he had collected the letter from Donal O'Shea, a broker of Dublin. After consultations with **MI5**, Eastwood was allowed to continue to act as a conduit and was entrusted with a letter for an **Abwehr** agent, Dr. Hermann Goertz, who was in prison. MI5 was able to monitor the case through ISOS, and one intercept revealed a plan to recruit an anti-Communist army to be led by a man named Duffy. G-2's cryptographer, Dr. Richard Hayes, broke Goertz's code, thus allowing both organizations to read his correspondence. Eventually the Abwehr in Lisbon learned that Tomas had been acting for the British and attempted, unsuccessfully, to persuade Eastwood to desert his ship at Huelva. Instead, he was arrested upon his return to Dublin.

ECCLESIASTIC. The **Secret Intelligence Service** code name for a **double agent** who was used as a channel for information intended to discredit OSTRO.

EDITH. Secret Intelligence Service code name for a seaman employed in 1942 as a **double agent** in **Lisbon**.

EDOUARD. Code name for a French-run **double agent** in **Algiers**, a sergeant employed in the intelligence branch of the French XIX Corps. For much of 1943 his relatively low-level information was transmitted by radio to Paris by RAM.

EFFIGY. British code name for the member of a German stay-behind organization, and **double agent**, operating a transmitter in Athens after the liberation of Greece in October 1944.

EFFREMOV, KONSTANTIN. An experienced, 32-year-old **GRU** officer and chemical warfare expert who had been operating in western Europe under student cover since about 1936, Capt. Konstantin Effremov was code-named PASCAL and had trained as an engineer and used a genuine Finnish passport issued in the United States in the name of Jernstroem. However, shortly before the arrest of **Johann Wenzel** in July 1942, Effremov prudently decided to switch to a new identity.

Effremov, who had worked with **Henri Robinson**, had run a sizable network of Soviet sources in Holland and lived for a period before the war in Zurich. He had arrived in Brussels in September 1939, ostensibly as a student enrolled at the École Polytechnique, to run an independent network, but he used Wenzel as his radio link and in March 1942 he had been instructed to meet **Leopold Trepper**. Thus he acquired considerable knowledge of the rings operating in **Belgium** and of **Viktor Guryevitch**'s contacts in Holland. Through one of his many contacts, he had been put in touch with a corrupt Belgian police officer, Chief Inspector Charles Mathieu, who had access to Belgian travel documents and had proved useful in the past. However, Mathieu was also working for the Germans as an informant, and he arranged for Effremov to be arrested when they met on 22 July 1942. Under pressure, and anxious about the fate of his young wife in Russia, the Ukrainian from Sawotzki had agreed to cooperate with the **Abwehr** and divulged enough information to compromise **Simex**, the GRU's commercial cover n Paris.

A jealous anti-Semite, Effremov hated being subordinate to the Jews who dominated the GRU and made radio contact with Moscow, under the direction of the Germans. He also lured two of his contacts into a trap: Herman Isbutsky had been running his own organization in his native Antwerp and had relied upon Wenzel for his communications. He was executed soon after his arrest in late July 1942 and a radio link developed code-named BOB in his absence. Effremov's second victim was Maurice Peper, a Jew from Amsterdam who had been recruited into the GRU while a seaman in the Dutch merchant marine. Both Peper and Isbutsky were arrested together at a meeting called by Effremov, but only Peper agreed to help the Germans. He admitted his role as a liaison officer with a separate Dutch network code-named HILDA and led his captors to its leader in Amsterdam, Anton Winterink. A prominent Dutch Communist, Winterink was arrested in an Amsterdam restaurant in August 1942 and, after two weeks of interrogation, agreed to reestablish a wireless link to Moscow, code-named TANNE by the Germans, on the radio that had been discovered at his home. The Abwehr regarded Winterink's capture as a significant coup because they had already suspected him of being TINO, the head of a dangerous Communist Party cell.

Winterink's attempt to deceive the GRU initially appeared to fail because Moscow had been warned of Winterink's capture by other members of HILDA who had witnessed his arrest, but TINO seems to have persuaded the Soviets that he had escaped. Accordingly Moscow maintained the wireless link with him until March or April

1944, when he was instructed to stop transmitting and join the resistance. This order proved to be a death sentence, because the Germans no longer had any use for him and he was executed.

Effremov continued to run the PASCAL radio link from Breendonck prison until April 1944 when he was moved to a house at 63 rue de Courcelles, where Guryevitch was being held.

EGGS. MI5 code name for an informant in London.

EL ALAMEIN. The defeat of the Afrika Korps at El Alamein proved to be a significant milestone in the Allied prosecution of the war. At the massive land battle, fought in October 1942, the Eighth Army's commander, Gen. Bernard Montgomery, struck a major strategic blow against the enemy, but was greatly assisted by comprehensive intelligence concerning his adversary's tactics, intentions, troop strengths, armored reserves, fuel supplies, ammunition stocks, and much else supplied by **Bletchley Park** and its regional branch, the **Combined Bureau Middle East** in **Cairo**. Montgomery's chief intelligence officer, Brig. Bill Williams, shrewdly exploited the ULTRA intercepts and ensured that the Germans were outmaneuvered and outgunned. His information was so complete that he even had access to his adversary's private medical bulletins, reports from Professor Hörster describing Field Marshal Erwin Rommel's low blood pressure.

In a prelude to the main offensive, Rommel had attempted at the end of August 1942 to break through British defenses at El Alamein to reach Alexandria, Cairo, and the Suez Canal, but his plans had been compromised by ULTRA. Instead of taking Montgomery by surprise and sweeping through relatively weak lines, many of Rommel's 203 tanks unexpectedly found themselves in a minefield sown with 18,000 mines and attacked from the air at night under the light of parachute flares. Worse, Rommel had gambled on the arrival of six ships from Italy loaded with fuel and ammunition, but ULTRA had identified the vulnerability and four of the merchantmen had already been found and sunk; while the battle raged, the last two tankers, the *Sanandrea* and the *Picci Fascio*, were destroyed as they approached Tobruk. After six days of intense fighting, in which the Afrika Korps lost 38 tanks and 400 trucks, Rommel began to withdraw, blaming the failure on a leak by the Italians.

When Montgomery counterattacked in October, Rommel was caught off-guard and, short of fuel and ammunition, lost most of his tanks to new Allied weaponry. Overestimating his adversary's strength and down to his last 32 tanks, Rommel led his 70,000 men on a long retreat 800 miles across the desert, constantly harassed by the Eighth Army and the Royal Air Force.

EL GITANO. French code name for a Catalan hairdresser in Oran recruited as a stay-behind agent by the Germans in December 1942 and the Italians June 1943. He was run as a **double agent** by the French until February 1944.

ELLIOTT, NICHOLAS. Having served briefly in **MI5**'s **B1(a)**, Nicholas Elliott joined the **Secret Intelligence Service**'s **(MI6) Section V** in 1941 and was posted to **Istanbul**, where he supervised the **defection** of **Erich Vermehren**. At the end of 1944, he was replaced by Richard Arnold-Baker and transferred to Switzerland to head the MI6 station in **Bern**.

ELLIS, C. H. ("DICK"). An Australian-born career **Secret Intelligence Service (MI6)** officer, Dick Ellis worked on diplomatic telephone interception in England in 1939, concentrating on the German embassy, and in 1941 was appointed deputy director of **British Security Coordination**. Before the war, he had worked under **Passport Control** cover in Berlin and Paris and, short of money, had sold classified information about MI6's internal structure to the **Sicherheitsdienst**. Identified under postwar interrogation by **Walter Schellenberg** as one of his most valued sources, Ellis eventually confessed to having passed MI6 secrets to the Nazis through his former brother-in-law in Paris.

ENGELS, ALBRECHT. An electrical engineer who had fought in World War I and had been wounded in 1917, Albrecht Engels graduated from the technical university in Berlin and immigrated to **Brazil** where he found work with a subsidiary of the German firm AEG. In September 1939, while on a holiday with his Brazilian wife in Europe, Engels was recruited by the **Abwehr**, and upon his return to Rio, he was contacted by Lt. Hermann Bohny. Together the pair transformed a rather ineffective, amateurish Abwehr network, run by an indiscreet Austrian officer, Capt. Erich Immer, into a highly professional organization, and when a senior Abwehr officer, Julius Stiege, conducted a tour of inspection in December 1940, he gave his consent to their takeover.

Early the following year, Engels, now code-named ALFREDO, was sent a **microdot** letter containing a hand cipher based on *The Collected Works of German Authors* and was instructed to establish radio contact with Hamburg. This was not achieved until June 1941 when call sign CEL, operated at his home in Santa Tereza by Benno Sobisch, a Telefunken engineer, began to exchange signals with ALD in Berlin; the transmissions were first noticed and monitored by the **Radio Intelligence Division** on 4 July 1941. Soon afterward, a second wireless was established in the Rio suburb of Jacarépagua by Ernst Ramez, code-named ERNESTO, the owner of an electrical store who was another World War I veteran. The traffic consisted of shipping reports collected by more than a dozen agents who had access to the waterfront, along with political gossip supplied by a corrupt member of the Brazilian Foreign Office who had been seconded to the presidential palace.

By February 1942, when a **Federal Bureau of Investigation (FBI)** report described CEL as "the most important station in a chain of clandestine German radios in South America," Engels had supervised 325 messages to ALD, and his network had received $112,500 from the Abwehr. However, it was all to come to grief over the arrest of a playboy, Hans Kurt Meyer-Clason, who had been approached to take a microdot to the United States by a member of the Bohny-Engels organization. The son of a German general, Meyer-Clason's ambitions to become a spy foundered when he was refused a U.S. visa. Nevertheless, when he was picked by the **Direção da Ordem Política e Social (DOPS)** in Porto Alegre at the end of January 1942, having been denounced as a Nazi, he knew enough, extracted under DOPS's characteristically ruthless interrogation, to implicate Eduard Arnold, the Abwehr agent who had attempted to recruit him. Arnold was promptly arrested by DOPS in São Paulo and, after receiving the same treatment as Meyer-Clason, signed a confession in which Engels was named as his spymaster. Encouraged by Jack West of the FBI's **Special Intelligence Service**, who provided a list of agents gleaned from the CEL, LIR and CIT intercepts, the DOPS chief, Felisberto Teixeira, authorized a further two dozen arrests in the middle of March 1942, among them Engels and Friedrich Kempter.

West's dossier on Engels had been supplied to him by the local British **Secret Intelligence Service (MI6)** station commander, Comdr. Philip Johns, who had run two **double agents** against him. The first was **Hans von Kotze**, a German aristocrat married to an Englishwoman, who had in June 1941 been dispatched on a Linee Aeree Transcontinentali Italiane (LATI) flight from Rome to Brazil to join the Engels organization as FRED, but instead had offered his services to MI6 and supplied Johns with a wealth of information about ALFREDO. Von Kotze also revealed that, accompanied by his beautiful Hungarian girlfriend, he had visited Buenos Aires in late August 1941 to confer with naval attaché Dietrich Niebuhr and had also had dealings with the German military attaché in Brazil, Gen. Günter Niedenfuhr, who apparently had expressed his disapproval of the frequency with which von Kotze had been spotted at the gaming tables in Santos accompanied by conspicuously attractive young women. Doubtless it was Gen. Neidenfuhr's attempt to instill some discipline in his subordinate that had prompted him to approach the British, although he may also have been unnerved by some unsubtle DOPS surveillance, which included snatching a few photographs of him relaxing on a beach near Santos.

The other double agent to compromise Engels was **Dusan Popov**, a colorful Yugoslav playboy run by MI5 as TRICYCLE. By the time Engels was detained by DOPS, Popov had returned safely to London to continue his role as a double agent.

ENGLANDSPIEL. The **Abwehr** code name for a counterintelligence operation conducted jointly with the **Gestapo** in Holland to penetrate and take control of British intelligence and resistance networks in Holland. *See also* DUTCH INTELLIGENCE; NORDPOL.

ENIGMA. The German electromechanical cipher machine developed for commercial use by continental banks that became the mainstay of Axis communications and the subject of concentrated attack by prewar French, Polish, and British cryptographers. The version adopted by the various German armed services was improved in 1930 by a modification, the plugboard, which vastly increased the cipher's complexity, and by 1939 more than 20,000 machines were in use. Limited success achieved by the Polish **Biuro Szyfrow** in 1938, using artificial aids to reverse-engineer the daily key settings retrospectively, led to greater resources being applied to the problem at **Bletchley Park**, where **Abwehr** hand ciphers compromised by **double agents** provided access to duplicated texts relayed on the enemy's Enigma circuits. Decrypts were given limited circulation, code-named first BONIFACE and then ULTRA, and had a significant impact on Allied counterintelligence operations, as well as playing a decisive role in the battles of the **Atlantic**, **El Alamein**, and **Kursk** and the **D-Day** invasion. *See also* CLAYMORE; GARBO; *MÜNCHEN*; POLISH INTELLIGENCE; SNOW; U-33; U-110.

ENORMOZ. Soviet intelligence code name for a combined **GRU** and **NKVD** operation conducted in Great Britain and the United States to penetrate the Anglo-American atomic bomb development program, the **Manhattan Project**. The operation was considered such a priority by Josef Stalin that he placed **Lavrenti Beria** in charge of it and authorized the two organizations to establish joint *rezidenturas* abroad, designated **XY**, to collect information from nuclear physicists employed at the Los Alamos, Berkeley, Oak Ridge, and Argonne laboratories in the United States, Chalk River in **Canada**, and the Culham and Cavendish laboratories in England. The Soviets achieved considerable success in recruiting well-placed sources, and only three Manhattan Project employees, Allan Nunn May, Klaus Fuchs, and David Greenglass, were ever convicted of having betrayed secrets from inside the project.

ERROR. The first **deception** of the Burma Campaign, undertaken at the end of April 1942 by **Peter Fleming**, was based on Richard Meinertzhagen's ruse during the 1917 battle for Gaza. Fleming prepared a briefcase, purporting to belong to Gen. Sir Archie Wavell, filled with his personal effects, and documents suggesting that India was much more heavily defended than the Japanese believed. The valise, bearing the commander-in-chief's initials, was left in a staff car abandoned near what remained of the Ava Bridge at Sagaing, after it had been blown up during the retreat.

ESTELLA, JOSÉ. A Spanish saboteur arrested in **Gibraltar** in February 1942, tried in London in May, and hanged at Wandsworth in July.

EXAMINATION UNIT. The innocuous title of the **Canadian** National Research Council's cryptographic branch, which intercepted and decrypted enemy wireless traffic.

– F –

FACKENHEIM, ERNST PAUL. Decorated with the Iron Cross during World War I, Ernst Fackenheim was a German Jew trained by the **Abwehr** for a mission to England in 1940 but then dropped into Palestine in October 1941 to report on troop movements. He offered his services to **Security Intelligence Middle East** as a **double agent** but was suspected of being a triple agent and prosecuted for espionage.

FALANGE. Ostensibly the Spanish Fascist political party that seized power during the Spanish Civil War, the Falange contained a Servicio de Información e Investigación, headed by David Jato Miranda, which was split into two secret bodies, the Servicio Exterior, which acted as an intelligence-collection agency, and the Falange del Mar, which checked on the political credentials of the crews of Spanish ships.

FALCON. Supreme Headquarters Allied Expeditionary Force code name for Georges Gaspari, a Corsican parachuted into liberated territory near Dijon, France, in February 1945 and run as a **double agent** from Lyons until the end of hostilities.

FAN. Code name for a radio operator in the French Navy who crossed the lines in Normandy on 4 August 1944 and was caught by British troops. He confessed he had been dispatched by Trupp 121 on a tactical mission. He was interrogated at **Camp 020** and was recruited as a **double agent**. However, by the time he was returned to Normandy and installed in a remote farmhouse, his short-range frequencies proved of limited value.

FANNY. British code name for a Syrian triple agent in Damascus. The Germans knew he had come under Allied control so he was supplied with information accordingly.

FAR EAST COMBINED BUREAU (FECB). The principal British cryptographic organization in the Far East, established in Hong Kong in March 1935. Shortly before the 1942 surrender, the FECB's staff was evacuated on HMS *Birmingham* to Kranji, Singapore, and remained there until its capture in February 1942. The remnants were then withdrawn to Kalinidi, near Mombasa, Kenya, before finally settling at HMS *Anderson*, a golf course outside Colombo in Ceylon. The FECB, reinforced by the transfer of personnel from **Bletchley Park**'s Hut 7, achieved considerable success in reading the Japanese naval codes designated JN-25 and JN-11 and made a decisive contribution to the Allied victory in the region. In 1945 many of the final sea battles of the war, including the sinking of the Japanese battle cruiser *Haguro* in May, were influenced by the cryptographers, whom Lord Mountbatten described as being "worth 10 divisions."

FATHER. MI5 code name for a Belgian pilot and **double agent**, Pierre Henri Arents, who reached England from **Lisbon** in June 1941. In June 1943 he was posted to India to avoid answering some increasingly difficult technical questions submitted by the **Abwehr** and was supplied with a transmitter code-named DUCK, which became operational in August 1944. When FATHER was posted back to **Belgium** in October 1944, his radio was operated until the end of the war by a police officer in Calcutta, supposedly a disaffected Indian courier based at the Strategic Air Force's headquarters.

FEDERAL BUREAU OF INVESTIGATION (FBI). An organization with virtually no prewar counterintelligence experience, the FBI was slow to grasp the implications of **Soviet**, **German**, **Japanese**, and **Italian** espionage, but successfully exploited the first major case of a Nazi spy ring in the United States, the **Frederick Duquesne** network compromised by **William Sebold**. Following a visit to London by Hugh Clegg and Clarence Hince in December 1940, the FBI obtained permission from President Franklin D. Roosevelt to establish a **Special Intelligence Service** to collect information in Latin America.

The law enforcement ethos engendered by FBI Director **J. Edgar Hoover** inhibited his subordinates from taking full advantage of the initial opportunities offered by **double agents** such as **Dusan Popov** in 1941. However, by 1944 the FBI had developed a capability for handling double agents initiated by liaison services in Europe, and in the example of PEASANT, it embraced the **deception** principles associated with the creation and management of **notional agents**.

The FBI failed to understand the Soviet threat, having submitted a complacent memorandum on the subject to the White House on 24 October 1940, in which Hoover effectively dismissed the problem and cited not a single case of domestic Soviet espionage. He concluded by claiming that "the movements, contacts and financial transactions" of "those Consular representatives whose conduct is reported to be detrimental to the United States" in "a most discreet and careful manner" are 'the subject of constant observation and study." Hoover's attitude would change in August 1943 when an anonymous letter, addressed to the director personally and typewritten in Cyrillic script, described an entire clandestine network headed by the **NKVD** *rezident*, identified accurately as Col. **Vasili Zubilin**, which led to him being placed belatedly under constant surveillance. This expedient led the FBI to unravel an extensive Soviet espionage offensive that encompassed the **Communist Party of the United States of America (CPUSA)**; the trading company Amtorg, which employed 2,300 at its headquarters on Madison Avenue; and numerous other professionals operating under diplomatic and consular cover, with much of it directed against the **Manhattan Project**, into which the FBI was not fully indoctrinated until October 1944. Later the FBI would become adept at piecing together the clues to the counterintelligence puzzle provided by CPUSA **defectors** such as Louis Budenz and **Elizabeth Bentley**, and double agents like Boris Morros.

Hoover entrusted his counterespionage operations to his assistant, Edward Tamm, who supervised Mickey Ladd's Domestic Intelligence Division, which included an Espionage Section headed by Harry Kimball (who would be succeeded by Robert H. Cunningham). The Espionage Section consisted of a General Desk and a Major Case Desk and handled all the Axis and Soviet investigations. Liaison with **MI5** in London was conducted through Arthur Thurston, posted to the U.S. embassy as a legal attaché. *See also* UNITED STATES INTELLIGENCE.

FELLERS, BONNER F. The U.S. military attaché in Cairo between October 1940 and August 1942, Col. Bonner Fellers transmitted regular reports to Washington, D.C., on current and future British military operations, but he did so in a cipher, the Black Code, that had been compromised. A copy of the cipher had been copied in August 1941 by the **Servizio di Informazione Militare (SIM)**, having broken into the safe of the American military attaché in Rome, Col. Norman Fiske. Naturally, SIM had shared its loot with the **Abwehr** and thus enabled the entire channel to be intercepted and the traffic read. As Fellers attended Gen. Claude Auchinleck's daily GHQ staff conferences, he was in an excellent position to submit detailed assessments of Allied strengths and weaknesses, as illustrated by his cable dated 8 January 1942, which offered the Afrika Korps's Erwin Rommel a detailed insight into recent British Eighth Army tank losses: "Estimates (Cairo) on equipment (British army) serviceable tanks in Libya: 328; repairable tanks in Libya: 521. Tanks destroyed last campaign: 374."

On 11 June 1942, Fellers unwittingly provided the Germans with useful advance notice of a nighttime clandestine operation set for the following night, which was intended to destroy Italian and Luftwaffe aircraft on the ground: "Night of June 12/13 British sabotage units plan simultaneous sticker bomb attacks against aircraft on 9 Axis aerodromes. Plans to reach objectives by parachutes and long range desert patrol. The method of attack offers tremendous possibility for destruction, risk is slight compared with possible gains."

When the attack took place at the German airfield at Derna, deep behind enemy lines, the team of saboteurs led by Capt. Herbert Buck was decimated. Only Buck and a French officer, Lt. Augustin Jordan survived. Among those who perished was a group of a dozen German Jewish refugees, volunteers from the **Special Interrogation Group**, and a pair of Germans who had served in the French Foreign Legion.

Fellers's accurate messages, describing his personal observations, recording his own comments, and summarizing his visits to the front, proved of immense value to Rommel, who waited each evening for the arrival of the next intercept before issuing his own instructions to subordinates. Whenever Fellers left Cairo for an extended tour of the battlefield, Rommel was temporarily disadvantaged and starved of information, but was invariably rewarded soon afterward by the updated intelligence contained in his dispatches.

The leak was discovered at the end of June 1942, when ULTRA intercepts of Luftwaffe traffic indicated that what the Germans had referred to as "the good source" had revealed that the British had learned the precise location of the Luftwaffe's headquarters. This had led to an extensive molehunt to find a traitor, but then in July 1942 Australian troops captured a forward Afrika Korps intercept station at Tel-el-Eisa, taking numerous prisoners and recovering a wealth of cryptographic material, including evidence that the Black Code had been compromised. The cipher was promptly replaced, but by then significant damage had been sustained across North Africa and the entire Mediterranean theater. Fellers continued a distinguished military career, unaware of his unintended indiscretion.

FICKLE. Supreme Headquarters Allied Expeditionary Force code name for Pierre Laurent, a spy dropped into Allied territory with FISH in February 1945 with the intention of working from Lyons, but never fully developed as a **double agent**.

FIDO. MI5 code name for a French pilot, Roger Grosjean, who arrived in London in July 1943 from **Lisbon**. When he underwent screening at the **Royal Victoria Patriotic School**, Grosjean confessed that he had been recruited as an **Abwehr** spy and instructed to steal a plane, preferably a Mosquito, and fly it to Nazi-occupied territory. He was enrolled as a **double agent** by **MI5** but actually worked for the **Bureau Central de Renseignements et d'Action** at its headquarters in Duke Street, St. James's, before being transferred in July 1944 to **Algiers** for a posting to a squadron at Meknes in Morocco, adopting the alias François Perrin. His contact with the Abwehr ceased in February 1944 when a last attempt to obtain further instructions from the Germans failed. In April 1954 Grosjean completed a manuscript, *The Sun Is in Leo*, in which he described his adventures, but it was not published before his death in Corsica in June 1975.

FIDRMUC, PAUL. Code-named OSTRO by **MI5**, Paul Fidrmuc was a Yugoslav in **Lisbon** who fabricated information for the **Abwehr**, some of which proved uncomfortably accurate and prompted the **Secret Intelligence Service** to consider eliminating him. Instead, a British **double agent**, ECCLESIASTIC, was supplied with material intended to undermine his credibility.

FINCKENSTEIN. A senior German intelligence officer named Finckenstein was captured by the Royal Navy during an attack on the *Freese*, off Jan Mayen Island on 17 November 1940. Accompanied by colleague named Hansen, Finckenstein was interrogated at **Camp 020**.

FINLAND. During the course of the Winter War of 1939–1940 with the Soviet Union, the Finnish intelligence service acquired valuable expertise in studying the enemy's cipher systems. Its cryptographic attack was assisted by covert cooperation with their Japanese counterparts, one part of which was the exchange of cryptographic data, much of which had been gleaned from material recovered in the ruins of the Soviet consulate at the port of Lonahamari in Petsamo, in the extreme north of the country, which had been overrun by Finnish troops on 22 June 1941 before the **NKVD** staff could destroy their codebooks. The isolated building, which also housed the British, German, and Swedish consulates, overlooked the deep, iceless harbor that was a valuable Finnish asset at the end of the narrow Petsamo corridor, providing valuable access to the Barents Sea.

The Soviet 104th and 52nd Divisions had occupied the port since the December offensive, which had resulted in a dictated peace the following March. The Lonahamari documents, four partially burned diplomatic codebooks, had allowed the Finns—who had established a listening post at Otanien, just to the west of Helsinki, to monitor Soviet and U.S. diplomatic traffic—to read some Soviet messages, and their experience, shared with the Japanese, enabled Tokyo to break into the traffic, too. The four items were a diplomatic codebook designated "Kod-26," the NKVD "Pobeda" code, a code for use by the **GRU** military intelligence service, and another for the **Naval GRU**. Studied in conjunction with the medium-grade military crypto items recovered on the battlefield, which included at least one NKVD Border Guards codebook, the material allowed the Finnish analysts to understand how the Soviets adapted military terminology in their systems, built code tables, and relied on a very straightforward mathematical formula to encode emergency signals. The Finns placed a heavy emphasis on cryptography, and Field Marshal Carl Gustaf Mannerheim's crucial victory against the Soviet 44th Division at Suomussalmi, a turning point in the Winter War, was largely due to advance knowledge of the enemy's strategy gleaned from intercepted signals.

Although not a formal member of the Axis and technically neutral for the first two years of the war, Finland participated in the assault on the Soviet Union the following year. By the time Great Britain finally declared war on Finland on 6 December 1941, the Helsinki authorities had developed a strong relationship with the Tripartite countries. The fact that an NKVD codebook had fallen into Japanese hands and had been passed to the Germans was soon reported to Moscow by Harro Schulze-Boysen, an Air Ministry official in Berlin and GRU spy whose wife, Libertas, was having an affair with another member of his network, Horst Heilmann, an **Abwehr** cryptographer.

At the end of hostilities on 17 September 1944, the Finns feared that, as had happened in Romania, the country would be occupied by the Soviets, and a group of nearly 800 intelligence officers and their families, led by the chief of military intelligence, Col. Aladar Paasonen, and the head of the signals intelligence section, Col. Reino Hallamaa, participated in Operation STELLA POLARIS. Paasonen, the father of Finnish cryptography, was a brilliant linguist who had been taught most European languages by his Hungarian mother. Although he had studied Soviet cipher systems in Germany, Poland, and the Baltic and had made the first purchases of intercept equipment in Italy in the 1920s, the principal figure in STELLA POLARIS was Hallamaa, who was convinced that Finland was about to become a Soviet surrogate and feared the consequences if the Communist Party seized his personnel or files.

Paasonen also ran a commando battalion, designated ErP4, which operated behind Soviet lines, and its membership was at considerable risk. Accordingly, with the tacit approval of the Finnish president, Field Marshal Carl Gustav Mannerheim, and his military chief of staff, Erik Heinrichs, Hallamaa invited his Swedish counterpart, Maj. Carl Petersén, the director of Defence Staff's intelligence branch, known as the C-Bureau, to open negotiations at his villa in June 1944 at Sökö, just outside Helsinki. His objective was to gain Swedish consent to his plan to reestablish his entire organization in Sweden and continue operations against the Soviets.

For their part, the Swedes knew that if Finland fell to the Soviets, their own territory would then become the front line, and few then doubted that Stalin's ambitions included the whole of Scandinavia. Petersén was also aware that, as well as possessing useful assets across the Soviet frontier, the Finnish codebreakers had accomplished far more than the Swedish Försvarsväsendets Radioanstalt (FRA), then headed by Comdr. Torgil Thorén. Relations between the FRA, which had been created in 1942, and the Finns had been sufficiently close to allow Thorén to second one of his subordinates, Capt. Ake Rossby, to Helsinki during part of the Russian-Finnish War, and he was again chosen to negotiate with Hallamaa. However, Thorén himself was kept deliberately isolated from the STELLA POLARIS plans because he had become distrustful of the Finns following an incident earlier in the war when the Finnish military attaché in **Stockholm**, Col. Stewenly, had tipped off the Abwehr to the success the Swedes had achieved in intercepting and decrypting teletype traffic on the German Oslo–Berlin landline, which happened to pass through the capital's telegraph exchange.

The talks conducted by Hallamaa, Petersén, and Rossby were officially authorized by Mannerheim, and the chief of the Finnish Defense Staff, Gen. A. E. Heinrichs, also knew of the scheme, as did the chief of the Swedish Defense Staff, Maj. Gen. C. A. Ehrensvärd. Hallamaa assigned two subordinates, Lt. Capt. Heikki Paulio and Lt. Veikko Virkkunen, to plan STELLA POLARIS, and they completed the preparations at the end of August 1944. A secret meeting was held by Hallamaa at his headquarters at Mikkeli to brief the heads of his five intelligence units—Lt. Comdr. Pekka Visa, his brother Capt. Paavo Visa, and Captains Mauri Hartikainen, Aarre Tunkelo, and Bror Erkki Sten Pale—who were instructed to gather their equipment and families at the ports of Härpes, near Kaskö and Nystad, ready to embark on the *Seagull* and two other coastal steamers for the voyage to Sweden. To ensure a proper reception, Virkkunen was transferred to the Finnish legation in Stockholm as assistant military attaché with instructions to represent the C-Bureau and make contact with his Axis counterparts, the Japanese general Makoto Onodera and the Abwehr's Büro Wagner. Elsewhere, the other two STELLA POLARIS components were put into action, with Col. Jussi Sovio leading the ErP4 commandos to Liminkai, conveniently close to the Swedish frontier, while the ErP4 vehicles, trailers packed with signals intelligence equipment, were moved to Tornea, with orders to drive over the border to Haparanda at a moment's notice.

The first group of intelligence personnel left Härpes for Härnösand on 20 September 1944 aboard the *Maininki* and *Georg*, followed by the others on the *Osmo*, which left the next day for Gävle. Upon arrival most of the "refugees" were accommodated at a displaced persons camp while their archives and equipment was taken by ship in more than 700 crates to a secret Swedish army store in a cave outside Härnösand, then moved not to the FRA's headquarters on the island of Lövön, but to a separate FRA facility in Stockholm at Karlaplan 4. Finally, the cipher documents were moved to the cellars of the Hotel Aston, where, over a period, they were photographed by Pale and put onto microfiche using equipment supplied by Finnish press attaché Heikki Brotherus. The film was then sent to Col. Uljas Käkönen in Helsinki for processing, and when Pale finally left Stockholm in March 1945, he was carrying 3,000 feet of undeveloped film, which was later returned to his C-Bureau successor in Stockholm, Lt. Pentti Hartikainen.

In November 1944, once the "Stellists" were safely established in Sweden, a delegation of senior Finnish officers, led by the chief of staff and including Lt. Gen. Harald Öhquist, Chief of Military Finance Col. Runar Bäckström, Finnish military attaché Col. Martin Stewen, Col. Hans von Essen, Maj. Emil Lautkari, and Capt. Erkki Pale, arrived in Stockholm to negotiate the sale of all the crypto equipment to the FRA director, Cmmdr. Thorén, for 252,875 crowns. The deal, which was completed on 10 January 1945 in Stockholm's Grand Hotel and included the boxes of Soviet ciphers and codes, was backdated to 1 July 1944, the day before the armistice, and the name of a Swedish manufacturer was placed on the actual bill of sale, together with that of Col. Johan Staahlstrom. According to Gen. Öhquist, the Soviet material was crucial to the sale, which the Swedes would not conclude without it, and a separate annex was completed that gave the Swedes control over the archival material for 50 years. This was signed by the general on behalf of Finnish defense minister Gen. Rudolf Walden, but the exact nature of the "property owned by the Finnish Defence Forces" sold was not specified, so as to ensure that the transaction was a strictly private one between Finnish officials and Swedish individuals.

Altogether, 100 boxes of Soviet cryptographic material were transferred by Capt. Pale in March 1945 to a mansion run by the FRA, and Maj. Lautkari delivered the other archives to an FRA flat. In addition,

Lautkari supervised the construction by the Stellist refugees of a radio facility at Lidongö, outside Stockholm, which was used to open a radio channel with Col. Paasonen in Helsinki. There, Col. Uljas Käkönen and Lt. Tauno Kylmönoja developed what amounted to a stay-behind network in anticipation of a Soviet takeover. *See also* SOVIET INTELLIGENCE; SWEDISH INTELLIGENCE.

FISH. Supreme Headquarters Allied Expeditionary Force code name for a German spy parachuted with FICKLE near Rheims, France, in February 1945. Both men surrendered immediately, and their transmitter was operated from Troyes.

FLAME. Code name for a Belgian member of a **Sicherheitsdienst** stay-behind network, a Fleming recruited as a **double agent** after he had surrendered to the British in Ghent, **Belgium**, on 23 September 1944. A former soldier in the Belgian Army, he had found a job in 1941 as a sanitary engineer at the Luftwaffe's headquarters in Brussels, and this had led to an approach from the **Abwehr**, who trained him as an agent in The Hague and Paris. He operated initially from Brussels, and then from Rumst.

FLASH. MI5 code name for a **Belgian** recruited as a **double agent**.

FLEMING, PETER. A successful world traveler, explorer, London *Times* journalist, *Spectator* columnist, and author prewar, Peter Fleming was the immensely successful husband of actress Celia Johnson who joined his regiment, the Grenadier Guards, on the outbreak of war and served in the Norwegian campaign before returning to England to organize the stay-behind Auxiliary Units, groups of armed volunteers who would resist a Nazi invasion. Posted to Egypt, he reached Greece in time for the evacuation, but learned the principles of strategic **deception** from Dudley Clarke. When he was transferred to Gen. Sir Archie Wavell's staff in Delhi in March 1942, he worked for his director of military intelligence (DMI), Brig. Walter Cawthorn, as a specialist in deception in GSI(d) and devised ERROR, a scheme intended to persuade the Japanese that India was heavily defended and that the arrival of more reinforcements was imminent. Believed successful, Fleming was encouraged to develop links with

Gen. Cheng K'ai-min, Chiang Kai-shek's DMI, and his American counterpart.

In January 1944 Fleming proposed the creation of **D Division**, responsible for the planning and execution of all deception projects in the Southeast Asia theater, and he remained in command until the end of hostilities, when he was preparing a project suggesting the existence of a large Allied espionage network on the Japanese mainland. *See also* JAPANESE INTELLIGENCE.

FLORADORA. **Government Communications Headquarters (GCHQ)** code name for German Foreign Ministry cipher traffic encrypted using **one-time pads (OTPs)** but successfully intercepted and broken at GCHQ's **Diplomatic Section**, whose cryptographers learned that the OTP numbers had been generated on a device manufactured by Siemens and therefore were not strictly random.

FLORIST. Supreme Headquarters Allied Expeditionary Force code name for Roger Hardouin, a French **double agent** operating in Cannes.

FOOTE, ALLAN. Born in Kirkdale, Liverpool, in 1905, Foote was a member of the **Communist Party of Great Britain** who volunteered to fight in the Spanish Civil War. Upon his return to London in September 1938, he was recruited as a courier by a lady in St. John's Wood, London—later identified as Birgette Lewis, née Kuczynski—and dispatched to Geneva, where he was met by another woman in the Central Post Office, who was Birgette's sister, **Ursula Kuczynski**. For the next three years, until his arrest at his apartment in Lausanne by the **Bundespolizei** in November 1943, Foote worked first as a spy based in Munich, where he had fallen in love with a beautiful young Kommunistische Partei Deutschlands courier, and later as a radio operator for a Soviet network that had succeeded in penetrating Germany. While living in Lausanne, Foote played the role of a wealthy Englishman in poor health who was disinclined to return to London while the war continued.

During lengthy postwar interviews with **MI5**'s Courtenay Young, which later became the basis of his memoirs, *Handbook for Spies*, Foote accurately identified almost all the other members of the

Soviet network with whom he had come into contact, and not unnaturally enhanced his own importance in the ring to the detriment of those members he had disliked. After his release from a Swiss jail in September 1944, he had reported to the Soviet military mission in Paris, where Col. Novikov of the **NKVD** had arranged for him to be flown to Moscow, accompanied by two other agents scheduled for repatriation: **Leopold Trepper**, the Polish Jew who had masterminded a **GRU** network that had stretched the breadth of Europe and survived the Nazi occupation, and **Alexander Rado**, the Hungarian who had headed the Swiss branch. Their flight was routed through Egypt and Persia, requiring a 48-hour stopover in **Cairo**, where Rado had disappeared, leaving Foote and Trepper to complete the journey on their own. The GRU, ever suspicious of treachery, had put the worst possible interpretation on Rado's reluctance to rejoin the flight and had subjected Foote and Trepper to months of harrowing interrogation. Eventually Foote was able to satisfy his inquisitors and was sent to a GRU training center at Sehjodia, 25 miles northwest of Moscow, in preparation for a new assignment, supposedly to Mexico.

Foote's story dovetailed with data gleaned from the postwar interrogation of German personnel, among whom was Wilhelm Flicke, a cryptographer who had studied nearly 5,500 intercepted Soviet signals that had been exchanged between Moscow and three illicit transmitters in Switzerland. When compared to the Bundespolizei reports and the very substantial quantity of Soviet wireless messages deciphered by the Swiss, it became clear that, apart from a few memory lapses and a tendency to inflate his own significance, Foote's recollection was entirely accurate. Evidently the **Sicherheitsdienst** had been aware of the existence of a Swiss branch of the **Rote Kapelle** and had made several attempts at penetration, but each had been detected and rejected. Nevertheless the German records gave further clues to the Soviet network, which evidently had been remarkably cosmopolitan in its membership and had been run with virtually no contact from the Soviet embassy or the local Communist Party. *See also* SOVIET INTELLIGENCE.

FOREIGN EXCELLENT RAINCOAT COMPANY. The commercial cover adopted by the **GRU** network in western Europe, based in Brussels and headed by **Leopold Trepper**.

FOREST. Code name for Lucien Hervieu, a French pilot recruited by the Germans in 1944 but run by **Supreme Headquarters Allied Expeditionary Force** as a **double agent** and notionally a fugitive hiding at a farm near Draguignan. Hervieu reported to his controllers by radio, passing observations he supposedly had made in Nice.

FORGE. Code name for a Belgian chauffeur who was a **Sicherheitsdienst** stay-behind agent sent through the lines in southern Holland in November 1944. Having been interrogated at **Camp 020** in mid-December, he was recruited as a **double agent** to be run by the Belgian Deuxieme Direction. As his mission was to find a transmitter and make contact with a secret resistance organization in Brussels, his case was considered a priority but by the time he returned to **Belgium** in February 1945 the Germans had lost interest in him.

FORTITUDE. Allied code name for a **deception** campaign undertaken in 1944 to persuade the Nazis that the invasion of **France** would take place in the Pas-de-Calais. The objective was to protect Operation OVERLORD, the **D-Day** landings in Normandy. The scheme included the creation of a fictitious military force, the First United States Army Group (FUSAG), which appeared to generate wireless traffic indicating a concentration of its component units in East Anglia. Bogus radio transmissions, false reports from **double agents**, and the construction of dummy planes and landing craft combined to enhance the impression conveyed to the enemy that FUSAG, commanded by Gen. George Patton, would embark in southeast England for the Pas-de-Calais some weeks after an initial feint had diverted German troops to Normandy. Captured intelligence indicates that the Germans accepted FUSAG as genuine and overestimated Allied strength. Many of the agent observations were made by GARBO, BRUTUS, and TATE, the latter supposedly having seen the U.S. 11th Infantry Division on the move near Cambridge. At the railway station, he supposedly observed the U.S. XX Corps heading west from Norwich, and the 25th Armored Division was spotted on its way south. Each item conveyed the impression that a second, more important amphibious assault was imminent, and this helped to tie down large numbers of enemy units in **Belgium** and northern France while an Allied beachhead was established in Normandy.

FORTITUDE NORTH. Allied code name for a **deception** campaign undertaken in 1944 to persuade the Nazis that an invasion of **Norway** was imminent. The objective was to tie up German forces in Norway and prevent them from being deployed more usefully elsewhere.

FORTY COMMITTEE. The Allied counterintelligence group created under the chairmanship of Michael Crichton to coordinate Allied **deception** and **double agent** activities in North Africa. The Forty Committee controlled subcommittees in Oran, Casablanca, Tunis, and **Gibraltar**. After the invasion of Italy, further committees were established in Bari, Naples, Rome, and Florence. *See also* THIRTY COMMITTEE; TWENTY COMMITTEE.

FOURTH DEPARTMENT. The Soviet designation of the military intelligence service, the **GRU**, known officially as the Fourth Department of the Red Army's General Staff.

FOXWORTH, PERCY E. ("SAM"). Having joined the **Federal Bureau of Investigation** in 1932, Percy "Sam" Foxworth was appointed **J. Edgar Hoover**'s administrative assistant four years later. In September 1939, he was appointed assistant director in charge of the New York Field Office as well as head of the National Defense Office. In 1942, he was chosen to lead the **Special Intelligence Service**, a role he fulfilled, with Special Agent Harold D. Haberfield, until shortly before his death in Dutch Guiana in January 1943, in an air accident while en route to North Africa.

FRAIL. Supreme Headquarters Allied Expeditionary Force code name for Jacques Michel, a French **double agent** dropped into the Haute-Savoie in April 1945 with a wireless transmitter and arrested immediately.

FRANK. Code name for a **Belgian** collaborator and member of the Rexist Party since 1940 who was recruited as a **double agent** in 1942. Upon the liberation of Brussels, FRANK, who edited a sports newspaper, revealed that he was part of a **Sicherheitsdienst** stay-behind network that included René Delhay; Arthur Garitte, code-named MEADOW; Yvon Roy, his radio operator; a young Walloon code-named

MERCY; and MAGNET. FRANK's radio in Cenval made contact with his controller, Marcel Zschunke, on 15 September 1944 and was used as a channel for **deception** until the end of hostilities. Soon afterward, Zschunke turned up with his wife at FRANK's home and was hidden for the next two months, unaware that FRANK had switched sides and was planning to travel to the United States. However, when Zschunke admitted that he had committed atrocities on the Russian Front, he was arrested in an elaborate trap intended to protect FRANK, but the ruse proved unnecessary because under interrogation, he betrayed FRANK.

FREAK. MI5 code name for Marquis Frano de Bona, an aristocrat from Dubrovnik and an old family friend of **Dusan Popov**. De Bona had undergone an **Abwehr** training course in the use of secret ink and Morse code and had also been provided with a radio transmitter, which he handed over when he was welcomed to **Madrid** by Popov. The Marquis eventually reached London via **Gibraltar** in December 1943, where he was assigned the cryptonym FREAK by **MI5** and began using his wireless to signal his German controllers as soon as Popov returned from **Lisbon** the following month. He remained in contact with his controllers until May 1944.

FREMDE HEERE OST (FHO). The intelligence branch of the Oberkommando der Wehrmacht responsible for the analysis of information about opposing forces on the Eastern Front and the preparation of assessments of the enemy order of battle. Headed by Col. Reinhard Gehlen, the FHO recruited hundreds of agents from captured Soviet military personnel and ran extensive networks across the Russian Front. After the war, the Soviets revealed that almost all of these organizations had been penetrated and run by the **NKVD** from Moscow. *See also* GERMAN INTELLIGENCE; MONASTERY; SOVIET INTELLIGENCE; ZEPPELIN.

FREMDE HEERE WEST (FHW). The intelligence branch of the Oberkommando der Wehrmacht responsible for the analysis of information about opposing forces on the Western Front and the preparation of assessments of the enemy order of battle. Headed by Col. Alexis von Roenne from March 1943, the FHW distributed daily estimates of Allied intentions prior to **D-Day**. *See also* GERMAN INTELLIGENCE.

FRENCH INTELLIGENCE. At the outbreak of war, the two principal French intelligence agencies were the Deuxieme Bureau, run by Gen. Gauche, and the **Service de Renseignements**, headed by Col. **Louis Rivet**. Both organizations worked closely with Wilfred Dunderdale's Paris station of the **Secret Intelligence Service**, based in the rue Joubert.

Upon the German occupation of Paris, the Deuxieme Bureau moved into the unoccupied zone, while two additional organizations, the **Bureau Central de Renseignements et d'Action** and **Direction des Services de Renseignements et des Services de Securité Militaire**, were created in London by the Free French forces under the control of Charles de Gaulle. When the Deuxieme Bureau reformed in **Algiers** under the leadership of **Paul Paillole** and Rivet, conflict developed with the Free French in London, controlled by André Dewavrin, and Paillole and Rivet resigned. *See also* VICHY INTELLIGENCE.

FRIEDMAN, WILLIAM. A cryptographer with experience dating back to World War I, when he and his wife Elizabeth had worked on German ciphers, William Friedman was a civilian employee of the U.S. War Department who was appointed chief of the Signal Intelligence Service within the army's Signal Corps in 1930. In 1940 he played a major part in reconstructing the Japanese PURPLE code and even built a replica PURPLE cipher machine, but the achievement took a toll on his mental health, and he underwent psychiatric treatment until April 1941. Two years later, Friedman flew to London to negotiate an agreement with **Government Communications Headquarters' Edward Travis** to divide their research effort and share the results. After the war, Friedman remained in the Signal Security Agency until his retirement from the newly created National Security Agency in 1955.

FUNKSPIEL. The German term for the wireless games such as **NORDPOL** played by counterintelligence personnel against Allied organizations, principally **Special Operations Executive**.

– G –

G-2. The Republic of Ireland's intelligence service. G-2 was headed by Col. Liam Archer and then Col. Dan Bryan, who worked in close but covert association with Cecil Liddell of the Security Service's Irish Section, B-21, later **B1(h)**. The two organizations exchanged information regularly, without the formal authorization of their governments, and tips from **MI5** enabled G-2 to arrest numerous **Abwehr** agents in Eire, including Walter Simon, Willy Preetz, Ernst Weber-Drohl, Herbert Tributh, Henry Obed, and Dieter Gaertner, all in 1940. The following year, Gunther Schütz, Werner Unland, and Hermann Goertz were arrested. The last two parachutists to be caught, named Kenny and O'Reilly, dropped into County Clare in December 1943, equipped with powerful transmitters. One of them was injured and hospitalized with pneumonia, and both had been in the Channel Islands on the outbreak of war. Another was found to have been a broadcaster, making radio propaganda from Germany.

G-2 would prove effective in countering the activities of German agents, and in the case of Goertz, embarked on a **deception** campaign intended to make him believe that he was in direct communication with Berlin.

GABAS. MI5 code name for an **Abwehr** field officer recruited as a **double agent**.

GAERTNER, FRIEDLE. Code-named GELATINE by **MI5**, Friedle Gaertner was already known to the Germans as a Nazi sympathizer who had been a frequent visitor to Joachim von Ribbentrop's embassy in London before the war. In reality, however, she had acted as an agent provocateur for the Security Service, identifying other contacts who were suspected of disloyalty. This had enabled MI5 to arrest and intern a large number of potentially dangerous enemy aliens on the outbreak of war. Code-named GELATINE because Billy Luke thought her "a jolly little thing," she was to become a key **double agent**, supplying the **Abwehr** with political gossip. She was in an especially good position to do this because her equally beautiful sister, Lisel, had married Ian Menzies, whose elder brother **Stewart Menzies** was **chief** of the **Secret Intelligence Service**. The Abwehr believed it maintained contact with Friedle through **Dusan Popov**, who was himself another double agent.

GALA. British code name for Anna Agiraki, once the mistress of the Italian **Servizio di Informazione Militare** chief in Athens, but sent on a mission in August 1942 to Syria. Arrested and imprisoned in Palestine, she **notionally** acted as a prostitute in Beirut, collecting information from British troops for QUICKSILVER.

GANDER. **MI5** code name for **double agent** Carl Grosse, who was parachuted into northern England in October 1940, but remained active for only a month because he had not been given the means, on his short-term mission, to receive instructions from the **Abwehr**.

GAOL. Code name for a French Air Force radio operator recruited by the **Gestapo** in Paris and dropped into **Algiers** in August 1943. He immediately turned himself in and was run as a **double agent**, sending reports **notionally** from the Algiers airport. At the end of August 1944, he was notionally transferred to France, reestablishing contact in October 1944, supposedly from Le Bourget in Paris.

GARBO. **MI5** code name for a Spanish **double agent**, **Juan Pujol**, recruited in **Lisbon** in April 1942 by the **Secret Intelligence Service** as BOVRIL.

GARTENFELD, KARL. Luftwaffe pilot Capt. Karl Gartenfeld was the **Abwehr**'s principal pilot on clandestine agent infiltration operations, flying a special matte-black Heinkel-111 bomber. His crew included Leutnant Nebel as copilot, Sergeant Wagner as wireless operator, Sgt. Karl-Heinz Suessmann as observer, and Corporal Achtelik as dispatcher.

GEHEIMSCHREIBER. The German cipher machine manufactured by Siemens that was used to encrypt long-distance teleprinter traffic. Many of the intercepted texts were decrypted at **Bletchley Park** by cryptanalysts operating COLOSSUS.

GELATINE. **MI5** code name for a **B1(a) double agent**, **Friedle Gaertner**, whose sister was married to **Stewart Menzies**'s brother

Ian. Born in Austria, she had worked for MI5 before the war identifying Nazi sympathizers in contact with the German embassy in London. Recruited by **Dusan Popov** in May 1941, she remained in contact with the **Abwehr** until the end of the war.

GEORGE WOOD. The **Office of Strategic Services** code name for **Fritz Kolbe**.

GERMAN INTELLIGENCE. The two principal German wartime intelligence agencies were the **Abwehr**, headed by Adm. **Wilhelm Canaris**, which accommodated branches for the Luftwaffe, Kriegsmarine, and Luftwaffe, and the **Reichssicherheitshauptamt**, headed by **Reinhard Heydrich**, followed by Heinrich Himmler and Ernst Kaltenbrunner, which included the **Sicherheitsdienst** and the **Gestapo**.

The collection and analysis of intelligence concerning the Western Front was the responsibility of **Fremde Heere West**, based at the General Staff's headquarters at Zossen, while intelligence on the Eastern Front was supervised by the **Fremde Heere Ost**, led from April 1942 by Reinhard Gehlen and based at the Führer's headquarters in East Prussia.

Signals intelligence operations were conducted by the Chiffrierabteilung (Chi) and the **Beobachtungdienst** (B-Dienst) and achieved considerable success against the American M-209 cipher machine and the Royal Navy's hand ciphers.

GESTAPO. An abbreviation for the Geheime Staatspolizei, the Gestapo was the principal Nazi instrument of repression in Germany and occupied territories, with a reputation for the torture and maltreatment of prisoners. The Gestapo was largely staffed by professional police officers who conducted investigations, leaving more complex counterintelligence activities to their **Abwehr** and **Sicherheitsdienst** colleagues. *See also* GERMAN INTELLIGENCE.

GIBRALTAR. The British colony of Gibraltar, at the strategically vital entrance to the Mediterranean, provided a base for **MI5**, represented by the **defence security officer (DSO)**, the **Secret Intelligence Service (MI6)**, and **MI9**. "The Rock," ceded to Great Britain in the 1713 Treaty of Utrecht, was also an important Royal Navy dockyard and a target for Axis espionage. The harbor was kept under constant observation by the **Abwehr** in La Lineas, Spain, and Tangier, Morocco; by the Spanish in Algeciras; and by Italian saboteurs operating from bases concealed in wrecks in Spanish waters. The DSO was Col. "Tito" Medlam, his MI6 counterpart was Col. John Codrington, and the MI9 representative was Donald Darling. By the end of the war, two enemy saboteurs had been arrested and hanged.

GILBERT. (1) **Special Operations Executive** code name for Henri Dericourt, the air movements officer for F Section responsible for supervising clandestine flights in and out of occupied France. A prewar pilot, Dericourt proved hugely successful and never lost a single aircraft to enemy action, mainly because he was a long-term agent of the Paris **Sicherheitsdienst**. After the war, he was prosecuted on charges of collaboration with the enemy but acquitted.

(2) British code name for **double agent** André Latham, who was a French Army officer, St. Cyr graduate, and member of an **Abwehr** stay-behind network in Tunis. He turned himself over to the British, along with his deputy, Capt. Durey-Marisse, code-named LE DUC, when the Afrika Korps surrendered, and in the autumn of 1944, they moved to Marseilles. Their radio operator, a petty officer in the French Navy named Blondeau, was code-named ALBERT, and another member of the organization was Charmain, code-named LE MULET, who was dropped by parachute into North Africa in October 1943 equipped with money and a new hand cipher. He was followed in July 1944 by Maj. Falguiere, code-named LE MOCO, who operated a second transmitter, code-named ATLAS II, from **Algiers**.

GIRAFFE. MI5 code name for a Czech **double agent**, **Georges Graf**, who was run against the **Abwehr** during September 1940, after his arrival in Great Britain. A former member of the French Foreign Legion, he volunteered to join the Free French in the Middle East.

GISEVIUS, HANS BERND. A senior **Gestapo** official, Hans Bernd Gisevius was able to travel to **Bern**, where he supplied information first to the British **Secret Intelligence Service** and then to the **Office of Strategic Services** representative, **Allen Dulles**. After the fall of

Paris, Gisevius had been based under vice consular cover in Bern until his complicity in the 20 July 1944 plot against Adolf Hitler had made his position impossible. He had been the recipient of a thrice-weekly diplomatic pouch to the consulate from **Abwehr** headquarters in Berlin and, as well as being in touch with Dulles, was in contact with the Swiss authorities, **Rudolph Rössler** and Georges Blun. In his postwar memoirs, Gisevius never admitted having been a source for the Soviets, despite his sympathies for the Kremlin's cause, but he had emphasized that "**Oster** seemed to be organizing an intelligence service of his own, within the counter-intelligence service. . . . One of the most important of his activities was to install his own confidential agents in the most diverse positions."

GLAD, TOR. Code-named JEFF by **MI5**, Tor Glad was a Norwegian.

GLAVNOYE RAZVEDYVATEL'NOE UPRAVLENIE. *See* GRU.

GLEAM. MI5 code name for Therea Jardine, a **notional agent** of the ARABEL network and lover of DICK, an Indian poet. Supposedly employed as a WREN and known to the **Abwehr** as JAVELINE, she was transferred to the South-East Asia Command's headquarters in Kandy, Ceylon, in 1944, where she recruited a series of equally notional sources, including ANDRIES, a Dutch liaison officer; Dave Close of the U.S. Navy; JACK, a Royal Air Force wing commander; a Royal Navy officer code-named EDWARD; and BILL, supposedly a colonel on Lord Louis Mountbatten's staff, but ceased writing her letters following a road accident.

GLUCKSMANN, REUBEN. An Austrian, Reuben Glucksmann was arrested in London in May 1940 and interned as an enemy alien, although **MI5** suspected, based on information from **Walter Krivitsky**, that he was a Soviet **GRU** agent. Glucksmann's firm, the Far Eastern Trading Company, was raided, and Kate Rank, his British secretary of Polish origin, was served with a detention order. According to MI5's files, the company had been founded by two well-known GRU staff officers who had been active in Germany and **China**, the brothers Aaron and Abraham Ehrenlieb.

GODFREY, JOHN. The **director of naval intelligence** since 1939, Adm. John Godfrey was replaced in September 1942 by Capt. Edmund Rushbrooke. Despite the efforts of his secretary, Edward Merrett, and his several assistants, of whom one was Ian Fleming, Godfrey proved a difficult personality who failed to gain the confidence of the other service intelligence directors, and he was finally removed from office after protests from the Joint Intelligence Committee to the Admiralty about his lack of cooperation.

GOOSE. MI5 code name for a **B1(a) double agent**, **Kurt Grosse**.

GORSKY, ANATOLI V. The **NKVD** acting *rezident* in London since the recall of *rezident* Grigori B. Grafpen, alias Grigori Blank, in December 1938, Gorsky was himself withdrawn to Moscow in February 1940 because of **Lavrenti Beria**'s mistaken belief that the *rezidentura* had been penetrated. He returned 10 months later, via Vladivostok, Alaska, and New York, to continue running **John Cairncross** and **Donald Maclean**, using the code name VADIM. His small *rezidentura* at the Soviet embassy consisted of Vladimir Barkovsky, who concentrated on technical intelligence, and Pavel D. Yerzin, with André Graur joining them in 1941.

In September 1943, Gorsky, adopting the alias "Anatoli Gromov," was reassigned to Washington, D.C., where Maclean had been posted in July, leaving Boris Krotov, code-named BOB, as his replacement. In August 1944, Gorsky succeeded **Vasili Zubilin** as *rezident* until his departure in 1946. The **Federal Bureau of Investigation** hoped to entrap Gorsky when he was identified by **Elizabeth Bentley** as her controller, but he broke off contact with her.

GOVERNMENT CODE AND CYPHER SCHOOL (GC&CS). The original name for **Government Communications Headquarters**, the British government's principal cryptographic organization, responsible for the creation of secure cipher systems and solving foreign codes. Initially located at 54 **Broadway**, the headquarters of the **Secret Intelligence Service**, GC&CS was transferred to its war station at **Bletchley Park** shortly before the outbreak of hostilities.

GOVERNMENT COMMUNICATIONS HEADQUARTERS (GCHQ). Originally titled the **Government Code and Cypher School**, GCHQ was responsible for the cryptographic attack on the cipher systems employed by foreign governments and for the development of secure methods of communication. Headed first by an administrator, **Alastair Denniston**, who was a veteran of Admiralty's Room 40, he was succeeded as director in January 1942 by (Sir) **Edward Travis**. Based at **Bletchley Park** and dependent on a worldwide network of intercept stations staffed by the three armed services, GCHQ established regional bases at Sarafand, **Cairo**, Singapore, and Delhi.

GCHQ's product, initially circulated as BONIFACE, was redesignated ULTRA in 1942 and remained strictly under the control of the **Secret Intelligence Service**, which exercised extreme caution in managing its distribution.

GRAF, GEORGES. Code-named GIRAFFE by **MI5**, Georges Graf had been talent-spotted for the **Abwehr** after he had arrived in **Lisbon** as a refugee earlier in the summer of 1940. He was just 22 years old and in 1939 had joined the French Army with a companion, Ivan Spaneil. They both attended the artillery school at Poitiers, and then had fled across the Pyrenees with the intention of joining the Free French forces in England. While in Portugal, they both accepted an offer from **Albrecht von Auenrode** to spy for the Germans, but they never intended to spy, hoping instead to use the Abwehr as a means of facilitating their journey to London. In any event, the person who had recommended their recruitment, a Frenchman named Wiesner, was himself working for Richman Stopford of the **Secret Intelligence Service (MI6)** as a **double agent** under the code name SWEETIE, so the approach had become known to MI6 almost as soon as von Auenrode decided to make it. Wiesner said that he cooperated with the Germans under duress because his family was still in Nazi-occupied territory and therefore vulnerable to reprisals. When Graf and Spaneil reached England in September, they immediately volunteered details of their clandestine roles to the British authorities and willingly agreed to work as **double agents**. MI5 assigned John Bingham as their case officer, gave them the cryptonyms GIRAFFE and SPANEHL, respectively, and supervised their supposedly illicit correspondence with the Abwehr's postal address in Lisbon. At no time did the Germans show any sign of realizing that Wiesner, Graf, or Spaneil had fallen under British control.

GRAF SPEE. *See ADMIRAL GRAF SPEE.*

GRAND, LAURENCE. The head of MI6's **Section D**, Laurence Grand was a pioneer of unorthodox warfare, but his clandestine organization was absorbed into **Special Operations Executive** in July 1940. Hitherto it had engaged in a series of unsuccessful sabotage operations in Sweden and Yugoslavia intended to disrupt Nazi acquisition of strategic minerals, including iron ore and oil from Ploesti.

GREEN, OLIVER. A veteran of the International Brigade who fought in the Spanish Civil War, Oliver Green was a London printer who was arrested for counterfeiting gasoline coupons. When his premises were searched, a large quantity of classified documents was recovered. Under interrogation, Green confessed that he was part of a much larger Soviet espionage network based on a membership of other Communists.

GREIF. German code name for an operation to infiltrate 150 English-speaking soldiers behind enemy lines during the Ardennes offensive in December 1944 organized by Obersturmbannführer Otto Skorzeny. The saboteurs, some dressed in the uniforms of U.S. military police, led by Wilhelm Giel, misdirected Allied convoys, destroyed bridges, and caused chaos as the 1st Panzer Division advanced toward Malmédy. In August 1947, Skorzeny and other officers of Panzerbrigade 150 were prosecuted for war crimes, including the murder of a group of American prisoners of war at Baugnez during the Battle of the Bulge, but they were all acquitted.

GROSSE, KURT. True name of **MI5**'s **double agent** code-named GOOSE.

GROSSVOGEL, LEON. A French Jew of Polish extraction and a **GRU** agent, Leon Grossvogel had worked for **Simex**, a garment manufacturer since 1926, as had his sister Sarah, who was married to one of the directors, Louis Kapelowitz. The business had been developed to export its well-established and popular product to Scandinavia, with the English market as another objective. Apart from Grossvogel's involvement, the firm was entirely respectable; Jules Jaspar, formerly the Belgian consul in Indochina, whose brother had been prime minister of **Belgium**, was on its board. Grossvogel's Communist sympathies and his checkered past (he had been cited in a divorce action and had been imprisoned briefly on an assault charge) were known to the company's directors, and they had welcomed with relief his decision to initiate an export-orientated subsidiary. **Leopold Trepper**, posing as a wealthy Canadian businessman named Mikler, supplied Grossvogel with the necessary capital to open foreign branches in **Stockholm** and Copenhagen as a preliminary to operating in London, a city he visited several times in 1937 and 1938.

GRU. The Glavnoye Razvedyvatel'noe Upravlenie (GRU) was the principal Soviet military intelligence service, also known as the **Fourth Department** of the Red Army's General Staff. It was headed from 1938 until July 1940 by Gen. Ivan A. Proskurov and ran extensive networks across the globe with personnel based at diplomatic premises and numerous illegals. Always referred to as the DIREKTOR, Proskurov was replaced by Gen. Filip I. Golikov, having developed the GRU into a large organization based at Znamensky 19, the General Staff headquarters in Moscow. Golikov's opposition to the Molotov-Ribbentrop Pact led to his arrest and execution. He was then succeeded by Aleksei P. Panfilov, until July 1942 when he too was shot; briefly by Leonid I. Ilyichev, who was purged; and then by Fedor F. Kuznetsov in April 1943.

Prior to the declassification of VENONA, the best-known **GRU** spies were **Ursula Kuczynski** and **Richard Sorge**. Very little was understood in the West about the GRU until the **defector Walter Krivitsky** was interviewed in London by **MI5**'s **Jane Archer** and **Guy Liddell** in February 1940. GRU officer **Ismail Akhmedov** defected in Turkey in May 1942, but he was not made available for interview by any Allied services until 1945. Further information about the GRU's wartime activities were disclosed in September 1945 by a code clerk,

Igor Gouzenko, who had been based in Ottawa since 1942 working for **Nikolai Zabotin**. During the war, the GRU organized sophisticated illegal networks in Brussels, the **Rote Kapelle**, and in London, the **X Group**, managed by the GRU's legal *rezident,* Ivan Sklyarov.

Gouzenko's information revealed the existence of a large network in **Canada**, while the VENONA decrypts identified the code names of more than 40 local sources, few of whom were ever identified. Those GRU sources that were caught, among them **Oliver Green**, **Douglas Springhall**, **Ormond Uren**, and **Olive Sheehan**, did not seem to appear in the traffic. *See also* SOVIET INTELLIGENCE.

GUDGEON, **USS.** The first Japanese naval loss of World War II occurred on 27 January 1942 when the submarine *Gudgeon* torpedoed the submarine I-27, having been vectored to the target 240 miles west of Midway by signals intelligence. I-27's position had been located by radio direction-finding and cryptanalysis, and the submarine sank with no survivors.

GUINEA. Secret Intelligence Service code name for James Ponsonby, the trade attaché at the British consulate in Tangier who pretended in July 1943 to be a **Special Operations Executive (SOE)** officer in financial trouble, prompting him to sell classified documents to the Germans. Actually the papers were part of a **deception** campaign intended to mislead the enemy about the Salerno landings. Ponsonby was later transferred to **Lisbon**, where his indiscretions led to his transfer back to London. Convinced he would be arrested and executed, Ponsonby attempted to ensure his safety by telling SOE that he had left letters in Portugal that would compromise the organization's operations in North Africa if he was detained. Instead Ponsonby was awarded an MBE.

GUN. Supreme Headquarters Allied Expeditionary Force code name for Guy Godot-la-Loi, a Frenchman infiltrated into Bordeaux in March 1945, arrested soon afterward, and run as a **double agent**.

GURYEVICH, VIKTOR. Code-named KENT by the **GRU**, Viktor Guryevitch was a veteran of the Spanish Civil War who had been born in St. Petersburg in 1911 but traveled on a Uruguayan passport in the name of Vincente Sierra from Montevideo, issued in New York in April 1936. Prior to his arrival in Ghent in July 1939, where he kept a rendezvous with **Leopold Trepper**, Guryevitch had spent two years in France, based in Marseilles, and had operated briefly in Germany, probably as a courier. Once in **Belgium**, he enrolled as a student of languages at Brussels University and, later that summer, made a trip to Switzerland to introduce himself to the GRU's local network. However, in addition to taking a course in commerce, he was taught cipher procedures by Trepper and acquired a wealthy mistress, Margarete Barcza, who happened to have an apartment in the same building as his, in the avenue Émile de Beco. When Barcza's Czech husband died in March 1940, she moved in with Guryevitch and subsequently introduced him to friends whom he persuaded to join the board of **Simex**, his import-export company, thus lending it an air of respectability when it was registered in March 1941. Despite a magnetic personality and all his undoubted skills as an illegal, Guryevitch never shook off his peasant origins.

When the Germans swept through Belgium in May 1940, Trepper's network was unprepared. **Mikhail Makarov**'s Ostend branch of the **Foreign Excellent Raincoat Company** was bombed out by the Luftwaffe, and Trepper was forced to make a hazardous journey to the resort town of Knokke-le-Zoute to retrieve a wireless transmitter hidden in a seaside villa. A measure of protection for Trepper's party, which included **Leon Grossvogel**, was afforded by the presence of the (apparently innocent) Bulgarian consul who drove the car in an attempt to trace Bulgarians isolated on the coast by the fighting. Another motive for the dangerous trip was to obtain accurate information about the Wehrmacht's advance through Belgium. Having survived the German invasion, Makarov moved to Brussels, and early in July Trepper fled to France, leaving his network in Guryevitch's hands.

From March 1943, Guryevitch operated the MARS transmitter while accommodated in a 10-bedroom villa at 40 avenue Victor Hugo in Neuilly, the residence of Sturmbannführer Karl Boemelburg, the head of the **Sicherheitsdienst** in Paris. That Guryevitch and his mistress Barcza enjoyed a considerable degree of freedom is evident from the birth of their son, Michel, in April 1944. The German decision to develop MARS was rewarded on 14 March 1943 when

Guryevitch was instructed by Moscow to make contact with a hitherto undiscovered network run by Waldemar Ozols, a former Latvian general who had fought with the International Brigade in the Spanish Civil War. Guryevitch found him at the address supplied by Moscow and learned from Ozols that he and his small organization had been run by the Soviet air attaché in Paris but when the Soviets withdrew from France in 1940 he had been left with a wireless transmitter but no operator. Accordingly, Ozols had gone underground, waiting to be contacted. Under Guryevitch's directions, Ozols reformed his network and linked up with MITHRIDATE, a resistance group in Marseilles headed by Col. Bressac and an elderly captain in the reserve, Paul Legendre. As a consequence, MITHRIDATE effectively came under German control, but only one of its members seems to have realized what had happened. He was Marcel Droubaix, a Frenchman who had been educated in England and had served in the Royal Horse Artillery during World War I. Droubaix suspected German penetration in June 1944 but he was arrested the following month while attending a meeting with Guryevitch in Paris and was to die at Buchenwald in February 1945.

Guryevitch survived the war but was imprisoned upon his return to the Soviet Union. Released from the KGB prison at Vorkonta in 1956, he settled in his native St. Petersburg.

GUSTAVO. Code name for a Polish journalist in Buenos Aires, **Argentina**, who worked as an interpreter for the Domei News Agency and supplied information to Saburo Suzuki, the local correspondent for *Mainichi*. In fact GUSTAVO was a **double agent**, run by the U.S. military attaché and supposedly in weekly contact with Hessell Tiltman in Washington, D.C., formerly the *Daily Express* correspondent in Tokyo.

GUY FAWKES. MI5 code name for an act of sabotage in November 1941, the detonation of an incendiary device in a foodstore in Wealdstone intended to bolster the reputation of **G.W.**, supposedly an extremist Welsh nationalist but actually a **double agent**.

G.W. MI5 code name for a **double agent**, **Gwilym Williams**.

– H –

HALDANE, J. B. S. A leading scientist of his era, Prof. J. B. S. Haldane undertook classified experimental work for the Admiralty and advised the British government on air raid precautions. According to **GRU** VENONA decrypts in 1940, Haldane was also a Soviet spy codenamed INTELLIGENSIA who headed a network known as the **X Group**.

HAMBURGER, WILLI. An Austrian **Abwehr** officer based in **Istanbul**, Dr. Willi Hamburger was ordered to return to Berlin following the **defection** of **Erich Vermehren** in December 1943. Rather than face a **Gestapo** interrogation, Hamburger, who had been embroiled in an affair with glamorous Hungarian actress Adrienne Molnar, was persuaded by her to defect to the American **Office of Strategic Services**.

HAMLET. The **Secret Intelligence Service** code name for Dr. Koestler, a Jewish businessman, former Austrian cavalry officer, and **double agent** recruited in **Lisbon** by MULLETT in 1941 and active until May 1944.

HANS. Code name for Dr. Friedrich Hack, a former economic adviser to the Japanese Navy resident in **Bern** and in contact with the U.S. military attaché. From early 1945, Hack unwittingly supplied misleading information to Cmmdr. Fujimura, a Japanese diplomat in radio contact with Tokyo.

HARKER, JASPER. Director of **MI5**'s B Division until June 1940, when he took over the role of acting director-general until the appointment of Sir **David Petrie** in March 1941.

HARLEQUIN. MI5 code name for an **Abwehr defector** named Wurmann who was captured in North Africa in December 1943 and proved very willing to cooperate in return for the promise of British citizenship.

HARRIS, KITTY. A long-term Soviet spy and former companion of Earl Browder, the leader of the **Communist Party of the United**

States of America, Kitty Harris had been born in London but brought up in Canada before moving with her family to Detroit. By 1939, after completing assignments for the **NKVD** in **China**, she was posted to London as an illegal and ran **Donald Maclean**. She followed him to Paris and was romantically involved with him until his evacuation in May 1940. She then returned to Moscow and was sent to **Mexico** to handle a network engaged in penetrating the **Manhattan Project** at Los Alamos. In some VENONA traffic from Mexico City in April 1944, she is identified with the code name ADA.

HART, HERBERT. MI5 officer and academic who worked as a counterintelligence analyst before returning to Oxford and his appointment as professor of jurisprudence. *See also* HART, JENIFER.

HART, JENIFER. A prewar member of the **Communist Party of Great Britain**, Jenifer Fischer Williams married **Herbert Hart** and worked in the Home Office as personal secretary to the permanent undersecretary, Sir Alexander Maxwell, with responsibility for preparing **MI5**'s applications for telephone intercept warrants. In 1998 she published her autobiography, *Ask Me No More*, in which she recalled meeting her Soviet contact, Arnold Deutsch, at a secret rendezvous in Kew Gardens.

HATCHET. MI5 code name for **Albert de Jaeger**.

HAT TRICK. British code name for a group of eight Indian agents landed from a Japanese submarine on the Malabar coast in April 1944. All were caught, although the arrest of the pair destined for Trichinopoly was publicized, making it impossible to employ them as **double agents**. Two of the others were recruited as DOUBTFUL and AUDREY and operated from Madras and Ramaswaram, respectively, transmitting **deception** material until the end of hostilities.

HEADLAND. Supreme Headquarters Allied Expeditionary Force code name for a French **double agent** active in Vannes from February 1945.

HEENAN, PATRICK. Born illegitimately in New Zealand in 1910 to an Irish mother, Patrick Heenan was educated in England at

Sevenoaks School and joined the army in 1935. He was posted to India to join the Royal Warwicks, but transferred to the 16th Punjabis in 1936 and soon afterward won India's heavyweight boxing championship. He saw action on the Northwest Frontier, and in 1938 took his accumulated long-leave in Japan, where he learned the language and acquired a Japanese mistress.

In October 1940 Capt. Heenan's battalion was posted to Singapore, where the Japanese consulate-general accommodated an extensive intelligence office headed by Dr. Tsune Ouchi, some of whose signals were intercepted by British cryptographers at the locally based **Far East Combined Bureau** and by Americans working from the Philippines. The traffic revealed the existence of an extensive Japanese espionage organization in Singapore and that the enemy possessed detailed knowledge about the island's air defenses. When Heenan was sent to Kota Baru, Malaya, as an air liaison officer to assist in defending an airfield, his queries and attempts to access classified plans raised suspicions, and he was arrested in December 1941. He was found to be in possession of a miniature transmitter and attempted to escape. He was court-martialed in January 1942 and executed on 13 February 1942 as Singapore fell to the Japanese.

HEIR. **Supreme Headquarters Allied Expeditionary Force** code name for a French **double agent** in Paris whose transmitter was dug up in Gerardmer.

HENRY. The Turkish wife of a German Jewish refugee in **Lisbon**, and formerly the mistress of the local Japanese naval attaché, HENRY unwittingly supplied information to the Japanese military attaché from early 1945 until the end of hostilities.

HERMAN. The **Federal Bureau of Investigation** code name for a **notional** subagent of PAT J, supposedly a seaman employed in the Philadelphia Navy Yard.

HEYDRICH, REINHARD. Born in 1904, Reinhard Heydrich joined the German Navy but was dismissed in March 1941 following a court of honor ruling over an allegation of misconduct toward a woman. He immediately joined the Nazi Party and was appointed by Heinrich Himmler to establish a security branch, the **Sicherheitsdienst (SD)**.

In 1939 the SD, having masterminded Operation TANNENBERG, was combined with the Kriminalpolizei and the **Gestapo** to form the **Reichssicherheitshauptamt**. In September 1941, Heydrich was appointed *protektor* of Bohemia and Moravia, and in May the following year died of wounds inflicted by two British-trained assassins who attacked him as he was driven through Prague.

HICCOUGHS. A completely **notional** network of British stay-behind agents in Burma that received information from July 1942 poorly concealed in broadcasts made by All-India Radio.

HITTITE. MI5 code name for a **double agent** recruited by the German consul in New Orleans, who instructed him to make contact with his new controller at the Regent Palace Hotel in London before the end of November 1940. HITTITE attended the suggested rendezvous, but met nobody. *See also* DUTCH INTELLIGENCE.

HOLTZ. The **Federal Bureau of Investigation** code name for a notion subsource of PAT J, supposedly a U.S. Navy seaman of German extraction.

HOOVER, J. EDGAR. The long-serving director of the **Federal Bureau of Investigation (FBI)**, J. Edgar Hoover had been appointed by the Justice Department in 1924. His organization was the principal federal counterintelligence authority but had little experience in that area until December 1939, when Hoover dispatched Hugh Clegg and Clarence Hince to London to tour **MI5** and the **Secret Intelligence Service**. Thereafter the FBI achieved early success against the **Abwehr** with the recruitment of **William Sebold** as a **double agent** in 1941.

Although Hoover was eager to develop the FBI's **Special Intelligence Service** in South America, he was reluctant to transform his organization into a counterintelligence agency, and most cases were run with a view to prosecution and publicity. Always a self-promoter, Hoover often supplied the media with misleading accounts of espionage cases, the PASTORIUS landings being a good example, for it would have been impossible to discover from the published versions that the entire investigation had been initiated by Georg Dasch, who had turned himself in to the FBI. Similarly, Hoover himself released a very distorted tale concerning **Dusan Popov** that suggested that he had been a Nazi spy detected by the FBI's vigilance, whereas he had always been a British double agent, as the director well knew.

HOST. **Supreme Headquarters Allied Expeditionary Force** code name for Pierre Schmidt, a **Sicherheitsdienst** interpreter from Alsace who was part of a stay-behind network in Strasbourg, but surrendered to the Americans with his wife Elizabeth Steuler, code-named HOST-ESS, in December 1944.

HUYSMANN, JOHANNES. Deported to England from **Lisbon** in May 1941, Johannes Huysmann was a Belgian recruited by the **Abwehr**. He made a full confession at **Camp 020**, where he acted as a stool pigeon until the end of the war, when he was returned to **Belgium** and sentenced to life imprisonment.

– I –

IMPERIAL CENSORSHIP. Upon the declaration of war, Imperial Censorship, based in Liverpool, intercepted and scrutinized all mail leaving the United Kingdom, and subordinate offices were established in **Bermuda**, **Gibraltar**, and **Trinidad**. Whereas the Liverpool headquarters examined mail destined for overseas addressees, copying suspect material intended for names appearing on **MI5**'s stop-list, the other branches monitored mail sent from the Western Hemisphere to Europe and proved an effective counterespionage instrument, enabling correspondence to compromise other members of spy rings.

IMPULSE. **Supreme Headquarters Allied Expeditionary Force** code name for a German stay-behind agent who was captured in Amiens, France. It was intended to use him as a **double agent**, but his controller was suspicious and instructed him to cease operations.

INDIAN POLITICAL INTELLIGENCE BUREAU (IPI). Headed by Sir **Philip Vickery**, the IPI collected and collated information about subversion in the subcontinent and liaised with the **Delhi**

Intelligence Bureau. As Indian nationalists, led by Subhas Chandra Bose, were recruited by the Japanese as spies, the huge card index of suspect personalities accumulated by the IPI became an increasingly valuable counterintelligence resource.

INFAMOUS. Secret Intelligence Service code name for a Turkish carpet dealer of Armenian extraction and **double agent** who offered to supply false information to the **Abwehr** in **Istanbul**. His offer was accepted, and he was later the conduit for a payment to QUICKSILVER in 1944.

INK. Code name for a **notional double agent**, supposedly a Chinese official in Chungking with access to reports written by Gen. Feng Yi, the Chinese representative at Lord Mountbatten's headquarters in Kandy, Ceylon, who transmitted to a Japanese controller in Macao.

INTELLIGENSIA. GRU code name for Prof. **J. B. S. Haldane**, a leading member of the **X Group** in London in 1940 and 1941, according to the relevant VENONA decrypts. A leading scientist, Haldane had been appointed a government adviser on air raid precautions following a study he had undertaken in **Madrid** during the Spanish Civil War, and later he conducted classified underwater experiments for the Admiralty. A lifelong member of the **Communist Party of Great Britain**, Haldane was not identified as INTELLIGENSIA until after his death.

INTERALLIÉ. British **Secret Intelligence Service (MI6)** code word for the first major network in Nazi-occupied France, established in 1940 after the fall of Paris. The mainly Polish network boasted several transmitters and a cell structure designed to ensure internal security and was controlled by the Polish director of military intelligence in London, Col. Stefan Mayer. Most of its personnel were displaced Poles with military backgrounds who were well disciplined, knew what to look out for, and recognized what they saw. These were no amateurs unable to distinguish different types of aircraft or tank models, but trained observers who had a good grasp of the kind of information required by the intelligence analysts in London. Their productivity was first-rate and insulated from the political intrigues that handicapped other Polish activities.

INTERALLIÉ was so impressive that its organizer, Roman Garby-Czerniawski (**BRUTUS**) of the Polish air force, was invited to London to confer with MI6's Wilfred Dunderdale and Polish commander-in-chief Gen. Wladyslaw Sikorski. A rendezvous with a Lysander from Tempsford was arranged, and on 11 October Garby-Czerniawski was delivered to London in a flawless operation, the first pickup from German-occupied territory of the war. Garby-Czerniawski then spent nine days at **Broadway** and with the Poles at the Rubens Hotel, always accompanied by Phillip Schneidau as his MI6 conducting officer, before receiving an urgent message from France alerting him to a bitter quarrel between his cipher clerk and mistress, **Mathilde Carré**, and the organization's chief radio operator, Gane.

Cutting short his visit, Garby-Czerniawski parachuted back "blind" into the Loire Valley and, upon his return to Paris learned that his two subordinates had fallen out. Worse, on 3 November the **Abwehr** in Cherbourg arrested Raoul Kiffer, one of INTERALLIÉ's principal subagents. Under duress, the former French air force noncommissioned officer had implicated one of Garby-Czerniawski's assistants, Bernard Krutki. When both men were left alone in an interrogation room in the Abwehr's headquarters in the Hotel Edouard VII in the avenue de l'Opera, their conversation was recorded and Krutki unwittingly disclosed Garby-Czerniawski's address in St. Germain-en-Laye.

Garby-Czerniawski was arrested on 17 November 1941, and within three days, his entire network had been rounded up. Carré swiftly transferred her allegiances to the Abwehr and became the mistress of Sgt. Hugo Bleicher, one of the Abwehr's most successful and imaginative investigators. It was his idea, now that he was in possession of four of INTERALLIÉ's transmitters, to have Carré resume contact with London to report the arrest of Garby-Czerniawski and her intention to take over the network. None of the Polish wireless operators would collaborate, but Carré told her captors of a Frenchman, Henri Tabet, who had previously left INTERALLIÉ after a disagreement. Under coercion, he agreed to send a signal, carefully enciphered by Carré. The transmission was duly acknowledged, and there then followed three months of a sophisticated radio game that gave the Abwehr a unique insight into MI6's activities. Unfortunately it also led to the elimination of the AUTOGIRO **circuit** run by **Special Operations Executive (SOE)**.

On 24 October 1941, AUTOGIRO had experienced the loss of its wireless operator, Georges Begue, who was arrested when he called at a compromised address in Marseilles. This left the circuit with only one operator, Georges Bloch, who had been dropped on 6/7 September. Unfortunately, he too was arrested, by police equipped with direction-finders in Le Mans around 13 November, which meant that the organization's leader, Pierre de Vomécourt, was without any means of communicating with London. Undeterred, he searched Paris for another radio and, just after Christmas, was introduced to Carré, who revealed her link with London and offered to service AUTOGIRO.

Disastrously, MI6 decided to accept AUTOGIRO's messages via INTERALLIÉ, and thereby doubled the Germans' knowledge of the resistance structure. If MI6 and SOE had maintained different lines of communications, such a step would probably have been rejected, but MI6 had only recently fought and won a bitter bureaucratic struggle in London to retain its control over SOE's signals. SOE was perfectly aware of the pressures imposed on it by MI6, but was powerless to do anything but protest. Apart from the operational restrictions on SOE's access to the Channel, aircraft, and the French coastline, there was a continuing problem over communications. All of SOE's radio links were relayed through Whaddon Hall, the main MI6 reception station. SOE suspected, quite rightly, that all its most sensitive messages were being read and circulated inside Broadway Buildings. In April 1941 this anxiety had been translated into a formal request for an independent cipher system and a separate communications channel. The proposal had been resisted strenuously, and MI6 had prevailed with the assertion that "SOE's methods were insecure."

De Vomécourt made the initial approach to Carré via her lawyer, who happened to be known to him, and once London's acknowledgment was received, via the **Canadian** legation in Vichy, de Vomécourt was fully satisfied that Carré could be trusted. Accordingly, he channeled all his communications through her, which meant that from November 1941 her Abwehr lover, Bleicher, was reading every item.

After nearly two months of working with Carré, de Vomécourt eventually realized that all was not well and challenged her with being in contact with the enemy. He had noticed a strange delay in her transmissions and had been suspicious about the arrest of a courier. Also, she seemed to be able to obtain German travel stamps for documents without much difficulty. Upon being confronted, Carré admitted her liaison with the Abwehr, which placed de Vomécourt in considerable difficulty. He had no other method of warning London that both AUTOGIRO and INTERALLIÉ had been compromised, and he could neither simply disappear nor take any overt steps to warn the rest of his circuit. Indeed, he had just been sent another agent, Jack Fincken, as an assistant. Nor did he explain to London that INTERALLIÉ's link was being used by the Abwehr to supply misleading information, including some false intelligence about the *Scharnhorst, Gneisenau*, and the *Prinz Eugen*, which were able to escape from Brest and return up the Channel to Germany unscathed.

Instead, de Vomécourt persuaded Carré to switch sides again and operate as a triple agent. It was an extraordinary gamble, but it led the Germans to endorse a bold plan: de Vomécourt would be allowed to return to London with Carré, where she proposed to work for the Abwehr; he would later return to France with a British general. Thus on 12/13 February an MI6 fast motor gunboat, the MGB 314, attempted to collect Carré and de Vomécourt from a beach in Brittany. It failed to pick up the two agents, but did deliver another pair, Claude Redding and his wireless operator, G. W. Abbott. Both were quickly arrested, together with their Royal Navy escort, Sublieutenant Ivan Black. The MGB 314's commander, a peacetime solicitor and yachtsman, Dunstan Curtis, was unaware of the drama on the beach and, bound by a strict timetable, headed for home with his depleted crew as dawn approached.

A more successful pickup was fixed for 26/27 February, and on this occasion de Vomécourt and Carré were taken to Dartmouth. De Vomécourt promptly revealed Carré's duplicity and the fate of INTERALLIÉ. This must have been devastating news for MI6, especially as it had relayed bogus information to the Admiralty about the German cruisers at Brest and, according to Pierre's brother Philippe de Vomécourt, who was then still in France, SOE had requested intelligence about St. Nazaire, the strategically important French port on Normandy's Atlantic coast and now a vital base for the Kriegsmarine.

In 1961 Philippe de Vomécourt disclosed that some of the messages handled by Carré, and therefore the Abwehr, had referred to St.

Nazaire, which had been selected as the target for CHARIOT, an ambitious attack against the lock gates of the port's massive dry dock. SOE had played a vital role in preparing the plans for the operation, and many of the participants had been trained at SOE's school at Aston House, near Hertford. CHARIOT took place on the night of 28/29 March, nearly a month after MI6 and SOE had been notified that all INTERALLIÉ's communications had been betrayed to the Abwehr.

Pierre de Vomécourt was given a warm welcome in London and was received by the chief of the Imperial General Staff, Gen. Sir Alan Brooke; Anthony Eden; and Lord Selborne, the minister of economic warfare. Meanwhile, Carré was interrogated by MI5, MI6, and SOE before being imprisoned, first at Holloway and then Aylesbury.

De Vomécourt's intention had been to return to France with Carré, and—once his version of events had been confirmed by Ben Cowburn, another member of AUTOGIRO, a tough Lancastrian in the oil business, who had made his own way to England via **Madrid** after the failure of the first rendezvous the previous month—he was allowed to parachute back alone on 1 April. He landed on his brother's estate near Limoges and proceeded to Paris, where Roger Cottin had been running AUTOGIRO in his absence. In order to buy time from Bleicher, who had been expecting Carré accompanied by a **notional** British general, the Abwehr was told via its INTERALLIÉ wireless that de Vomécourt had been delayed in London but would be back by the next full moon. Isolated from this dangerous radio link, and without a wireless operator, de Vomécourt was obliged to communicate with SOE's network by courier via Virginia Hall, an American journalist working for the *New York Post* who ran a safe house in Lyons. Despite the handicap of having a wooden leg, Hall was a highly successful SOE agent and later became a senior officer in the Central Intelligence Agency's Latin America division.

Once Hall's courier had been caught and Bleicher realized that de Vomécourt had slipped back into France, AUTOGIRO was doomed. Cottin, who had been kept under constant German surveillance, was arrested immediately, and soon afterward Leon Walters, the Belgian in whose apartment de Vomécourt was staying, was taken in for questioning. On 25 April, Bleicher caught up with de Vomécourt in a café while he was meeting Jack Fincken. Noel Burdeyron, who had represented AUTOGIRO in Normandy since the previous July, was next, and then the Comte du Puy. Last of all was Christopher Burney, another SOE agent who was dropped near Le Mans on 31 May with instructions to contact AUTOGIRO's man in Caen and then work for Burdeyron. He was eventually arrested on 1 August, by which time Hall had learned of the roundup and alerted London. The AUTOGIRO debacle had led to the arrest of Abbott, Redding, Black, Cottin, Burdeyron, Walters, Fincken, and Pierre de Vomécourt. Altogether 15 members of AUTOGIRO were arrested, as well as de Vomécourt's brothers Philippe and Jean. Only the latter did not survive the war.

INTERDEPARTMENTAL INTELLIGENCE CONFERENCE (IIC). Convened by **J. Edgar Hoover** in the Department of Justice Building in Washington, D.C., in June 1939, the IIC was a forum in which the **Federal Bureau of Investigation**, the War Department's Military Intelligence Division, and the **Office of Naval Intelligence** could meet weekly to exchange information and plan operations. Much of the work of the IIC was conducted by two subcommittees, one dealing with current investigations, chaired by Stanley J. Tracy, and the other, chaired by W. Richard Glavin, which considered policy issues.

INTER-SERVICES LIAISON DEPARTMENT (ISLD). The cover title of the British **Secret Intelligence Service** in the Middle East and the Far East. ISLD was headed in those two regions, respectively, by Cmmdr. Cuthbert Bowlby in **Cairo** and Wng-Cmmdr. Pile in Delhi.

IRISH INTELLIGENCE. *See* G-2.

IRISH REPUBLICAN ARMY (IRA). In 1939 the Irish Republican Army conducted a terrorist campaign in England by leaving letter bombs in Royal Mail postboxes. There were no casualties, but the incidents persuaded the **Abwehr** that the IRA represented an opponent to the British that had already established a network across the country. Accordingly, contact was established between the IRA and Berlin, with the IRA's chief of staff Sean Russell acting as an emissary. Thereafter a series of German agents were parachuted into Ireland, among them Ernst Weber-Drohl and and Dr. Hermann Goertz, with instructions to liaise with the IRA. Although Goertz succeeded in retaining his liberty in Dublin for 17 months, he was eventually arrested and detained until the end of the war. Russell died of a perforated ulcer while attempting to reach Ireland in August 1940 aboard a U-boat.

ISK. Government Communications Headquarters code name for decrypts of **Abwehr Enigma** machine cipher traffic first broken by Dillwyn Knox. Reluctant to rely on vulnerable landlines for their most sensitive communications, the Germans came to depend on Enigma channels to exchange messages between individual *Abstellen* and Berlin. Knox was able to solve some of these intercepts through access to the original clear texts supplied by **double agents** under **MI5** and **Secret Intelligence Service (MI6)** control. ISK became MI6's principal source of information, and a separate branch, **Section V**, was established to process the material, investigate leads, and protect its security.

ISOS. Government Communications Headquarters code name for decrypts of **Abwehr** hand ciphers first broken by Oliver Strachey. These relatively primitive systems were employed by all *Abstellen* when communicating by radio with their substations that were not equipped with **Enigma** machines.

ISTANBUL. A veritable hive of espionage activity, Istanbul was the main route out of Europe to the Middle East, and all travelers were photographed by the efficient Turkish Sûreté, which collaborated closely with Harold Gibson, the head of the local **Secret Intelligence Service** station. The station contained a **Section V** officer, Nicholas Elliott, who was succeeded in 1944 by Keith Guthrie. The Germans were also active in the city, although the **defection** of **Erich Vermehren** and his wife, followed by the **Kleczkowskis** and **Willi Hamburger**, proved a severe setback for the local **Abwehr**, headed by Dr. Paul Leverkühn.

ITALIAN INTELLIGENCE. The principal Italian intelligence agencies were the formidable **Servizio di Informazione Militare**, the **Servizio di Informazione Segrete**, the **Servizio di Informazioni**

Aeronautiche, and the ruthless Fascist security apparatus, the **Opera Volontaria di Repressione dell'Antifascismo**.

IVAN. Abwehr code name for **Dusan Popov**.

– J –

JADE. AMICOL was a resistance organization created in 1940 by Father Arnould in Bordeaux, who called himself "Colonel Claude Ollivier," and another Roman Catholic, Philippe Keun, known as "L'Amiral." Their organization was centered on the Convent of the Sisters of St. Agonie in the rue de Santé in Paris. By **D-Day**, more than 1,000 sub-agents had been recruited, many of them working in individual cell units headed by a leader with the code name of a gemstone. JADE was a branch with a membership of railway men.

JADE/AMICOL was in direct contact with the **Secret Intelligence Service**'s French country section, headed by Wilfred Dunderdale, and survived Keun's betrayal in July 1944, soon after his return from a visit to London. He was executed two months later, but his organization proved highly successful and most resistant to hostile penetration.

JAEGER, ALBERT DE. Code-named HATCHET by **MI5**, Albert de Jaeger was a **Sicherheitsdienst** officer who arrived in Great Britain in 1941 from **Lisbon** and volunteered to act as a **double agent**.

JAHNKE, KURT. Implicated in the explosion on Black Tom Island in New York Harbor in July 1916, Kurt Jahnke was a veteran German intelligence officer and later a Prussian deputy who before the war had developed his own independent organization for the deputy Führer, Rudolf Hess. Jahnke had been named by **Walter Krivitsky**, when interviewed by **MI5** in February 1940, as having been in contact with the **GRU** in 1927, and in 1940 he approached the **Secret Intelligence Service (MI6)** claiming to have been passed copies of Ambassador Joseph Kennedy's telegrams to President Franklin D. Roosevelt, supposedly by someone in the British Foreign Office or by a woman connected to him. An investigation implicated Harold Fletcher, a **Government Communications Headquarters** cipher clerk who had already reported a prewar conversation with Capt. Pfefer, a German intelligence officer associated with Jahnke, and with Pfefer's wife Gulla, with whom he had been conducting an affair in England. Jahnke's offer to cooperate with MI6 was rejected, but his information led to the detention of Gulla Pfefer in London. Jahnke's activities were closed down by the **Gestapo** in 1942, but **Walter Schellenberg** then employed him to undertake certain negotiations with Chiang Kai-shek, and thereafter he remained in contact with various Chinese military attachés.

At the end of November 1944, Jahnke's secretary, Karl Marcus, who used the alias "Marienhofer," **defected** by slipping through the lines as a deserter and reached Paris, where he asked to be put in contact with MI6. When questioned by Frank Foley, he offered information about a Nazi atomic bomb and suggested that Jahnke and Schellenberg might try to reach Switzerland to negotiate with the Allies. He was brought to London for further interviews, but nothing transpired, and Jahnke was arrested in Berlin by the Soviets in 1945. Both Jahnke and Marcus were later released and remained in Germany.

JAKOBS, JOSEF. A 43-year-old German dentist, Josef Jakobs was a parachute agent who landed in a potato field in Huntingdonshire on 1 February 1941. He was court-martialed in August 1941 and shot at the Tower of London 10 days later. His imminent arrival had been signaled to **Arthur Owens**, who had supplied the **Abwehr** with his cover name, "James Rymer," and other information that was found on his forged identity card. **MI5** had been confident of catching "Rymer" because Owens had been instructed to make contact with him, but an unforeseen accident had wrecked the scheme. Jakobs had broken both ankles when he hit the ground and had been arrested a few hours later as he lay in agony beside his parachute. The circumstances of his capture near Ramsey were widely known in the neighborhood, so there was considerable risk to employing him as a **double agent**. As a result, Jakobs became a prime candidate for prosecution.

JANOWSKY, WALDEMAR. An **Abwehr double agent** in **Canada**, code-named WATCHDOG by **MI5**.

JAPANESE INTELLIGENCE. In Tokyo, the Foreign office, the Greater East Asia Ministry, and the General Staffs of the Imperial Army and Navy all maintained their own separate intelligence organizations. The Imperial Army's Second Division included the secret military police branch, the **Kempeitai**; an espionage branch, the Tokumu Kikan; and a codebreaking unit, the Central Special Intelligence Department, which concentrated on Chinese traffic. Although the Second Division had been active in Malaya since 1934, its operations elsewhere were limited; in Europe, they were restricted to Germany, Spain, Portugal, Sweden, Switzerland, and Turkey.

Japanese naval intelligence, designated the Naval Staff's Third Division and headed by Rear Adm. Maeda, was separated into four geographical sections, covering the United States, **China** and Manchuria, Russia and Europe, and Southeast Asia.

JEBSEN, JOHANNES. An **Abwehr** officer based in **Lisbon**, "Johnny" Jebsen recruited and ran his university friend **Dusan Popov** but when he realized Popov was cooperating with the British, he volunteered to **defect**. His offer was declined on the grounds that if he did so, he would compromise several double agents, including Popov and his subagents GELATINE and BALLOON.

In 1944 Jebsen offered to defect, and his suggestion was spiced with item of information that the Abwehr officer had calculated would make his proposition extremely attractive to the Allies: He had told Popov that he knew the true identity of the top German agent in England, a man who was exceptionally well placed and was in charge of a whole network of compartmented subagents. To Popov, this nugget made Jebsen extremely valuable, but there were a couple of further dimensions to the matter that Popov had no knowledge of.

Popov's own opinion was that Jebsen could be trusted and that his participation would guarantee the success of his escape line from Switzerland. Although he knew nothing of GARBO, he was "absolutely sure" Jebsen realized that Popov was secretly working for the British, and in view of that, there was little to be lost in bringing him into the fold as well. In addition, there was a further possible benefit to enlisting Jebsen. When he had last seen Popov, in mid-September, Jebsen had warned him to move out of central London because rockets were to be fired at the capital from launch sites along the French coast. This morsel had been received with particular interest in Whitehall, where Duncan Sandys was already chairing a secret committee to investigate similar reports. Finding out more about this weapon had been given a high priority by the War Cabinet, and Jebsen appeared to be a potentially useful source in this regard. The weight of opinion gradually leaned in favor of trusting Jebsen, and this was the view that finally prevailed within the Security Service, although a few still had severe reservations about the wisdom of confiding in Jebsen. Some of these diminished toward the end of September when, in response to a query from Popov, Jebsen indicated that he would be willing to remain in place rather than physically defect to England.

Accordingly, in November 1943, Popov returned to the Portuguese resort of Estoril in the guise of a diplomatic courier to convey the good news to Jebsen, who had by then taken up residence in a villa there and thenceforth was to be code-named ARTIST in **MI5**'s files and put in touch with Cecil Gledhill at the local **Secret Intelligence Service (MI6)** station. This single act of acceptance had suddenly put Jebsen in a position of unprecedented power over a substantial proportion of MI5's **double cross** operations. If he had not already been certain, he now knew definitely that the Abwehr's three main agents in Great Britain—Popov, **Juan Pujol**, and TATE—were all under MI5's control. For this knowledge to be imparted to any single individual was serious enough. The fact that Jebsen was also an Abwehr officer made the whole matter extraordinarily sensitive and was the subject of many high-level conferences in London. What would happen if Jebsen's loyalties changed again? Might his circumstances change and present him with a chance of betraying everything that MI5 had built up with such care? These worries were to be the cause of constant anxiety over the coming months.

What complicated these preoccupations was the very secret fact, withheld from Popov, that Jebsen was not the only Abwehr officer in the Iberian Peninsula to have offered to switch sides. MI5 and MI6 both were aware of another potential defector, code-named JUNIOR, since February 1941 when Walter Dicketts, one of MI5's many double agents, had held a very profitable rendezvous with him in Lisbon. Dicketts, known to MI5 as CELERY, had returned to London and given his MI5 case officer a detailed account of his dealings with the Abwehr.

Jebsen's official motive for moving to **Madrid** during late 1943 had been to facilitate the Spanish end of Popov's new escape route from Switzerland, but he confided to Col. Walter Wren, the MI6 station commander, that his financial dealings had landed him in trouble with the **Gestapo** and he felt he could not return to Germany. He was anxious to know whether MI6 would be willing to exfiltrate him if the need arose. While this contact gave Wren a splendid opportunity to conduct a prolonged debriefing of Jebsen and learn more about Germany's new rocket-powered weapons, it placed JUNIOR in a much too powerful position, so he was smuggled to England in November so as to remove him from the scene. In his absence, Jebsen moved closer to MI6 and finalized the arrangements for Popov's Yugoslav evaders.

During his discussions in Lisbon, Popov had made various suggestions for expanding BALLOON's dwindling activities, but the Abwehr reaction had been negative. Thus, in mid-November 1943, while Popov was still in Portugal, BALLOON was effectively abandoned by his German controllers, who justified the action by saying that other members of Popov's network could fulfill his function just as easily. While this was partly true, it was to be interpreted as the first ominous sign that the enemy was not entirely content with Popov's ring. Then, after Popov's return to London in the new year, there was a lack of response to **Stefan Zeis**'s letters. The information he had conveyed to the Abwehr in earlier correspondence had covered a range of military topics, but in January it appeared that his enemy controllers were losing interest in him, too.

Popov flew back to Lisbon at the end of February 1944 to confer with the Abwehr and persuaded them to bring his brother, Ivo, to Lisbon. He stayed there for nearly two months, and when he returned in April, he was able to reassure his MI5 case officers of the high standing he still enjoyed. He brought back two Abwehr questionnaires and one from the **Sicherheitsdienst (SD)**, five reports from Jebsen, and a message to King Peter from Draza Mihailovic, the royalist leader of the Cetnik guerrillas still fighting in the mountains. These were welcomed by MI5 and MI6, but the situation in England had altered quite considerably. By now the Security Service had experienced a perceptible change in its strategic role, and the confidence Popov expressed was to have exactly the opposite effect to that which he had intended, for two related reasons. The first was Popov's confirmation that Jebsen was still willing to continue operating as ARTIST. Although there had been some discussion about the possibility of Jebsen slipping away to England, he had been dissuaded from doing so. Jebsen had apparently said that his position would continue to be secure so long as the Abwehr protected him from the Gestapo, of whom he lived in understandable dread. The second nagging worry was the perilous position of the Abwehr, which, unbeknownst to Popov, was struggling for independence from its archrival, the powerful SD. The internecine warfare had been watched from afar by the intelligence analysts who had been deciphering the Abwehr's internal wireless traffic, and they reported that a dangerous climax was approaching.

Whereas, up until New Year's Day 1944 MI5 had fulfilled what was largely a tactical function by taking and maintaining overall control of the enemy's intelligence networks in Britain, the impending invasion had completely changed the situation, and the new priority was not to just exert control but actually to manipulate the spy rings. Instead of concentrating on the more domestic issue of organizing the enemy's espionage, the double cross system was to be exploited as a conduit of strategic **deception**. The objective now was to persuade the enemy that the Allied assault was destined for the Pas-de-Calais, and both GARBO and TATE had been assigned key parts in the campaign.

The realization that there was suddenly rather more in the balance than the lives of the families left in enemy-occupied territory had a considerable impact on the case officers charged with ensuring the integrity of their agents. Prior to the change in MI5's role, the double cross game had been played without any great risk. However, entrusting the fate of a wholesale offensive on the intended scale of **OVERLORD** to a handful of double agents was quite a different matter, especially when it was recognized that they in turn were wholly dependent upon Johannes Jebsen, an enemy intelligence officer. Certainly Tomas Harris, GARBO's MI5 case officer, was profoundly uneasy about placing so much reliance on ARTIST, and in February 1944 he recommended that Pujol should not be used for deception purposes. In justification, Harris pointed out that it was too great a gamble to risk an entire military operation on ARTIST's doubtful loyalty.

Two dramatic developments were to change the situation. One was the removal of Adm. Wilhelm Canaris from the Abwehr in February 1944, an event that was quickly followed by the organization's effective subordination to the SD in April. Paradoxically, the decline of the Abwehr that placed Jebsen in greater jeopardy had been hastened by MI6, which had successfully engineered the defection in **Istanbul** of a senior Abwehr officer, **Erich Vermehren**. A staunch Anglophile and devout Catholic, Vermehren's decision to switch sides, so soon after JUNIOR's disappearance, had a profound effect in Berlin and acted as the catalyst for the Abwehr's eventual subsumption. MI5 was able to monitor the situation through the medium of the Abwehr's wireless traffic and was appalled to learn that Jebsen, who had held a meeting with his MI6 contact Gledhill on 28 April, had been abducted by the Gestapo later the same day and driven back to Germany. This was exactly the eventuality that Harris, for one, had foreseen, but his worst fears were not to materialize. It seemed that Jebsen had been involved in fraudulent currency transactions and the Gestapo had kidnapped him in order to prevent his anticipated defection.

The news that Jebsen had been arrested was devastating in London, and it was little consolation that, as yet anyway, he was not apparently suspected of having already made contact with the British. MI5 decided that Popov's entire network should be closed down, but opted to continue with GARBO, at least until there was some evidence that Jebsen had been forced to reveal what he knew. Fortunately, the Gestapo never suspected Jebsen of the more serious crime, but he was executed at Oranienburg anyway.

JEDBURGH. Code name for three man inter-Allied paramilitary teams, usually consisting of **Office of Strategic Services**, **Special Operations Executive**, and Free French personnel, who were dropped into Nazi-occupied territory in 1944, some shortly before, but most after, **D-Day**, to coordinate local resistance groups in France and Norway.

JEFF. MI5 code name for **Tor Glad**.

JEST. Code name for a French stay-behind agent in Toulon in 1944 who was run as a **double agent** until February 1945 when ISOS intercepts suggested he had tipped off his German controllers.

JEWEL. Code name for a French **double agent**, an expert on agricultural gases sent to North Africa in 1941, run against his German controllers first from Casablanca and then from **Algiers**.

JIGGER. MI5 code name for an **Abwehr** noncommissioned officer caught in Paris upon the liberation in August 1944. He had worked in the Hotel Lutetia and had removed the organization's files on stay-behind networks and future targets of sabotage missions. JIGGER proved to be an enthusiastic collaborator with his British interrogators and compromised numerous enemy operations.

JOB, OSWALD. A Briton resident in Paris before the war, Oswald Job was interned during the Nazi occupation but was released to act as a spy for the **Abwehr** in London. Betrayed by ISK, Job was arrested in November 1943 in possession of a diamond-studded tiepin that he had been instructed to hand over to another spy, DRAGONFLY. MI5's interrogation of Job proved sensitive because of the need to protect DRAGONFLY, who could also compromise FATHER and another valued double agent. Having stuck to his cover story and lied to his interrogators, Job was hanged at Pentonville in March 1944.

JONASSON, HUGO. On 23 September 1940, two **Abwehr** agents, Hugo Jonasson and Gerald Libot, were taken into custody in Plymouth. Both had been on *La Part Bien*, a small French boat that had been escorted into port by a Royal Navy offshore patrol. Under interrogation, the Swede and Belgian had admitted to having been recruited by the Abwehr for a sabotage mission.

JONES, REGINALD V. The principal scientific adviser to the British **Secret Intelligence Service**, R. V. Jones was transferred from the Air Ministry in 1939, and one of his first tasks was to authenticate the information contained in the **Oslo Report**. Thereafter Jones was in the forefront of Allied technical intelligence collection and played a key role in assessing the enemy's development of radar, guided missiles, and magnetic mines. *See also* MAYER, HANS.

JOSEF. MI5 code name for a Russian seaman and **double agent** active between August 1942 and December 1944 against the Japanese in **Lisbon**.

JOSEPHINE. A mysterious source of high-value information from London, JOSEPHINE was supposedly the code name of a contact of the Swedish air attaché, Count Oxenstierna. Study of the traffic suggested the **Abwehr** in **Stockholm**, represented by Karl-Heinz Krämer, had recruited either the Count or someone close to him, and a study was conducted by **MI5** to identify JOSEPHINE's identity. The Count eventually was expelled, and Peter Falk, the **Secret Intelligence Service**'s **Section V** officer in Sweden, concluded that the spy had been a secretary in the headquarters of the Swedish High Command. Falk had recruited Krämer's maid as a source and solved the mystery of JOSEPHINE and a subsource, HEKTOR, who had been credited with reports of high-level conversations in London, supposedly held between Sir Stafford Cripps and Air Marshals Charles Portal and Arthur Harris. HEKTOR also claimed access to British Ministry of Aircraft Production figures, which, upon close examination, turned out to have been fabricated, but not before the Swedish air attaché in London, Frank Cervell, had been placed under surveillance.

JUNIOR. An **Abwehr** officer based in **Lisbon**, **Hans Ruser** suggested to CELERY that he might be interested in **defecting** to the British. A year later, code-named JUNIOR, he approached the **Secret Intelligence Service (MI6)** station in Lisbon with a view to defecting, but he was rebuffed, on **MI5**'s advice, for fear of jeopardizing **Dusan Popov**, who had been known to him because of his meetings with **Albrecht von Auenrode**. To MI5's relief, JUNIOR pursued the matter no further at the time, but in January 1943 he was transferred to the German embassy in **Madrid**, where he had made another pitch to MI6. On this occasion, he was accepted, but on the condition he remain in place. JUNIOR agreed to these terms, and fortunately this arrangement worked well, although it presented a definite risk for Popov because

JUNIOR had been able to deduce that Popov must have been operating as a **double agent**. The unexpected complexity arose when, later in the year, JUNIOR was consulted by **Johannes Jebsen** when the latter visited Madrid and was put in touch with Col. Walter Wren, then the new MI6 station commander.

– K –

KAPP, NELLIE. A secretary employed by the **Sicherheitsdienst** in **Ankara**, Nellie Kapp defected to the U.S. **Office of Strategic Services** in 1944. The daughter of the prewar German consul in Cleveland, Ohio, Kapp had fallen in love with an American officer, Ewart Seager, and was able to supply information concerning CICERO.

KEEL. **Supreme Headquarters Allied Expeditionary Force** code name for Jean Carrere, a French stay-behind agent recruited by the **Sicherheitsdienst** in Paris. Upon the city's liberation, he gave himself up and was run as a **double agent** until the end of September, when he was abducted and murdered by members of the resistance. Thereafter, until April 1945, his wireless was operated by an **Office of Strategic Services** case officer for a further five months who claimed that KEEL had broken his wrist in an accident to explain the difference in the Morse technique.

KELLY. Code name for a Portuguese Army officer who unwittingly supplied bogus information he received from the U.S. military attaché to the Japanese.

KEMPEITAI. The principal **Japanese** secret police organization, staffed by military personnel drawn from the army, the Kempeitai fulfilled counterintelligence and counterespionage functions and acquired a reputation in occupied territories for ruthless interrogation, torture, and executions. The power of the Kempeitai was greatly enhanced when one of its officers, Hideki Tojo, who had headed the organization in Kanto Prefecture since September 1935, was appointed prime minister in October 1941.

KENT. GRU code name for **Viktor Guryevitch**.

KENT, TYLER G. A 29-year-old U.S. embassy clerk arrested in May 1940 in London and convicted of unauthorized possession of classified information at his apartment, Tyler Kent was imprisoned for seven years. Also convicted was his coconspirator, **Anna Wolkoff**, who received 10 years. Until his arrival in London in September 1939, Kent had served for five and a half years in Moscow, where he had acquired a beautiful mistress, Tanya Ilovaiskaya, with links to the **NKVD**.

When **MI5** received a tip from **Kurt Jahnke** that some of Ambassador Joseph Kennedy's telegrams were reaching Berlin, the news was passed to the State Department, but the investigation uncovered no leaks until October 1939 when Kent was seen visiting a suspected Nazi agent, Ludwig Mathias, at a hotel in London. Kent was placed under surveillance and watched while he associated with members of the Right Club, a pro-Nazi group of political activists that included Wolkoff. His new Moscow-born mistress, meanwhile, was Irene Danischewsky, the wife of an army officer who was away from home.

Kennedy waived Kent's diplomatic status for a search to be made of his apartment on 20 May, and it was found to contain copies of some 1,900 confidential embassy cables, among them secret messages passed between **Winston Churchill** and Franklin D. Roosevelt, and other material, including duplicate keys to the embassy's code room. Under interrogation, Kent admitted that he had photographed some documents using a camera left to him by a colleague, another cipher clerk who had since been posted to the U.S. embassy in **Madrid**. This disclosure prompted a massive operation conducted by the **Federal Bureau of Investigation**'s **(FBI)** Edward Tamm, who sent undercover special agents, posing as State Department couriers, to Madrid, Moscow, Berlin, Rome, and **Lisbon** to test the local security. Special Agent Louis Beck, who received the Moscow assignment, quickly discovered that the vice consul, Donald Nichols, had been having an affair with Tanya Ilovaiskaya who, if she was not herself an NKVD officer, at least possessed a driving license issued by the NKVD and had permission to travel abroad. Beck uncovered numerous other security lapses, including a homosexual relationship between a cipher clerk, Robert Hall, and the ambassador's secretary, George Filton.

Much of the material Kent had removed from the embassy suggested that he had been in league with the Soviets, not the Nazis, because some of the letters referred to MI5 interest in current FBI cases, including Evelyn Strand, a Comintern agent trained in Moscow as a radio operator but then working at the New York headquarters of the **Communist Party of the United States of America**, and Terence E. Stephens, a veteran of the International Brigade in Spain. Another purloined telegram was a request from MI5's **Guy Liddell** for FBI surveillance on two suspects, Armand Feldman and Willie Brandes, both implicated in the 1938 Woolwich Arsenal case in which Soviet spies had stolen secret blueprints of Royal Navy weaponry. Kent was deported at the end of the war and until his death in 1988 always denied having spied for the Soviets.

KESSLER, ERIC. Code-named ORANGE by **MI5**, Eric Kessler had been a Swiss journalist in London before the war. Appointed the Swiss press attaché, he was recruited by his homosexual lover, Guy Burgess, and supplied information from inside the Swiss embassy until he was appointed editor of the *Neue Zürcher Zeitung* in 1944.

KEYNOTE. Supreme Headquarters Allied Expeditionary Force code name for Louis Valette, a French stay-behind agent in Bordeaux, run as a **double agent** after his arrest in November 1944.

KHEIFETS, GRIGORI P. An experienced Jewish intelligence officer who had acted as secretary to Vladimir Lenin's widow, Nadezhda Krupskaya, Grigori Kheifets served as deputy *rezident* in Italy before the war. While working as an illegal in Germany, he obtained a diploma at the Jena Polytechnical Institute, and he spoke fluent English, French, and German. Later, as the wartime **NKVD** *rezident* in San Francisco, under consular cover and code-named CHARON, he conducted an affair with Louise Bransten, the wealthy former wife of Bruce Minton, a **Communist Party of the United States of America (CPUSA)** sponsor denounced by **Elizabeth Bentley**, crediting him with being one of Jakob Golos's recruiters and a contributor to the CPUSA's journal *New Masses*. Bransten, the heiress to the Rosenberg dried fruit fortune, was a popular socialite who used her status to hold frequent soirees that were attended by NKVD personnel and targets in the **Manhattan Project** intended for cultivation. Although Kheifets was both sophisticated and professional, he adopted the alias "Mr. Brown" to run unwittingly at least one **double agent** who reported to the **Federal Bureau of Investigation**, so the local field office never harbored any doubts about his dual role. Kheifets was succeeded in May 1944 by Grigori P. Kasparov, code-named GIFT, when he was recalled to Berlin to participate in the investigation into **Vasili Zubilin**, and he was later transferred to Mexico City.

KIEBOOM, CHARLES VAN DEN. A 26-year-old Dutchman, Charles Van Den Kieboom was landed by boat at Dymchurch in September 1940 with **Sjord Pons**. He was tried in November and hanged at Pentonville in December.

KIENER, BERNIE. An **MI5 double agent** code-named RAINBOW.

KING, ANDREW. A **Secret Intelligence Service** officer and former member of the **Z Organisation** working under commercial cover, Andrew King was based in Zurich and handled **Halina Szymanska**.

KING, JOHN. A Soviet spy working in the Foreign Office in London as a cipher clerk, Capt. John King was arrested in September 1939 after being betrayed by a **GRU defector**, **Walter Krivitsky**. King, the first spy to be convicted of espionage in Great Britain in World War II, confessed that he had sold large quantities of classified material to his Soviet contacts between 1934 and 1937, and he was sentenced to 10 years' imprisonment.

KISS. Security Intelligence Middle East code name for an Iranian student recruited by BLACKGUARD in 1943 for an **Abwehr** mission to Tehran. Arrested in Persia, KISS acted as a **double agent** for the **Combined Intelligence Centre Iraq** and passed **deception** material to the Germans for a year from March 1944.

KISS, EUGENIO ZILAHY. A Hungarian diplomat in **Argentina**, Eugenio Zilahy Kiss officially was the agricultural adviser to the

Hungarian legation who had arrived in 1941, but he was suspected of running two clandestine Axis wireless stations under the supervision of the chargé d'affaires, Count Andor Sempsey. However, when Kiss was scheduled to return to Budapest in May 1943, he approached the **Federal Bureau of Investigation (FBI)** and offered to pass on information by radio or secret writing. When, on his voyage home, he reached Port of Spain, he was interviewed at length and admitted having run a radio for the Germans in Buenos Aires. The FBI accepted his offer, and after his arrival in Hungary, an intermediary in Buenos Aires, Andres Miklos, received a letter bearing a sign indicating it concealed a message in secret writing. Unfortunately, the FBI was unable to read it and later heard that Count Sempsey had denounced Kiss to the authorities in Budapest, where he was briefly placed under arrest but somehow managed to negotiate his release. The FBI later heard from Miklos that he had received a telephone call from Kiss, demonstrating that he had regained his liberty, but this effort at running him as a **double agent** went no further.

KLATT. The **Abwehr** code name for Richard Klauder, a German officer employed in Sofia, Bulgaria, and Bucharest, Romania, who persisted in authenticating information supplied by MAX, a Soviet **double agent** supposedly operating freely behind the Soviet lines on the Eastern Front with access to top level plans. After the war, Klauder was captured in Vienna by American intelligence personnel, and under interrogation he acknowledged having acted as a double agent for the **NKVD**.

KLECZKOWSKIS. Following the **defection** of **Erich Vermehren** and his wife from **Istanbul** in December 1943, the **Abwehr** suffered the loss of the Kleczkowskis, a Jewish husband-and-wife team working in Turkey under journalistic cover who preferred not to answer a recall to Moscow to give evidence to an internal investigation.

KLEISS, HANS. An **Abwehr** courier working for the Hamburg-America Line, Hans Kleiss was a member of the spy ring in New York headed by **Frederick Duquesne**. Although employed as a chef on the SS *America*, he maintained an apartment on 89th Street, where he was arrested on 28 June 1941, together with 33 other suspects.

For the next two weeks, Kleiss underwent interrogation. He started off by claiming total innocence of espionage and ignorance of **William Sebold**. He also denied knowing Paul Fehse, Franz Stigler, and Erwin Siegler—nor their aliases of "Fink," "Aufzug," and "Metzger"—and was emphatic he had not visited Room 627 of the Newsweek Building on 25 January 1941. However, worn down by the depth of the **Federal Bureau of Investigation**'s **(FBI)** knowledge about his movements and background, he eventually realized there was no point in resisting further and made a brief confession to Assistant U.S. Attorneys James D. Saver and Vincent Quinn, transcribed by an FBI stenographer.

Kleiss, who had been born in August 1896 in Frankfurt, had become a naturalized U.S. citizen in 1931, but in 1936 had moved his wife and 16-year-old daughter to Germany. Soon afterward, he had been caught smuggling currency out of the Reich, and this had brought him into contact with the **Gestapo** and ultimately led to his recruitment as a courier, working first on the SS *President Harding* and then the SS *America*. According to his statement, Kleiss had come to the United States originally under rather unusual circumstances, as an interned seaman. During World War I, he had served on the *Kronprinz Wilhelm*, a German surface raider that had preyed on British shipping in the Atlantic, but had been forced into Newport News, Virginia, in April 1915 for repairs, where the crew had been interned, having sunk 14 merchantmen. Proud of his wartime service, Kleiss had been released from a POW camp in Georgia in October 1919 and shipped back to Germany, where he stayed with his parents in Gena until he joined the *George Washington* as a cook in August 1921. On arrival in New York he had been hired by the *Orantec*, of the Polish-American Line, as a cook, but in May 1922 Kleiss had rejoined the United States Line, where he had been employed until May 1941.

Kleiss claimed that his recruitment had taken place in February 1940 in the Hotel Mira Mara, near the railway station in Genoa, when he was approached by two men who were unknown to him but asked him whether he wanted to help the Fatherland and whether he would take a package for them back to New York for a fee of $100. At the time, Kleiss had been working aboard the *Manhattan* and was on his second voyage to Genoa, and he had declined the request. He was then sent to Newport News to supervise the construction of the kitchens on SS *America.*

Although Kleiss denied having known either of the two men in Genoa, whom he never saw again, he did admit that an acquaintance of his in New York, Jimmy Schmidt, whom he had met in the Hotel New Yorker, had told him that one of the men had been named Gerhoff. Schmidt had invited him to mail some letters for him on his next trip to Genoa, but he had declined, saying that he was on vacation and anyway based in Newport News. Kleiss then encountered Schmidt again unexpectedly on the street in Newport News, and on this occasion he was asked to take a two-page letter back to New York, allegedly for Schmidt's brother, whom he agreed to meet at the corner of 35th Street and Fifth Avenue. He denied the accusation that there was no such person as Schmidt and that he had been the person responsible for collecting information in Newport News.

During the course of the interrogation, Kleiss came to realize that the FBI knew all about his visit to Sebold's office in the Newsweek Building on the evening of 25 January 1941, when he had met Paul Fehse and handed Franz Stigler a full set of the blueprints for the SS *America,* together with a letter addressed to Gerhoff, copies of which were in the FBI's possession. He had also given Sebold $40 and asked him to buy him a camera, which had been delivered to him the following day by Erwin Siegler.

Kleiss was confronted with the evidence of his complicity in espionage, including copies of his correspondence, which was matched to a portable typewriter recovered from his apartment, and a receipt in his name for its purchase from the International Typewriter Company of 240 East 86th Street. Kleiss claimed that he had sold the typewriter to a soldier in the U.S. Army named Richard Gerdts. The FBI had encountered that name previously in a conversation recorded between Sebold and Richard Strunck. Gerdts was a seaman who had deserted his ship, the SS *Siboney,* in **Lisbon** in May 1941, and subsequently had been flown to Germany.

The incriminating letters typed on this machine included one dated 15 July 1940 containing naval information from Newport News describing the construction of a fast motor torpedo boat, "60' long, 12' wide, Wright motor, with explosive gasoline, 60 knots, have been built at Navy Yard, Washington, 4 torpedoes, 3-inch guns, 5-man crew." It ended with the words "via Fink from Hard."

There was another, signed "E. Rychner, Neustadtgasse 7, Zurich," which Kleiss admitted he had delivered to either Erwin Seigler or Franz Stigler in New York, from Jimmy Schmidt, for onward transmission to Germany. A third, dated 17 September 1940, signed by "Jimmy Hard," was addressed to a Herr Gerlach in Hamburg, but had been handed to Sebold by Stigler. Kleiss was also confronted with a four-page letter, dated 2 March 1941, containing information about shipping he had observed in the Panama Canal, and an account of a ship sunk in the Indian Ocean, mailed by him from Havana to "Harry Sawyer, PO Box 67, Madison Square Station," and he had some difficulty explaining how he had come to receive mail under the name of "Richard Herman" at the firm of W. L. Ertinger & Co., at 50 Broadway, an alias that he had attributed to Schmidt.

Kleiss denied he was a Nazi, but he did acknowledge that on one occasion in 1940 he had been in **Gibraltar** where he had seen some British submarines and that whatever he had witnessed there had had a powerful impact on him.

KLOP. *See* USTINOV, IONA.

KNIGHT, MAX. A brilliant **MI5** case officer, Maxwell Knight specialized in running agents in suspect political organizations and achieved success early in the war by breaking up the spy ring headed by **Tyler Kent** and **Anna Wolkoff**. Knight also penetrated the **Communist Party of Great Britain**, but his employment of Harald Kurtz was to cause the Security Service considerable embarrassment when it emerged that his evidence against Ben Greene had been fabricated.

KOLBE, FRITZ. A member of the German Foreign Ministry, Fritz Kolbe visited **Bern** regularly as a diplomatic courier and took the opportunity to deliver copies of telegrams to the **Office of Strategic Services** representative, **Allen Dulles**, who dubbed the source GEORGE WOOD.

KONDOR. Abwehr code name for Johannes Eppler, a spy infiltrated with Peter Sandstetter into **Cairo** in June 1942 by Count Laszlo Almasy, the Hungarian explorer. Both agents, on a mission code-named SALAAM that had been compromised by ISK, were arrested in September 1942 and under interrogation by **Security Intelligence Middle East** cooperated with their captors.

KOTZE, HANS VON. Code-named SPRINGBOK by **MI5**, Hans von Kotze was a German aristocrat, married to an Englishwoman, who had immigrated to **South Africa** in 1929 to work as a fur buyer and miner. Soon after the outbreak of war, hoping to avoid internment as an enemy alien, he had moved to Portuguese East Africa but had been expelled. In a further attempt to avoid internment, he had taken a passage to Europe but had been captured by a French ship and detained in Morocco until July 1940. When he was finally released, he was offered the option of serving in the Wehrmacht or working for the **Abwehr** and had chosen the latter.

In June 1941, von Kotze was dispatched to **Brazil** to join the **Albrecht Engels** organization under commercial cover as a buyer in the leather trade, but what he really wanted to do was reestablish contact with his wife, who had been interned in South Africa, and their children. When finally in March 1942 he was ordered to move to South Africa, he wrote to the British Consulate in São Paulo and offered his services to the **Secret Intelligence Service (MI6).**

In exchange for a British passport after the war, some money, and the opportunity to be reunited with his wife without being arrested, von Kotze supplied information about the Abwehr's network in Brazil, its members, and its codes. In addition, he had much to say about an Abwehr spy ring in South Africa. MI6 quickly agreed terms and enrolled von Kotze as SPRINGBOK, but the plan to let him go to South Africa collapsed when the authorities there refused him entry. Instead, von Kotze suggested he might try North America and, with the Abwehr's consent, he made his way using the alias "Johannes van Huges" to **Canada**, where he attempted to establish wireless contact with Germany through Werner Waltemath, code-named ANTONIO, one of the radio operators in the Engels network working the INC–MNT circuit, whom coincidentally he had met on the flight to Recife from Rome. Although he was a trained Wehrmacht technician, Waltemath experienced considerable problems with his homemade transmitter in São Paulo and, despite a lengthy correspondence conducted in 13 letters and 10 telegrams in a code based on *The Martyrdom of Man*, was unable to help von Kotze.

SPRINGBOK, by now ostensibly working for a British company, Vickers & Benson Ltd., in Toronto, tried to reach the Germans at a postbox address in **Lisbon**, but by the time his letter arrived, on a slow mailship, instead of by airmail on the transatlantic clipper, the **Direção da Ordem Política e Social (DOPS)** had pounced on the Engels network, and Waltemath had gone into hiding.

When eventually Waltemath was caught by DOPS, in June 1943, he accepted an offer from MI6 to reopen the INC–MNT link as a **double agent**, but his controllers in Germany were not fooled and the connection was severed, leaving Waltemath facing a prison sentence of 27 years. Meanwhile SPRINGBOK, out of touch with the Germans, became a nuisance to **British Security Coordination (BSC)**, especially after he seduced Dorothy Hyde, the wife of his case officer, Harford Montgomery Hyde. His role as a double agent ended in August 1943 when his name was released in Brazil, and he was sentenced *in absentia* to 27 years' imprisonment. Although BSC arranged for the Royal Canadian Mounted Police to announce his arrest so as to protect his cooperation, von Kotze was allowed to sail to England from Halifax in February 1945.

KREMER, SIMON. The **GRU** *rezident* in London, Simon Kremer operated under diplomatic cover as secretary to the Soviet military attaché.

KRIVITSKY, WALTER. A **GRU defector**, Walter Krivitsky was brought to England in February 1940 from the United States to be interviewed by **MI5**'s **Jane Archer** because he had information about Soviet spies in England. His credentials had been established in September 1993 when he identified Capt. **John King**, then a senior cipher clerk employed in the Foreign Office, as a mole.

KUCZYNSKI, URSULA. Code-named SONIA by the **GRU** and always an ideological zealot, Ursula Kuczynski had traveled widely even before she was recruited into the GRU by **Richard Sorge**. At the age of 22, she had moved to New York, where she helped run the Henry Street Settlement to accommodate poor Jewish families with the legendary Lillian Wald. Later she would marry Rudi Hamburger and participate in a GRU network in Shanghai before being posted to Switzerland, where she worked with the **Rote Drei** and encountered **Allan Foote**. In February 1940, she married **Len Beurton** to obtain a legitimate British passport and moved to Oxford, where she ran several spies, including Klaus Fuchs. She remained in England after the war, but made a hasty return to Germany when she was identified to **MI5** as a wartime Soviet spy by Foote.

KÜHLENTHAL, KARL-ERICH. Formerly an assistant to the chief of **German intelligence** in Spain during the Spanish Civil War, Karl-Erich Kühlenthal headed the *Abstelle* in **Madrid** and personally recruited **Juan Pujol**. Partly Jewish, he was granted a certificate confirming his Aryan parentage in 1941. He remained in Spain at the end of hostilities.

KUOMINTANG (KMT). *See* CHINA.

KURSK, BATTLE OF. The largest tank battle of all time until 1973, the Nazi defeat during the battle of the Kursk Salient in July 1943 is regarded as a turning point in the war, and it was influenced significantly by faulty intelligence and strategic **deception**. To divert attention away from the imminent offensive, the **NKVD** employed nine controlled enemy wireless sets, operated by **double agents** working from five different cities. Their messages misled the Nazis, leaving them vulnerable to a surprise attack. On the day before the main German assault, code-named ZITADELLE, Luftwaffe aircraft were destroyed on the ground at airfields, the locations of which had been identified in England from ULTRA intercepts and passed to the Soviets by **John Cairncross**, then working at **Bletchley Park**. The Nazi attack on 5 July, intended to be the last of the summer campaign, consisted of 900,000 men and 11 Panzer divisions, some equipped with the new Tiger tanks. Opposing them were 3,600 tanks, supposedly spread thinly along a front 1,000 miles long. In reality, the Soviets, with the benefit of advance knowledge, concentrated their armor on the Kursk Salient. The German offensive was resisted, and a counterattack on 12 July led to a breakthrough north of Kursk that proved unstoppable.

– L –

LAHOUSEN, ERWIN VON. The head of Abteilung II, the **Abwehr**'s sabotage branch, Maj. Gen. Erwin von Lahousen-Vivremont was a monocled Roman Catholic Austrian nobleman and close confidant of Adm. **Wilhelm Canaris**, who had joined the organization in 1938 after having headed the Central European bureau of the disbanded Austrian military intelligence service. After graduating from the Wiener Neustadt staff college fluent in French, Polish, Czech, and Hungarian, Lahousen had opted for intelligence and established a liaison relationship with the French Deuxieme Bureau while running operations in Poland and Czechoslovakia. Also an anti-Nazi, he was transferred to the Russian Front in August 1943, but he survived to appear as a prosecution witness at the Nuremberg trials. Lahousen died in 1955, having concealed from his Allied interrogators the existence of his secret war diaries, which documented many of the sabotage operations he had conducted, including details of his frustrating relationship with Sean Russell of the **Irish Republican Army**, his links with the grand mufti of Jerusalem and the Indian nationalist Subhas Chandra Bose, his recruitment of the sultan of Morocco, and his failure to persuade Francisco Franco to collude in Operation FE-LIX, an attack on **Gibraltar** scheduled for January 1941.

LALOU, RAYMOND. ISOS identified Raymond Lalou, a Belgian recruited by the **Abwehr** in Cologne, as a spy who was in contact with a cover address in **Lisbon**. He was interrogated upon his arrival in 1941 and detained at **Camp 020**, but permission to prosecute him was denied.

LAND SPIDER. Secret Intelligence Service code name for the Icelandic **double agent** Ib Riis.

LANG, HERMAN. A member of the **Abwehr** spy ring in New York City headed by **Frederick Duquesne**, Herman Lang commuted daily from his home in Glendale, Queens, to work in Manhattan at the Lafayette Street offices of the L. C. Norden Company, which manufactured the famous bombsight under a secret patent. Age 27, Lang had been brought to the United States from Germany in 1927 but had remained passionately patriotic, although he had taken care not to confide in his wife or daughter about his thefts of the bombsight's blueprints. His accomplice, who worked as an engineering inspector at the Sperry Gyroscope plant in Brooklyn, was 44-year-old Everett

Roeder, also German-born and an enthusiastic spy who apparently was waiting to be activated.

LANGBEIN, ALFRED. An **Abwehr** agent who had been landed in **Canada** at St. Martins, New Brunswick, from a U-boat in the spring of 1942, Alfred Langbein gave himself up to the Royal Canadian Mounted Police in October 1944. Between his arrival and his surrender, Langbein had lived in a rented room in Ottawa until his money had run out. Under interrogation by **MI5**'s Cyril Mills, Langbein revealed that he had lived in Winnipeg and Montreal before the war. When he returned to Bremen, he had been recruited by the Abwehr, in preference to being called up for military service, and undertook missions in **Belgium** and Bulgaria before being selected for Operation GRETE, the name of his wife. On 25 April he joined the U-213, a Type VII submarine commanded by Ahmelund von Vahrendorff, which sailed from Brest and delivered him to Canada. On the U-boat's next voyage, it was sunk on 21 July 1942 off the Azores.

Upon landing on the shore of the Big Salmon River, Langbein buried his wireless transmitter and made his way to Ottawa, where he checked into hotel. Having effectively abandoned his mission, Langbein was of no value as a potential **double agent**, and he was interned at Fredericton until the end of the war.

LATHAM, ANDRÉ. Code-named GILBERT, André Latham operated as a **double agent** in Tunis from 1943 until the end of hostilities.

LAUREYSSENS, JOSEPH. A merchant seaman, Joseph Laureyssens was arrested on 17 February after an investigation lasting less than a fortnight. One of his letters, addressed to an **Abwehr** postbox in **Lisbon**, had been detected by the mail censors during a routine chemical test for secret writing. Concealed in an apparently innocuous text was a firsthand description of a German attack on a convoy. Laureyssens was quickly traced as its author, and under interrogation he admitted that over a period of months he had written 16 such illicit letters and had made contact with numerous other agents in Great Britain. His claims about the existence of Abwehr spies unknown to **MI5**, though causing a flurry of trepidation at the time, were subsequently proved to be fiction, but in the meantime MI5 was particularly anxious to obtain his cooperation. This was yet another reason why Lord Swinton's rigid guidelines were considered impractical by the case officers charged with combating enemy espionage.

LAZY. Code name for Anneliese Peters, a 19-year-old Luftwaffe wireless operator and member of the RHINEMAIDENS, a German stay-behind network in the Mönchengladbach area. Recruited as a **double agent** in March 1945, she and BLAZE maintained contact with the enemy from Rheydt until the end of hostilities.

LEGION. Supreme Headquarters Allied Expeditionary Force code name for Robert Pennors, a Frenchman dropped near Lyons in December 1944 and run as a **double agent** in Metz from January 1945. There he was contacted in March by an **Argentine** courier, Jacques Moglia, code-named IDOL.

THE LEMONS. Security Intelligence Middle East code name for a pair of **Abwehr** agents, both Greek Cypriots, who landed in Cyprus in 1943 posing as refugees. The radio operator, LITTLE LEMON, denounced his leader, BIG LEMON, to the British, and he was enrolled as a **double agent.** LITTLE LEMON continued to transmit **deceptive** information to the Germans until September 1944. Among LITTLE LEMON's **notional** sources was a genuine troupe of chorus girls working in Nicosia cabarets, consisting of a Belgian code-named MARIA; a Bulgarian, MARKI; a Romanian, SWING-TIT; an Austrian, TRUDI; and a Hungarian, GABBIE.

LENA. The **Abwehr** code name for an intelligence collection operation personally approved by Adolf Hitler, intended to infiltrate spies into Great Britain during the autumn of 1940. Operation LENA was supervised largely by the Hamburg *Abstelle* and dispatched agents by sea and parachute. All were captured, with the exception of **Jan Willen Ter Braak**, who committed suicide in April 1941.

LIDDELL, GUY. Appointed director of **MI5**'s B Division in 1940, Capt. Guy Liddell had joined the Security Service from the Metropolitan Police Special Branch in 1931. Throughout the war, he kept a daily diary, which he dictated each evening to his secretary, Margot

Huggins. The document was declassified in 2004 and remains a unique record of MI5's counterespionage operations between August 1939 and June 1945.

LIEBBRANDT, ROBEY. The 1937 heavyweight boxing champion of **South Africa**, who had represented his country at the 1936 Berlin Olympic Games, Robey Liebbrandt was a student in Germany when war broke out and, being an anti-British Afrikaaner, joined the **Abwehr** to participate in Operation WIESSDORN. After attending a sabotage course at Quentzsee, near Brandenburg, Liebbrandt joined yachtsman Christian Nissen in Brittany to sail back to South Africa aboard the 40-ton *Kyloe* in April 1940. After an epic voyage of 67 days, the *Kyloe* completed the 8,000 miles, and Liebbrandt was dropped off along the coast of Namaqualand on 9 June with a radio and a suitcase of explosives. He took the next week to reach Cape Town, 150 miles to the south. Meanwhile, Nissen sailed the *Kyloe* to the Spanish colonial port of Villa Cisneros, where he gave the yacht to the local German consul and flew home to Hamburg via **Madrid**.

In Cape Town, Liebbrandt made contact with the pro-Nazi Osswega Brandwag ("Guards of the Oxwagons"), but he could not persuade the organization's kommandant-general, Dr. van Rensburg, who disapproved of his sabotage mission, to take him seriously. Instead, he gathered a group of supporters around him and hid in a farm north of Pretoria, aware that rumors of his return had circulated widely and had reached the police. The first raid on the farm, by the Transvaal police in September, was undertaken by Boer sympathizers who allowed Liebbrandt to escape, and a second attempt to arrest him, at his uncle's home in Pretoria, also failed to catch him. However, he was then lured into a trap in Johannesburg by a police informer and was arrested. Liebbrandt was convicted of treason in November 1942 and sentenced to death, but the sentence was commuted to life imprisonment. He was released in 1948 when Field Marshal Jan Smuts's government was defeated by the nationalists.

LINEE AEREE TRANSCONTINENTALI ITALIANE (LATI). *See* BRAZIL.

LIPSTICK. MI5 code name for **double agent** Josef Terradellas, a Catalan separatist who was sent by the **Abwehr** to Great Britain in November 1942. He declared his mission and his secret writing instructions to the **Secret Intelligence Service** station in **Madrid** before his departure and was managed until December 1944 by MI5, although his political activism became increasingly embarrassing to his handlers.

LISBON. The capital of neutral Portugal, Lisbon became an international crossroads when transatlantic civil air traffic was limited to the route flown by flying boats operating between Baltimore and **Bermuda**. The large **Secret Intelligence Service (MI6)** station, located in the British **Passport Control Office** in the rua Emenda, was headed successively by Austin Walsh, Richman Stopford, Cecil Gledhill, and finally Philip Johns, with Charles de Salis and then Ralph Jarvis looking after **Section V**'s interests. In addition, local agents were run by Graham Maingot, Eugene Risso-Gill, Rita Winsor, and a fruit merchant, Jack Ivens. **MI9**'s local representative, in the British Repatriation Office, was Donald Darling, while Jack Beevor headed the **Special Operations Executive** unit attached to the embassy in the rua do Sacramento a Lapa. MI6's operations in Portugal were supervised in London by a former Shell Oil executive, Basil Fenwick, and Dick Brooman-White.

The **Abwehr**'s representative, at the German legation in rua de Buenos Aires, was an aristocrat, **Albrecht von Auenrode**, assisted by Fritz Kramer. The senior **Sicherheitsdienst** officer was Erich Schroeder, listed as the police attaché at the consulate in the rua Joaquim António de Aguiar, supported by subordinates named Henss, Haack, Spreu, and Salsieder.

Monitoring the activities of both organizations was the **Polícia do Vigilância e Defesa do Estado (PVDE)**, Antonio Salazar's ruthless secret police, which turned a blind eye to Nazi espionage, which was very extensive. By the end of hostilities, the MI6 station's registry included cards on 1,900 confirmed enemy agents, 350 suspected ones, 200 German businessmen, and 46 suspect commercial fronts.

Lisbon proved to be such a hotbed of Axis espionage that it was the only neutral capital in which a special coordinating unit, designated the Sixty Committee, was created to supervise Allied counterintelligence and **deception** operations.

LITTLE, W. HAEBURN. An Irish artist and Royal Naval Reserve officer employed by the Admiralty's office in **Lisbon**, Lt. Haeburn Little was investigated in January 1941 as a German spy following the discovery of his name in **Kuno Weltzien**'s card index.

LONDON CAGE. The London District Holding Centre in Kensington Palace Gardens accommodated enemy prisoners of war while they were undergoing preliminary interrogation before being assigned to a permanent camp. The mansion acquired some notoriety after hostilities when one of the staff, Col. **Alexander Scotland**, published *The London Cage*.

LONG JUMP (LÄNGESPRINGE). **Sicherheitsdienst (SD)** code name for an attempt to assassinate President Franklin D. Roosevelt, Prime Minister **Winston Churchill**, and Marshal Josef Stalin at Tehran during their stay in the city between 28 November and 2 December 1943. As soon as the Germans learned from the Persian authorities that the "Big Three" were to gather for a tripartite conference in Iran, plans code-named LÄNGESPRINGE were made to infiltrate agents into the country in support of the remnants of a network formerly headed by Franz Mayr, a spy who had been arrested in August 1943. Between 22 and 27 November, six groups of parachutists, code-named ELEPHANT and led by Sturmbannfuhrer Rudolf von Holten-Pflug, landed undetected near Qum, and a further eight, led by Vladimir Shkvarev and amounting to nearly 60 men, landed near Qazvin. However, as soon as Shkvarev's agents attempted to contact the local network, they were arrested by **NKVD** troops attached to the occupation forces and interrogated at Tabriz. The other parachutists were sheltered by SD agents Lothar Schöllhorn and Sturmbannfuhrer Dr. Winifred Oberg, who were in radio contact with Berlin, unaware that they had been compromised by ISOS traffic and information extracted from Mayr.

Churchill arrived at Amerabad on 28 November and lodged at the British embassy, which was directly adjacent to the Soviet legation, while Roosevelt flew into the military airfield at Gale Morghe from **Cairo**, having landed off the battleship USS *Iowa* in Oran. Their host, Stalin, had been the first to arrive, on 26 November, but had failed to persuade his guests to stay with him. Instead, Roosevelt had insisted on driving to and from the American embassy, across the city. It was to be on one of these hazardous journeys, or on the road back to the airport, that the German commandos planned to ambush one or all of their targets, but on the night of 31 November, all but von Holten-Pflug and five of his companions were arrested in police raids orchestrated by the British **Combined Intelligence Centre Iraq**. Two days later, the six Germans who had escaped capture were lured to a trap set by a Swiss double agent, Ernst Merser, and all were taken into custody, with the exception of Holten-Pflug's interpreter, an Iranian named Gorechi, who was shot dead as he attempted to throw a grenade. All three leaders returned to their capitals a day earlier than expected because of a forecast of poor weather, untroubled by the Nazi plot.

LUCY. GRU code name for **Rudolf Rössler**.

LUKE, CAROLA. A secretary employed in **MI5**'s registry, Carola Luke falsely confessed in July 1943 that she had passed information to the **Communist Party of Great Britain** (**CPGB**), including the identity of **M-8**, **Max Knight**'s agent inside the CPGB.

– M –

M-8. MI5 code name for Tom Driberg, an agent run by **Max Knight** who had penetrated the **Communist Party of Great Britain** (**CPGB**). When Driberg was expelled from the Party by the secretary-general, Harry Pollit, he was accused of being a mole code-named M-8. Informed of this, Knight realized his organization had been penetrated and Driberg compromised. Eventually the source was identified as **Anthony Blunt**, but not before another CPGB member and MI5 secretary, **Carola Luke**, made a false confession in which she admitted to having leaked Driberg's identity.

MACLEAN, DONALD. A long-term Soviet spy recruited by the **NKVD** in 1935, Donald Maclean entered the Foreign Office and passed information from his post in the Paris embassy to his contact **Kitty Harris** until he was evacuated in May 1940. Thereafter he served in the British embassy in Washington, D.C., and in April 1951 was compromised by VENONA texts, which implicated him as a 1944 source code-named HOMER who had supplied copies of President Franklin D. Roosevelt's secret correspondence with Prime Minister **Winston Churchill**.

MADRID. A center of espionage throughout the war because of Spain's supposed neutrality, Madrid's diplomatic missions included substantial intelligence staffs. At the German embassy, the **Abwehr** was headed by **Karl-Erich Kühlenthal**, assisted by Gustave Knittel. At the British embassy, the **Secret Intelligence Service** station was headed first by Col. Edward de Renzy-Martin and then by Hamilton Stokes, with **Section V** represented by Kenneth Benton. The British naval attaché, Comdr. Alan Hillgarth, was also active in collecting information while **MI9**'s Michael Cresswell supervised the repatriation of evaders, but the ambassador, Sir Samuel Hoare, limited his intelligence staff's activities to prevent any diplomatic incidents. *See also* GIBRALTAR; LISBON.

MAKAROV, MIKHAIL. In March 1939, Lt. Mikhail Makarov, a **GRU** officer who had fought in the Spanish Civil War as a pilot, traveled to Brussels on a circuitous route via **Stockholm**, Copenhagen, and Paris. In Brussels, he had adopted the identity of a Uruguayan named Carlos Alamo to work as an illegal. Reputedly the nephew of Soviet Foreign Minister Vyacheslav Molotov, Makarov had been born in Leningrad and first entered **Belgium** in January 1934, at age 31, while in transit to America. Once established in Belgium, Makarov was posted to Ostend, where he took over the management of the local branch of the **Foreign Excellent Raincoat Company**, which had previously been run by **Leon Grossvogel**'s wife, Jeanne Pesant. Makarov was to use the company as a cover for his true role, that of wireless operator offering technical courses to **Leopold Trepper**'s recruits.

MANAGER. The **Federal Bureau of Investigation** code name for a **notional** subsource run by PEASANT, supposedly another Shell Oil manager based in Washington, D.C.

MANHATTAN PROJECT. Cover name for the U.S. Army Corps of Engineers project headed by Gen. Leslie Groves to develop an Anglo-American atomic bomb. The name came from the Manhattan Engineering District, which was the unit responsible within the Corps of Engineers. *See also* ENORMOZ.

MARTIN. French code name for Auguste Mauboussin, a German stay-behind agent in Rouen who was run by **Supreme Headquarters Allied Expeditionary Force** as a **double agent** code-named ASSASSIN from December 1944.

MASTERMAN, JOHN. In 1940, Christ Church, Oxford, scholar J. C. Masterman joined **MI5** and in January 1941 was appointed chairman of the **Twenty Committee**. At the conclusion of hostilities, he was commissioned to write an internal history of the **Double Cross System**, which was declassified and published in 1972.

MAX. German code name for a spy on the Eastern Front known to the **NKVD** as HEINE. MAX's true name was Aleksandr Demyanov, supposedly a deserter and an adherent of an anti-Soviet monarchist organization known as Prestol ("Throne"), but actually he acted as a **double agent** from the moment in March 1942 when the Germans parachuted him back into Soviet territory near Yaroslavl. Claiming to have become a Soviet staff officer with access to top-level plans, MAX persuaded his German controller to send a further 22 agents, code-named KURIERY ("Couriers") and 13 radios to his network, all of whom fell directly into Soviet hands. An extension of the operation was code-named BEREZINO and played a significant role in misleading the enemy about Soviet intentions. By the end of hostilities, the operation, supervised by Pavel Sudoplatov and Leonid Eitingon, had resulted in 39 deliveries by the Luftwaffe of 255 shipments of weapons and materiel, an account of which covered 117 volumes in the NKVD's archive. Some of MAX's wireless traffic was monitored by the British **Radio Security Service**, leading **Winston Churchill** to warn Josef Stalin in 1943 that the Red Army's General Staff had been penetrated. **Anthony Blunt** also alerted his NKVD contact in London to MAX's activities, leaving him baffled that apparently no action was taken to silence the source.

MAYER, HANS. An electrical engineer employed by Siemens, Dr. Hans Mayer was the author of the **Oslo Report**, a document delivered anonymously to the British embassy in Norway in November 1939 detailing numerous German scientific developments, including guided missiles, proximity fuses, magnetic mines, and other breakthroughs with a military application. The information was authenticated by the **Secret Intelligence Service**'s principal scientific adviser, **Reginald Jones**, who learned of Mayer's identity only after the war.

MEADOW. Code name for Arthur Garitte, a Flemish nationalist operated by the **Belgian** Sûreté as a **double agent** against the **Abwehr** from 1939. A writer by profession, MEADOW revealed himself in 1944 to have been part of a German stay-behind network in Brussels.

MECHANIC. Code name for a **Belgian** ship captain who was taken prisoner after his vessel had been torpedoed. At a camp near Bremen, he accepted an offer from the **Abwehr** to go on a mission to North or South America. He was awaiting further instructions in October 1944 at a hotel near Antwerp, run by another spy named Van Meldert, when the area was liberated. MECHANIC gave himself up and identified Van Meldert as a stay-behind agent. An attempt was made, through a letter delivered to the Germans in **Lisbon**, to reestablish radio contact, but it failed.

MEIER, CARL. A 24-year-old Dutchman from Koblenz, Carl Meier was landed by boat at Lydd in Kent in September 1940 with **Sjord Pons**. He was tried in November and hanged at Pentonville in December.

MENEZES, ROGEIRO DE. Having arrived in London in July 1942 to work at the Portuguese legation as a junior diplomat, Rogeiro de Menezes began writing letters to his sister in **Lisbon**, enclosing another note using secret ink addressed to a man named Mendez. His mail had been included in the Portuguese diplomatic bag, which was surreptitiously opened and examined by TRIPLEX. His role as a **Sicherheitsdienst** spy had been betrayed by an ISOS intercept even before he landed, and he was watched inside the legation by an **MI5**

agent, and outside by MI5 surveillance teams. According to Jack Bingham, an MI5 officer who befriended him, he seemed particularly interested in antiaircraft defenses.

In February 1943, the evidence was presented to Ambassador Monteiro, who was reminded that three other Portuguese—Gastão de Freitas, Maria dos Santos, and **Ernesto Simoes**—had already been caught spying. After he had consulted Lisbon, Monteiro agreed to withdraw Menezes' immunity. When arrested, Menezes claimed that he had spied under duress because he had relatives in Germany who were under threat. In his confession, he identified "Mendez" as a man named Marcello who worked for an **Italian intelligence** officer named Umerte. He claimed to have been introduced to them by a Portuguese air force officer, Col. Miranda, and also mentioned a cipher clerk named Ramos in the Portuguese Foreign Ministry. Nevertheless, he was convicted under the Treachery Act in April 1943 and sentenced to death, but was reprieved after a plea from his ambassador. Instead, Menezes was imprisoned at Dartmoor, and on the instructions of the lord chief justice, no public statement was made concerning the trial or the reprieve.

As a result of the case, the **Polícia do Vigilância e Defesa do Estado** in Lisbon arrested 23 members of the **Abwehr**'s local organization, including **Kuno Weltzien**. Menezes was freed and deported back to Portugal in December 1949.

MENZIES, STEWART. Appointed **chief** of the **Secret Intelligence Service** in November 1939 upon the death of Adm. Sir **Hugh Sinclair**, Stewart Menzies remained in the post throughout the war. An experienced intelligence professional who had served on Field Marshal Sir Douglas Haig's staff in France in World War I, Menzies traveled overseas only once, to attend a conference in 1943 in **Algiers**, and surrounded himself with personnel drawn from his own social circle. He made himself indispensable to the prime minister by personally delivering selected intercepts daily, and he engendered considerable personal loyalty from his subordinates. Always approachable, Menzies made most of his senior appointments himself and gave morale-boosting interviews to new officers and those undertaking assignments overseas.

MERCY. Code name for a **Belgian double agent** and member of FRANK's **Sicherheitsdienst** stay-behind network in Brussels. Arrested in 1944, his wireless transmitter was supposed to be a backup for FRANK.

METCALFE, DICKIE. Code-named BALLOON by **MI5**, in part because of his rotund stature, Dickie Metcalfe was recruited as a German spy by **Dusan Popov**. His story, partly true, was that he had been obliged to resign his army commission when he had got into financial difficulties after a racehorse deal failed. He now ran a company based in Piccadilly trading in small arms and had agreed, at MI5's suggestion, to pose as a willing source of data regarding weapons.

METEOR. MI5 code name for **Eugn Sostaric**, a Yugoslav pilot and **double agent** in contact with his friend **Dusan Popov** from April 1943. He cut his contact with the **Abwehr** in May 1944.

MEXICO. Heavily influenced by Spain, the **Falange** supervised two local subsidiaries in Mexico, the Acción National and the Sinarquistas, which the **Federal Bureau of Investigation** estimated enjoyed a following of 500,000 and a definite appeal to Latinos north of the Rio Grande.

MI5. The official War Office designation of the Security Service. At the outbreak of hostilities, the organization had been headed for the previous 30 years by Sir Vernon Kell. It expanded rapidly to cope with the threat posed by German and Italian espionage and by the large numbers of enemy aliens resident in Great Britain. MI5 would go on to establish a network of **defence security officers** across the empire, develop a regional organization based in **Cairo** (**Security Intelligence Middle East**), and attach a representative to **British Security Coordination** in New York.

After Kell's replacement in June 1940 by **Jasper Harker**, followed in September 1940 by Sir **David Petrie**, MI5 was placed under the control of the newly created **Security Executive** and concentrated on the interment of aliens, the detention of political extremists, the monitoring by the **Radio Security Service**'s Voluntary Interceptors of illicit radio transmissions, and the development of counterintelligence operations through the manipulation of **double agents**. Initially MI5's stable of controlled enemy agents was restricted to **Arthur Owens**, code-named SNOW, but shrewd management of his network by **T. A. Robertson**, together with success in reading the **Abwehr**'s ISOS traffic, led to the creation in January 1941 of a **Double Cross** Committee to supervise a growing number of captured enemy spies incarcerated at **Camp 020** and volunteers among refugees from the Continent screened at the **Royal Victoria Patriotic School**.

Although MI5 was reliant on confidential informants, liaison with county police forces through a network of regional security liaison officers and the more conventional sources of telephone intercepts and diversion of diplomatic pouches, it operated within a strict legal framework and was anxious to avoid controversy or accusations of indulging in **Gestapo** tactics. Through a bias for the recruitment, using mainly personal contacts, of academics and prewar members of the legal profession, MI5 was successful in maintaining political support for the organization while still maintaining its traditional secrecy about its activities.

Although anxious about Fifth Columnists, British Union of Fascist blackshirts, and **Communist Party of Great Britain (CPGB)** agitation, MI5 proved adept at monitoring potentially subversive groups, and it placed agents inside targets across the political spectrum from the Peace Pledge Union to the Right Club and the Link. MI5's B Division, responsible for counterespionage, also cemented relations with Ireland's **G-2** to plug any leaks to Germany via the **Irish Republican Army** or the German diplomatic mission in Dublin. Altogether 13 German spies were executed in London, all but **Josef Jakobs** hanged after having been convicted under the Treachery Act of 1940. Jakobs alone was shot in the Tower of London, and an additional two spies, Luis Cordon-Cuenca and José Munoz were executed in **Gibraltar**.

While largely successful, and self-financing thanks to some ingenious schemes to support some **notional** enemy spy rings, MI5's performance was marred by the suicide in May 1940 of a retiree, William Rolph, who unwisely attempted to sell information about the organization to the enemy through SNOW; by the mistaken detention of Gen. Charles de Gaulle's deputy, Adm. Émile Muselier, on fabricated evidence; and by the equally embarrassing arrest of Benjamin

Greene on false testimony from an MI5 agent provocateur. Only after the war was it learned with certainty that MI5 had been penetrated both by the CPGB, through registry clerk **Carola Luke**, and by the **NKVD**, through **Anthony Blunt**, a Cambridge-educated mole who occupied several senior positions, including personal assistant to B Division's director, **Guy Liddell**.

By 1942, MI5 had moved from its temporary accommodations in **Wormwood Scrubs** prison to **Blenheim Palace** in Oxfordshire, with operational offices in St. James's Street. Under the direction of Liddell, it had begun to exploit its grip over the Abwehr's espionage inside Great Britain by undertaking increasingly bold **deception** campaigns, culminating in FORTITUDE, an ingenious scheme intended to mislead the enemy about the objectives of **D-Day**. Close coordination with **Section V** of the **Secret Intelligence Service**, institutionalized in 1943 by the establishment of a jointly run War Room, ensured that debilitating interagency rivalries were minimized and that American **Office of Strategic Services X-2** personnel were integrated.

MI6. *See* SECRET INTELLIGENCE SERVICE (MI6).

MI9. The escape and evasion branch of the **Secret Intelligence Service**. MI9 was created at the end of December 1939 and was headed by Norman Crockatt and Jimmy Langley. Based in Ebury Street, Belgravia, with a training unit in Hampstead, MI9 established representatives in **Lisbon**, **Madrid**, **Bern**, **Stockholm**, and **Gibraltar** to assist in the repatriation of Allied military personnel. It also ran a training school in Highgate to prepare selected noncommissioned officers for life as prisoners of war (POWs) and give them the means of communicating clandestinely with London in the event of their capture.

By the end of hostilities, MI9 was in direct radio contact with dozens of POW camps in Germany and Poland and had developed numerous commercial and charitable covers to distribute contraband, such as maps, compasses, inks, forged identity cards, currency, and other escape paraphernalia concealed inside tins of food, games, and similar ostensibly innocuous items to which prisoners were allowed access by their unsuspecting captors. Because nonofficers were allowed, under the terms of the Geneva Convention, to undertake industrial work outside their camps, their observations provided a useful source of information from inside the Reich.

MICRODOTS. The technique of concealing messages in photographs that have been so reduced in size that they can be read only with the aid of a microscope or similar apparatus. Microphotography was developed shortly before World War II and was perfected by the **Abwehr**, which routinely hid microdots under postage stamps attached to apparently innocuous postcards and letters. The communications system was hard to detect but correspondence addressed to, or sent from, suspect addresses were the subject of intensive scrutiny by Allied censorship examiners trained to spot what **MI5** code-named DUFF.

The procedure required that an item be photographed and then reduced in size by a ratio of 200:1, down to a dot that required specialist knowledge, training, and equipment to read. It was a major breakthrough in concealed writing, which hitherto had depended on secret inks that could be detected under certain lighting conditions or chemical treatment. The **Federal Bureau of Investigation** first encountered the technique in 1941 when it was revealed by **William Sebold**, whereupon an optical expert, James E. Dunlop, was hired from the medical laboratory at Johns Hopkins Hospital to study photoreduction techniques. *See also* IMPERIAL CENSORSHIP.

MIDAS. Code name for an **MI5** scheme developed in 1941 by **Dusan Popov** to enable the **Abwehr** to make a deposit in a neutral country and arrange for someone already in England to dispense a similar sum to the Abwehr's nominee. Popov's plan received the backing of Martin Toeppen, the Abwehr's financial supervisor, and Maj. **Albrecht von Auenrode** was particularly impressed by his suggestion for a nominee, a Jewish theatrical agent who, Popov asserted, had made a tidy sum in London and was anxious to export his cash to America. The fact that the theatrical agent was Austrian originally added authenticity to Popov's proposal, although the person in question, Eric Glass, had absolutely no knowledge of what was being done in his name. Upon his return to London, Popov agreed to obtain the details of an account in New York into which the Abwehr should transfer $100,000 and make arrangements for the equivalent amount in sterling to be made available at Glass's place of business. In reality, MI5 had placed one of its own staff as a receptionist at 15 Haymarket in anticipation of receiving a request for money from an unknown German spy. When the project eventually got under way in July 1941, no less than £20,000 was handed over to TATE, thus confirming his standing in German eyes. The arrangement was later abandoned when Toeppen was arrested by the **Gestapo** for having embezzled some of the Abwehr's foreign currency reserves.

MIDDLE EAST INTELLIGENCE CENTRE (MEIC). Led by Illtyd Clayton, MEIC acted as a coordinating unit in the Middle East region, supervising the work of the **Inter-Services Liaison Department** and **Security Intelligence Middle East**, under the political control of the Middle East Intelligence Committee headed by Henry Hopkinson.

MIDWAY, BATTLE OF. The Japanese plan to attack the strategically important Hawaiian archipelago island of Midway in the Pacific in June 1942 was compromised when U.S. Navy cryptographers headed by Joseph J. Rochefort solved the HYPO cipher and read messages indicating that Adm. Isoroku Yamamoto had gathered an invasion force of 162 ships, including 4 of his navy's 10 carriers, to attack a target designated "AF." To verify his hypothesis that AF was Midway, Capt. Wilfred Holmes, a submariner turned codebreaker, suggested that the local command transmit an important message in a low-grade cipher concerning a breakdown in Midway's desalination plant. Soon afterward, he decrypted a Japanese signal reporting a water shortage on AF, and the site of the Japanese attack was confirmed.

With the advantage of knowing the enemy's order of battle and intentions, Adm. Chester W. Nimitz reinforced the local garrison and air defenses and then set out to ambush his adversary with a task force led by four carriers. Surprised by unexpectedly heavy air defenses over Midway, Yamamoto learned of the presence of an American carrier and immediately ordered his aircraft to rearm with torpedoes to eliminate the threat. However, his planes aboard the *Kagu* and *Arkagi* were caught where they were most vulnerable, on deck, by American bombers from the USS *Enterprise* and *Hornet*. The *Soryu* was then attacked by the *Yorktown*, a survivor of the Battle of the

Coral Sea, and finally the *Hiryu* was sunk. Yamamoto lost 322 air-craft, all four carriers, a heavy cruiser, and two destroyers, while Nimitz saw the *Yorktown* and her destroyer escort, the *Hammann*, torpedoed by a Japanese submarine. Midway remained in American hands, enabling the Aleutians to be defended, a victory largely attrib-utable to the role played by Nimitz's fleet intelligence officer, Edwin T. Layton, and his codebreakers.

The triumph proved short-lived, for news that the U.S. Navy had acquired advance knowledge of the Japanese fleet was published within days by the *Chicago Tribune*, a shocking breach of security that led to a grand jury investigation. No one was indicted for the leak, but the Japanese changed their cipher and call-sign systems in August 1942.

MIKE. Federal Bureau of Investigation (FBI) code name for Michael Letsch, a Dutch movie producer who revealed to the Amer-ican embassy in **Madrid** in November 1944 that he had been sent on a mission as a courier to New York to replenish PAT J's funds. The FBI opened a file, MICASE, and ran him as a **double agent** until the end of hostilities.

MINARET. British **Secret Intelligence Service** code name for Jorge José Mosquera, an **Argentine** leather trader based in Buenos Aires who had been recruited by the **Abwehr** in Hamburg before the war. In November 1941, he contacted the U.S. embassy in Montevideo to declare his new mission to New York, and upon his arrival, he was handled by the **Federal Bureau of Investigation (FBI)** under the code name RUDLOFF. Under the supervision of Special Agent Gil Levy, Mosquera made radio contact with his German con-trollers and developed a network consisting of **notional agents**, among them NEVI, OFFICER, OSTEN, REP, WASCH, and UNNAMED FRIEND. MINARET became a source of friction between the FBI and the British when it emerged that a **deception** plan, suggesting that Tokyo was to be bombed in an air raid, was conveyed to the Ger-mans just three days before the city really was raided by Col. James Doolittle's bombers on 18 April 1942. The FBI's Mickey Ladd found it hard to accept British assurances that this was a coinci-dence and not evidence of a leak.

MINCEMEAT. MI5 code name for a **deception** scheme intended to persuade the enemy that the Allied invasion planned for the Mediterranean in 1943 would take place in Sardinia, not Sicily. The operation involved planting a dead body in the sea off Huelva, Spain, with a briefcase attached to his wrist containing skillfully forged documents; it was later the subject of a novel, *Operation Heartbreak*, by Duff Cooper, and a film, *The Man Who Never Was*. The corpse, supposedly a Royal Marine, Maj. William Martin, was actually that of a Welsh tramp, although his identity documents bore the photograph of an **MI5** officer, Ronnie Reed. A photo of Martin's girlfriend, included in his pocket litter, was actually a Naval Intelligence Division secretary, Paddy Bennett.

The operation had been inspired by a security lapse in October 1942 when a Free French courier, Lt. Clamorgan, was killed when his Catalina crashed off the Spanish coast en route to **Gibraltar**. Clamorgan had been carrying sensitive **Special Operations Executive** documents intended to brief U.S. forces in North Africa, but ISOS intercepts proved that they had been washed ashore and passed to the **Abwehr** in **Madrid**.

MINISTER. The **GRU** code name for an unidentified spy and a member of the **X Group** active in London in 1940 and 1941, according to the relevant VENONA decrypts.

MINT. Code name for a **double agent**, the son of the former **Belgian** consul in Zurich. MINT was parachuted into Allied territory on 18 March 1945, and he remained active until the end of hostilities, although he was considered unreliable. His other contact, whom he identified to the Belgian Deuxieme Direction, turned out to be **DERRICK**'s courier.

MODEL. Code name for a **Belgian**, an officer in the Queen's Own Cameron Highlanders of **Canada**, who was identified in November 1944 as a **Sicherheitsdienst** stay-behind agent who had volunteered to join the Canadian Army. When challenged, MODEL, who had been active in the black market in Antwerp during the Nazi occupation, admitted that he had been recruited to spy in Antwerp, and in February 1945 agreed to cross the lines to reestablish contact with his controller. He was eventually picked up again when northern Holland was liberated, and it was learned that he had so impressed the Germans that he had been promised an Iron Cross.

MOE, JOHN. Code-named MUTT by **MI5**, John Moe was a trainee hairdresser in Oslo with dual British citizenship who was landed by a Luftwaffe seaplane off the coast of Scotland in April 1941 on a sabotage mission. Accompanied by JEFF, Moe immediately surrendered to the police and acted as a **double agent** until 1944 when he joined the Norwegian Army and participated in FORTITUDE NORTH.

MONASTERY. The Soviet code name for a network of **double agents** reporting from the Eastern Front, among whom was MAX.

MONTAGU, EWEN. The Naval Intelligence Division representative on the **Twenty Committee**, Ewen Montagu played a significant role in MINCEMEAT. In 1953, he wrote an authorized account of the operation, *The Man Who Never Was,* which was subsequently released as a movie. *See also* MONTAGU, IVOR.

MONTAGU, IVOR. The youngest son of Lord Swaythling, Ivor Montagu was a lifelong **Communist Party of Great Britain** member and in 1939 was appointed war correspondent of the party's newspaper, the *Daily Worker.* In 1965 he was identified as a Soviet spy who, according to references to him under the code name NOBILITY in VENONA texts, had been active in 1940 in an espionage network known as the **X Group.** His elder brother, **Ewen Montagu,** knew him to be Communist, but was unaware that he was also a spy.

MOONBEAM. A **notional agent** in Toronto in 1943, supposedly recruited by his Venezuelan brother, BENEDICT, who was GARBO's principal subagent and deputy. Known to the **Federal Bureau of Investigation** as GLOCASE, the fictitious MOONBEAM moved to Montreal and established radio contact with GARBO in England in early 1945. He supplied information from his cousin in Buffalo, New York, code-named CON.

MOONLIGHT SONATA. The Luftwaffe code name for a massed air raid on the Midlands industrial center of Coventry on 14 November

1940. Advance notice of an attack had been given two days earlier by a captured German pilot who, under interrogation, had claimed that "every bomber in the Luftwaffe" would participate in a major air operation. The code phrase MOONLIGHT SONATA had been disclosed in decrypted **Enigma** messages, and the Royal Air Force (RAF) had responded with COLD WATER, a preemptive strike against enemy airfields in northern France, and ASPIRIN, electronic countermeasures designed to "bend" the navigation beams followed by German aircraft. The COLD WATER raids proved ineffective. By the time, in the early evening, that Enigma intercepts revealed that Coventry was to be the target, RAF's 80 Wing expressed confidence that the planes would be deflected by ASPIRIN. However, the ASPIRIN jamming equipment was accidentally set to the wrong frequencies so the enemy raiders found their targets without difficulty.

MORAVEC, FRANTISEK. The Czech director of military intelligence, Frantisek Moravec fled to London with his staff shortly before the Nazis occupied Prague. Although he and his organization existed under the sponsorship of the **Secret Intelligence Service**, Moravec was suspected of having fallen under Soviet influence, although there is no hint of this in his postwar autobiography, *Master of Spies. See also* CZECH INTELLIGENCE.

MORTON, DESMOND. A former **Secret Intelligence Service (MI6)** officer and director of the Industrial Intelligence Centre, Maj. Desmond Morton was **Winston Churchill**'s principal intelligence adviser. Wounded in France in 1917, where he had served as an artillery officer, Morton had acted as an aide-de-camp to Field Marshal Sir Douglas Haig, and in that capacity had met and escorted Churchill, then the minister of munitions. They remained close friends thereafter, while Morton served in senior posts in MI6, and on the outbreak of war in September 1939 he was appointed director of intelligence at the Ministry of Economic Warfare. When Churchill became prime minister in May 1940, Morton moved into 10 Downing Street and remained there until July 1945, participating in all the major Allied intelligence decisions of the conflict and sitting as a member of the **Security Executive** and the Committee on Foreign Allied Resistance. He also acted as the prime minister's personal representative to various Allied intelligence services, including **Dutch intelligence** and the Free **French intelligence**, and as a link to the other British security and intelligence agencies. After the war, he transferred to the Treasury, retiring in April 1953. He died in July 1971 at the age of 79. *See also* BRITISH INTELLIGENCE.

MOST SECRET SOURCES. The euphemism adopted by **Winston Churchill** in his grand opus *History of the Second World War* for signals intelligence, being mainly **BJ**, BONIFACE, and ULTRA.

MULLETT. MI5 code name for a **double agent**, a Briton born in **Belgium** named Thornton who supplied information to HAMLET and was active between December 1941 and May 1944.

MÜNCHEN. A 306-ton armed trawler based in Drontheim, the *München* was captured on 7 May 1941 north of Iceland by a Royal Navy force of three cruisers and four destroyers. The *München* was an important target because she was equipped with an **Enigma** machine and was sending regular weather reports to Germany. The cipher machine was thrown overboard by the crew before they abandoned ship, but Capt. Jasper Haines, a specially briefed Naval Intelligence Division officer, climbed aboard and recovered cryptographic documents, which were immediately sent to Scapa Flow on HMS *Nestor*. When they were examined at **Bletchley Park**, they provided the DOLPHIN Home Waters keys for June, the first time that Kriegsmarine traffic could be read by **Government Communications Headquarters** without a delay.

MUTT. MI5 code name for **John Moe**.

MYTCHETT PLACE. Code-named **Camp Z**, Mytchett Place was the large mansion near Aldershot that accommodated the German deputy Führer, Rudolph Hess, in 1941.

– N –

NARODNYI KOMMISARIAT VNUTRENNYKH DEL. *See* NKVD.

NAVAL GRU. The Soviet Red Banner Fleet's naval intelligence branch was referred to within Western intelligence circles as Naval Glavnoye Razvedyvatel'noe Upravlenie (GRU).

NEPTUNE. Allied code name for the naval component of **D-Day**, compromised by the **Sicherheitsdienst** spy CICERO.

NETTLE. The **Secret Intelligence Service** code name for Helmut Goldschmidt, a **double agent** who acted as a talent-spotter for the **Abwehr** in Spain before he was sent on a mission to England and the United States. He reached Washington, D.C., in August 1944, where he was **notionally** employed by Shell Oil but was actually run as PEASANT by the **Federal Bureau of Investigation**.

NEUKERMANS, PIERRE. A **Belgian** pilot sent to England as a refugee to spy for the **Abwehr**, Pierre Neukermans was arrested after he had been cleared for entry, having been denounced by another agent named Wyckaert. Initially Neukermans held up under interrogation, but eventually he confessed that he had succeeded in taking secret ink undetected through **MI5**'s London Reception Center and had reported his safe arrival to the Germans in two letters that had been passed by censorship. At his trial, he pleaded insanity, but was nevertheless convicted and executed.

NEVI. **Federal Bureau of Investigation** code name for a member of RUDLOFF's network, a **notional agent** supposedly a civilian employee of the Navy Department in Washington, D.C.

NKVD. The principal Soviet foreign intelligence service, the Narodnyi Komissariat Vnutrennykh Del was headed in Moscow by **Lavrenti Beria** and operated across the globe through legal and illegal *rezidenturas*, run by the head of foreign intelligence, Pavel Fitin, which were heavily dependent on local Communist parties for support and sources. Considered the sword and the shield of the Communist Party of the Soviet Union, the NKVD concentrated on the acquisition of technology and industrial processes before the war, but later concentrated on political intelligence and atomic data.

NKVD *rezidenturas* were usually concealed in either diplomatic or trade missions headed by a *resident*, who supervised a team of subordinates that managed networks of agents, either directly or through intermediaries. Their operations were directed in detail from Moscow, as was learned subsequently from the study of the relevant VENONA traffic, which revealed aspects of NKVD wartime agent management in Mexico City, Washington, D.C., San Francisco, New York, London, and **Stockholm**. Evidently the NKVD's ability to function in western Europe following the Nazi repudiation of the Ribbentrop-Molotov Pact in June 1941 was severely handicapped, leaving the Soviets devoid of legal *rezidenturas* in Berlin, Copenhagen, Paris, The Hague, Oslo, Rome, Prague, **Bern**, Belgrade, Bucharest, Budapest, Warsaw, Helsinki, Tallinn, Riga, Vilnius, and possibly **Madrid** and **Lisbon**, too. This placed a heavy burden on the *rezidenturas* in London, Ottawa, Mexico City, Stockholm, the three in the United States, and eventually Buenos Aires when a *rezident* was posted there in 1944.

In London, the NKVD declared a *rezident*, Ivan Chichayev, to his hosts for liaison purposes, but in reality continued to conduct local intelligence-gathering operations through numerous agents, among them Guy Burgess, **Kim Philby**, Leo Long, and **Anthony Blunt**, who penetrated various branches of **British intelligence** under the direction of the undeclared *rezident*, **Anatoli Gorsky**. In addition, Melita Norwood, Klaus Fuchs, and Allan Nunn May passed information to the NKVD from inside the British atomic weapons development program.

In Ottawa, the NKVD *rezident*, Vitali Pavlov, ran few independent operations, because the local Communist Party had been embraced by his GRU counterpart, **Nikolai Zabotin**. In **Mexico**, **Lev Vasilevsky** ran the embassy *rezidentura* under the alias Lev Tarasov and was largely dependent on Spanish Republican refugees. In Stockholm, the *rezidentura* was headed by a Mrs. Yartseva and then Vasili Razin, and it concentrated on the development of local political figures.

Gorsky (code-named VADIM, alias Anatoli Gromov) was appointed *rezident* in Washington, D.C., in September 1944, a post he held until December the following year, when he was transferred to Buenos Aires. In March 1945, the New York *rezident*, Stepan Apresyan, was posted to San Francisco, a *rezidentura* that had been opened in December 1941 by **Grigori M. Kheifets** (code-named CHARON), with a *subrezidentura* in Los Angeles. Kheifets was recalled to Moscow in

January 1945 and replaced by Grigori P. Kasparov (code-named GIFT). Apresyan's replacement in New York was Pavel Fedosimov (code-named STEPAN). Together, these NKVD officers ran more than 200 spies, of whom 115 were later identified as U.S. citizens with a further 100 undetected.

On the Eastern Front, the NKVD gained a ruthless reputation for capturing enemy agents and managing entire networks of **double agents**, often at the expense of having to sacrifice authentic information to enhance the standing of their **deception** campaigns. In the 18 months up to September 1943, the NKVD turned 80 captured enemy agents equipped with wireless transmitters, and by the end of hostilities, it had run 185 double agents with radios. *See also* GRU; KLATT; MAX; MONASTERY; SMERSH; SOVIET INTELLIGENCE.

NOBILITY. GRU code name for **Ivor Montagu**.

NORBERT. Code name for a sergeant in the French Air Force who headed a small network of **double agents** in **Algiers**, consisting of EDOUARD and their radio operator, RAM.

NORDPOL. Abwehr code name for a *funkspiel* played in Holland against networks run by **Special Operations Executive (SOE)**.

The first agent to be dropped into Nazi-occupied Holland was Lt. Lodo van Hamel of the Royal Netherlands Navy, who landed "blind" near Sassenheim on 27 August 1940 and proceeded to develop a small **circuit**, including a radio operator, Johan van Hattem, who had built his own wireless set. However, six weeks later, Van Hamel was arrested by Dutch police while on his way to a rendezvous with a Dutch amphibious aircraft that was supposed to land on Tjeuke Lake. Van Hamel was handed over to the Germans for interrogation, and an ambush was prepared for the seaplane. The Fokker T8, piloted by Comdr. Hidde Scappe, landed on the night of 13/14 August but just managed to escape the trap. Van Hamel was executed on 16 June 1941 but he had resisted the **Gestapo**'s interrogation, thus ensuring that Van Hattem could remain at liberty and continue his activities for a further 18 months.

Three days earlier, on 13 June, a pair of **Secret Intelligence Service (MI6)** agents—a young naval cadet named Hans Zomer and a former police inspector, Wiek Schrage—had been dropped and had established themselves in Bilthoven. Zomer was soon spotted by German radio direction-finding, and he was arrested on 31 August 1941 while transmitting a signal. After interrogation, Zomer agreed to send a message to London under German control, but the ploy was detected. Thereafter Zomer was tried for espionage and executed on 11 May 1942, leaving Schrage trying to find a means of escape to England.

On 6/7 September 1941 Ab Homburg and Corre Sporre were parachuted into Holland by SOE, both intending to make a short reconnaissance before being picked up from the beach. The rendezvous never materialized, so both men established themselves in Haarlem, where Homburg was recognized and betrayed to the Gestapo on 6 October 1941. He was subsequently sentenced to death, but managed to escape from prison the night before his scheduled execution. He eventually made his way back to Great Britain by trawler from Ijmuiden, arriving in February 1942. Meanwhile, Sporre had avoided arrest and made contact with Schrage. Together they tried to escape by boat in November, but they were never heard of again.

A month later, two more agents, Huub Lawers and Thys Taconis, were sent to look for them. This pair, who shared a background of having worked in the Far East until the outbreak of hostilities, landed safely, but their radio proved to be faulty so their first message to London was not transmitted until 3 January 1942. Soon afterward, Taconis traced Homburg and reported his arrest and subsequent escape. SOE's reply was an instruction that Homburg should make his own way back to England and that, because there was still no sign of Sporre, it must be assumed that he had drowned while attempting to cross the North Sea by boat with Homburg. Lauwers and Taconis based themselves in The Hague and maintained a regular radio schedule with London. Using this channel, they arranged a supply drop on 28 February that went largely according to plan (except that one of the two containers was lost). However, Lauwers was arrested a week later, on 6 March, when German direction-finding equipment isolated the address in The Hague from which he had been transmitting. The Germans also recovered his wireless and a quantity of his previous signals. Three days later, Taconis was also taken into custody.

During intensive interrogation, Lauwers was persuaded to use his radio to transmit, under German control, back to London. This he did on 12 March, confident that SOE would spot the telltale omission of his security check, the procedure of inserting a deliberate mistake at a predetermined position in every message to indicate that the operator was not working under duress. Surprisingly, SOE not only acknowledged the signal but also announced the imminent arrival of another agent, Lt. Arnold Baatsen, formerly a professional photographer, who duly landed on the night of 27/28 March. He was to be the first victim of a long **deception** campaign that netted the Germans more than 50 Dutch agents.

On the question of whether SOE had registered Lauwers's missing security check, Robin Brook gave the following explanation in October 1949 to the Parliamentary Commission of Enquiry conducted by the Dutch: "This fact was established and it was weighted against other arguments which testified to the conclusion that this agent was at liberty. In view of this consideration it was decided to continue the traffic."

The Abwehr's control over Lauwers, Taconis, and Baatsen coincided with a dramatic escalation in N Section's activities. The night after Baatsen was dropped, two teams landed. The first, which landed safely, consisted of a student who had been studying in England named Han Jordaan, and Gosse Ras, a trader in textiles. The second pair was not so lucky. Their radio was smashed on impact, and Jan Molenaar was mortally injured, leaving his companion, a 29-year-old student in holy orders named Leonard Andringa, to administer a suicide pill. Thereafter Andringa made his way to Amsterdam where, devoid of contacts, he lived rough for a while. A third team, of Hendrik Sebes, who was a veteran of Dunkirk, and Barend Klooss, who had recently returned from Southeast Asia, followed on 5/6 April and established themselves in Hengelo without incident.

The next arrival, on 8/9 April, was Jan De Haas, who was landed by a British motor torpedo boat with the objective of linking up with Lauwers and Taconis, not realizing both were already in German custody. His search failed, but on 27 April, Lauwers received a fatal message from London instructing him to go to Haarlem to meet De Haas. Instead, the Germans moved in and cornered both De Haas and Andringa, who had become increasingly desperate following the death of his partner and had been forced to seek help from his friends. Andringa was coerced into attending a rendezvous in a café with Ras, Jordaan and Klooss on 1 May. However, just before the Germans sprang their trap, Jordaan slipped away and was able to alert SOE headquarters in London to the arrest of his companions. His liberty lasted only a few hours, however, for both he and Sebes were caught using information extracted from the others.

Indeed, the German triumph was completed when they substituted their own operator for Jordaan and reestablished contact with SOE—a coup made possible only because Jordaan had recently requested permission to recruit and train his own operator in the field, a highly unusual departure from the standard security procedures. SOE had granted the request, and this message had been discovered among Jordaan's effects. Thus the Abwehr was presented with an ideal opportunity to run and exploit a second captured radio.

This in turn resulted in another parachute operation, on 29 May, which delivered two saboteurs, Antonius van Steen and Herman Parlevliet, both former Dutch gendarmes, straight into the hands of the enemy and provided the Germans with a third and fourth active wireless link with London. More were to follow. Jan van Rietschoten, a technical college student who had rowed to England the previous year, and his radio operator, Johannes Buizer, arrived near Assen on 23/24 June and were forced to send a "safe landing" signal. Then, a month later, Gerard van Hamert dropped straight into an enemy reception committee and was obliged to hand over his radio. When they searched him, the Germans found some orders addressed to Taconis, whom they had imprisoned in March, which amounted to confirmation that SOE had not an inkling of the extraordinary deception game now under way involving six separate wireless channels.

In Van Hamert's case, the Germans went to elaborate lengths to pretend that Taconis had at least attempted to complete the mission assigned to him by Van Hamert, the destruction of a radio station mast at Kootwijk. Allied direction-finding had identified this location as one of the bases used to transmit signals to the U-boat fleet, so it was considered a target of some strategic importance. An assault was planned for 8 August 1942, and Lauwers reported the next day that the attackers had been beaten off by an unexpectedly large number of sentries. This bogus explanation, backed up by a fireworks display at the appropriate moment, satisfied SOE that Taconis had mounted a daring raid. SOE sent commiserations to Taconis and even announced that he had been decorated with the Military Medal.

The Germans nearly achieved a seventh SOE transmitter when a South African named George Dessing was dropped accidentally into the middle of an SS training camp on 27/28 February 1942. He casually walked out, giving Nazi salutes to the guards, who assumed he was authorized to be there. Later he had another lucky escape when the Germans tried to use Andringa to entrap him in a café. Sensing that something was wrong, Dessing casually walked out, straight past Andringa's German escort, thereby narrowly avoiding capture for the second time. Realizing that his friend Andringa was under enemy control, Dessing decided to get out of Holland as soon as possible, but he was unable to warn London of what had happened because he had no independent means of communication. Molenaar, the agent who had been killed on landing, had been intended to become his radio operator, and without him Dessing was powerless. He eventually made his way to Switzerland, but he would not reach London until the autumn of 1943.

In the meantime, the duplicity continued. On 26 June 1942, Prof. George Jambroes, a senior and influential figure in the Dutch government-in-exile, and his wireless operator Sjef Bukkens were dropped straight into a German reception committee, and Bukkens's radio was used to report on the supposed low morale and security of the Orde Dienst resistance movement.

On 4/5 September 1942, four more agents followed Jambroes: a young student, Knees Drooglever, and an engineer, Karel Beukema, were taken, and the former's transmitter became the eighth to join the game; Arie Mooy and Cmmdr. Jongelie were next, but the latter, a tough naval officer who had worked undercover in the Dutch East Indies, refused to cooperate, so the Germans sent a message to London indicating that he had been fatally injured in the landing. Once again, SOE raised no objection. Indeed, London was so keen to hear from Jambroes, who was supposed to be liaising with the Orde Dienst, that he was put in touch with a contact in Paris so he could be exfiltrated down an escape line. This clue was pursued by the **Sicherheitsdienst** in France with ruthless efficiency and almost led to the collapse of SOE's French networks.

Gradually the Germans had taken control of a substantial part of SOE's network in Holland, but at least it had been operated in isolation from MI6's circuits, which were every bit as extensive and had experienced their own difficulties. One handicap had been the loss in March 1942 of a British naval officer and a Dutch sailor.

Euan Rabagliati, the head of the Dutch country section of MI6, had been attempting to send over two agents, again by boat across the North Sea, but the first operation proved a complete disaster. On 11 March 1942, a brand new vessel, MGB 325, commanded by a peacetime solicitor, Peter Williams, was assigned the task of taking two agents to Holland. MGB 325 was a 110-foot Fairmile "C" Type capable of 27 knots and carrying a crew of 16. The two agents, one of whom was a Dutch sailor named Maessen, were accompanied by an MI6 officer, Angus Letty. Having reached the Dutch coast, the agents were rowed ashore by Charles Elwell, the MGB 325's first lieutenant. Unfortunately, their craft capsized and a German patrol caught both men. Maessen was subsequently shot, and Elwell went to a POW camp, ending up at Colditz, but not after he too had been questioned. He was later to comment that his chief inquisitor "not only knew the actual numbers of his gunboat, but also the names of many of the officers" based at Great Yarmouth, where the 15th Motor Gunboat Flotilla was based. Indeed, he believed the Germans knew more about MI6's clandestine operations than he did.

Rabagliati's principal asset in Holland was Aart Alblas, a 21-year-old merchant seaman who had been operating independently since his arrival on 5/6 July 1941. After the arrest of Hans Zomer, the naval cadet who had been caught by direction-finders in Bilthoven, MI6 had decided that Alblas's codes might have been compromised and used a former naval signalman, Wim van der Reyden, to deliver a new set. This courier parachuted into northern Holland in September 1941 and duly handed over the material, but in February 1942 he was arrested in the company of another Secret Intelligence Service agent, Johannes Ter Laak, who had been delivered to Scheveningen by boat on 21 November 1941 but whose wireless had fallen into the water and was in need of repair. The arrest of van der Reyden and the courier was a chance encounter for the Gestapo, and although they tried to raise London on the radio, MI6 spotted the absence of the all-important security checks and declined to acknowledge the signal.

However, under interrogation, van der Reyden confirmed the existence of the third agent, Alblas, and his signals were monitored. Eventually, in early July 1942, he too was trapped, but when the Germans tried to exploit his transmitter, MI6 spotted the ruse and signed off instantly.

In the coming months, more MI6 agents were swept up. Ernst De Jonge, who had been landed by boat in February 1942, was caught with 10 other members of the Ijmuiden resistance on 18 May 1942. Once again, MI6 refused to respond to De Jonge's transmitter when it was operated under enemy control. Soon afterward, three more MI6 agents, Jan Emmer, Evert Radema, and Felix Ortt, were arrested.

MI6 responded to these losses by dropping Willem Niemayer in the spring of 1942, but by October the former journalist had run short of funds and Rabagliati asked SOE to deliver a roll of banknotes to his agent. The courier was a Dutch naval officer, Aat van der Giessen, who was also handed a set of emergency identity papers for Niemayer that contained his photograph. Accordingly, when Van der Giessen was received by the Gestapo, it did not take them long to trace Niemayer. He was promptly arrested, but yet again MI6 would not respond to his radio signals, realizing from his faulty security check that he had come under enemy control.

This, however, was not to be the last of the game. SOE still had no clue to the unfolding tragedy and stepped up the number of agents being dropped to Holland. Nine went in October, with a further four in November. By December 1942, the Germans had captured 43 British agents and were controlling 14 different radio channels.

By April 1943, another 13 SOE men had been dispatched, as well as a woman from **MI9**, Beatrix Terwindt, whose mission had been to build an escape line. She, too, was accommodated at the seminary in Haaren that the Abwehr and Gestapo had acquired to isolate their prisoners. However, the German policy of securing all their captives in the same place led to a leak, which eventually reached the British embassy in **Bern** in June 1943. For the first time, SOE received word that eight British parachutists, including Pieter Dourlein who had arrived on 1/2 March, were in German custody, but the warning was ignored.

In May, Anton Mink, Laurens Punt, and Oscar de Brey arrived at the cells in Haaren and gave an 18th radio link to the Germans. Ingeniously, it was one of these channels that the Abwehr used to smear two of the agents, Dourlein and Johan Ubbink, when they escaped from Haaren on 30 August 1943. Realizing that the entire deception was threatened by this resourceful pair, the Germans reported to London that they had actually been captured by the Gestapo and allowed to escape, having been turned. When Dourlein and Ubbink eventually reached Bern on 22 November 1943 and gave a detailed account of their experiences, this report was transmitted by the MI6 head of station in Bern, Count Frederick Vanden Heuvel:

> Lt. Johan Bernhard Ubbink, cover-name Edema and code letters CEN, parachuted into Holland during the night of 1 December 1942, and Sergeant Pieter Dourlein, cover-name Diepenbroek, code letters ACO, dropped during the night of 10 March 1943, have both arrived here. Both report that they were met by a reception committee who knew their cover-names yet turned out to consist of Dutch Nazis and German SD, who immediately arrested them. During their interrogations it became clear that the Germans were completely aware of the whole organization with its codes and passwords. For a long time the Germans have been transmitting to England pretending to be agents. They guess that at least 130 men have been arrested in this way so that the whole organization is in German hands. During the night of 30 August 1943 they escaped from prison. They suspect Maj. Bingham of treachery without daring to accuse him outright and press for the utmost caution with this message. On 25 November I can send them to Spain using our normal route, but arrangements have to be made to ensure that they spend as little time as possible in Spain, in view of the importance, in my opinion, of their information. Do you agree with this or do MI6 want to give them a new assignment? Please let me know immediately if they really are who they say they are. Description of first mentioned. Height 1.82m, face long and thin, hair blond, blue grey eyes, quite a large nose and somewhat crooked, scar on left knee. Of the second, height 1.78m, face thin and somewhat triangular shaped heavy chin, prominent jaw, dark blond hair, eyes green grey, heavy eyebrows, nose long and thin, damaged middle finger left hand, on right arm tattooed anchor.

This signal, with its grave accusation, caused chaos in London and prompted MI6 to circulate a damning message to all its agents warning of SOE's insecurity: "Sister service totally infiltrated by Germans. We therefore urge you to break off all contact with their agents and keep clear of them. Please warn any other organizations."

This, of course, was intercepted and read by the Germans, who finally realized that the game was up. Ironically, the two agents who conveyed the bad news to SOE, Ubbink and Dourlein, received harsh treatment when they finally reached England, via **Gibraltar**, on 1 February 1944. They were interrogated at length in London and then moved under open arrest to Guildford. In May, they were transferred to Brixton Prison, and then released, to be told that one of those who had helped them to escape from Holland, a former police inspector from Tilberg named Van Bilsen, had been assassinated by the resistance.

At the end of the war, an investigation was launched to discover the fate of the agents sent to Holland by MI6 and SOE during the 20 months of what had become known as "der Englandspiel," and it was revealed that virtually all of them had perished in the Nazi concentration camp at Mauthausen early in September 1944. Of the SOE agents, only Lauwers, Dessing, and the two escapees lived through the experience.

An investigation into the disaster revealed that MI6 had learned of the German penetration in May 1943 and had warned SOE immediately and that several assessments had been made by SOE following irregularities in the security checks but, "after taking into consideration the personalities and characters of the agents," the decision had been made by SOE to maintain contact. In SOE's view, the security check was not the sole arbiter of the continued integrity of a particular agent. In difficult field conditions, under constant stress, and with the fatigue of hours spent encoding messages, agents invariably made mistakes in their procedures. As Dourlein himself later admitted, "Agents who were at liberty forgot their check or used it incorrectly."

After the Nazi surrender, the principal enemy counterespionage personnel were brought to London for detailed interrogation, and an intensive study was made of captured documents. One in particular made damning reading. Dated 6 December 1943, the paper listed 46 agents who had been taken prisoner during the *spiel*, of whom only 17 were described as not having collaborated in any way. SOE's determination to insulate their latest agents from those tainted by the Englandspiel proved in one case to be counterproductive. In November 1943 three more prisoners followed the example set by Dourlein and Ubbink and escaped from Haaren: Anton Wegner, Jan van Rietschoten, and Aat van der Giessen rejoined the resistance and eventually tried to contact London via Peter Gerbrands, the agent who had managed to avoid arrest. However, Ivor Dobson was by this time so wary of people claiming to be escapees that none were returned to England. On this occasion at least, the trio was genuine, and their version of what was happening at Haaren would have been invaluable to SOE's damage control exercise, then fully under way.

During the course of the Englandspiel, more than 4,000 signals were exchanged, unwittingly, by SOE with the enemy. After the war, the Dutch military intelligence service claimed that of this total, less than 200 had been shared with them. The breakthrough into MI6's cipher system (which was at that time shared by SOE) that had made the whole deception feasible had been the capture of a single MI6 agent, Wim van der Reyden, together with some of his past messages.

The full impact of what had happened to SOE under the leadership of Richard Laming, Charles Blizard, and Seymour Bingham became apparent only when the Abwehr, in recognition that the Englandspiel had come to an end, on 31 March 1944 sent an identical message on 10 separate channels, in plain language, addressed to SOE's Bingham and, significantly, to Blizard, using his nom-de-guerre, "Blunt":

> To Messrs Blunt Bingham and Successors Ltd. You are trying to make business in the Netherlands without our assistance. We think this is rather unfair in view of our long and successful cooperation as your sole agent. But never mind whenever you will come to pay a visit to the Continent you may be assured you will be received with same care and result as those you sent us before. So long.

This signal was routinely acknowledged by 6 of the 10 SOE circuits used.

NORWAY. Shortly before the German occupation of Norway, Leslie Mitchell, who knew Norway well from before the war, visited the **Secret Intelligence Service (MI6)** station there and, with Frank Foley, laid the foundations for one of MI6's most successful radio operations. By the end of 1940, he was receiving signals from POLLUX, OLDELL, and SKYLARK, the first of nearly 100 MI6 wireless agents, and had set up a base in the Shetlands to receive Norwegian escapees. He experienced only one mishap: Konrad Lindberg and Fritjof Pedersen, who had made their way to Aberdeen in August 1940 and had been sent home with a faulty radio, were arrested soon after their arrival. They were executed by the Germans on 11 August 1941.

NOTIONAL AGENTS. Spies who exist only on paper, or in the minds of ingenious **double agents**, are known as notional agents and are usually associated with **deception** campaigns.

NO. 30 ASSAULT UNIT (30 AU). Established in November 1943, following a proposal made the previous March by Ian Fleming, No. 30 Assault Unit was based on the **Abwehr**'s model *Kommando* led by Kapitan-Leutnant Obladen and intended to seize sensitive documents and equipment of intelligence value, which had proved highly effective during the battle for **Crete** in May 1941. Personnel for 30 AU were drawn from 30 Commando, Royal Marines, who were based at a camp outside Chichester and directed from the Admiralty by NID 30.

The unit was intended to play a role in the Dieppe raid in August 1942 but was unable to land because of the intensity of the fighting on the beach. Commanded by a polar explorer, Quentin Riley, and a veteran of the St. Nazaire raid, Dunstan Curtis, 30 AU performed better during the TORCH landing in North Africa in November 1942 and captured the Italian naval headquarters in **Algiers**. On **D-Day**, 30 AU landed at Arromanches to dismantle an enemy radar station before it was destroyed, and on D+4 another section landed on UTAH beach at Varreville, en route to the naval headquarters in Cherbourg. Later in Germany, Comdr. Jim Glanville led 30 AU to Tambach, where the Kreigsmarine and Führer war conference archive was located, and the unit's war was concluded in Bremen and Bremerhaven.

– O –

OBED, HENRY. Henry Obed was arrested in August 1940 by the Irish Garda with two South African students, Herbert Tributh and Dieter Gaertner, having landed in Baltimore Bay from a yacht, the *Soizic*, which had sailed from Brest. All three were sentenced to seven years' imprisonment at Mountjoy Prison.

OFFICE OF NAVAL INTELLIGENCE (ONI). Created in March 1882 and subsequently designated OP-16, the U.S. Office of Naval Intelligence collected information on the Japanese. OP-20G, based at the Communications Annex in the Munitions Building on Michigan Avenue in Washington, D.C., studied intercepted Japanese naval traffic encrypted with the JN-25 cipher, which had been introduced in June 1939 and was broken partially in September 1940. The cipher was replaced in December 1940 with JN-25B, which succumbed in November 1941. OP-20G's interception and decryption activities were centered on Station CAST at Corregidor in the Philippines, Station HYPO at **Pearl Harbor**, and NEGAT at the Washington Navy Yard.

OFFICE OF STRATEGIC SERVICES (OSS). Created in June 1942 under the leadership of Gen. **William ("Wild Bill") Donovan**, the Office of Strategic Services consisted of four branches: Secret Intelligence (SI), Special Operations (SO), Morale Operations (MO), and Research and Analysis (R&A). Counterintelligence was conducted by the **X-2** subsection of SI. The OSS established training camps in the **United States**, including one located at "Area F," the Congressional Country Club in Maryland, and sent candidates to the Special Training School run by **Special Operations Executive (SOE)** in Osahwa, **Canada**. The OSS would operate in Europe, Southeast Asia, and the Far East, but in the Mediterranean theater it was heavily dependent on the British for communications and transport. The organization was closed by order of President Harry Truman in October 1945, against the recommendation of Gen. Donovan, who recommended its continuation into the peace.

The OSS developed a close relationship with its British counterparts and, based in an office at 72 Grosvenor Street in London's Mayfair, attached personnel to **MI5**, SOE, and the **Secret Intelligence Service (MI6)**. A joint War Room was created in 1943 to coordinate counterintelligence operations with MI5 and MI6, and although there was friction between the agencies in the Middle and Far East because of differing political objectives and priorities, cooperation in Europe resulted in considerable success, particularly in North Africa, Italy, France, and Yugoslavia.

OFFICER. Federal Bureau of Investigation code name for a member of RUDLOFF's network, a **notional agent** that was supposedly a friend of WASCH's, working for the U.S. Army in San Francisco.

ONE-TIME PAD (OTP). A system of encrypting text using tables of five-figure groups that are used only once, thereby theoretically offering a high degree of security. However, cryptanalysts seeking to exploit patterns and repetition discovered that, if the numbers were generated by machine, they were unlikely to be truly random and therefore were vulnerable to cryptographic attack. Codebreakers at **Bletchley Park** achieved considerable success against German Foreign Ministry OTPs and distributed the product as FLORADORA, while the U.S. Army Security Agency attacked Soviet OTPs, a source that would develop into VENONA.

OPERATIONAL INTELLIGENCE CENTRE (OIC). Accommodated in the bombproof citadel constructed on the surface in the Mall next to the Admiralty in London, the OIC gathered information from all sources and plotted the movements of enemy submarines in the Atlantic. Headed by a peacetime barrister, Rodger Winn, the OIC was in direct contact with the Naval Section at **Bletchley Park**, the Royal Air Force Coastal Command, the **Y Service**, and Headquarters Western Approaches at Derby House, Liverpool, to monitor the routes of Allied convoys and vector aircraft and surface warships to the known location of wolfpacks posing a threat to the transatlantic convoys.

OPERA VOLONTARIA DI REPRESSIONE DELL'ANTIFAS-CISMO (OVRA). The principal Italian security agency, OVRA was an instrument of Benito Mussolini's Fascist Party and gained a reputation for ruthlessness comparable to the **Gestapo**. Headed by the former prefect of Genoa, Arturo Bocchini, OVRA employed a permanent staff of 700 and countless thousands of informants.

ORANGE. MI5 code name for Swiss diplomat **Eric Kessler**.

OSHIMA, HIROSHI. The Japanese ambassador in Berlin, Baron Hiroshi Oshima's regular reports to Tokyo contained important strategic information that was encrypted on a PURPLE machine, which had been solved by **William Friedman.** Formerly the long-serving Japanese military attaché in Berlin, Oshima maintained a close relationship with Adolf Hitler and reported his frequent conversations with him almost verbatim in his lengthy messages to Tokyo.

OSLO REPORT. A package delivered anonymously to the British legation in Norway in November 1939 contained a lengthy description of German scientific developments that became known as the Oslo Report, along with an example of a proximity fuse. The report was assessed as genuine by the **Secret Intelligence Service**'s scientific adviser, **Reginald V. Jones**, who later established that the author had been a Siemens electrical engineer, **Hans Mayer.**

OSTEN, ULRICH VON DER. On 18 March 1941, Maj. Ulrich von der Osten was hit by a taxi in Times Square, New York, having only just arrived in Manhattan from Hawaii and Shanghai, and died the following day in Bellevue Hospital. Von der Osten, traveling under a false Spanish passport, was a senior **Abwehr** officer who had operated in Castile and Burgos throughout the Spanish Civil War. He was one of the Abwehr's few experts on America, with members of his family already in the United States, including his brother Carl Wilhelm who was living in Denver. Incriminating evidence recovered from von der Osten's room in the Taft Hotel indicated that he had been intended to be a key organizer for the Abwehr in the United States.

OSTER, HANS. The anti-Nazi deputy chief of the **Abwehr**, Maj. Gen. Hans Oster was implicated in the 20 July 1944 plot against Adolf Hitler and was executed. Earlier in the war, he had given very categorical and well-documented warnings to the Allies, via the Dutch military attaché in Berlin, of the imminent Nazi invasions of Holland and Norway.

OSTRO. MI5 code name for **Paul Fidrmuc**.

OTHMER, MAXIMILIAN G. W. The request by Maximilian Othmer to a Trenton, New Jersey, dentist for a prescription for Pyramidon, a well-known ingredient for secret ink, led the **Federal Bureau of**

Investigation to check his mail. It intercepted letters addressed to "R. A. Hombery" at 46 Via Gran Sassa in Milan containing naval information. This turned out to be a postbox used by other **Abwehr** agents, and Othmer was exposed as the leader of an extensive German spy ring.

OTTO. The **Federal Bureau of Investigation** code name for a **notional** subsource of PAT J's, supposedly a laborer in the Brooklyn Naval Yard of German extraction.

OUTCAST. MI5 code name for a **double agent** in London in contact with Gen. Onodera, the Japanese military attaché in **Stockholm**. OUT-CAST claimed to have a White Russian friend in the United States, code-named JAM, who supplied him with information, but a plan in March 1945 to put JAM in direct contact with Onodera failed.

OVERLORD. The code name for the Allied **D-Day** invasion of Normandy in June 1944.

OWENS, ARTHUR. The real name of the **B1(a) double agent** SNOW. Owens was a highly dubious figure who had worked for the **Secret Intelligence Service (MI6)** and the **Abwehr** long before he came into contact with **MI5** in September 1939. His career as a double agent was to come to an end in March 1941 following a visit to **Lisbon** made in the company of another MI5 nominee, Walter Dicketts, code-named CELERY. Owens had been invited to Portugal in February and was entertained there while Dicketts spent three weeks in Germany undergoing an intensive training course. Exactly what happened next is unclear. Owens told his MI6 contact in Lisbon that the Germans had charged him with being a double agent, working for the British almost as soon as he had arrived, and he had admitted only to having been in contact with MI5 for the past two or three months or so. Dicketts, however, told an entirely different story. He insisted that the Germans had never expressed any lack of confidence in him, and he produced £10,000 and some sabotage materiel as proof of the Abwehr's trust.

Also denounced by his son and mistress, on 21 April 1941 Owens was detained at Dartmoor Prison, where he languished for the remainder of the war. The explanation relayed over SNOW's wireless link to the Germans was that Owens, known to the Abwehr as JOHNNY, had fallen gravely ill and had hidden his transmitter. While this explanation covered Owens's removal from the scene, it was to jeopardize all the other connected double agents, including TATE, whose address had been given to Owens so he could send him some cash. Contact with RAINBOW and TATE was maintained, but MI5 allowed two other agents closely associated with Owens and Dicketts to cease operations. In the months that followed, MI5 subjected all of RAINBOW's letters and TATE's wireless signals to intense analysis, and it was deduced that the Abwehr had indeed accepted much of what Owens had told them, but they had mistakenly concluded that Dicketts had denounced Owens to the authorities after their return to Great Britain in March 1941. After the war, Owens was released to immigrate to Canada, and he died in Ireland.

– P –

PAGET, SIR JAMES. The **Secret Intelligence Service** head of station in New York upon the outbreak of war, Capt. Sir James Paget was replaced in July 1940 by **William Stephenson**.

PAILLOLE, PAUL. A graduate of St. Cyr and deputy head of the Deuxieme Bureau's counterespionage branch at the outbreak of war, Paul Paillole established **Travaux Ruraux (TR)** with the tacit approval of the Vichy authorities, but in contact with the **Secret Intelligence Service (MI6)**, until the Nazis took over the unoccupied zone of France in November 1942, forcing TR to withdraw to **Algiers**. There, from January 1943, Paillole worked closely with MI6 and independently of Charles de Gaulle's organization, running sources in France and North Africa. In November 1944 he resigned when he was ordered to subordinate his networks to the newly formed **Direction Générale des Services Spéciaux**. *See also* VICHY INTELLIGENCE.

PANDORA. Government Communications Headquarters code name for a German Foreign Ministry cipher encrypted on **one-time**

pads and exchanged between Dublin and Berlin. The German minister in Dublin, Dr. Edouard Hempel, was the recipient of high-level messages and this material proved to be exceptionally valuable.

PASSPORT CONTROL OFFICER (PCO). The prewar cover adopted by **Secret Intelligence Service (MI6)** personnel in New York, **Lisbon**, **Madrid**, Paris, Brussels, Oslo, The Hague, Vienna, Berlin, Prague, Bucharest, Belgrade, Budapest, Riga, Tallinn, and Athens. It had the advantage of offering official status to some MI6 staff, but the arrangement was so transparent, and so compromised, that its premises were often the subject of hostile surveillance and occasional penetration. The expedient avoided causing diplomatic embarrassment to ambassadors and ministers, but made individual officers vulnerable to arrest and compromise. In 1938, Thomas Kendrick, the PCO in Vienna, was detained briefly by the **Gestapo**, and in 1939 the PCO in The Hague, Maj. **Richard Stevens**, was abducted by the **Sicherheitsdienst**.

PASTORIUS. The **Abwehr** code name for an attempt to infiltrate eight saboteurs into the United States by submarine. On 18 June 1942, the U-584 dropped four saboteurs onto the beach at Ponte Vedra, 25 miles south of Jacksonville, Florida. Having buried some boxes of equipment and explosives in the sand dunes, they walked to a store on Highway 140 and then caught a bus to Jacksonville, where Edward J. Kerling and Herman Neubauer checked into the Seminole Hotel. Their companions, Herbert Haupt and Werner Thiel, checked into another hotel and the following day all the men caught two different trains to Cincinnati, Ohio. All had been born in Germany but had lived in the United States before the war. They were led by Kerling, age 33, who had worked for four years in New York.

Haupt did not stay in Cincinnati like the others, but instead traveled on to Chicago, where he had been brought up and trained as an apprentice optician. He was followed there on 20 June by Neubauer, a former chef on the SS *Hamburg*. Meanwhile Kerling and Thiel went to New York, unaware that Georg Dasch, the 39-year-old head of Operation PASTORIUS, who had landed on Long Island, New York, on 14 June from the same U-boat, had turned himself in to the **Federal Bureau of Investigation** in Washington, D.C., revealing that three companions who had landed with him were staying at the Governor Clinton Hotel in New York. Those three were quickly arrested, and another suspect, Helmut Leiner, whose name had been found on a list of 16 contacts supplied to Dasch written in secret writing on a handkerchief, was placed under surveillance. Leiner was observed meeting Kerling, who was then followed to a rendezvous with Thiel. All three were arrested, and on 27 June Haupt was arrested in Chicago. Under interrogation, he revealed that Neubauer was staying at a hotel in Chicago, and later the same evening Neubauer was arrested at the Sheridan Plaza. All eight men were then reunited in Washington, D.C., where they were placed on trial and convicted of espionage.

PAT J. Federal Bureau of Investigation (FBI) code name for Alfred Meiler, a Dutch diamond cutter and long-term German spy who revealed his mission to New York for the **Abwehr** to the Netherlands embassy in **Madrid** in 1942. Upon his arrival, PAT J was run by the FBI, and he eventually developed a network that included three **notional** subsources: HERMAN, HOLTZ, and OTTO. In November 1944, PAT J received additional funds from a courier, MIKE.

PEACH. MI5 code name for a **double agent**.

PEARL HARBOR. The Japanese raid on the U.S. Navy's Pacific Fleet's anchorage on Oahu, Hawaii, on 7 December 1941, code-named Operation Z, took the country by surprise and destroyed or damaged 18 American warships, including 7 battleships, along with 188 aircraft. Japanese losses amounted to 29 aircraft and 5 midget submarines.

The attack had been planned meticulously and the local Japanese consulate provided cover for Takeo Yoshikawa, an experienced naval intelligence officer and graduate of the Eta Jima academy. Yoshikawa, who had arrived on the island in March 1941 under the alias "Morimura Ito," made daily observations and reported to Tokyo using the PURPLE machine cipher usually reserved for the consul-general, Kita Nagao. Hitherto, intelligence messages from Kita had consisted of information supplied by a former German naval officer, Otto Kühn, who had lived in Honolulu since October 1936, ostensibly running a furniture business while his wife Friedle Birk worked as a hairdresser with her daughter Ruth.

After the Pearl Harbor attacks and the U.S. declaration of war, Yoshikawa was interned with the other consular staff. His true identity undetected, he was repatriated in August 1942 to continue his career in naval intelligence. Yoshikawa died in Japan in 1993, insistent that he had received no help from the 160,000 Japanese Americans resident in Hawaii. Kühn was convicted of espionage in February 1942, sentenced to death, reprieved and sentenced to 50 years' hard labor, and finally released in 1946 because he had cooperated with the **Federal Bureau of Investigation**.

Significantly, some of Yoshikawa's messages had been decrypted in Washington, D.C., including a signal from Tokyo dated 24 September 1941 that requested information on the precise location of warships moored in Pearl Harbor and provided a grid system, known as a "bomb plot," to identify the exact position of each.

As the political atmosphere deteriorated and the diplomatic traffic reflected the increasing tension, intercepts of PURPLE traffic, known as MAGIC, revealed the coded arrangements made for action to be taken when particular messages were received. These contingency plans included the destruction of sensitive cipher equipment, but the texts were not interpreted as an indication that hostilities were imminent. Therefore, the senior local naval and military commanders on Oahu, Adm. Husband E. Kimmel and Gen. Walter Short, were given, on 27 November, only the vaguest warnings about war; neither was indoctrinated into MAGIC. Subsequently both Kimmel and Short were severely criticized, relieved of their duties, and went into retirement, neither aware of the nature of the cryptographic intelligence that had accumulated in Washington.

In 1978, Yoshikawa revealed that, as he had listened in on his shortwave radio and heard the "East winds: Rain" signal that indicated a total breakdown in relations, he could also hear the Zero fighters attacking Pearl Harbor.

PEASANT. Federal Bureau of Investigation code name for Helmut Goldschmidt, a **double agent** run in **Lisbon** by the British **Secret Intelligence Service** with the code name NETTLE. A Dutch Jew, Goldschmidt ran an entirely **notional** network in Washington, D.C., which consisted of BATES, KLEIN, MANAGER, ROBERTS, SAUNDERS, and WAVE, under the supervision of special agent Mark Felt.

PEDANT. British code name for a **double agent** who was a member of a German stay-behind network in Athens discovered upon the city's liberation in October 1944. PEDANT's wireless was used briefly to convey **deception** material to the enemy.

PEG. MI5 code name for a saboteur in **Gibraltar**.

PEPPERMINT. MI5 code name for José Brugada Wood, a **double agent** run inside the Spanish embassy in London between December 1941 and April 1943.

PESSIMISTS. Security Intelligence Middle East code name for a group of three **double agents** run in Syria, but originally recruited by the **Secret Intelligence Service (MI6)**. The trio landed in Tripoli in October 1942 on a mission to Damascus, and they were quickly captured and turned against their **Abwehr** controllers in Athens. They consisted of PESSIMIST X, a Swiss-Italian named Costa who **notionally** acted as a courier for PESSIMIST Y, the group's wireless operator and a professional singer. Known to the Germans as MIMI, he was a Greek, originally from Alexandria, Egypt, and collected information from PESSIMIST Z, a thug with a criminal past involving drug smuggling. Of the three, only PESSIMIST Y retained his liberty, living in the same house as QUICKSILVER.

PETERS. MI5 code name for a **double agent**.

PETRIE, DAVID. Appointed **director-general of the Security Service** in March 1941, Sir David Petrie had previously headed the **Indian Political Intelligence Bureau** in Delhi. Petrie was succeeded on 1 May 1946 by Sir Percy Sillitoe.

PHILBY, KIM. Recruited by **Special Operations Executive** from *The Times* in 1940, Harold A. R. "Kim" Philby joined the **Secret Intelligence Service (MI6)** in September 1941 and worked as a signals intelligence analyst on ISOS traffic in **Section V**'s Iberian Section, designated V(d), until 1944, when he transferred to Section IX to supervise MI6's anti-Soviet operations. The following year, he was posted to **Istanbul**, where he interviewed a **GRU defector, Ismail Akhmedov**. In November 1951, Philby was dismissed after he came under suspicion as a Soviet mole, and in January 1963 he wrote a confession in which he admitted that he had been recruited by the **NKVD** soon after graduating from Cambridge University.

Having been a Soviet spy since his recruitment by Dr. Arnold Deutsch in London in 1934, Philby hemorrhaged MI6 secrets to his NKVD controllers. His first marriage, to Litzi Friedman, who had been a Communist activist in Vienna, ended soon after her friend Edith Tudor Hart (née Suschitzsky) had introduced him to Deutsch. Thereafter he lived with Aileen Furse, who died in December 1957, apparently of natural causes although she had accused her husband of attempting to murder her.

During World War II, Philby maintained contact with the NKVD through the *rezident* in London, **Anatoli Gorsky**, who worked at the embassy under diplomatic cover, and in Gorsky's temporary absence in 1940, through a **Communist Party of Great Britain** official, Bob Stuart. The first member of the Cambridge Five spy ring, Philby was close to his friends **Anthony Blunt** and Guy Burgess, but scarcely knew **Donald Maclean** and may have been unaware of **John Cairncross**'s espionage.

PHILLIPS, WALLACE. In March 1942 the **Federal Bureau of Investigation** learned that Wallace B. Phillips, who had developed an **Office of Naval Intelligence (ONI)** network of four men along the west coast of Mexico and in Baja California to investigate reports of Japanese espionage in 1941, had joined **Coordinator of Information (CoI) William Donovan**'s organization. This prompted a fierce protest from **J. Edgar Hoover**, who suspected the CoI had also acquired Phillips's undercover network. In fact nothing of the kind had occurred, but there had been a period of six weeks of overlap as Phillips moved from ONI to his new post. Ever suspicious, Hoover's accusation was unfounded and the CoI never poached the ONI's organization, and certainly had not established, as alleged, 90 agents in Latin America. Similarly, the State Department was infuriated when it was informed that a CoI officer, Donald Downes, was active in

Mexico City, whereas in fact he was merely a courier on a mission approved by Hoover to obtain a list of Axis spy suspects volunteered by a group of Spanish republican refugees. The feuding was damped down, but not before numerous memoranda had been exchanged and the White House had been drawn into the arguments.

PIP. The code name of a 21-year-old Flemish saboteur, radio operator, and **double agent** dropped by parachute near Malines in February 1945 with SQUEAK and WILFRED. His two companions were taken into custody in Antwerp after PIP identified them, and they remained active under the control of the **Belgian** Deuxieme Direction until the end of hostilities, although they were not sent any further agents as they had been promised.

POGO. MI5 code name for a Spanish journalist named del Pozo, identified by ISOS as an **Abwehr** spy in London.

POLIAKOVA, MARIA. A Russian Jew and dedicated Communist, Maria Poliakova was a senior **GRU** officer who spoke several languages fluently. She was sent to Switzerland in 1936 to supervise **Alexander Rado**, even though her brother, husband, and father had all perished in Josef Stalin's purges. In 1941 she returned to Moscow, but her continued involvement in the network was evident from her distinctive Marxist style, which manifested itself in so many of the signals that were exchanged between Moscow and Switzerland and were intercepted. According to **Allan Foote**, Poliakova was switched to head the GRU's Spanish section in 1944 and was probably liquidated "in about May 1946."

Before the war, Poliakova had served as the GRU's illegal *rezident* in Germany and **Belgium** and had operated independently in France and Switzerland. When senior GRU organizer **Ismail Akhmedov** had undertaken tours of inspection in Europe, Poliakova had acted as his deputy in Moscow. Even though many of her colleagues disappeared during the purges, Poliakova survived, probably because her knowledge of the GRU's files was regarded as indispensable. When Foote and **Leopold Trepper** reached Moscow in January 1945, they were interrogated by Poliakova, and she remained at her post until April 1946 when she fell ill. Soon afterward, she disappeared.

POLÍCIA DO VIGILÂNCIA E DEFESA DO ESTADO (PVDE). The feared Portuguese secret police, the PVDE had been run since 1933 by the secretary-general, José Ernesto do Vale Catela, with Capt. Agostinho Lourenço as executive director. Based in the rua Antonio Maria Cardoso, the PVDE acted as a surrogate for the Germans and maintained hostile surveillance on suspected Allied intelligence personnel. Lourenço was cultivated by the U.S. military attaché in **Lisbon** and even assigned the code name JIMMY, but was used only briefly in 1945 as the source of misleading information intended for the Japanese minister.

POLISH INTELLIGENCE. Following the Nazi occupation of Warsaw, the Polish Sixth Bureau, headed by Col. Stefan Mayer, was evacuated to London, where Stanislaw Gano established a new headquarters under the sponsorship of the British **Secret Intelligence Service (MI6)** in the Rubens Hotel, Victoria, with a radio station at Funny Neuk, at Woldingham in Kent. Gano retained control over Polish intelligence personnel stationed overseas, and his representatives in **Bern** and **Madrid** provided MI6 with useful information, although the office in **Lisbon** headed by Col. Pan was penetrated by the **Abwehr**.

POLITICAL WARFARE EXECUTIVE (PWE). Responsible for the dissemination of Allied propaganda, including the use of "**black radio**," PWE distributed subversive literature, rumors, and news across Europe and the Western Hemisphere.

POLLITT, HARRY. The general-secretary of the **Communist Party of Great Britain**, Harry Pollitt was known to have maintained a clandestine radio link with Moscow before the war, and his activities were monitored by **MI5** in the belief that he had supervised underground cells engaged in espionage for the Soviets.

PONS, SJORD. One of four Dutchmen who landed in a boat near Dungeness on 3 September 1940, Sjord Pons was accompanied by **Charles Van Den Kieboom**, **Carl Meier**, and **José Waldburg**. They had been instructed to report on British coastal defenses and on army reserves in Kent on the road to London. Under interrogation, they said that there was a concentration of mounted troops equipped with mules at Le Touquet, information later confirmed by the **Secret Intelligence Service**, and that they had been told that an invasion would take place before the middle of September. In the meantime, they were to report anything over their radio transmitters. They were to work in pairs, and each had been equipped with £60 and food for a week. They were given no contacts in Britain and, according to **MI5**, "were singularly badly directed and to anybody with any knowledge of conditions in this country should have been apparent that none of these could hope to succeed. All of them had been misled about conditions in this country, probably as an inducement to them to come over." The only one of the four to be acquitted of charges under the Treachery Act, Pons was nevertheless detained until the end of hostilities.

POPOV, DUSAN. Code-named TRICYCLE by **MI5** and SCOUT by the **Secret Intelligence Service (MI6)**, Dusan ("Dusko") Popov, the son of a wealthy Dubrovnik merchant, had studied law at Freiberg University and been recruited by his fellow student **Johannes Jebsen** for the **Abwehr**. His mission was to go to England as a spy, leaving his older brother **Ivo Popov** and their youngest brother, Vlada, in Yugoslavia. Once in London, Popov, code-named IVAN, was to make contact with a friend who Popov had claimed would be willing to gather information for the Nazis. In reality, no such person existed outside Popov's fertile imagination.

In mid-December 1940, Popov turned up at **Lisbon** and left a prearranged message at the British **Passport Control Office** for Richman Stopford, the local MI6 head of station. Stopford arranged for his flight on 20 December to Bristol, where he was met by a suitably briefed **MI5** officer, Jock Horsfall, a former racing driver, who escorted him to the Savoy Hotel in London.

When debriefed, Popov revealed that his German contact in Lisbon, "Ludovico von Karstoff" (actually **Albrecht von Auenrode**), was attached to the German legation and that he had been given the identity of an emergency contact in London, a Czech named **Georges Graf**. Popov was introduced to "Bill Matthews," who was to act as his handler and was actually William Luke. Popov's task of creating an import-export firm was assisted by MI5, which installed him in a prestigious office in Imperial House, Regent Street, of a company entitled Tarlair Ltd., a name devised by **T. A. Robertson**. Popov's secretary, Gisela Ashley, was also thoughtfully provided by MI5, as was his manager, Mrs. Brander, and although Popov never spotted it, he was kept under constant surveillance and his apartment on Park Street was fitted with hidden listening devices.

In January 1941, Popov returned to Lisbon to report on his progress to von Auenrode and then traveled to **Madrid**, where he was met for further debriefing by Jebsen. In between his meetings with the Germans, he kept secret appointments with MI6's Ralph Jarvis and reported that he had received instructions to develop his operation in London a stage further by recruiting two of his contacts, his attractive Austrian girlfriend, **Friedle Gaertner**, and a former army officer, **Dickie Metcalfe**.

As Popov acquired his two subagents, MI5 gave him a new, more appropriate cryptonym, TRICYCLE. After his return from Lisbon in February 1941, Popov handed MI5 a questionnaire that he had been instructed to complete, which provided a useful insight into the enemy's intelligence requirements and revealed the quality of the information already in its possession:

> Do Vickers Armstrong possess factories at Brighton and Hawarden to the west of the aerodrome? Have the buildings which were near the aerodromes and which were used for army purposes now been taken over by Vickers for manufacturing? How many Wellingtons do Armstrong make each month? Where else are Wellingtons or parts for Wellingtons made? We want sketches showing sites for Vickers at Weybridge and Vickers near Crayford.

In addition, Popov was requested to complete a detailed study of the defenses along a stretch of the English coastline from the Wash in Norfolk to Southampton. He was also specifically asked, "When are five battleships of *King George V* class ready?"

Popov revealed that the purpose of recruiting GELATINE and BALLOON was so they could continue operations in England, leaving him free to undertake a special mission in the United States. This new assignment was discussed by von Auenrode and Popov when they met again in Lisbon at the end of February 1941, as Popov delivered a favorable report on his two new subagents. He also offered a solution to the Abwehr's problem of establishing a permanent, reliable conduit to its agents in England through which they could receive money. Popov's ingenious solution was to suggest Plan MIDAS.

Popov was to go back to Lisbon in March 1941 to make one last interim report before his U.S. assignment and to finalize MIDAS. While the Abwehr was keen to proceed with the plan to finance TATE, it showed less enthusiasm for a map Popov pretended he had obtained from an acquaintance in the Royal Navy. It supposedly charted the location of minefields along Great Britain's east coast, but the matter was pursued no further, apparently because the Germans believed the document to be out of date. The remainder of the visit was spent in preparation of Popov's forthcoming voyage across the Atlantic, which was to be made, theoretically at least, on behalf of the Ministry of Information in London to assess the effect of British propaganda on Yugoslavs in America.

Popov traveled to Portugal, for the fourth time that year, on 26 June and received a briefing from von Auenrode concerning the tasks he was to undertake while in the States. In addition, he was given a questionnaire which, using **microdots**, had been reduced to the size of six full stops on a telegram so as to escape any search Popov would be put through in **Bermuda** or New York. This development created great interest in London, because microphotography was then quite a novelty and this was one of the very first examples of its operational use. As for the questionnaire itself, a large part of it related to naval installations in Hawaii, which, though poorly translated by the **Federal Bureau of Investigation (FBI)**, was to take on a greater significance after the Japanese attack on **Pearl Harbor** four months hence:

> Decay of Uran. According to some information obtained, there is reason to believe that the scientific works for the utilization of the atomic-kernel energy are being driven into a certain direction in the US partly by the use of helium. Continuous informations about the tests made on this subject are required and particularly: (1) What process is practised in the US for the sending of heavy uran? (2) Where are being made tests with more important quantities of uran? (Universities, industrial laboratories, etc.) (3) Which other raw materials are being used at these tests? It is to be recommended to entrust only best experts with this test, and if not available, to abstain from it.

Popov arrived in Manhattan on 12 August 1941, escorted by MI6's John Pepper and Hamish Mitchell, whom he had met in Bermuda.

While MI5 had been delighted by the **double agent**'s performance, the FBI was decidedly cool to the prospect of an enemy agent's arrival. Nevertheless, **British Security Coordination (BSC)** had arranged for Popov to be interviewed by Lt. Chambers from the U.S. **Office of Naval Intelligence** and Capt. Murray of Army Intelligence at the Waldorf Hotel on Saturday, 14 August. According to the official report of the encounter, Popov had information about "five or six German agents operating in the U.S." This news was passed to the FBI on the following Monday morning.

The FBI's initial reaction to Popov's arrival appears to have been lukewarm, judging by the 12-page report written by FBI Assistant Director Earl J. Connelley, following a three-hour meeting held on Wednesday, 18 August, a full six days after Popov's arrival. The next morning, he was introduced to **Percy E. Foxworth**, the FBI special agent assigned to his case, and it was on this occasion that Popov showed him his personal codebook, based on the novel *Night and Day*, and a sample of the crystals the Abwehr had given him to make secret ink. It has been suggested that **J. Edgar Hoover** did not much care for Popov's behavior or his morals. Certainly on one occasion the FBI wrecked an amorous weekend and brought Popov back to New York after he had attempted to take a girlfriend to Florida in September, thereby crossing state lines for an immoral purpose, contrary to the federal statute known as the Mann Act.

While Popov was in the States, responsibility for supervision of his day-to-day conduct lay with Charles F. Lanman, a special agent reluctantly assigned to his case by the FBI. Popov entrusted Lanman with his code and established himself in an apartment at 530 Park Avenue in Manhattan, spending the weekends at a cottage in Locust Valley, Long Island, with his newly acquired girlfriends, Terry Brown and the French movie actress Simone Simon. As agreed with the FBI, he mailed a few reports to Portugal, but by October he had received no acknowledgment of them, which led MI5 to fear the Abwehr was losing interest in him. The situation was saved by a message from Lisbon ordering Popov to travel to **Brazil** and report to **Albrecht Engels**, code-named ALFREDO, at the German firm AEG in Rio.

During his three weeks in Rio de Janeiro, Popov held several meetings with ALFREDO and received instructions to establish a radio station in the United States to communicate with Rio and Lisbon. He was also told to collect information on war production, the composition and destination of transatlantic convoys, and technical developments in the field of antisubmarine warfare. Popov's extended contact with the personable Engels served to compromise him, especially when Engels topped up IVAN's dwindling funds.

Popov returned by ship to New York triumphant, but the FBI remained uncooperative in helping him to collect suitable information for his wireless link, to the point that in March 1942 MI6 disclosed that it had learned that the Abwehr was having second thoughts about IVAN's loyalty and that there was a belief that he had come under the FBI's control since his arrival in the United States the previous August. This had been revealed in ISOS decrypts, which, inexplicably, MI6 had refused to share with MI5 until the following May, by which time the situation had deteriorated into a major crisis.

Finally MI6 revealed an ISOS text from Berlin to Lisbon, dated 21 March, instructing IVAN's handler to test him with a question about his salary. Once again, Popov was running low on funds, had failed to pay several overdue bills, including one on his telephone, and the FBI refused to finance his extravagant partying. Popov replied to the query from Lisbon entirely unaware that it had been designed to confirm his bona fides, and he was not told that another ISOS intercept from Berlin, dated 5 May, advised that the Abwehr's Luftwaffe branch had concluded that IVAN had been "turned." In August, an exasperated FBI asked MI6 to withdraw Popov, and two months later he returned to Portugal, escorted by MI5's Ian Wilson, having been warned by BSC that he might receive a less than warm welcome.

Ignorant of the full circumstances or that the Abwehr had become very suspicious of him, Popov put on a bravura performance in Lisbon, complaining that German parsimony had handicapped his ability to fulfill his mission and was rewarded with a new assignment in London and $20,000. Naturally, these events were monitored through ISOS, although Popov was never indoctrinated into the source used by MI5 to check on his status and integrity. Not all the 36 letters he had mailed from the United States had been received at their destination, and there was some dissatisfaction that he had been unable to travel to Hawaii. Popov defended himself vigorously, claiming that the shortage of funds had reduced his efficiency, and he gradually won the Abwehr over. They rewarded him with an additional $26,000 and

75,000 escudos and on 17 October reported to Berlin that Popov's integrity as a German spy was undiminished.

Popov's 14 months in the Western Hemisphere served to highlight the different attitudes prevailing in London and Washington about the way double agents should be exploited, but the experience, although damaging for the FBI's increasingly tense relationship with BSC, proved helpful in solving the problem of authorizing the release of information suitable for distribution to double agents—an obstacle that had hamstrung Popov—with the January 1943 creation of an Anglo-American coordinating body known as Joint Security Control.

Popov spent a week in Lisbon placating his German controllers, and then flew back to London with the seeds of yet another ingenious scheme in mind, this time to free some of his brother's friends from Yugoslavia, among them **Eugn Sostaric**, on the pretext that they could be recruited as agents.

Following his success, Popov decided to try the same trick again, and in mid-July 1943, he flew to Portugal. This time, instead of traveling under his civilian cover as an international commercial lawyer, he went with a diplomatic passport, having been called up for Yugoslav military service—or so he told Jebsen, who met him in Lisbon. The idea was to persuade the Abwehr to allow a group of Yugoslav officers who had been interned in Switzerland to escape to Spain. As Popov had anticipated, the Germans seized on the proposal because it presented them with a useful method of infiltrating agents into the Allied forces. Indeed, the Abwehr was so taken with the scheme that they asked Ivo Popov, who had now been enrolled into the organization with officer rank, to supervise the Yugoslav end of the escape route. This was exactly what Popov had wanted, for it left him with an officially sponsored underground railroad across Europe on which Ivo could send friends with little fear of enemy interference.

Popov remained in Lisbon, shuttling to and from Madrid on his diplomatic passport, until mid-September when he received an engineer, another old friend, **Stefan Zeis**. His arrival, after a journey via Switzerland lasting more than a year, was to prove critical because he confirmed what Popov had already come to suspect: that Ivo's principal contact in the Abwehr, Jebsen, was himself a candidate for **defection** to the Allied side. This extraordinary turn of events required delicate handling, so Popov flew straight back to England with Jebsen's proposal to actively cooperate with the British. He also brought a wireless transmitter with him, as proof of his acceptance by the Germans, and a large sum of cash.

The prospect of recruiting a genuine Abwehr agent handler sparked a mixed reaction in London. While it had the superficial attraction of getting valuable insight into the enemy camp, it was not entirely without risk. If Jebsen either lost his nerve or accidentally did something to betray himself, he would immediately jeopardize the whole of Popov's ring. Indeed, the consequences might be even more serious, and the Abwehr might be tempted, if conducting a full-scale investigation, to weigh up the loyalties of some of its other agents, too. But rejecting Jebsen's offer would not be without its hazards either. Such a move might serve to prove to him that all his agents were already under hostile control.

The dilemma was deepened by another consideration, known only to a relative handful of senior intelligence officers: most of the Abwehr's wireless traffic was being routinely intercepted and decrypted, and this invaluable source provided such a comprehensive overview of the enemy's activities that there was no operational need to treat with defectors. This debate continued throughout October 1943 while Zeis was established in MI5's books as THE WORM, a reflection of his unattractive personality, and put to work writing letters in secret ink to a cover address on the Continent.

The chosen method of bringing Popov's spy ring to a close was particularly ingenious, intended to allay any lingering doubts the Germans might have had. Popov wrote a letter to Lisbon stating that the most recent wireless signal from the Marquis de Bona (FREAK), on 19 May, was to be his last, as he had fallen under suspicion following a leak from Draza Mihailovic that he might be a German agent. Surprisingly, the Germans failed to acknowledge Popov's letter and continued to try to contact de Bona by radio. Eventually, at the end of June, de Bona responded, claiming that he had been ordered to New York in his new capacity as aide-de camp to King Peter of Yugoslavia. This excuse was accepted reluctantly by the Germans, and the network came to an end officially when, in August 1944, Ivo Popov was flown out of Yugoslavia by the Royal Air Force.

Dusan Popov eventually published an account of his wartime adventures, *SpyCounterspy*, in which he changed the names of the members of his network. He died at his home, once the bishop's palace in Opio near Valbonne in the Alpes-Maritimes, southern France, on 10 August 1981.

POPOV, IVO. A Yugoslav physician, code-named DREADNOUGHT by **MI5**, Ivo was **Dusan Popov**'s older brother. Also recruited by the **Abwehr**, he acted as a **double agent** from April 1943 until he was able to escape to Italy in August 1944.

PORTUGAL. The principal Portuguese intelligence agency was the **Polícia do Vigilância e Defesa do Estado (PVDE)**, which was considered by the Allies to act as a surrogate for the Germans. President Antonio Salazar's regime was generally sympathetic to the Nazis during the first half of the war, but as the tide turned, the Portuguese reached an accommodation with the United States over the use of an airbase in the Azores and acquiesced in their occupation. **Lisbon** remained a hotbed of espionage throughout the conflict because of its geographic location on the civilian transatlantic air route between **Bermuda** and Bristol. Accommodation addresses in Lisbon and Estoril were routinely employed by the **Abwehr** for the receipt of letters written in secret ink by spies from Great Britain and the United States.

POST, KENNETH. Suspected by **MI5** of having been a Soviet spy active in the **X Group** in 1940 and 1941 with the code name RESERVIST, Col. Kenneth Post worked in the Ministry of Supply and was seconded to the **Crossbow** Committee in 1943.

PUENTER, OTTO. Code-named PAKBO, Otto Puenter was a member of the **GRU**'s spy ring in Switzerland known as the **Rote Drei**. An experienced GRU agent with a useful journalistic cover, Puenter had maintained good contacts with the Swiss military establishment and had run some sources into Italy, whence he received reports on Italian naval movements. His main source was GABEL, a Yugoslav former pilot who acted as the Spanish consul in Susak, a port on the Yugoslavian coast close to the Italian frontier. Although GABEL harbored republican sympathies, he had been in regular touch with Gen. Francisco Franco's official representative in Belgrade and had acquired some interesting intelligence concerning Spain and Italy for Puenter. As well as GABEL, Puenter also managed **Georges Blun**, a French political correspondent based in Zurich code-named LONG.

Puenter's third main source was a former German Social Democrat code-named POISSON who had taken Swiss nationality after fleeing from his home in the Saarland, where he had participated in the League of Nations administration before the 1935 plebiscite. Puenter, who moved to East Berlin after the war, obtained considerable financial support for the network by the expedient of promising Swiss businessmen lucrative postwar contracts with the Soviets in return for immediate cash aid. One person who cooperated with Puenter to give money and information was Emil Guehrle, a director of the Oerlikon arms manufacturing firm who featured in a couple of messages and made regular contributions to the Rote Drei's dwindling funds.

PUJOL, JUAN. True name of the **MI5 double agent** code-named GARBO by MI5 and ALARIC by the **Abwehr**, who submitted reports fabricated in **Lisbon** to his German handler in **Madrid** from October 1941. Contacted by the **Secret Intelligence Service (MI6)**, which gave him the code name BOVRIL, Pujol was escorted to London in April 1942 and remained in contact with **Karl-Erich Kühlenthal** until the end of hostilities.

Supervised by MI5's Tomas Harris, GARBO invented 22 **notional** subagents, including a KLM pilot who supposedly acted as a courier, carrying his messages to Lisbon; a Royal Air Force (RAF) officer assigned to Fighter Command; a Spaniard in the Ministry of Information who obtained a job for GARBO; a left-wing Ministry of Information official; a lovelorn secretary in the War Office; a Portuguese businessman code-named CARVALHO based in Newport, Monmouth, overlooking the Bristol Channel and in touch with Welsh nationalists; William Gerbers, a married Swiss businessman in Bootle who died of cancer in October 1942; William Gerbers's widow; a wealthy Venezuelan student, code-named BENEDICT, who acted as ALARIC's deputy and had a brother in **Canada**, code-named MOONBEAM; a non-commissioned RAF officer; a lieutenant in the British 49th Division; a Greek Communist seaman who deserted from the merchant navy and believed he was working for the Soviets; a **Gibraltarian** waiter, code-named FRED, who worked in a storage depot in the Chislehurst caves; a Spanish republican, code-named ALMURA, who worked as ALARIC's radio operator; a guard in the Chislehurst munitions depot, recruited by FRED; MOONBEAM's cousin, code-named CON; a South African, code-named DICK, who was killed in North Africa in July 1943; a Welsh nationalist seaman from Swansea, known as Stanley and code-named DAGOBERT; a soldier in the British 9th Armoured Division who supplied information to DAGOBERT; a retired seaman named David, living in Dover and leading the World Aryan Order, code-named DONNY; Theresa Jardine, a WREN code-named GLEAM; an Indian poet living in Brighton code-named DICK; a cousin of DONNY's living in Swansea; and the treasurer of the World Aryan Order, living in Harwich and code-named DORICK.

GARBO participated in numerous **deception** schemes, including the principal role in FORTITUDE. He operated undetected until the end of hostilities, when he visited Kühlenthal in Spain to be paid off. Altogether GARBO received in excess of £40,000 from the Abwehr, which paid for much of MI5's wartime cost.

PUPPET. The **Secret Intelligence Service** code name for a **double agent** named Fanto, a British businessman in contact with HAMLET who was also a friend of Gen. von Falkenhausen, the German military governor of **Belgium**. He was active between April 1943 and May 1945.

PURPLE. American code name for the Japanese cipher machine used to encrypt top-level diplomatic messages. By 1935, after five years of toil, the U.S. Army's Signal Intelligence Service (SIS) had achieved considerable success against RED, the "Type A" cipher machine used by Japanese naval attachés to encrypt messages that were handed over to commercial carriers for onward transmission to Tokyo. As the Axis began to take shape, the huge volume of Japanese Foreign Ministry telegrams placed an increasing strain on the SIS's very limited resources, which boasted a staff of just seven, and an arrangement was made with U.S. **Office of Naval Intelligence** cryptographers of OP-20G to share the burden, with SIS handling traffic on even calendar days and the navy dealing with the odd days. This collaboration worked well, with SIS doubling its staff to 14, until March 1939 when the flow of decrypts suddenly ceased due to the unexpected introduction of a more sophisticated replacement unit, the "Type B," code-named PURPLE.

The PURPLE cipher generated by the Type B resisted the decoders until 25 September 1940, when the first complete text succumbed and was distributed to the very limited group indoctrinated into the highly classified program. The breakthrough occurred after 20 months of pure cryptanalysis by a team led by **William Friedman**, who promptly underwent a nervous collapse. Friedman's subordinate, Frank B. Rowlett, had been able to reconstruct the PURPLE cipher—and thereby develop a replica Type B machine—by exploiting two flaws in Japanese procedures. The first was a common error, known as the "stereotype," which resulted from the stilted diplomatic language that convention dictated should begin and end individual telegrams. The predictable repetition of the pedantic phrase "I have the honour to inform your excellency" allowed the experts to glimpse the construction of particular messages, as did the Japanese habit of reproducing word for word the content of U.S. State Department communiqués. Since the cryptanalysts, among them Genevieve Grotjan, worked with copies of the original texts, they had little difficulty in retracing the process by which the Japanese had transformed the text into cipher. Once Friedman had grasped the principles upon which PURPLE was based, Lt. Leo Rosen was able to build an electromagnetic device from telephone exchange relays that would duplicate the original machine, and by January 1941 a model had been delivered to OP-20G in Washington, D.C., and another had been donated to **Bletchley Park**, which hitherto had concentrated on the Japanese Navy's hand ciphers.

PUTLITZ, WOLFGANG ZU. MI5's prewar source inside the German embassy in London, handled by **Iona Ustinov** and **Dick White**, Wolfgang zu Putlitz was compromised when serving at The Hague in 1940 and was exfiltrated to London. He subsequently traveled to the Caribbean, but returned to Great Britain where he was employed broadcasting on the "**black radio**" stations managed by the **Political Warfare Executive**.

– Q –

QUAIL. Supreme Headquarters Allied Expeditionary Force code name for Pierre Schmidttbuhl, an **Abwehr** agent since 1933 who was parachuted into the Metz area in February 1945.

QUEEN BEE. MI5 code name for German rockets.

QUICKSILVER. British code name for George Liossis, a Greek air force officer and nephew of Gen. Liossis who was dispatched on a mission for the **Abwehr** in August 1942 with Anna Agiraki, code-named GALA, and a **Gestapo** thug named Bonzos, code-named RIO. Upon his arrival in Beirut, Liossis, who had been in contact with the **Secret Intelligence Service (MI6)** in Athens before the war, surrendered to Douglas Roberts, the local **defence security officer**, who assigned John Wills of **Security Intelligence Middle East** to supervise the contact made with his German controllers by radio in October 1942, after GALA and RIO had been imprisoned. QUICKSILVER's **notional** network also included KHALIL, a laundryman working for the British Ninth Army, and KYRIAKIDES, supposedly a Greek businessmen with royalist connections in **Cairo**, where he was a frequent visitor. In 1944 QUICKSILVER's diminishing funds were replenished with 200 gold sovereigns supplied by INFAMOUS, a Turkish **double agent** under MI6 control who had been friendly with the **Belgian** consul in Beirut, and therefore was considered suspect. Famously his **Inter-Services Liaison Department** case officer in Beirut, Charles Dundas, complained to Cairo that "plans which appear well-prepared at your end seem half-baked at ours." Despite the protest, INFAMOUS was allowed to make his delivery, but took the opportunity to smuggle some watches into Lebanon, where he was caught and briefly imprisoned. This incident appeared to have no impact on QUICKSILVER's standing with the Abwehr, and in August 1944 he was appointed provost marshal of the Royal Hellenic Air Force in Egypt.

– R –

RADIO INTELLIGENCE DIVISION (RID). On 1 July 1940, the Federal Communications Commission (FCC) received a secret allocation of $1.6 million from the White House and appointed George E. Sterling to create a Radio Intelligence Division, based on the British **Radio Security Service**, initially from seven sites in the United States, to monitor illicit transmissions. Known as the National Defense Communications Section, it quickly built an eighth monitoring station in Laredo, Texas, and arranged through the army to use facilities at a further 30 military posts.

Although, prior to the breakthrough provided by **William Sebold**, the RID had not possessed the means to read the intercepted traffic, it was able to do so from June 1941 on, with advice from Paul A. Napier, the head of the cryptology section of the **Federal Bureau of Investigation (FBI)** technical laboratory. For example, the RID had been monitoring a transmitter in **Chile** with the call sign FMK since April 1941, but had not succeeded in breaking its code. The advantage gained from Sebold allowed the FBI to routinely intercept and read almost every **Abwehr** message transmitted from Latin America throughout the rest of the war, in a coup comparable to the ISOS success achieved by British cryptographers based at **Bletchley Park**. As well as helping the codebreakers, Sebold performed a further valuable service by relaying Abwehr signals from South America. At certain times of the year and certain times of the day, it was almost impossible to exchange shortwave signals between Latin America and central Europe, so Sebold was employed to relay the traffic in both directions, which was a considerable relief to the intercept operators.

To coordinate its activities with other agencies, including the FBI, the FCC late in the autumn of 1940 created a Defense Communications Board, with representatives from the State Department, coast guard, army, and navy, and gained approval from the Treasury in January 1941 to expand the intercept network by an additional five primary stations, with support from a further 60 smaller ones, so as to provide comprehensive monitoring 24 hours a day. With the FBI's help, exploiting information from Sebold, the RID became highly proficient at reading the enemy's traffic, to the point that some technicians even suspected the Abwehr might have been deliberately providing the material to divert their attention from "more sinister operations of a professional nature." They were bemused by the frequent lapses in the most fundamental security procedures, such as the occasions when PYL in Chile and LIR in **Brazil** even mentioned in clear text the titles of the novels their ciphers were based on!

The RID's interception operations were not restricted to North America, for one of its radio direction-finding experts from Laredo, Robert Linx, was posted to Rio de Janeiro in late March 1941, for a temporary assignment that was to last four years, and John de Bardeleben was sent to Chile. With Linx's help, the Brazilian authorities developed their own radio direction-finding (RDF) system, located at six coastal sites as well as São Paulo, Belo Horizonte, and Porto Alegre, which proved very effective and provided the basis of the evidence used to initiate the mass arrests of August 1942 that silenced all five clandestine transmitters. De Bardeleben's experience in Chile was one of rather less cooperation, and he was obliged to work independently of the pro-Axis authorities, with the help from two **Special Intelligence Service** special agents, and operate his RDF equipment while the trio traveled the country to monitor the PYL transmitter, masquerading as miners.

RADIO SECURITY SERVICE (RSS). The **British intelligence** organization dedicated to the interception of illicit wireless broadcasts, which, in the absence of traffic to monitor, concentrated on **Abwehr** communications. Headed by Lord Sandhurst, an enthusiastic member of the Radio Society of Great Britain, and based at Arkley in North London, RSS provided high-quality intercepts to an analytic section consisting of Hugh Trevor-Roper, Gilbert Ryle, and Stuart Hampshire. With help from Oliver Strachey of the **Government Code and Cypher School**, RSS read many of the enemy's hand ciphers, codenamed ISOS, which opened the way for the exploitation of the machine ciphers where there was a helpful duplication.

RADO, ALEXANDER. Code-named DORA by the **GRU**, Alexander (Sandor) Rado was recruited in Moscow in 1935. Subsequently he tried to gain a residency permit in Brussels, but was rejected by the local police. Instead, the GRU directed him to Geneva, where in May 1936 he opened a map publishing agency called Geopress. In reality, it was a front for the GRU's operations mounted against Italy and supervised from the Soviet embassy in Paris. However, in April 1938, Rado was put in touch with **Otto Puenter**, a generously proportioned lawyer code-named PAKBO who worked as a journalist reporting parliamentary proceedings in **Bern** for his own INSA Socialist press agency.

Originally from Budapest, where he had been born Radolfi and had become a prominent member of the Communist Party, Rado had studied in Germany and had married Helene, Vladimir Lenin's secretary, in Moscow in 1923. Thereafter he had worked as a geographer in Berlin, Vienna, and Paris before starting his branch of Impress in Geneva. Geopress was an ideal cover for espionage, and Rado proved an exceptionally talented illegal, with Helene acting as his wireless operator, servicing a large network. When **Ursula Kuczynski** was ordered to England in 1941, she passed **Allan Foote** on to Rado, and although the two men often clashed, they continued to work together.

On 13 October 1943, the **Bundespolizei** seized two illicit Soviet transmitters in Geneva and a little over a month later, they caught Foote in his apartment in Lausanne. Enough cryptographic material was recovered in the three raids to compromise Rado, who promptly disappeared from sight, and one of his principal subagents, **Rudolf Rössler**, who was taken into custody in June 1944. To the embarrassment of the Bundespolizei, Rössler turned out to enjoy close links with Swiss military intelligence — or at least close enough to persuade the authorities that it would not be worth prosecuting either him or **Rachel Dübendorfer**, who had been arrested at about the same time, so both were released without charge. While Rössler stayed in Switzerland and would be arrested again on a charge of espionage in October 1945 (on which he was acquitted), Dübendorfer disappeared in France and was believed to have escaped back to Moscow.

Rado later identified most of his sources and has disclosed the true names of many of the sources that appeared in his wireless messages disguised by cryptonyms: Louis Suss, of the French legation in Bern, was SALTER; Dr. Eugen Bircher, of the Swiss medical delegation to Germany, was another key source; PETER was a director of the Bosch works and a frequent visitor to Zurich laden with data about German munitions; and LOUISE was a generic cover for the Swiss General Staff. According to Rado, "Rudolf Rössler only became LUCY in November 1942 when we established contact with him on a regular basis. Before that, all we had received from him were bits and pieces that TAYLOR [Christian Schneider] had passed on to us without telling Rössler he was doing so" (Rado, *Codename Dora*).

In January 1945, Rado tried to **defect** to the British as he was being flown back to Moscow, and then he attempted suicide. He was handed over to the Soviets in July and persuaded to complete his journey to Moscow. Upon arrival, he was arrested, and he remained in Soviet prisons until 1955, when he was released to take up an academic post in Budapest.

RAINBOW. MI5 code name for **double agent** Bernie Kiener, a Briton educated in Germany who returned to England in 1939 to work as a pianist in a dance band in Weston-super-Mare. RAINBOW remained in contact with his German controllers until June 1943.

RAM. Code name for a **double agent**, a French Army sergeant who acted as a radio operator in **Algiers** during 1943 for EDOUARD and NORBERT. Recruited by the **Abwehr** in Paris, he had been dispatched to North Africa at the end of 1942 on a mission to penetrate a **French intelligence** organization.

RATS. MI5 code name for **José Estella**, a Spanish saboteur captured in **Gibraltar**.

REICHSSICHERHEITSHAUPTAMT (RHSA). Created in September 1939 through an amalgamation of the **Sicherheitsdienst**, the **Gestapo**, and the Kriminalpolizei, the RHSA was headed by **Reinhard Heydrich** until his assassination in May 1942. The RHSA was divided into six departments: I, Personnel; II, Administration; III, Domestic Security; IV, Gestapo; V, Detectives; and VI, Foreign Intelligence. A seventh, dealing with ideological research, was added later.

Heydrich was succeeded briefly by Heinrich Himmler, but in January 1943 Himmler appointed an Austrian lawyer, Ernst Kaltenbrunner, as his replacement. In February 1944 the **Abwehr** was absorbed into the RHSA. *See also* GERMAN INTELLIGENCE.

REINBERGER, HELLMUTH. On 10 January 1940, an Me-108, lost in fog on a courier flight between Münster and Cologne, carrying a German parachute commander, made a forced landing in poor weather at Mechelen-sur-Meuse in **Belgium**. When Maj. Reinberger of the 7th Airborne Division was searched, he was found to be carrying important documents, including plans relating to operation GELB, an imminent surprise attack by the Sixth Army, describing how paratroops would seize the Meuse bridges. Clearly crestfallen, Reinberger had attempted to burn the papers when he was arrested and made another attempt to destroy them in a stove while he was interrogated by a Belgian intelligence officer, Capt. Rodrique. Initially believing the material to be part of a **deception** campaign, the Belgians allowed Reinberger and his pilot, Maj. Erich Hoenmanns to be interviewed by the German air attaché in Brussels, Gen. Wenniger, but were persuaded of their authenticity when the prisoners were heard to lie to their visitor and assure him all secret papers had been destroyed.

REP. Federal Bureau of Investigation code name for a member of RUDLOFF's network, a **notional agent** who was supposedly an engineer employed by Republic Aviation on Long Island and was WASCH's brother.

RESERVIST. The **GRU** code name for a spy and member of the **X Group** active in London in 1941. According to the relevant VENONA decrypts, he was a territorial officer who had been wounded in France and subsequently employed by the Ministry of Supply as a tank expert. The description was found to fit Col. **Kenneth Post**, a member of the **Crossbow** Committee created to advise the British government on the development by the Nazis of rockets and other secret weapons.

REYSEN, HANS. A member of the Wehrmacht who landed by parachute in the north of England on the night of 3/4 October 1940 with instructions to report on defenses in the northwest of Great Britain in anticipation of an invasion. He was discovered sheltering in a barn by a farmer and subsequently made a full statement to **MI5** in which he identified his unit as the Lehr **Brandenburger Regiment**. At the time of his capture, he had been in civilian clothes but was carrying a Wehrmacht paybook and a Luftwaffe uniform. Reysen was accepted as a **double agent** even though his mission was obviously intended to be very short term—he had been given just £140, his radio was found to have no receiver, so he could only transmit messages, and he had been told to expect an invasion within a fortnight after his arrival. Reysen was enrolled in MI5's books as GANDER, but it soon became apparent that MI5 possessed no authority whatever to make any such offers. He transmitted daily weather reports and what purported to be assessments of morale in the Midlands under MI5's supervision, but by November his money and his mission had been exhausted. MI5 honored its promise and detained him until the end of the war.

RHINEMAIDENS, THE. British code name for five young Luftwaffe radio operators, trained by Trupp 122, who formed a stay-behind network near their homes in Mönchengladbach in 1945. One of the RHINEMAIDENS, Anneliese Peters, code-named LAZY, betrayed the others, and she and Ingeborg Schotes, code-named BLAZE, agreed to transmit **deception** material for the Allies from Rheydt until the end of hostilities. Their reports, concerning local Allied troop movements, were believed, and they were both awarded Iron Crosses.

RICHTER, KAREL. A Sudetan German, Karel Richter had worked on the Hamburg-America Line before the war and was parachuted into Hertfordshire in May 1941. He arrived with a false identity card in the name of Fred Snyder, bearing an address thoughtfully provided by **Arthur Owens** and two passports in his own name; the Czech one was genuine, but the Swedish document had been forged. Richter landed near London Colney, Hertfordshire, early on 14 May 1941 but was arrested a few hours later by a suspicious police constable. When searched, Richter was found to be carrying $1,000 and £300, some of which had been intended for "Harry Williamson," an alias used by **Wulf Schmidt**.

Under interrogation at **Camp 020**, Richter admitted that his mission's objective was not only to hand over a crystal and the money to Schmidt but also to act independently. In the latter capacity, his first task had been to check on Schmidt and ensure he had not fallen into enemy hands. His conclusions were to be reported to Hamburg either over his own wireless set or via secret writing to a cover address on the Continent. Oddly, he had not been supplied with the necessary secret ink, but only the chemical formula with which to make it. Its principal ingredient, amidopyrine, was available in England, but only from pharmacies, where he would have been required by the law to declare his name and address in the poison book.

Richter's arrest, which took place in rather too public circumstances for **MI5**'s liking, placed the Security Service in a very awkward position and was to lead to the German's execution under the Treachery Act, which had been introduced the previous year to deal with cases of espionage. Until its enactment, enemy agents had been prosecuted under the Official Secrets Act, which had not proved very satisfactory and in any event did not include provision for a death penalty. The terms of the Treachery Act, rushed through Parliament during the summer of 1940, were much more severe, and already three German spies had been convicted under the new law and hanged. On 10 December 1941, Richter met a grisly death on the scaffold when, at the very last moment and with his head in the noose, he lost his self-control and struggled terribly.

RITTER, NIKOLAUS. A senior **Abwehr** officer who had recruited **William Sebold** in Hamburg, **Herman Lang** in New York, and many others. Ritter's textile business in the United States had collapsed during the Depression, so after 10 years there, he had returned to Germany and followed a new career as an intelligence officer with excellent English and an ability for talent-spotting suitable agents. At the end of the war, Ritter was captured by the British and was still bitter about Sebold's duplicity. His plan to leave the Abwehr and take a diplomatic appointment in Rio de Janeiro had been vetoed personally by Joachim von Ribbentrop, who complained that Ritter was too notorious and his disastrous spy rings had caused the Reich too much embarrassment.

RIVET, LOUIS. Formerly the head of the **Service de Renseignements**, in Vichy, Col. Louis Rivet established a Free **French intelligence** agency loyal to Gen. Henri Giraud in **Algiers** after the German invasion of the unoccupied zone of France in November 1942. *See also* VICHY INTELLIGENCE.

ROBERTSON, T. A. The first head of **B1(a)**, T. A. "Tommy" Robertson joined the **Security Service** in 1931 from his Scottish regiment, the Seaforth Highlanders, and handled SNOW personally. He also conducted the investigation of **John King** and Mathilde Krafft. An intuitive intelligence professional, much of the credit for the success of the **Double Cross System** is due to this modest officer, who after the war was appointed to head **Government Communications Head-quarters'** security branch.

ROBINSON, HENRI. A **GRU** agent born in 1897 in Germany, Henri Robinson studied in Geneva during World War I and became closely associated with the Communist Youth International. In 1936, he was working alongside the Soviet military attaché in Paris before being placed in charge of all the French and English networks the following year. Upon the outbreak of war, he was ordered to subordinate his activities to **Leopold Trepper**, and reluctantly he obeyed. There was no love lost between the two men, and their mutual hostility was later to be exploited by the Germans. Robinson perished while in German captivity, having been arrested in Paris in December 1942, betrayed by Trepper.

ROOM 055. The official postal address and interview suite at the War Office in Whitehall for **MI5**.

ROSBAUD, PAUL. An editor of German technical journals, Paul Rosbaud supplied information to the British **Secret Intelligence Service (MI6)** before World War II and contrived to remain in contact through **Stockholm** and **Bern** during hostilities. He is credited with having passed details of the Nazi atomic weapons development program to MI6. After the war, he became a partner in Pergamon Press, a publisher of academic periodicals.

RÖSSLER, RUDOLF. A German political refugee, Rudolf Rössler settled in Lucerne, Switzerland, in 1933 and opened a small publishing business, which in the summer of 1939 attracted the attention of Dr. Xavier Schneiper of the Swiss military intelligence service. While the Swiss were anxious to exploit Rössler's many anti-Nazi contacts still in Germany, the publisher was motivated primarily by money, and by the end of 1942 he was receiving a regular salary from the Swiss via Schneiper, and from **Rachel Dübendorfer** through a **GRU** cut out, Christian Schneider. Code-named LUCY, Rössler gained access to exceptionally accurate Swiss assessments of German troop movements, which his Swiss contacts knew he was relaying to the Soviets. When the **Bundespolizei** finally intervened on 14 October

1943 and seized two of **Alexander Rado**'s wireless operators, they found documents that could be traced to Rössler and to the Swiss General Staff. The Bundespolizei called the trio "der **Rote Drei**," but were unable to identify all his sources.

One person positively linked to Rössler's espionage was Ernst Lemmer, the German-born Berlin correspondent of the *Neue Zürcher Zeitung*, who was implicated in Rössler's second brush with the Swiss authorities after the war. A friend of the Swiss military attaché in Berlin, Lemmer was granted the cryptonym AGNES by LUCY and eventually was elected to the Federal Bundestag and appointed a cabinet minister.

The Central Intelligence Agency's postwar research into LUCY's sources also produced the name of Col. Fritz Boetzel, head of the High Command's cipher department until 1939, when he had been transferred to the South-East Army Group's intelligence evaluation office. Boetzel had been known to **Hans Oster** and **Wilhelm Canaris** and had fit the anti-Nazi profile of Rössler's contacts. Another candidate was Carl Goerdeler, formerly the lord mayor of Leipzig, who was Reichchancellor for price control until his execution in October 1944 for involvement in the plot to assassinate Adolf Hitler.

As well as dealing with the Swiss and the Rote Drei, Rössler was also in touch with the Czechs through Col. **Karel Sedlacek**, who operated under journalistic cover in Zurich as a correspondent for the Prague daily *Narodni Listy*. Using the alias "Karl Selzinger," Sedlacek had cultivated Rössler and become friendly with a Swiss intelligence officer, Maj. Hans Hausamann. Both gave information to Sedlacek, who transmitted it to his superior in London, Col. **Frantisek Moravec**, over a period of three years. Proof that Sedlacek and Hausamann had relied almost entirely upon Rössler for their information can be deduced from the fact that when LUCY was detained by the Bundespolizei, between May and September 1944, the quality of Sedlacek's reports to Moravec deteriorated markedly. After the war, Sedlacek was appointed the Czech military attaché in **Bern**, and recruited Rössler as his agent.

ROTE DREI. The **GRU** network in Switzerland was dubbed Der Rote Drei ("The Red Three") by the **Bundespolizei** because of the three wireless transmitters confiscated in raids conducted in October and

November 1943 on the homes of **Allan Foote**, **Alexander Rado**, and **Rudolf Rössler**. Until the **defection** of Foote, knowledge of the Rote Drei had been limited to the interrogation reports of suspects kept by the Bundespolizei, an impressive quantity of Soviet radio signals that had been successfully deciphered by Swiss cryptographer Marc Payot, and an analysis of an estimated 5,500 clandestine wireless messages exchanged between Moscow and Switzerland intercepted by Wilhelm F. Flicke, a 13-year veteran of the **Abwehr**'s communications branch.

When examined by the analysts, it became obvious that Foote's messages had come from Rado, who had received the information from Rössler, apparently without asking its provenance. The network's architect was **Maria Poliakova**, who was known to Foote as VERA. She had laid the foundations of the Rote Drei in 1936 when she supervised the activities of the GRU's network in Switzerland, which at that time had consisted of **Rachel Dübendorfer** and **Otto Puenter** in **Bern**, and Rado in Geneva. In December 1939 Rado had been joined in Geneva by **Ursula Kuczynski**, who as SONIA had been assigned the task of facilitating Rado's communications in the event that his channel—microfilm carried by couriers to the embassy in Paris—was interrupted. She in turn had handled Dübendorfer, the Polish woman and Kommunistische Partei Deutschlands (KPD) activist who had acquired Swiss citizenship through a marriage of convenience and then had found employment as an interpreter and typist with the International Labor Organization in Geneva. Dübendorfer lived with Paul Boettcher, a former member of the KPD's Central Committee who had fled to Switzerland when the Nazis had seized power in Germany. SONIA had also run the GRU's two British volunteers, Foote and **Len Beurton**, both veterans of the International Brigade. "She taught them the rules of conspiracy, how to use secret codes and operate a radio, and in fact everything an intelligence agent needs to know," recalled Rado.

Although the Rote Drei must have provided Moscow with some useful items of information, including some from Belgrade where Rado had been dispatched briefly in October 1940, the organization did not produce any really strategically significant intelligence until the autumn of 1942, when Rössler started supplying high-quality material to Rado via Puenter.

The Bundespolizei's first move against the Rote Drei was a raid on the Geneva home of Edmond and Olga Hamel, timed to coincide with the arrest of Margaret Bolli and a search of her apartment. The Hamels and Bolli had been Rado's radio operators, and the fact that he had needed three different transmitters to send his material to Moscow is an indication of the volume involved. The Bundespolizei had been listening to the traffic for a considerable period and in the raid recovered two transmitters, a partial record of Rado's accounts, and enough information about Soviet cipher techniques for Payot to begin decrypting the thousands of signals that had been intercepted.

As soon as he learned of the raids, Rado dropped from sight by checking himself into a clinic. He asked Louis Suss to approach the British for help, but before he could obtain a reply, Moscow vetoed the idea. On 20 November 1943, Foote was arrested in his flat in Lausanne in the act of receiving a lengthy message from Moscow, thus suddenly bringing the Rote Drei to an end. The detainees underwent six months of solitary confinement and interrogation, and on 19 April 1944, Dübendorfer, Boettcher, and Christian Schneider were taken into custody. A month later, Rössler was arrested and charged with espionage.

Thanks to some unofficial assistance from the **Abwehr**, the Bundespolizei reconstructed much of Rado's network and identified its members from photographs taken covertly during a lengthy surveillance operation. Payot succeeded in deciphering a large quantity of Rado's messages, and most of those imprisoned gave statements that incriminated either themselves or their contacts. The result was that the Hamels were released on bail in July 1944, having received a suspended prison sentence, and a fine was paid by Puenter, who was never charged. Rado escaped to Paris in September 1944, where he was reunited with Foote, who had been released earlier in the month. Dübendorfer was released soon after her arrest, and she promptly disappeared, reportedly to Paris and then Moscow where she was imprisoned again. In her absence, she was sentenced by the Swiss to two years' imprisonment and 15 years of exclusion from Switzerland. Her lover, Boettcher, was transferred to a refugee camp at Sichem, but he escaped in July 1945 and apparently was spotted with Dübendorfer in Paris in August 1945. Thereafter, neither was seen again. He had received a similar sentence from the Swiss. In contrast, Schneider cooperated with his interrogators and was set free within a month.

The arrest of Rössler early in June 1944 proved highly embarrassing for the Swiss, and after three months in custody he was granted his freedom. He was eventually charged with espionage in October 1945, but was acquitted.

Prior to the autumn of 1943, when Rössler's material came on stream, Rado's signals had contained relatively trivial data that had emanated from a handful of leftist sources who were personal contacts developed by Puenter. Postwar analysis of the Rote Drei's messages confirmed the authenticity of their content and the extraordinary speed with which they had reached the Soviets. Much of it could be traced back to Rössler, but he had resisted all the attempts made by Moscow Center, evident in the traffic, to make him identify his contacts. In his signals LUCY had referred constantly to four sub-agents: WERTHER, TEDDY, OLGA, and ANNA.

After the war, the Central Intelligence Agency (CIA) and the Swiss devoted considerable resources to finding names for these cryptonyms. The CIA obtained copies of 437 signals, calculated to be around 8 percent of the total messages exchanged, in which 55 separate sources are indicated. Regrettably, there was minimal internal evidence to suggest the identities of the sources, for the intelligence conveyed was of an extraordinarily diverse nature. Statistically, the 437 texts were considered sufficiently large to make some deductions, the most important of which was that LUCY's four key sources had been responsible for 42.5 percent of the radio traffic passing from Switzerland to Moscow. After lengthy study, the CIA positively identified 15 of the cryptonyms and put possible names to a further 16, leaving 24 unaccounted for. Nor was this the complete picture, for there were certainly people on the periphery of the Rote Drei who had never merited a mention in a signal to Moscow. Of the 332 texts traced to Rado, WERTHER had appeared in 20 percent, making him by far the most important and productive source, with TEDDY at 10 percent and OLGA and ANNA trailing in at 8 and 3.5 percent, respectively.

The CIA concluded that the speed with which the German data consistently reached Switzerland meant that the original German sources must have had access to some official communications channel. Shortly before he died, Rössler hinted to a friend that **Hans Oster** and **Hans Bernd Gisevius**, two well-known anti-Nazi conspirators, had been his sources, suggesting that they had misused the Abwehr's internal channels for their own purposes.

ROTE KAPELLE. The name ("Red Orchestra") given to a **GRU** network uncovered by the **Abwehr** in Brussels in 1941. It was headed by **Leopold Trepper**, an experienced GRU officer who had lived in France and Palestine before his assignment to build a network in western Europe. On the night of 12/13 December 1941 the Abwehr, guided by radio direction-finders, raided 101 rue des Attrebates in the Etterbeck district of Brussels and arrested an illicit wireless operator who gave his name as de Smets. In fact, de Smets was Lt. **Anton Danilov** of the GRU, who had been posted to Paris as an assistant military attaché in 1938 and had subsequently worked in that capacity in Vichy. In mid-1941, he had moved to Brussels to work for **Viktor Guryevitch** as a communications expert.

Danilov had been transmitting early in the morning as the Germans burst into the house and, in a fierce struggle, he was injured and overcome. A few hours later, his controller, Trepper, who happened to be visiting Brussels, called at the house and was questioned by the Germans, but he was sufficiently well equipped with authentic Todt Organization permits to bluff his way out of a potentially very awkward situation. Alerted to Danilov's arrest, Trepper succeeded in warning Guryevitch of what had happened, and he promptly fled to Paris, but **Mikhail Makarov** was not so lucky. He also called at the house on the day of Danilov's arrest and was taken into custody.

Once the Germans had solved **Johann Wenzel**'s ciphers, they were able to backtrack, and the Abwehr's principal cryptographer, Dr. Wilhelm Vauck, succeeded in decrypting around 200 of the Rote Kapelle's signals that had been intercepted and recorded. On 15 July 1942, Vauck tackled a message from the DIREKTOR, Moscow, dated 10 October 1941 and addressed to a certain KENT, one of several texts that disclosed data of the highest significance to the counterespionage investigators:

KL 3 DE RTX 1010-1725 WDS GBT FROM DIREKTOR TO KENT PERSONAL:

Proceed immediately Berlin three addresses indicated and determine causes failure radio connections. If interruptions recur take over broadcasts. Work three Berlin groups and transmission information top priority. Addresses: Neuwestend, Altenburger allee 19, third right; Coro Charlottenburg, Frederikstrasse 26a second left, Wolf-Friedenau, Kaiserstrasse 18 fourth left. Bauer. Call name here "Eulenspiegel"

Password: "Direktor." Report before 20 October. New plan repeat new
in force for three stations GBT ARi KLS RTX.

It did not take the **Gestapo** long to establish the identities of the
occupants of these three suspect addresses, who were placed under
surveillance. They were Harro Schulze-Boysen of the Air Ministry;
Arvid von Harnack, a respected academic; and Adam Kuckhoff, a
film producer. Another of these compromising messages, decoded by
Vauck, referred to Saalestrasse 36, the Berlin address of a young
woman named Ilse who was also of some importance. If the Germans
had any doubts about her identity, the grotesque indiscretion that had
compromised so many agents was compounded by a signal dated 28
August 1941, decrypted retrospectively, which made it clear that Ilse
was her true name: "An important agent known as ILSE will in the future be designated under the cover name ALTE."

Gestapo inquiries showed Ilse Stoebe to be working for Theodor
Wolff at the German Foreign Ministry; before the war, she had been
a correspondent for various Swiss newspapers. She was arrested by
the Gestapo in Hamburg, and under interrogation she revealed that
she had been the mistress of Rudolf Herrnstadt, a notorious *Berliner
Tageblatt* journalist who had **defected** to Moscow in 1933. Despite
the seniority and sensitivity of her post, Stoebe had kept in touch with
Herrnstadt, who became a senior GRU officer supervising clandestine air drops into Germany, and had even allowed her address to be
given to GRU parachutists as a safe house. Before her execution on
22 December 1942, Stoebe implicated Schulze-Boysen, von Harnack, and Rudolf von Scheliha, a diplomat in the information section
of the German Foreign Ministry. Once Stoebe had named the three,
their entire network amounting to 80 subagents was rounded up and
either hanged or beheaded.

A subsequent **Reichssicherheitshauptamt** investigation concluded that von Harnack and Schulze-Boysen, both Communist activists for many years, had been recruited by the GRU quite recently,
in 1941. They had been given a wireless transmitter by Alexander
Erdberg, of the Soviet Trade Delegation in Berlin before its withdrawal in June 1941, but they never achieved direct contact with
Moscow as intended. In August 1941, Guryevitch had given them another set, but again they failed to establish direct contact and instead
had relied upon couriers to pass messages to the Soviet embassy in

Stockholm and to Wenzel in Brussels. This was the fatal flaw in an otherwise well-organized network, for it led to Wenzel's arrest and the capture of his ciphers.

Certainly the quality of the material reaching Moscow from Berlin was unprecedented, for among the members of the ring were Herbert Gollnow, an Abwehr liaison officer at Oberkommandowehrmacht headquarters responsible for supervising clandestine air operations on the Eastern Front; Lt. Wolfgang Havemann of naval intelligence; and Horst Heilmann, an Abwehr cryptographer who was having an affair with Schulze-Boysen's wife, Libertas. All were interrogated and then hanged at Ploetzensee Prison.

Von Scheliha, a more experienced Soviet agent, suffered the same fate. He had been recruited while serving at the German embassy in Warsaw in 1934 and had been paid for his information through a Swiss bank. As well as being compromised by Stoebe, he was incriminated by Heinrich Koenen, a German Communist who parachuted into Osterode in eastern Prussia in October 1942 with instructions to contact Stoebe. By the time he landed, she was already in the hands of the Gestapo, and when he was arrested on 22 October, he was found carrying a receipt confirming a transfer of $7,500 to von Scheliha's bank account.

The Rote Kapelle's commercial front **Simex** survived the German occupation until November 1942, when raids were mounted simultaneously in both Brussels and Paris. The companies had fallen under suspicion soon after the arrest of **Konstantin Effremov**, an experienced GRU officer and chemical warfare expert who had been operating in western Europe under student cover since about 1936. Under pressure, the Ukrainian had agreed to cooperate with the Abwehr and divulged enough information to compromise Simex in Paris, which had led them to Trepper.

Catching Trepper gave the Germans a tremendous advantage, for he volunteered to help them, apparently motivated by the very justifiable fear that the Soviets would execute his entire family if they learned of his arrest. Not only did Trepper betray **Henri Robinson**, **Leon Grossvogel**, Isadore Springer, and other members of the network, but he also agreed to start transmitting to Moscow as a **double agent**. While the **Sicherheitsdienst (SD)** negotiated with Trepper, they took elaborate steps to prevent the news of his arrest from leaking.

Most of the Rote Kapelle suspects were kept in the isolation cells in a special wing of Fresnes Prison, but Trepper was held separately, in a suite of rooms on the ground floor of the building in the rue des Saussaies that formerly had been the headquarters of the Sûreté. The remainder of the Sonderkommando, a special joint counterintelligence unit, was accommodated on the fifth floor.

Trepper's capture came only a fortnight after the arrest in Marseilles of Guryevitch and his mistress, Margarete Barcza. Unwisely, Guryevitch had opened a branch of Simex in Marseilles after he had fled from **Belgium** following the arrests there, and once Effremov had started to help the enemy, the Simex cover was worse than useless. Guryevitch was escorted to Berlin for interrogation, where he admitted his GRU code name KENT, and in March 1943 agreed to transmit to Moscow from Paris as MARS, under the SD's control.

By Christmas 1942, the Germans had unraveled an extraordinary series of interlocking networks and taken control of most of the senior Soviet personnel. Trepper seemed entirely cooperative and initiated a wireless link with Moscow code-named EIFFEL. He ensured Robinson's arrest and arranged for the entrapment of Grossvogel, together with three others, at the Café de la Paix in Paris. He also denounced Springer and thereby betrayed an entire independent ring based in Lyons.

Trepper's help was of critical importance to the Germans because, through him, they were able to recover the famous Robinson Papers, a virtual archive of Soviet illegal activity in Europe dating back to the 1920s. When Robinson was arrested in December 1942, a search of his hotel room revealed a briefcase hidden under the floorboards, full of documents, forged identity papers, and texts of messages. Among the many branches of the GRU compromised by Robinson was an important wireless transmitter run by Dr. Hersog Sokol for the French Communist Party at his home in Le Rancy, through which Trepper had relayed messages to Moscow via London. Although Polish in origin, Sokol was a physician prominent in the Belgian Communist Party. He and his wife Mariam were arrested on 9 June 1942 and both later died in captivity.

As well as scrutinizing the veritable gold mine of the Robinson Papers and obtaining Trepper's apparently enthusiastic assistance, the Germans also persuaded Effremov to change sides and work as a double agent.

With Winterink, Effremov, and EIFFEL in radio contact with Moscow, and Guryevitch promising to cooperate, the Germans believed they had taken control of much of the GRU's illegal networks in Belgium, France, and the Netherlands and had eliminated the organization's entire branch in Germany, but the situation was actually rather more complicated. In fact, Trepper had succeeded in both winning the confidence of the Germans, who thought he had genuinely switched sides, and also in alerting Moscow Center to his arrest. Similarly Wenzel eluded his German captors in November 1942 and sent a message to the Soviet embassy in London that Effremov was in enemy hands and that his radio was operating under control.

Although Trepper appears to have betrayed a large number of his subordinates to the enemy, he kept a single contact at liberty and used this line of communication to keep Moscow informed of developments. The GRU responded by protecting their star agent and participating in a complicated triple game of wireless **deception**, a *funkspiel* that may have been part of a sophisticated contingency plan but certainly one that was maintained until Trepper's escape from German captivity in September 1943.

Trepper was later to insist that his escape had been prompted by his discovery that the Abwehr had closed down a previously unknown transmitter run by the French Communist Party near Lyons and recovered a large quantity of backtraffic that was to be scrutinized by the celebrated Dr. Vauck. Trepper feared that the Sonderkommando was on the point of learning how he had duped his captors. Accordingly, he eluded his escort while under guard in the center of Paris and went into hiding for the rest of the war. Intriguingly, Trepper wrote four letters to the Sonderkommando, in which he pretended to have been the victim of an abduction, and reassured Heinz Paulsen, a senior SD officer, that Moscow remained ignorant of the funkspiel.

Notwithstanding Trepper's escape, and despite the Abwehr's confidence that the Rote Kapelle had been eliminated, the network continued to function, albeit under German supervision. Effremov, for example, ran the PASCAL radio link from Breendonck Prison until April 1944 when he was moved to a house at 63 rue de Courcelles, where Guryevitch was being held.

The German villa in Neuilly also accommodated various other captured GRU personnel. Trepper stayed there until his escape in September 1943, and his colleagues there included his assistant,

Hillel Katz, whom he had betrayed almost as soon as he was arrested. Like Trepper, Katz was a Polish Jew and had been a member of the Communist Party in Palestine. He was an important figure in the Rote Kapelle, as he had acted as Trepper's link with Grossvogel, Simex, and Robinson. He, too, willingly cooperated with the Germans, as did Otto Schumacher, a German who had fought for the Republicans during the Spanish Civil War. It had been at Schumacher's house in Laeken that Wenzel had been arrested in June 1942, and from that moment he had been a marked man. He had promptly fled to Lyons where he had joined Springer, but after Trepper's arrest, he had been moved to Paris where he had been caught early in 1943.

Robinson and Grossvogel died in German captivity, as did Springer and Schumacher. According to the most recent estimates, 217 arrests were made in connection with the Rote Kapelle investigation, of whom 143 committed suicide, died in captivity, or were executed.

At the end of the war, Allied investigators seized many of the German records of the Rote Kapelle investigation, and in later years a determined effort was made to piece together the fragments of the story. Guryevitch and Trepper maintained their silence for many years, but some of the Germans who had supervised the funkspiel were traced and interrogated. It became clear that in July 1942, when the scale of the Soviet network had emerged, a Sonderkommando had been formed under the leadership of an SD officer, Karl Giering. Giering had died of cancer in a Paris hospital in 1943, and his chief, Karl Boemelburg, died after an accident in Germany in December 1946, but there were others to be found. The first arrests, of Danilov and Makarov in November 1941 in Etterbeek, had been made by Capt. Henry Piepe of the Ghent branch of the Abwehr IIIF. Piepe had also been responsible for catching Wenzel and was later transferred to the Sonderkommando in Paris. Much later, when he had become a businessman in Hamburg, he agreed to describe Trepper's interrogation to the Central Intelligence Agency (CIA).

Piepe's version of events was largely confirmed by Wilhelm Berg, who had been Trepper's escort when he had slipped away, but the British suspected that the former Kriminalinspektor who had served as Joachim von Ribbentrop's bodyguard in Moscow may have fallen under the influence of the Soviets and might even have been recruited by Trepper (a charge he denied). Other useful SD sources were Horst Kopkow, who was interrogated in 1947, and Heinrich Reiser, a former prisoner of war in Great Britain during World War I who had been Giering's deputy. Obersturmbannführer Reiser was transferred from the Paris Sonderkommando to a Gestapo job in Karlsruhe during the summer of 1943, following the arrival of Paulsen and later wrote a book about the Rote Kapelle. He retired to Stuttgart and was interviewed.

Paulsen, who called himself Pannwitz, was posted to Paris in March 1943 following his investigation into the assassination of **Reinhard Heydrich** in Prague. Paulsen took charge of the Sonderkommando from Giering, who was in failing health. He remained in Paris until 16 August 1944 when he withdrew with Guryevitch and the rest of the Sonderkommando to Hornberg in the Black Forest and then to Würzburg in the Tauber Valley, where they burned what remained of their records. In May 1945 he and Guryevitch, who had moved into a chalet near Bludenz in Austria, surrendered to the local French occupation troops and were returned to Paris. On 7 June 1945, they were flown to Moscow on Stalin's personal plane, interrogated by the head of **Smersh**, the notorious Viktor S. Abakumov, and imprisoned.

Paulsen was sentenced to 25 years' imprisonment but was released in 1954 to return to Stuttgart, where he became a banker. He remarked to the CIA that the Germans succeeded not only in locating and liquidating the clandestine networks in Brussels, Berlin, Amsterdam, and Paris but also in doubling the Soviet agents, and by virtue of the funkspiel in "intoxicating the Soviets with false information." However, this was sharply contradicted by Trepper, who maintained that it was the Germans who were the victims of an elaborate deception campaign. He insists that he betrayed no one and that the Center made perfect use of the Great Game to ask, constantly, for more military information. After February 1943, the Germans were forced to give Moscow information that a normally functioning network, however powerful, would have had trouble obtaining.

ROVER. MI5 code name for a Polish naval officer and **double agent** who reached Great Britain in May 1944. His wireless transmitter remained active until the end of hostilities.

ROYAL VICTORIA PATRIOTIC SCHOOL (RVPS). MI5's refugee screening center on Wandsworth Common in South London was the reception center for civilian personnel claiming to have escaped from enemy-occupied territory. Mixed among them were numerous Nazi spies, who underwent interviews and, if expected because of advance information contained in ISOS, were challenged and then transferred to **Camp 020** for detailed interrogation. Most refugees understood the need to exercise caution, and the procedures could be completed in two days in cases where there were no suspicions aroused.

RUSER, HANS. A German journalist connected to the **Abwehr** in **Lisbon** since 1937, Dr. Hans Ruser **defected** to the British **Secret Intelligence Service (MI6)** in April 1942 on condition his mother could travel to the United States. The arrangements were negotiated by Col. Pan, the **Polish intelligence** representative in Portugal, with whom he was in contact following a threat that he might be called up for military service, and the deal was agreed to by **MI5**. However, ISOS revealed that Ruser was to be abducted by the Abwehr in **Madrid**, so MI6 exfiltrated him before he could compromise ARTIST, who was known to him. Upon his arrival in Great Britain, Ruser was incarcerated at **Camp 020**.

RUTLAND, FREDERICK. Known as "Rutland of Jutland" because of his heroic role in the World War I sea battle, Frederick Rutland was an expert on aircraft carriers and the development of undercarriages and shipborne airplane-recovery systems. He worked in Japan as a consultant to Mitsubishi and later moved to California, where he came under suspicion of continuing to maintain contact with the Japanese Navy. Rutland approached the British embassy in Washington, D.C., with an offer to act as a **double agent**. However, when he returned to London in December 1941, he was detained, but was released without charge in September 1943. He committed suicide in January 1949.

– S –

SAVAGES. The **Security Intelligence Middle East (SIME)** code name for a group of three **double agents** run by James Robertson's

Special Section in Egypt. The trio landed in Cyprus with a transmitter in July 1943, having sailed from Piraeus in a caique. SAVAGE I was the radio operator, a Greek Cypriot and former soldier in the Greek Army. After he was transferred to **Cairo**, he **notionally** obtained a job with the British General Headquarters, Middle East, which supposedly gave him access to important information. SAVAGE II was a Greek Cypriot doctor, recently married to SAVAGE III, a Greek lady who was also a doctor in Athens. All three had wanted to escape from Greece, but because they failed to be entirely candid upon their capture, SAVAGE II and his wife were interned until the end of hostilities, while SAVAGE I, who had been the best man at their wedding, remained at liberty under SIME's control.

SCHALBURG, VERA VON. Also known as Vera Erikson, Vera von Schalburg was arrested soon after she had arrived in Scotland, having rowed ashore at Portgordon from a Luftwaffe amphibious aircraft at the end of September 1940. She was an **Abwehr** agent, of Danish extraction, accompanied by **Karl Drücke** and **Werner Wälti**, but unlike them was never prosecuted and thus was saved from the gallows. She was held at Holloway Prison until the end of hostilities, and under interrogation at Aylesbury, she claimed to have acted as a Soviet spy in the past and admitted that her brother was a leading figure in the Danish Nazi Party.

SCHELLENBERG, WALTER. A participant in the **Venlo** incident in November 1939, Walter Schellenberg rose to the top of the **Sicherheitsdienst** and after the war was interrogated at length by the British at **Camp 020**. He was imprisoned briefly for war crimes, but was given early release and died in Italy after the publication of his autobiography, *The Schellenberg Memoirs.*

SCHMIDT, WULF. A Dane from Abenra in the German territory of Schleswig-Holstein, Wulf Schmidt parachuted into Cambridgeshire on the night of 19/20 September 1940 and was turned at **Camp 020** into an **MI5 double agent** code-named TATE.

Recruited by the **Abwehr** in 1939 after his return from working overseas, first as general manager on a cattle ranch in Argentina and then growing bananas for a fruit company in the Cameroons, Schmidt served in the Danish Army, stationed in Copenhagen. He had then volunteered for what he had believed would be a short stay in England. He spoke good English, albeit with a heavy accent, and his task was to carry out reconnaissance prior to a German invasion. Although he was to parachute in solo, he was actually one of several agents dropped into England during September 1940. Of the others, **Gósta Caroli**, a Swede by birth who had made two short visits to the Birmingham area just before the outbreak of hostilities, was known to him because they had been trained in Hamburg together, and they had arranged to meet in England.

Schmidt was flown to Cambridgeshire by an ace Luftwaffe pilot, Capt. Karl Gartenfeld, and was dropped over the Royal Air Force aerodrome at Oakington, close to the village of Willingham. He spent just a few short hours at liberty before he was challenged by a member of the local Home Guard in Willingham soon after he had completed his breakfast in a café. When he was searched, Schmidt was found to be carrying £132, $160, a genuine Danish passport in the name of Wulf Schmidt, and a forged British identity card bearing the details of "Harry Williamson" with an address in London that had been suggested to the Abwehr by another of MI5's double agents, **Arthur Owens**.

Under interrogation, Schmidt initially stuck rigidly to his cover story, but when MI5 demonstrated that Caroli had been in custody since his arrival and had already made a very full confession, Schmidt cracked. Finally, after a session with MI5's psychiatrist, Dr. Harold Dearden, Schmidt agreed to cooperate and accompanied his captors back to Willingham, where he recovered his parachute and radio from their hiding places. At midnight on 16 October, he transmitted his callsign, DFH, and reported to Hamburg, under the supervision of MI5's wireless expert, Ronnie Reed, that he had found lodgings near Barnet. In reality, he had been installed with Maj. **T. A. Robertson** and his wife at Roundbush House, Radlett.

MI5 was persuaded to accept Schmidt as a double agent by the transparent candor of his initial statement in which he identified a dance band pianist named Pierce as a key member of an existing Abwehr circuit whose name had been given to Schmidt in Hamburg in case of emergencies. In reality, the pianist was known to MI5 as RAINBOW and had been operating under Robertson's guidance since February. This item provided MI5 with useful confirmation that

Schmidt, now dubbed TATE (because of his resemblance to music hall comedian Harry Tate), was telling the truth and that the Abwehr continued to believe RAINBOW was an authentic source.

While claiming to have found work on a farm, Schmidt acquired a **notional** girlfriend named Mary, who often stayed with him on weekends and was a cipher clerk based at the Admiralty. In November 1942, she was supposedly loaned by the Admiralty to the U.S. Naval Mission and introduced Schmidt to British and American naval officers who, toward the end of 1942, carelessly left classified documents for him to read.

Schmidt also played a role in the **deception** campaign to cover the **D-Day** landings and was able to report Gen. Dwight D. Eisenhower's arrival in England in January 1944 to take up his appointment as Supreme Allied Commander even before the news had been officially released. His farm in Radlett was too far from the coast to make any useful observations, so Schmidt's employer sent him to spend the summer on a friend's farm near Wye in Kent. From this location, he monitored troop movements and participated in STARKEY, a deception mounted during the summer of 1943 designed to persuade the Germans of an imminent attack in the Pas-de-Calais region so as to reduce the pressure on the hard-fought Russian Front. As a precaution, a special landline from London was constructed to the notional remote transmitting site in Kent so that, if the Germans ever decided to use direction-finding equipment to check on the source of Schmidt's transmissions, it would confirm his location in the southeast. In March 1944, Schmidt supported the D-Day cover plan code-named **FORTITUDE NORTH**, intended to convey the impression that the forthcoming Allied assault on Europe would take place in Scandinavia. Schmidt reported that, by chance, he had learned that the British minister in **Stockholm**, Victor Mallett, had been brought home to London for urgent consultations with the Foreign Office.

After the success of D-Day, Schmidt was tasked by the Germans to collect data on the time and location of V-1 explosions. This information was vital for correcting the aim of the weapon system, and it was Whitehall's intention to suggest to the enemy that many of the rockets were overflying the capital, or at least impacting north of the center, so the Germans would shorten the range. On 21 September 1944, Schmidt passed a significant milestone, the transmission of his

1,000th signal. His message read: "On the occasion of this, my 1,000th message, I beg to ask you to convey to our Führer my humble greetings and ardent wishes for a speedy victorious termination of the war." Schmidt maintained contact with Hamburg until the very last days of the war and was decorated with the Iron Cross.

SCOOT. MI6 code name for **Dusan Popov**.

SCOTLAND, ALEXANDER. An **MI9** interrogator fluent in German who had served in the kaiser's forces in German South-West Africa before World War II. Based at the **London Cage** in Kensington Palace Gardens, Scotland's fluency in the language and familiarity with Wehrmacht terms led some captives to believe he was really a turncoat.

SCOUT. MI6 **code name** for **Dusan Popov**.

SCRUFFY. **MI5** code name for **double agent Alphons Timmerman**, a **Belgian** seaman run deliberately badly between September and November 1941 to demonstrate to the **Abwehr** that **MI5** had no experience controlling enemy agents.

SEBOLD, WILLIAM. A 40-year-old married engineer working for the Consolidated Aircraft Corporation in San Diego, William Sebold returned from a visit to his family in his native Germany, his first for 15 years, and in 1941 revealed to the **Federal Bureau of Investigation (FBI)** that he had been approached to spy for the Nazis. He had succumbed to an implied threat from officials purporting to be from the **Gestapo** and, for the sake of his mother, two brothers, and sister in Mülheim, Sebold reluctantly had agreed to be signed on by the Hamburg *Abstelle* in June 1939 with the code name TRAMP. However, dismayed by this episode, which occurred so soon after he had disembarked from the SS *Deutschland*, and the theft of his passport, Sebold had alerted the American Consulate in Cologne of his predicament and had been advised by the vice consul, Dale W. Maher, to pretend to cooperate with the Nazis. Thereafter Sebold underwent an intensive training course with the intention of placing him in charge of a transmitter so a clandestine radio channel could be opened between the East Coast and the Abwehr's radio station at Hamburg-Wohldorf. Meanwhile, Maher, conscious that his communications might be insecure, traveled to **Lisbon** to alert the State Department and provided the foundation for an FBI file under the cover name "S. T. Jenkins."

Once safely back in the United States in February 1941, having traveled aboard the SS *Washington* from Genoa on a new passport identifying him as Harry Sawyer, Sebold was contacted by Special Agent William G. Friedemann and made a detailed statement, explaining that he had fought for the kaiser during World War I and had been wounded in the Battle of the Somme. After the war, he had moved to America, changed his name from Wilhelm G. Debowski, and become a naturalized citizen and loyal American. He had agreed to follow the Abwehr's instructions and contact four other Abwehr agents, for whom he carrying a **microdot** questionnaire and was to provide a shortwave wireless link to speed their communications with Hamburg. This was the first time anyone at the FBI had encountered a microdot, which was an ingenious solution, patented in 1938 by Zeiss, to the problem of carrying potentially incriminating documents and messages.

Those Abwehr agents named, on a slip of onion-skin paper, were **Lily Stein**, an Austrian model of Jewish descent, living on East 54th Street in Manhattan; Everett Roeder of Merrick, Long Island; **Frederick R. Duquesne** of West 76th Street; and an engineer, **Herman Lang**. To aid communications, Sebold was told how to contact a courier, Erwin Siegler, a butcher on the United States Lines vessel SS *Manhattan*, and was given postal addresses in Shanghai, São Paulo, and Portugal.

Sebold also disclosed the hand cipher with which he had been entrusted by the Abwehr, which was then passed for cryptographic examination by Paul A. Napier, the head of the cryptology section of the Bureau's technical laboratory. This procedure revealed that the Germans relied on a relatively simple system known as single columnar transposition, which depended on a grid supplying alternative letters to encipher the message. The system's security lay in the choice of letters in the grid, which were taken from a particular page of a particular book. These could be changed, apparently randomly, with the agent inserting the "indicator" or page number in a prearranged position in the body of the message. The Abwehr's system was ingenious and superficially offered tremendous security, with the indicator being the sum of three figures: the number of the month and the number of the day of the month added to a permanent number assigned to a particular agent. Thus agent 21, enciphering on 5 February, would rely on page 28 of his particular novel. To convey this knowledge to the receiving station in Germany, the agent turned to the relevant page, took the last three letters on the page and, having reversed them, transmitted them as a call sign.

Without a copy of the selected book and knowledge of the indicator, the cipher was considered highly secure, but to increase its effectiveness, the Abwehr had added a refinement. Instead of choosing easily available classics, the Abwehr opted for the Albatross series of British and American classics, which were pirated editions and therefore generally unavailable in countries covered by international copyright agreements, including Great Britain and the United States. The flaw, spotted by Napier, was that each Albatross copy included on the dust jacket a list of the other titles in the series, and he simply acquired all of them from bookshops in neutral countries. In Sebold's case, the book was Rachel Field's *All This and Heaven Too*, and the indicator was concealed in the date of each message. Thus equipped, the Bureau was able to read almost all of the Abwehr's hand ciphers.

The FBI proceeded to exploit Sebold's leads and placed his contacts under surveillance. Using money provided by the Abwehr through Chase Manhattan Bank, a cottage was purchased in Centerport, Long Island, and a powerful shortwave transmitter installed, together with two special agents, James C. Ellsworth, who spoke fluent German, and Maurice H. Price, who held an amateur radio license. In May 1941, using the call sign CQDXVW2, and after several false starts, contact was established with AOR, the Abwehr's call sign in Hamburg. It was this channel that became Duquesne's preferred method of sending urgent messages to Germany, instead of through the accommodation addresses in Portugal and **Brazil**, although he continued to rely on a large team of transatlantic steamship couriers for bulky items that needed delivery to Hamburg.

Sebold also rented a three-room office, Suite 629 in the Knickerbocker Building at 152 West 42nd Street, under the name of the Diesel Research Company, but the FBI wired the room for sound and installed a two-way mirror on a wall-mounted medicine cabinet constructed by Special Agent Raymond F. Newkirk, behind which a 16mm movie camera, supervised by Special Agent Richard L. Johnson, filmed every visitor. Every word was recorded and a team of special agents fluent in German, consisting of Friedemann, Jim Kirkland, Tom Spencer, and Joseph T. Fellner, transcribed the conversations. Meanwhile, surveillance on the street outside was conducted by Special Agent Downey Rice, working from inside a parked truck.

While Sebold came to know most of the members of the ring, he was occasionally surprised by an unheralded arrival. On one occasion, an agent identifying himself as Leo Waalen, a shipyard painter from Yorkville, turned up unexpectedly and asked Sebold to use his microphotography equipment to turn a lengthy document into a microdot. Waalen was promptly placed under surveillance and eventually was sentenced to 12 years' imprisonment.

The only really anxious moment during the entire operation occurred when one of the couriers, Paul Fehse, one of the *Manhattan*'s cooks, was heard to express some doubts about Sebold and state his intention to return to Berlin to check up on him. To prevent him from doing so, the FBI promptly arrested Fehse, who was considered a senior figure in the network, and charged him under the Federal Registration Act, the statute requiring all foreign agents to declare their role. This effectively was a holding charge that allowed the Bureau to detain Fehse and neutralize him until it was ready to bring the more serious charges of espionage. Fehse pleaded guilty to the lesser charge and was sentenced to a year and a day in prison. It was only later, after Duquesne's arrest, that he was tried on the espionage charges, convicted, and sentenced to 15 years' imprisonment. The only other member of the spy ring to be taken into custody early was Bertram W. Zenzinger, a dental student living in Topanga Canyon, California, who was also charged with a violation of the Registration Act in April 1941.

SECRET INTELLIGENCE SERVICE (MI6). Known throughout the war by the cover military intelligence designation MI6, the Secret Intelligence Service commenced wartime operations at a distinct disadvantage because its principal overseas stations—in Paris, Brussels, Warsaw, Vienna, Belgrade, Berlin, Budapest, Bucharest, Athens,

Tallinn, Riga, and The Hague—had not organized stay-behind networks in anticipation of a Nazi occupation, and their primary role had been one of liaison with their hosts. Caught unawares by the speed with which the Nazis took control of Europe from the Pyrenees to the Norwegian Arctic, MI6 was left virtually devoid of assets on the Continent. It was also handicapped by the loss of **Sigismund Best** and Maj. **Richard Stevens**, who were abducted by the **Sicherheitsdienst** in November 1939 at **Venlo**, and a very comprehensive understanding of MI6's internal structure supplied to the Germans by an Australian MI6 officer, **C. H. Ellis**.

Headed by Col. **Stewart Menzies**, who succeeded Adm. Sir **Hugh Sinclair** upon his death in November 1939, MI6 reestablished its reputation by exercising control over the signals intelligence product of the **Government Code and Cypher School**, which initially exploited the **Abwehr**'s hand ciphers to solve the keys to some **Enigma** ciphers. MI6's largest branch, **Section V**, was dedicated to counterintelligence analysis of data gleaned from the Abwehr's communications channels, code-named ISK and ISOS. Close cooperation with the **Office of Strategic Services** led to the establishment of **X-2**, which ran **double agents** jointly and developed teams to roll up enemy stay-behind networks.

MI6's overseas organization was based on stations operating under **Passport Control Office** cover in the neutral capitals of **Bern**, **Lisbon**, **Madrid**, and **Stockholm**, with regional headquarters in **Cairo** and Delhi, under **Inter-Services Liaison Department (ISLD)** cover. The individual stations were controlled by regional "G" officers who passed on requests from Requirement Sections covering the army, navy, air, economic, and counterintelligence liaison units and supplied the results to Production Sections, which analyzed the material and sanitized it for distribution.

Exploiting the advantage of providing sanctuary, accommodations, and communications for its **Belgian**, **Dutch**, Estonian, **French**, **Czech**, **Polish**, Greek, Yugoslav, and **Norwegian** counterparts, and maintaining links to Spanish, Austrian, Hungarian, Bulgarian, Swedish, and Italian émigré opposition groups, MI6 adopted the role of sponsor in western Europe, enabling liaison services to run their own individual operations in enemy-occupied territory. Accordingly, MI6 developed a profitable relationship with the Free French **Bureau**

Central de Renseignements et d'Action and established the **AL-LIANCE** network, which survived until September 1943. Of MI6's ventures in occupied France, only JADE/AMICOL survived beyond June 1944. Unlike **Special Operations Executive (SOE)**, which employed a staff of around 13,200 and nearly 50 training schools, MI6 ran a single radio school in Sloane Square, a naval unit on the Helford River in Cornwall and on Shetland, and a discreet sanatorium at Tempsford Hall.

Relatively few clandestine MI6 missions were mounted in Europe, apart from in Greece and in the Balkans where liaison personnel were attached to British Military Missions sent to establish contact with indigenous resistance organizations. Operating after the liberation of the heel of Italy from a station headed by John Ennals, ISLD sent some British personnel into Axis-occupied territory, but the attrition rate from enemy action and local banditry was a significant deterrent. Bill Stuart, attached to SOE's TYPICAL mission, was killed in an air raid on Tito's headquarters in May 1943 and others were murdered for the money belt of gold sovereigns they were known to carry.

MI6's apparent reluctance to infiltrate agents into enemy-occupied territory was a consequence partly of the relative ease with which better information could be obtained through signals intelligence, but also because of the danger of hostile penetration. Such MI6 networks as existed in France and Holland occasionally encountered disastrously insecure **circuits** run by SOE, and the risk of contamination was considerable. Therefore, MI6 preferred to concentrate on counterintelligence activities based from stations in neutral countries while giving encouragement to others willing to act as surrogates. Put simply, **Bletchley Park** was a far more accurate and reliable source of intelligence than the teams infiltrated at heavy cost by agencies not indoctrinated into ULTRA. For example, when information about Nazi secret weapons became a priority, MI6 coordinated the various strands of air reconnaissance, diplomatic rumor, refugee reports, and **defector** claims to produce a comprehensive and accurate assessment of the threat that, when overlaid with signals intelligence, enabled the **Crossbow** Committee to make the appropriate recommendations. Similarly, MI6's Eric Welsh collated hints of atomic research from Germany and Norway, but apart from exfiltrating key witnesses such as Danish physicist Niels Bohr and Prof. Leif Tronstad from the

Norwegian heavy water plant at Vermork, MI6 left actual intervention to others, principally SOE.

MI6's posture in the Far East, in the absence of any existing Allied intelligence structures in French Indochina or the Dutch East Indies was rather more proactive, with ISLD's Colin Tooke cooperating closely with Colin Mackenzie, in charge of SOE's Force 136, to land parties onto Malayan beaches and drop parachutists into Burma. The impressive result was 90 missions dispatched, with 48 radio networks established in Japanese-held territory.

SECTION D. Known as the "Sabotage Service" in the higher echelons of Whitehall, Section D, as it was known to the cognoscenti, was run by a local British businessman, Julius Hanau. He headed a group of hand-picked saboteurs who, operating under commercial or journalistic cover, attempted to recruit Yugoslavs who were sympathetic to the Allied cause. The second covert structure was an intelligence-gathering group headed by Clement Hope, an experienced **Secret Intelligence Service** officer who acted as the **passport control officer** attached to the British legation in Belgrade.

SECTION V. Headed by a former officer in the Indian police, Maj. Felix Cowgill, Section V developed from a small prewar unit consisting of Cowgill, Col. Valentine Vivian, and a clerk into a large global network of specially cleared personnel with access to the extremely sensitive cryptographic source code-named ISK and ISOS. Cowgill was obliged to endure considerable criticism for his reluctance to share this vulnerable material with others, but he maintained strict security at his organization's headquarters at Glenalmond and Praewood, two large properties on Lord Verulam's estate in Hertfordshire.

Structured on geographical subdivisions, Section V processed intercepts, stored references to individuals and operations on cards, and created a mammoth index on which it was possible to cross-reference personalities and agent instructions. When leads needed to be pursued locally, the appropriate instructions were sent to a specially indoctrinated Section V officer posted to the relevant **Secret Intelligence Service** station who fully understood the source and the need to protect it. Ultimately Section V absorbed personnel from the **Radio Security Service**, the specialists at Barnet who had first broken the Abwehr hand ciphers, and it became a separate, secret compartment within an already highly secure organization, so when staff moved up to central London in 1943, it was accommodated in a different building, in Ryder Street, St. James's, from the rest of MI6's headquarters. By the end of the war, Section V had opened files on 3,575 enemy agents, of whom 675 were arrested.

SECURITY EXECUTIVE. The Home Defence Security Executive was created in June 1940 under the chairmanship of Lord Swinton to supervise the activities of **MI5**. Swinton was replaced in June 1942 by Duff Cooper. The deputy chairman was Sir Joseph Ball, and the other members were **Jasper Harker** from MI5, Valentine Vivian from the **Secret Intelligence Service**, Col. Roger Reynolds from the War Office, Sir Alan Hunter from the War Office's prisoner-of-war department, **Desmond Morton** from the prime minister's office at Downing Street, Arthur Rucker from the Ministry of Health, Arthur Hutchinson from the Home Office, trade union leader Alf Wall, Malcolm Frost from the BBC, and Isaac Foot, a former Liberal member of Parliament. The Security Executive was served by two secretaries, William Armstrong from the Board of Education and barrister Kenneth Diplock.

SECURITY INTELLIGENCE MIDDLE EAST (SIME). The regional **MI5** branch in the Middle East created in December 1939, SIME was represented in Aden, Palestine, Iraq, Turkey, and Syria by locally based **defence security officers**. Based in **Cairo**'s Grey Pillars compound and headed by a tank officer, Raymund J. Maunsell, SIME conducted counterespionage investigations and, through a Special Section headed by James Robertson, ran counterintelligence operations against the Axis in tandem with **"A" Force**. SIME's greatest achievements included CHEESE and the SAVAGES in Egypt; the PESSIMISTS, SMOOTH, CRUDE, and QUICKSILVER in Syria; KISS in Iraq; and DOLEFUL in Turkey.

SECURITY SERVICE. *See* MI5.

SEDLACEK, KAREL. The Czech military intelligence representative in Zurich on the outbreak of war, Karel Sedlacek traveled to England

and was later considered a candidate for the **GRU** agent code-named BARON in the 1941 VENONA traffic. Sedlacek's superior in London, Col. **Frantisek Moravec**, recalled in his memoirs Sedlacek's success:

> Reports arrived almost daily, giving details of men and material. We passed on these reports to the British, producing almost daily changes in the huge War Office maps on which the deployments of the German forces were plotted. The information was mainly rather technical data, such as movements of armies and divisions, changes in command, transportation and supply problems, innovation in equipment, but there were also comments and forecasts concerning the German invasion of the West. (Moravec, *Master of Spies*)

Much of Sedlacek's information is believed to have come from **Rudolf Rössler**. After the war, Sedlacek was appointed the Czech military attaché in **Bern**, and recruited Rössler as his agent.

SERGUEIEV, LILY. Code-named TREASURE by **MI5**, Lily Sergueiev was an **Abwehr** agent of Russian extraction, recruited in Paris by Émile Kliemann. She reached **Madrid** in June 1943, where she was interviewed by **Section V**'s Kenneth Benton, and reached London, via **Gibraltar**, in October. Sergueiev proved to be a volatile **double agent**, but from January 1944 maintained wireless contact with her Abwehr controllers and became a useful conduit for the **D-Day deception** campaign. Although she subsequently joined the French Army and was posted to Paris after the liberation, her radio channel continued to transmit for a further five months, operated by the **Radio Security Service**.

SERRE. French code name for André Schurmann, an **Abwehr** recruiter and merchant marine radio operator employed by the Germans in Le Havre since November 1941. He became a **double agent** in December 1944 and was code-named CAMOUFLAGE.

SERVICE DE RENSEIGNEMENTS (SR). The prewar foreign intelligence branch of the French Deuxieme Bureau, headed by Col. **Louis Rivet**, at 2bis avenue de Tourville, the Service de Renseignements was officially closed but continued to operate at Uzès, in the unoccupied zone, until November 1942 when it was forced to evacuate to **Algiers**. In November 1943 the SR was disbanded, and some of its personnel absorbed by Gen. Charles de Gaulle's Free French organization, the **Direction Générale de Services Speciaux**.

SERVIZIO DI INFORMAZIONE MILITARE (SIM). The principal Italian military intelligence agency, the SIM acquired an impressive reputation for running sophisticated espionage networks across the Balkans and the Middle East. Headed by Gen. Giacomo Carboni, who was replaced in November 1940 by his deputy, Gen. Caesar Amé, the SIM employed less than 1,000 personnel but had become proficient before the war at penetrating foreign diplomatic missions in Rome, including the British embassy, and establishing a sophisticated cryptographic center based at the Forte Bravetta, outside Rome. The SIM read large quantities of British, French, Greek, Turkish, and Yugoslav diplomatic cipher traffic and developed a sabotage and assassination unit that proved effective in Croatia, Macedonia, Palestine, and Ethiopia. Gen. Amé was dismissed by Marshal Badoglio in August 1943 and replaced by Carboni, who two months later was obliged to cooperate with the Allies. *See also* ITALIAN INTELLIGENCE.

SERVIZIO DI INFORMAZIONE SEGRETE (SIS). The Italian navy's intelligence branch, headed until May 1941 by Adm. Giuseppe Lombardo, the SIS concentrated on the collection of tactical information concerning France and Yugoslavia and was heavily reliant on signals intelligence. The SIS also achieved considerable success against British hand ciphers. Lombardo was succeeded by Adm. Franco Maugeri. *See also* ITALIAN INTELLIGENCE.

SERVIZIO DI INFORMAZIONI AERONAUTICHE (SIA). The intelligence branch of the Italian air force, the SIA was headed by Gen. Virgilio Saggeliotti, who was restricted to security operations to protect airfields and research of foreign technical developments. *See also* ITALIAN INTELLIGENCE.

SHADOW. MI5 code name for a **double agent**.

SHARK. Government Communications Headquarters code name for Kriegsmarine U-boat wireless traffic enciphered on a modified, four-rotor **Enigma** machine.

SHEEHAN, OLIVE. Arrested in 1942 after she had been identified as a source working for **Douglas Springhall**, Olive Sheehan was employed by the Air Ministry in London and supplied him with classified information concerning the development of jet engines. She was sentenced to three years' imprisonment.

SHEPHERD. MI5 code name for a Frenchman who was a **double agent** between March 1944 and May 1945.

SICHERHEITSDIENST (SD). Created in 1932 under the leadership of **Reinhard Heydrich** and located in a villa at Zuccaliststrasse 4 in Berlin, the SD consisted of three branches: I, administration; II, domestic intelligence; and III, foreign intelligence.

Originally the Nazi Party's own security apparatus, the SD was absorbed into the **Reichssicherheitshauptamt** in September 1939. Nevertheless, the SD worked independently of, but in parallel to, the **Abwehr**. The SD organization in Turkey acquired some notoriety when the local representative, Ludwig Moyszich, succeeded in recruiting the British ambassador's valet as an agent code-named CIC-ERO. *See also* GERMAN INTELLIGENCE.

SILVER. British code name for Bhagar Ram Talwat, a Hindu and Indian nationalist whose brother had been executed for assassinating a British official. Having participated in the escape of Subhas Chandra Bose to Afghanistan in 1941, he was recruited by the Germans in Kabul and by the **NKVD**. When his role was revealed to the British by the Soviets in 1942, he was arrested and agreed to be run as a **double agent**, posing as the head of an imaginary All-India Revolutionary Committee. From 1943, he made five visits to Kabul to see his controller at the German consulate, and in July 1943 established a radio link with Delhi, code-named MARY. He later made contact with TOM, a transmitter at Burg, near Magdeburg, a circuit that remained open until the end of hostilities. MARY also maintained contact with RHINO, Bhose's headquarters in Burma.

SIMEX. The Société Import-Export (Simex) was a commercial cover in Paris for a **GRU** network based in France and **Belgium**. The organization was compromised in July 1942 by the arrest of **Konstan-**

tin Effremov, but the subsequent raid on Simex initially yielded the **Abwehr** very little, as no evidence of espionage was recovered and there was no trace of "Jean Gilbert," the alias adopted by **Leopold Trepper**, who had become the Abwehr's principal target. However, interrogation of one of Simex's Paris directors, Alfred Corbin, suggested a clue. Corbin or his wife had recommended a dentist to Gilbert, and surveillance on the surgery led the Abwehr to arrest him on 5 December 1942 as he prepared to have his teeth treated.

SIMOES, ERNESTO. Even before his arrival at Poole from **Lisbon** at the end of July 1943, **MI5** was aware from ISOS that Ernesto Simoes had been recruited by the **Abwehr**. A well-traveled Portuguese, he was allowed to land partly to test the efficiency of the reception process in England and also to see if he had any other contacts. He was placed under surveillance and passed through the immigration controls without difficulty, and then was given discreet help to obtain a job at the Percival Aircraft factory in Luton, where he lodged with one of the other employees. He wrote a single letter to a German cover address in Lisbon, and apart from seducing his landlady, made no attempt to engage in espionage, even when he was encouraged to do so by an MI5 agent provocateur.

Simoes was arrested, questioned at Luton police station, and then interrogated by Tommy Harris of **B1(g)** at **Camp 020**, where he remained until September 1945, when he was deported to Portugal to be reunited with his wife and daughter. He escaped prosecution only because of the unsuccessful use of the agent provocateur but gave a detailed confession, acknowledging that he had been supplied with the ingredients for making secret ink, concealed in cotton wool stitched into the lining of his overcoat, and had been instructed to report on the arrival of American troops in Great Britain, the movement of troops, and anything else of interest. However, he insisted that he had never intended to engage in espionage and simply wanted to earn good wages in England, a country he could not have reached without German assistance.

SINCLAIR, HUGH. Appointed **chief** of the **Secret Intelligence Service (MI6)** in June 1923, Adm. Hugh Sinclair previously had been the Admiralty's **director of naval intelligence**. He died of cancer in November 1939 and was succeeded by **Stewart Menzies**.

Sinclair's wish to develop an effective worldwide organization was stymied by Treasury parsimony, and he once claimed that MI6's annual budget was less than the cost of maintaining a single destroyer in home waters. In 1935 Sinclair fought and won a battle with the Air Ministry and Stanley Baldwin's government over the extent of German rearmament and the size of the Luftwaffe. As chief, Sinclair came to rely on personnel overseas, often operating under **Passport Control** cover, who enjoyed private incomes, and MI6 sponsored a parallel network in Europe of expatriate businessmen and journalists, known as the **Z Organisation**, which gave part-time employment to patriotic volunteers. Sinclair's other lasting contribution was the purchase in 1938 of **Bletchley Park** as MI6's war station, which later accommodated **Government Communications Headquarters**.

SKULL. Supreme Headquarters Allied Expeditionary Force code name for an **Abwehr** staff officer recruited as a **double agent** after he had been compromised unwittingly by DESIRE. Arrested in August 1944, SKULL was one of seven agents run by the celebrated Friedrich Kaulen from Le Havre. After he had established radio contact in November, following a spell in **Camp 020**, he was appointed Kaulen's paymaster and given instructions to give DRAGOMAN some cash. SKULL was controlled by the 31st **Special Counter-Intelligence Unit**, which devised TRIPOD, a scheme to lure Kaulen to a rendezvous in Bordeaux where he could be captured by a team of selected French and American troops. Although Kaulen agreed to the meeting, at night on the banks of the Gironde on 6 April 1945, the ambush misfired and Kaulen was accidentally shot dead by a nervous soldier. DRAGOMAN himself was half-strangled, but the incident was not a complete fiasco, for a list of agents found on Kaulen's body showed that all of them actually were already under Allied control. The TRIPOD debacle was particularly disappointing because Kaulen—an experienced Abwehr spymaster who had undertaken three missions to England before the war and had only narrowly escaped to Ireland when hostilities were declared—was considered an important prize.

SMERSH. The Russian abbreviation for Smert Shpionam ("death to spies"), an **NKVD** paramilitary organization created by Viktor S.

Abakumov under the personal directive of Josef Stalin in 1942 to identify and liquidate Nazi stay-behind networks. Smersh acquired a ruthless reputation and was responsible for the elimination of unknown thousands of suspected collaborators and for the deportation of entire ethnic groups to remote areas of Kazakhstan and Siberia. Smersh was dismantled in March 1946, although many of its personnel continued to have successful careers within the NKVD, including Abakumov who was appointed minister for state security in October 1946, only to be purged in August 1951, released in March 1953, rearrested in December 1954, and finally executed.

SMOOTH. The British **Inter-Services Liaison Department (ISLD)** code name for a **double agent**, a Turkish customs officer in Antioch who supplied information to his German controllers allegedly supplied by HUMBLE, the **notional** proprietor of a fruit and vegetable shop in Aleppo, Syria. In turn, HUMBLE supposedly was in touch with KNOCK, a salesman in medical supplies who traveled frequently to and from Iran and Iraq. SMOOTH was run by ISLD's Michael Ionides, who was able to use him to identify two important **Abwehr** spies in Alexandretta, Turkey, Paula Koch and her Armenian son-in-law Joseph Ayvazian. HUMBLE's performance was so good that the Germans authorized him to recruit two more subagents, WIT and WAIT. It was later maintained that HUMBLE's reporting resulted in two American **Office of Strategic Services** officers spending several weeks in Aleppo trying to track him down.

SNARK, THE. **MI5** code name for a Yugoslav **double agent** named Mihailovic, a domestic servant active between July 1941 and March 1943.

SNIPER. **MI5** code name for a **double agent**, a Belgian pilot named Hans Bertrand, who reached Great Britain in November 1943. He was allowed to join a Belgian squadron of the Royal Air Force, and when he was posted back to **Belgium** in December 1944, he sent a letter in secret ink to his controller in **Lisbon**. At the end of March, he received confirmation that money for him had been buried near Aachen, but it was never recovered and the surrender happened before the case could be pursued any further.

SNOW. MI5 code name for **B1(a)**'s first **double agent**, **Arthur Owens**.

SOLBORG, ROBERT. The **Office of Strategic Services** representative in **Lisbon**, Col. Robert Solborg was exceptionally indiscreet and, according to ARTIST, a British source in the local **Abwehr**, was the sole source of leaks to the Germans.

SONIA. GRU code name for **Ursula Kuczynski**.

SORGE, RICHARD. Born in Baku, on the Caspian, to a German oilfield engineer, Richard Sorge had been wounded twice while fighting with the kaiser's forces during World War I. He became an active member of the Kommunistische Partei Deutschlands (KPD), attending its Second Congress in 1921 as an official delegate, and contributed to a leftist newspaper, *The Voice of the Mineworkers*, based at Solingen in the Ruhr. Despite leaving a trail of evidence concerning his political beliefs at Aachen University, in the mines where he had worked as an agitator, in the police files of Hamburg that recorded his party membership, and in the economic textbooks he had written, Sorge joined a Soviet intelligence network around 1924. Ostensibly he cut his links with the KPD and with his schoolteacher wife Christiane, who was later to immigrate to the United States, but in reality he went to Moscow for training and attended a radio course.

Sorge's first overseas mission appears to have taken him to Hollywood, where he wrote articles on the American movie industry for a German magazine. He used the same journalistic cover in Scandinavia and Holland. In 1929, he traveled to London, supposedly for the innocent purpose of studying British politics and economics. There, he was interviewed by a Metropolitan Police Special Branch detective, which, although a routine encounter at his hotel concerning the registration of aliens, had the effect of terminating his visit after just 10 weeks. Sorge subsequently turned up in Shanghai as correspondent for *Soziologische Magazin*, and it was here that he established his reputation as an unusually gifted intelligence officer. With the help of a radio operator, Seber Weingarten, Sorge developed a large ring for the **GRU** and was responsible for the recruitment in November 1930 of **Ursula Kuczynski** and her husband Rudi Hamburger.

When Sorge arrived in Tokyo, he did so as a respected German journalist equipped with authentic Nazi credentials. He was popular in the local expatriate community's club and established an extremely useful friendship with Col. Eugen Ott, with whom he had served in the same regiment during World War I. An artillery expert on attachment to the Imperial Army, Ott was later appointed military attaché at the German embassy and in 1940 succeeded Herbert von Dirksen as ambassador. Apparently Ott never suspected his friend, and it was on his recommendation that Sorge became the embassy's press attaché, a post that gave him useful access to German diplomatic cables, upon which he reported to Moscow. Evidently neither the Foreign Ministry in Berlin nor the **Gestapo** raised any obstacle to Sorge's appointment, apparent vindication of the wisdom of the GRU's decision to allow Sorge to use his own name while operating as an illegal. According to **Leopold Trepper**, Sorge himself raised this issue with his GRU controller, the legendary Jan Berzin, who allegedly replied "a man walks better in his own shoes."

Sorge's network in Japan fell under suspicion in June 1941 following the arrest by the **Kempeitai** of Ito Ritsu, a prominent member of the Japanese Communist Party. Under interrogation, he implicated Miyagi Yotoku, an American-educated Japanese artist, and he in turn led the Kempeitai to the journalist Ozaki Hozumi. By the end of October, 35 members of the ring were under arrest, including Sorge himself and his radio operator, Max Klausen, a KPD activist. Among the others taken into custody were Branko de Voukelitch, a Yugoslav who represented the French magazine *La Vue*, and Sorge's Japanese mistress, Mikaya Hanako.

Sorge and Ozaki were hanged on 7 November 1944, leaving only the summaries prepared by their principal interrogator, Yoshikawa Mitsusada, for study by postwar Allied investigators. De Voukelitch died serving a life sentence in 1945, but Klausen survived his imprisonment and was repatriated to Vladivostok, where he was promptly rearrested by the **NKVD** and taken under escort to Moscow for interrogation and to face charges of duplicity.

SOSO. MI5 code name for a Portuguese employee of the British legation in **Lisbon**.

SOSTARIC, EUGN. Code-named METEOR by **MI5**, Eugn Sostaric was a Yugoslav air force pilot recruited as an **Abwehr** agent by his friend **Dusan Popov**. Sostaric had been the king of Yugoslavia's aide-de-camp, but had been imprisoned after attempting to escape the German occupation via Salonika. On that occasion, Sostaric, who had intended to offer his services to the Royal Air Force, had been betrayed and sentenced to death. The intervention of **Ivo Popov** saved his life, having persuaded **Johannes Jebsen** that Sostaric, who was a strongly anti-Communist Croatian, would make an ideal agent. Eventually the Abwehr authorized Sostaric's release and his travel across Europe to **Madrid**, where he was received by the British embassy. Further delays were experienced while Sostaric waited in **Gibraltar** for transport to England and then, upon his arrival, while he underwent a security screening at the **Royal Victoria Patriotic School** in Wandsworth.

Finally, in April 1943, the airman was enrolled into Popov's network as METEOR, but there was an unexpected twist to his case. When Sostaric was introduced to MI5, he cheerfully revealed that he had been instructed by the Abwehr to confess his espionage to the British authorities at the first opportunity. He was to admit that he had been provided with an address in Portugal to which he was supposed to send apparently innocuous letters, in which messages were to be written in secret ink. Furthermore, the Germans had told him that, having admitted all this, he was to pretend to cooperate with MI5, and then proceed to correspond with another postbox, this time in Madrid, in a secret ink made from another formula that was to be withheld from the British. The Abwehr's clear intention was to run Sostaric as that most sophisticated of agents, the so-called triple cross. Sostaric neatly sabotaged the scheme by disclosing it in its entirety, and it was left to MI5's Ian Wilson, who was appointed his case officer, to devise two separate texts for enemy consumption. The first was to contain material that the Germans would perceive to be false, while the second would contain what the Abwehr was calculating on being an authentic report that they could rely upon. Astonishingly, this charade was maintained without a hitch until May 1944, when Sostaric was posted to the Mediterranean theater as a liaison officer to the Allied commander-in-chief's staff.

SOUTH AFRICA. South African military intelligence, headed by Col. E. G. Mulherbe, was preoccupied by the Osswega Brandwag (OB), a pro-Nazi organization that exercised considerable influence in the Afrikaaner nationalist community. One suspected member was the assistant chief of police, Lt. Coetzee.

Although Field Marshal Jan Smut's South African government was fully committed to the Allies, there was plenty of German espionage that went unchecked, if not actually encouraged. **MI5** was represented in Cape Town successively by William Luke and Michael Ryde, while the **Secret Intelligence Service** sent Mark Oliver, who liaised closely with Malcolm Muggeridge over the border in Lourenço Marques where the local German consul, Leopold Werz, was active. Of principal concern to the counterespionage authorities were the German consul in South Africa, Paasche, who was implicated by wireless intercepts, and Lothar Sittig, code-named FELIX, a notorious spy and head of the LEO network, who twice escaped from internment to Swaziland, apparently the beneficiary of OB collusion, despite the efforts of the local pro-Allied police chiefs, Brigadier Baston and his subordinate, Col. de Villers.

Knowledge of German espionage and sabotage originated from intercepts and from the interrogation of captured agents, among them **Robey Liebbrandt**. *See also* KOTZE, HANS VON.

SOVIET INTELLIGENCE. The two principal Soviet intelligence agencies during World War II were the **GRU** (Glavnoye Razvedyvatel'noe Upravlenie) military intelligence service and the **NKVD** (Narodnyi Komissariat Vnutrennykh Del). Both organizations were handicapped not by a lack of resources or access to information in target countries, but by Moscow's reluctance to accept advice that conflicted with Josef Stalin's prejudices. For example, the NKVD's excellent sources in London were discounted because the information supplied by them simply looked too good to be true. Similarly, numerous indications that the Nazis intended to launch an attack on the Soviet Union in June 1941 were disbelieved and dismissed as **deception** intended to undermine the Molotov-Ribbentrop pact.

While Soviet intelligence ran extensive operations throughout Europe, mainly exploiting local Communist Party sympathizers, its greatest success was ENORMOZ, the penetration of the **Manhattan Project**, the joint Anglo-American atomic bomb project. Soviet intelligence acquired a ruthless reputation for mounting sophisticated but costly deception campaigns on the Eastern Front, but achieved little when attempting to insert agents into Nazi-occupied territory, mainly because the personnel chosen turned out to be reluctant to embark on their missions once they had reached the west. To deal with turncoats and Nazi collaborators, Stalin approved the creation of **Smersh**, a paramilitary unit dedicated to the identification and liquidation of suspected opponents of the regime. *See also* ROTE KAPELLE.

SPANEHL. MI5 code name for a Czech **double agent** named Ivan Spaneil.

SPANISH INTELLIGENCE. The Alto Estado Mayor's (AEM, Supreme General Staff) Sección III, headed by Gen. Arsenio Martinez de Campos, included a subdivision, the Servicio Ofensivo, run by Col. Carmelo Medrano and Col. Juan Luis Roca de Togores, that supervised three Negociados, or branches, the first of which collected information about the United States and Great Britain, mainly through consular officials posted abroad, and acted as a surrogate for the **Abwehr**. Proof of this role was supplied by Andrés Blay and Jochim Baticón. The latter was arrested in **Trinidad** in February 1943, and his interrogation, combined with Blay's confession and ISOS information, led to the arrest of three more *Ybarra* stewards between June and August 1943 and, most significantly, to the capture of a valued prize, Manuel Perez, the Spanish police attaché in Buenos Aires. Perez was taken off his ship in Trinidad and ended his journey at **Camp 020**, where, with Joaquin Ruiz, one of the ship's officers responsible for guarding the Spanish diplomatic bag, he underwent a lengthy interrogation that served to demonstrate the collusion between the AEM and the Abwehr and to close this particular line of communication.

SPECIAL COMMUNICATIONS UNIT (SCU). The distribution network for the circulation of ULTRA intelligence from **Bletchley Park** to its authorized recipients was achieved through a channel managed by the **Secret Intelligence Service** and known as the Special Communications Unit.

SPECIAL COUNTER-INTELLIGENCE UNITS (SCI). In anticipation of **D-Day**, **Supreme Headquarters Allied Expeditionary Force**'s intelligence branch cooperated with the **Secret Intelligence Service** and **X-2** of the **Office of Strategic Services** to create two specialist units, designated SCI 103 and SCI 104, to handle captured enemy agents. The units, each consisting of four officers, four noncommissioned officers, two drivers, and a 15-cwt truck, were trained at Easthampstead Park, near Bracknell, before being accommodated in Chelsea Barracks in anticipation of deployment in August. They then moved to Rouen, Amiens, and finally Brussels in September. Both units were disbanded in August 1945, but during the 12 months of their existence, they handled 14 major **double agents**, under the direction of the 212 Committee, which met every Monday morning alternatively at 12th Army and 21st Army Group headquarters from 21 August 1944.

SPECIAL INTELLIGENCE BUREAU (SIB). The Australian Special Intelligence Bureau was established at Park Orchards, Melbourne, in April 1941 to solve Japanese ciphers. It initially was dependent on two intercept stations, located at Rownsville and Canberra. The SIB achieved considerable success, with help from **Bletchley Park** and American OP-20G personnel, on JN-25 traffic in the Pacific theater, liaising closely with Gen. Douglas MacArthur's Central Bureau, initially located at Cranleigh in Melbourne, but then at Henry Street, Brisbane, where the staff grew to 1,350 mainly Australian and American personnel.

Early in January 1944 a collection of enemy codebooks was recovered from Sio when Allied troops captured Madang from the Japanese 20th Division. These assisted the cryptographers to read a lengthy 13-part message dated 19 January 1944 that provided the entire order of battle in New Guinea and details of the defense strategy.

SPECIAL INTELLIGENCE SERVICE (SIS). The **Federal Bureau of Investigation**'s clandestine organization in Central and South America during World War II, the SIS was created in 1942 but was closed down on President Harry Truman's orders in March 1947.

FBI director **J. Edgar Hoover** became convinced that America needed a civilian intelligence agency, and in May and June 1940, he persuaded Assistant Secretary of State Adolph Berle, Gen. Miles of G-2, and Director of Naval Intelligence Adm. Walter S. Anderson to back his plan for a new agency to operate across Latin America to counter any threat from the Nazis. Its mission would be to combat "financial, economic, political and subversive activities detrimental to the security of the United States." President Franklin D. Roosevelt gave his secret approval, on 24 June, to the SIS's role of collecting nonmilitary intelligence in the Western Hemisphere.

Hoover's choice to head the SIS was Assistant Director **Percy E. Foxworth**, then in charge of Division Five, the National Defense Office in New York. The first SIS officers deployed into the field were sent under commercial cover. According to Don Whitehead's 1956 authorized history of the FBI, "One undercover agent went to South America as a soap salesman for an American concern whose officials never suspected his role in the FBI," while another "young man opened a stockbrokerage business" and established his own wire communications to New York from **Argentina**. This was Ken Crosby, working under Merrill Lynch cover, and "he turned a neat profit, but his reports to the FBI were even more informative than his reports to his stock customers."

The SIS concentrated on **Brazil**, Argentina, **Chile**, and **Mexico**, where there were large expatriate German communities. It was able to establish overt offices in Rio de Janeiro when Brazil cut diplomatic relations with the Axis in February 1942, followed by Argentina in 1944. Altogether about 360 SIS agents operated across Latin America, and by the end of the war the FBI had appointed official legal attachés, known simply as "legats," to liaise with the authorities in nine countries, where they were openly declared as the FBI's representatives based at the U.S. embassy. The SIS was especially successful in Colombia where, until June 1941 when his assets were frozen in the United States, a German trader had exercised a virtual monopoly on the platinum market. Thereafter this strategic commodity became the focus of various smugglers anxious to exploit the high prices offered by the Nazis. The SIS was instrumental in identifying Harold Ebury, a British banker based in California, as a key figure in the smuggling racket, and he was taken into custody by the FBI in July 1943.

While the SIS's personnel worked closely with the British **Secret Intelligence Service** stations throughout the region, and together they scored some notable successes, including the prevention of a pro-Axis coup in Bolivia, there was considerable tension between Hoover and the **Office of Strategic Services** and between the director and **British Security Coordination**. At one stage, suspicious of the friendship between **William Stephenson** and **William Donovan**, Hoover attempted to insert his SIS into a liaison role between the two organizations so as to vet any exchange of information between them, but despite support from Adolph Berle in the State Department, his bid failed in the Oval Office.

The SIS continued to operate until June 1946, when President Truman's National Intelligence Authority, chaired by Dean Acheson, transferred responsibility for all overseas intelligence-gathering to the newly created Central Intelligence Group, later the Central Intelligence Agency.

SPECIAL INTERROGATION GROUP (SIG). A unit created in England comprised of German refugees, mainly Jews, who volunteered to question prisoners of war and act as stool pigeons in Allied detention centers.

SPECIAL MATERIAL. MI5 designation for transcripts of intercepted telephone conversations conducted by target diplomats in London.

SPECIAL OPERATIONS EXECUTIVE (SOE). Established in July 1940 as an organization within the Ministry of Economic Warfare to encourage resistance and subversion in enemy-occupied territory, Special Operations Executive was headed by Sir Frank Nelson, a **Secret Intelligence Service (MI6)** officer and the former Conservative member of Parliament for Stroud. In the 21 months of its existence before it was officially disbanded on 30 June 1946, SOE trained and equipped more than 9,000 agents and inserted them into enemy-occupied territory with varying degrees of success. It operated on a global basis, running missions in **China**, Malaya, Africa, South America, and the Middle East as well as 19 European countries.

Initially SOE was an amalgam of two existing clandestine units: the black propaganda staff known as Electra House, headed by Sir Campbell Stuart; and MI6's sabotage branch, **Section D**, consisting of 140 hastily recruited intelligence officers. Together they formed the foundation of SOE, an ad hoc organization created to foment subversion across the world and, in **Winston Churchill**'s famous phrase, "set Europe ablaze."

Nelson was succeeded by a banker, Sir Charles Hambro, who had started SOE's Scandinavian country sections, and he was replaced by Maj. Gen. Sir Colin Gubbins, a regular army officer with unconventional ideas about guerrilla warfare. Their scope was deliberately restricted to prevent SOE from engaging in the collection of intelligence, an area retained as MI6's exclusive province.

SPIDER. MI5 code name for a Spanish seaman recruited as a **double agent**.

SPRINGBOK. MI5 code name for a **double agent Hans von Kotze**.

SPRINGHALL, DOUGLAS. A former commissar of the British Battalion of the International Brigade in the Spanish Civil War, Douglas "Dave" Springhall was national organizer of the **Communist Party of Great Britain** when he was convicted in June 1943 of running a Soviet espionage network in London and receiving classified information from Capt. **Ormond Uren** and **Olive Sheehan**. He was sentenced to seven years' imprisonment. His Soviet contact, André Graur, left London suddenly four days after Springhall's arrest.

SQUEAK. Code name for a Flemish saboteur recruited as a **double agent** and dropped by parachute near Malines in February 1945 with PIP and WILFRED. All three were taken into custody and remained active until the end of hostilities.

STARZICZY, JOSEF J. Having adopted the alias of a Danish engineer, Niels Christian Christiansen, Josef Starziczy arrived in Rio de Janeiro from Bordeaux on the German merchantman SS *Hermes* in April 1941 carrying an **Abwehr** *Agentfunk* suitcase radio and, with help from the local German consul in Santos, began to build his organization. Starziczy was arrested in March 1942 when he attempted to buy components for his transmitter, and a search of his home by the **Direção da Ordem Política e Social (DOPS)** and his deposit box at the Banco do Credito Mercantil revealed copies of all his past messages and meticulous financial accounts.

Confronted with this incriminating evidence, Starziczy gave DOPS a comprehensive account of his Abwehr connections and background. A German of Polish descent, Starziczy had served in the German Imperial Navy in World War I and afterward had graduated from the University of Breslau with a degree in mechanical engineering before finding work in England. At the outbreak of war, he had returned home, via **Denmark**, and had been invited to join the Abwehr by Adm. **Wilhelm Canaris** himself. After months of training in Hamburg, he had joined the *Hermes* in France, with instructions to help the elderly German consul in Santos, Maj. Otto Übele, to establish a transmitter and a network to supply details of Allied shipping. Once he had completed the first part of his mission, he was to travel to the United States.

Starziczy, when he arrived on the *Hermes* in Rio, was met by Hermann Bohny, then set about building his network, initially by installing his transmitter in the offices of the Theodore Wille Shipping Company, a Hamburg-based company of which Übele was a director. He also recruited two other Wille employees, Albert Schwab (codenamed SPENCER) and Karl Mügge, both enthusiastic Nazis, as wireless operators. Having previously depended on writing in secret ink to a mail drop in **Lisbon**, Starziczy made radio contact with Hamburg at the end of May 1941 on a Halicrafter bought by Mügge and installed at his home in Ipanema. During the following month, he transmitted 104 messages, of which 10 were devoted to technical matters, the remainder being shipping reports, including the news that the cruiser HMS *Newcastle* had just resupplied in Rio. The latter signals were accurate, potentially extremely dangerous, and certainly caught the attention of the Allied cryptanalysts reading the traffic.

By the middle of 1941, Schwab had made contact with Hamburg from his home in Leblon, and another recruit, Benno Sobisch, was transmitting from Santa Teresa. In August, Starziczy used an intermediary to rent a secluded house in Leblon, which became his headquarters and communications center, with a room dedicated to espionage, packed with chemicals for developing secret writing using various techniques, including dissolved Pyramidon tablets, and photographic equipment for producing **microdots**. With additional sources on the coast at Rio Grande do Sul and Porto Alegre, and a steward on the SS *Uruguay* who reported his observations of Allied convoys on his vessel's regular run to New York, the network was generating a very large quantity of intelligence. As well as reporting on Allied shipping, the ring also collected information from Natal, a vital stepping-stone on the transatlantic air link from the United States to Bathurst, the airbase in the British colony of The Gambia. Large numbers of American troops and engineers had poured into Parnamerim Airport, and the runway at Ibura was extended to accommodate large military aircraft.

When signals containing reports of these observations were intercepted and read in Washington, it served to heighten American anxieties about the **Brazilian** transmitters. Other messages, urging the recruitment of ADMIRALTY, an apparently promising source inside the British consulate in Santos, and the cultivation of an American businessman and former secretary of the American Chamber of Commerce in São Paulo with access to the U.S. consulate, also exacerbated the situation, increasing the need for urgent intervention.

Starziczy's role as the spymaster code-named THE KIND MAN began to unravel in December 1941 when he tried to assemble a new transmitter in São Vicente and found the apparatus was missing several components, including an ondometer. On a recommendation from Übele, he visited an electronics shop in São Paulo to buy the necessary items and gave the owner a false name and address. As Starziczy spoke no Portuguese, he made the purchase speaking English with a German accent, but gave the Portuguese name "Senhor O. Mendes." His suspicions aroused, the owner reported the matter to the police, and the DOPS security police kept the shop under surveillance. When Übele sent a subordinate to collect the order for the ondometer, he too was watched, and in March 1942 DOPS swooped. Although they recovered a transmitter from one of his contacts, they extracted little else from Übele, but a search of his office revealed correspondence with "Niels Christiansen" in Leblon. DOPS then arranged to raid Christiansen's address in Rio, where they found Starziczy and his Brazilian mistress Ondine Peixoto de Oliveira, as well as his radio and a mass of incriminating papers, including the text of a message transmitted the previous evening, reporting the departure of the *Queen Mary*, carrying 8,000 Canadian troops.

DOPS arranged for an urgent warning to be given to the British embassy, but in fact the liner was destined for the Far East, with 9,000 American troops aboard, and Tom O'Shaughnessy, a regular diplomat who liaised with the legal attaché's office, was invited to sit in on the subsequent interrogation. For four days, Starziczy stuck to his "Christiansen" cover story of an innocent Danish engineer, and then he concocted a story that he thought included only what the DOPS interrogators already knew, naming fellow-conspirators whom he was sure had left the country already and an entirely fictional, mysterious organizer named Hansen. His only slip was to mention Albert Schwab, with whom he had fallen out, who was one of the Wille Company employees who had passed him Allied shipping intelligence.

Based on the clue to Schwab's involvement and armed with a list of 48 suspects drawn up by the **Special Intelligence Service (SIS)**, DOPS chief Felisberto Teixeira began to arrest dozens of Abwehr agents, among them Herbert von Heyer, Karl Mügge, Friedrich Kempter, and **Albrecht Engels**, who turned himself in to the police. Suddenly the call signs CEL, LIR, and CIT went off the air, and it appeared that the Abwehr's principal spy rings in Brazil had been crushed. To make absolutely certain there was no backsliding, and to avoid any intervention from Filinto Muller, SIS head Jack West persuaded U.S. Ambassador Jefferson Caffery to give President Getúlio Vargas and two of his senior ministers copies of the intercepted CEL–ALD traffic, which showed the scale of the intelligence that had flowed to Berlin.

After a fortnight of continuous interrogation, and under pressure from a threat to make his mistress submit to a DOPS interrogation, Starziczy finally admitted his true identity, implicated Otto Übele, and led DOPS to his safe deposit box, which contained copies of all the LUCAS traffic since May 1941 and complete financial records of his network. The material was damning and was used by DOPS to great effect on Engels, who hitherto had kept silent. Disheartened by the evidence from Starziczy's safe deposit box, and after four days of what DOPS called *regime duro*, Engels finally confessed and named the house in São Cristovão where his transmitter was hidden.

The DOPS investigation, dogged by complaints of maltreatment and torture, resulted in several months of criminal prosecutions at the end of 1943 and the conviction of 58 spies who received a total of more than 1,000 years' imprisonment. As for Starziczy, who insisted he had never acted against Brazilian interests and claimed to have turned against the Abwehr when the first Brazilian ships were torpedoed, his offers to build an electronic device that would detect U-boats was turned down, and he was sentenced to 30 years' imprisonment.

STEIN, LILY. Of the contacts supplied to **William Sebold** by the **Abwehr** in February 1941, Lily Stein turned out to be one of the most significant. Formerly the mistress of an Abwehr officer, she had been recruited in Germany under duress after she had fled from Vienna during the *Anschluss* in 1938. She was unenthusiastic about the mission for which she had been trained in Hamburg, but was short of money, and the apartment to which she had moved, on East 79th Street in New York City, acted as a postbox for other members of the Abwehr's organization in the United States. One such source was Edmund Heine, a former Ford Motor Company executive who had managed one of the company's assembly plants in Germany and still enjoyed access to the headquarters in Detroit and to confidential production figures. While under surveillance, Heine was seen to masquerade as a current Ford employee and conduct an inspection of the Glenn Martin aircraft plant in Maryland.

STEINER, FLORENT. An **Abwehr** spy, Florent Steiner arrived in Great Britain in June 1941 but was not traced to Liverpool until eight months later. Under prolonged interrogation, he admitted possession of secret ink and two cover addresses in **Lisbon**, but as he had not contacted the Germans, he was not prosecuted but detained at **Camp 020** until the end of the war.

STEPHAN. **MI5** code name for an Austrian named Klein who was recruited as a **double agent**.

STEPHENSON, WILLIAM. Appointed head of **British Security Coordination (BSC)** in July 1940, William Stephenson replaced the former **Secret Intelligence Service (MI6) passport control officer in New York, Sir James Paget**. A **Canadian** of Icelandic parentage, Stephenson's organization was distrusted by the **Federal Bureau of Investigation** but nevertheless provided an umbrella for the regional activities of **Special Operations Executive**, **MI5**, MI6, and the Ministry of Economic Warfare. BSC was closed down in 1945. In 1962, one of Stephenson's subordinates, Harford Montgomery Hyde, wrote a reasonably accurate biography, *The Quiet Canadian*, which was followed by the fictional *A Man Called Intrepid*.

STEVENS, RICHARD. The **Secret Intelligence Service (MI6)** station commander in The Hague, Maj. Richard Stevens was abducted with **Sigismund Best** at the German frontier near **Venlo** in November 1939 by the **Sicherheitsdienst**. He was a relatively inexperienced MI6 officer, on his first posting overseas, but he resisted interrogation and survived the war in a concentration camp. After the conflict, he was accused of having betrayed sensitive information about MI6's structure to the enemy; his denials were disbelieved, and he was dismissed from MI6. Years later, it emerged that neither he nor his fellow abductee, Best, had been indiscreet, and that the culprit had been another senior MI6 officer, Col. **C. H. Ellis**.

STOCKHOLM. The capital of neutral **Sweden** became a significant center of wartime espionage, with the **Secret Intelligence Service (MI6)** and the **Abwehr** running operations monitored by the Swedish security police and the military intelligence service. Inhibited in mounting potentially embarrassing schemes, John Martin's MI6 station concentrated on learning the identity of the sources recruited by Karl-Heinz Krämer, the German controller of a network in London code-named JOSEPHINE. *See also* SWEDISH INTELLIGENCE.

STORK. MI5 code name for an agent in London.

STRONG, KENNETH. The former British assistant military attaché in Berlin, Kenneth Strong was appointed Gen. Dwight D. Eisenhower's chief of intelligence at **Supreme Headquarters Allied Expeditionary Force**.

SUMMER. MI5 B1(a) code name for **Gósta Caroli**, an **Abwehr** agent parachuted into England in September 1940. Arrested upon his arrival, he broke under interrogation and compromised his friend **Wulf Schmidt**, with whom he had trained. Initially Caroli made satisfactory, supervised wireless contact with his enemy controllers and was accommodated at the Old Parsonage in Hinxton, Cambridgeshire, **MI5**'s "Home for Incurables." But after he assaulted his guard, stole a motorcycle, and made an unsuccessful attempt to reach the coast, he was incarcerated at **Camp 020** for the remainder of the war.

SUNDAE. MI5 code name for a Spanish **double agent** in Algeciras.

SUPREME HEADQUARTERS ALLIED EXPEDITIONARY FORCE (SHAEF). Following the **D-Day** landings, responsibility for the rolling up of enemy stay-behind networks, the arrest of spies, and the management of **double agents** in the 21st Army theater fell to SHAEF's counterintelligence branch, headed by **Dick White**. **Deception** campaigns were supervised by a **Twenty Committee** offshoot, the 212 Committee.

SWEDISH INTELLIGENCE. The Swedish Joint Military Intelligence Service (JMIS) was established on 1 July 1937 with the Försvarsstaben, a joint defense staff that succeeded the former general and naval staffs. The JMIS consisted of the Underrättelseavdelningen (Intelligence Branch), headed by Col. Carlos Adlercreutz, formerly the military attaché in Helsinki, and Sektion II, which was created in September 1942. The former, with 22 officers, consisted of two subdivisions: one for foreign operations, the Utländsk Sektion; and the other for Swedish issues, the Svensk Sektion. Sektion II was divided into three units: Persona, for vetting of personnel, headed by Capt. Georg Berendt; Detectio, which dealt with industrial protection, headed by Lt. Lindberg; and Evidens, or counterespionage, run by Lt. Lindquist since the late spring of 1938. In October 1942 Adlercreutz was sent back to Helsinki and was succeeded by Commodore Daniel Landquist.

A Swedish cryptographic organization, the Försvarsväsendets Radioanstalt (FRA, National Defense Radio Establishment) was established in July 1942, headed by Commodore Torgil Thorén, to exploit taps on the two communications cables linking German forces in **Finland** and Norway to Berlin. The FRA succeeded in breaking the **Geheimschreiber** cipher, but the access to Geheimschreiber traffic proved temporary because the break was compromised by the Finnish military attaché, Col. Stewenly. The Swedish cipher experts failed to solve any **Enigma** keys.

Internal security in Sweden was the responsibility of the Stats-polisen, created in 1939 and led by Eric Hallgren, but the organization expanded dramatically following the occupation of Norway and **Denmark**, and the creation of a general security service, the Al-manna Sakerhetstjantsen, employing a central staff of 1,000 and a further 270 in telephone monitoring and 350 on mail interception. In April 1940, the Radiokontrollavdelningen was established to censor overseas telegrams.

Security in **Stockholm** was managed by Martin Lundqvist for the Almanna Sakerhetstjantsen with a staff of 191 working in four bu-reaus, three covering Soviet espionage and local Communists, run by Erik Lönn; Axis powers, headed by Wilhelm Magnusson and Torsten Söderström; and Allied powers, supervised by Nils Fahlander and later Otto Danielsson, and the fourth unit keeping the records. Lundqvist remained in charge of the Inrikesavdelningen (Information Bureau) until 1943 when he was forced to resign after pressure from the British, who complained of the zealous pursuit of evaders, particularly **Special Operations Executive (SOE)** escapers from Norway. He was replaced by Count Carl Bonde, the son of a royal equerry, who proved more amenable, but by then SOE's disas-trously counterproductive efforts—first to sabotage the Oxelösund iron ore docks, and then to recruit local Communists as saboteurs—had been stymied.

During the war, more than 1,800 individuals were arrested in Swe-den for suspected subversive activity, although most were not prose-cuted and often proved to be Norwegians who had crossed the border illegally. In 500 cases, there were prosecutions, resulting in 444 con-victions. Of these, 262 were Swedes and the remaining 182 were for-eigners. *See also* FINNISH INTELLIGENCE.

SWEETIE. Secret Intelligence Service code name for a Czech named Wiesner who was recruited as a **double agent**.

SWEET WILLIAM. MI5 code name for William Jackson, a **B1(a) double agent** active from August 1941 to August 1942.

SWISS INTELLIGENCE. As well as the **Bundespolizei** security apparatus, the Swiss military intelligence service, headed since 1937 by Brig. Roger Masson, consisted of three bureaus—designated D, F, and I, covering Germany, France, and Italy, respectively—initially with a staff of 10 that grew to 120. Masson also ran a semi-independent network known as the Buro Ha and headed by the secretary of the Union of Swiss Officers, Hans Hausamann, who was based at a large property at Kastanienbaum, near Lucerne, where he operated a press cutting agency. Hausamann had links to German Social Democrats, and his contact with them was maintained through Masson's liaison officer, Max Waibel, who had attended a staff college in Germany before the war. Thus the Buro Ha received information from a network code-named VIKING that stretched from Basel to Berlin. Another source for the Buro Ha was a German refugee, **Rudolf Rössler**, who owned a small publishing business in Lucerne. After the arrest by the Bundespolizei in April 1944 of one of his contacts, **Rachel Dübendorfer**, who was a Soviet agent code-named SISSY, Rössler was suspected of working for the Soviets or passing information he obtained from the Buro Ha to the **Rote Drei**.

SZYMANSKA, HALINA. The wife of the prewar Polish military attaché in Berlin, Halina Szymanska and her three daughters were in Poland when the Germans invaded in September 1939 and isolated from her husband, who had been detained by the Nazis and deported to the Soviet Union. She succeeded in making contact with Adm. **Wilhelm Canaris**, the **Abwehr** chief whom she had known in Berlin, and he arranged for her to travel from Poznan to Switzerland. Resettled in **Bern**, Szymanska became an agent for Capt. Szczesny Chojnacki of the **Polish intelligence** service, and for **Andrew King** of the British **Secret Intelligence Service (MI6)**, who provided her with forged French papers identifying her as "Marie Prenat." These she used to travel to Italy to meet Canaris, who supplied her with information to pass on to the Poles. Whether Canaris knew or suspected Szymanska was in touch with the British remains unclear, but his information, especially his advance warning of Operation BARBAROSSA, proved valuable. Szymanska remained in Bern until the end of hostilities, when the MI6 station commander, Nicholas Elliott, escorted her to England where her daughters completed their education. Col. Antoni Szymansky was believed to have perished while in Soviet captivity.

– T –

TACHIBANA, ITARU. The first Japanese naval officer to be arrested and charged with espionage, Comdr. Itaru Tachibana was caught by the U.S. **Office of Naval Intelligence** collecting information in California about shipyards, war production statistics, and West Coast defenses. He had approached a former U.S. Navy yeoman, Al Blake, for information, but Blake had contacted the authorities and acted as a **double agent**, enabling the other members of Tachibana's network to be identified. Among them were Inao Ohtani, Charlie Chaplin's former valet; Toraichi Kono; and a Dr. Furusawa. Tachibana submitted his reports to the naval attachés in Washington, D.C., and Los Angeles. He was expelled in June 1941 when the spy ring was closed down by the **Federal Bureau of Investigation**.

TANGERINE. Code name for an **MI5** agent.

TANGIER. An international crossroads at the western end of the Mediterranean, in Spanish-controlled neutral territory, Tangier became a convenient center for espionage, and the British consulate housed a small **Secret Intelligence Service** station headed by Toby Ellis. The **Abwehr** occupied a villa at 4 rue de la Falaise, which the local ISOS traffic revealed contained an infrared device, code-named BODDEN, designed to monitor Allied shipping transits through the Strait of **Gibraltar**. After lengthy negotiations with the British ambassador in **Madrid**, Sir Samuel Hoare, his reluctant consent was obtained for an operation, code-named FALAISE, to blow up the building and the apparatus, which was carried out successfully in January 1943. The station's other preoccupation was MAD DOG, a contingency plan for infiltrating saboteurs and a stay-behind organization into southern Spain in the event of Spain joining the Axis or of a German attack on Gibraltar.

TANNENBERG. The German code name for an operation conducted on the night of 31 August 1939 by a group of 150 **Sicherheitsdienst (SD)** personnel and Polish-speaking German soldiers, led by Alfred Naujocks and dressed in Polish uniforms, who attacked and seized a radio station at the frontier town of Gleiwitz while others destroyed the customs post at Hochlinden, on the road to Ratibor. A forestry lodge at Pitschen also came under fire, and corpses obtained from a concentration camp were scattered across the scene as proof of casualties for press photographers. A brief anti-Nazi broadcast was made from the radio station, thus establishing Polish blame for the incident, which was presented as a deliberate provocation, and Adolf Hitler's spurious pretext for the Nazi invasion of Poland, which followed swiftly the following day. After the war, an inquiry conducted by U.S. Attorney General Alfred Speiss at Nuremberg identified the SD's chief **Reinhard Heydrich** as one of the architects of the scheme.

TATE. MI5 code name for **Wulf Schmidt**, alias Harry Williamson, a Nazi spy who was parachuted into Cambridgeshire in September 1940, only to be captured the following day.

TEAPOT. MI5's code name for an **Abwehr** agent who arrived in England in January 1943, declared himself to be a triple agent, and was run successfully thereafter, communicating with the Abwehr by radio and occasionally meeting his controller. This case provided MI5 with a rare opportunity to make direct contact with the enemy and give them a demonstration of the Security Service's relative lack of skill at running double agents. The object of the exercise was to persuade the Abwehr that the British were quite untutored in the arcane arts, thereby lulling the Germans into a false sense of security. The case ran on until May 1945.

TER BRAAK, JAN WILLEN. The body of a 27-year-old man was found in an air raid shelter in Cambridge on 1 April 1941, a single gunshot wound to his head, carrying forged documents identifying him as a Dutch refugee named Jan Willen Ter Braak. An investigation conducted by MI5 established that Ter Braak was a Nazi spy who had landed by parachute in November 1940, but had probably committed suicide when he ran out of food coupons. His true identity was later established as Englebertus Fukkus.

THIRTY COMMITTEE. A regional extension of the **Twenty Committee**, the Thirty Committee was created in **Cairo** in March 1943 to supervise **deception** schemes and the handling of **double agents**. It consisted of representatives from **Security Intelligence Middle East**, the **Inter-Services Liaison Department**, and **"A" Force**. The Thirty Committee exercised control over five subcommittees based at various times in Beirut, Baghdad, Asmara, Tehran, **Istanbul**, Nairobi, Tripoli, Cyprus, and **Algiers**. *See also* THIRTY-ONE COMMITTEE; THIRTY-THREE COMMITTEE; THIRTY-TWO COMMITTEE.

THIRTY-ONE COMMITTEE. A local subordinate group headed by the **Thirty Committee** in **Cairo**, the Thirty-One Committee in Beirut was chaired by Rex Hamer from **"A" Force** and consisted of Viscount Astor from Naval Intelligence, John Wills from **Security Intelligence Middle East**, and Michael Ionides and Peter Chandor from the **Inter-Services Liaison Department**.

THIRTY-TWO COMMITTEE. A local subordinate group headed by the **Thirty Committee** in **Cairo**, the Thirty-Two Committee in Baghdad was chaired by David Mure of **"A" Force** and included Frank Giffey of the **Inter-Services Liaison Department**, who was succeeded by Reg Warry.

THIRTY-THREE COMMITTEE. A local subordinate group headed by the **Thirty Committee** in **Cairo**, the Thirty-Three Committee in Nicosia, Cyprus, was chaired by the **defence security officer**, Guy Thomson, with a single representative of the **Inter-Services Liaison Department**, Philip Druiff.

TIMMERMAN, ALPHONS. A **Belgian** seaman, Alphons Timmerman was arrested at the **Royal Victoria Patriotic School** in September 1941. Code-named SCRUFFY, Timmerman was a genuine **Abwehr** spy detected by his interrogators when he tried to enter Britain posing as a refugee. He was imprisoned at Wandsworth while an MI5 officer substituted for him, writing in secret ink to his cover address in Portugal. The letters were intentionally drafted to contain mistakes in the hope of proving that **MI5** was no match for its opponents, but inexplicably, SCRUFFY's German controllers in **Lisbon** continued to maintain the relationship by answering his letters, leaving it to the embarrassed British case officers to terminate the exercise. Timmerman himself was led to the gallows in July 1942, proving conclusively to the enemy that their agent had never been at liberty to operate and had always been under MI5's control. The episode, in which Timmerman himself had played no willing part, forced MI5 to conclude that perhaps the Abwehr did not boast the finesse and sophistication it had been credited with.

TRAVAUX RURAUX (TR). The name commonly given to Tous Renseignements, a clandestine **French intelligence** agency that operated in the unoccupied zone of France until November 1942, ostensibly for the Vichy regime, but actually working against German interests. It was headed by **Paul Paillole**.

TRAVIS, EDWARD. The director of the **Government Code and Cypher School (GC&CS)** appointed in 1944, Comdr. Edward Travis had been on Lord Jellicoe's staff until 1916 when he joined the Admiralty's Signals Division. In 1918 he was transferred to the cryptographic section at Room 40. Travis joined GC&CS in 1924 as **Alastair Denniston**'s deputy and head of the Naval Section. He remained director of the organization, subsequently renamed **Government Communication Headquarters**, until 1952.

TREASURE. MI5 code name for **Lily Sergueiev**.

TRELLIS. MI5 code name for a plan considered in July 1941 to send a London bank official of German extraction to **Lisbon** to volunteer to spy for the Abwehr, declaring himself to be a British **double agent**, with the intention of being enrolled as a triple agent.

TREPPER, LEOPOLD. In 1931, at age 27, Leopold Trepper arrived in **Belgium** carrying a Polish passport in his true name and, after studying political science at the Free University of Brussels, he subsequently traveled to the Soviet Union. His return, in March 1939, ostensibly from Quebec, marked the foundation of a major **GRU** network of illegals that Trepper had planned from Paris, where he was residing in December 1936, and was based on a commercial cover, the **Foreign Excellent Raincoat Company**, a subsidiary of the Roi du Caoutchouc, a well-established business whose general manager, **Leon Grossvogel**, was also a former Comintern agent as well as Trepper's acquaintance from Palestine, where they had both lived in the late 1920s.

Once in France, Trepper made contact with Gen. Susloparov, the Soviet military attaché in Vichy, and arranged for his wife and son to return to Moscow via Marseilles. After their departure in August 1940, Trepper established himself in Paris as a businessman named "Jean Gilbert" and opened the Société Import-Export (**Simex**) with Grossvogel. Once Simex had begun operating, Trepper ventured back to Brussels under his French identity to liaise with **Viktor Guryevitch** and see his beautiful American mistress, Georgie de Winter, who had borne him a son, Patrick, in September 1939. De Winter played no direct part in Trepper's network, but she believed the story he had told her, that he was a secret agent working for **British intelligence**. Meanwhile, Guryevitch had continued to run Simex without any adverse interference from the Germans and had succeeded in negotiating several useful contracts with the occupation forces. Simex's business relationship with the enemy flourished and not only provided useful cover for Trepper and his network but also gave them travel facilities.

Trepper remained in hiding in Paris until the end of the war, when he emerged and reported to Col. Novikov, the head of the Soviet military mission in Paris. Novikov arranged for Trepper to be flown to Moscow on 6 January 1945, where he was thrown into the Lubyanka Prison until March 1953 after the death of Josef Stalin. Trepper then returned to Poland, where he became a leader of what remained of the Jewish community, but he remained the subject of suspicion until 1973 when, after a lengthy international campaign, he eventually received permission to immigrate to Israel. His controversial memoirs, *The Great Game*, were published in Paris in 1975, but only after he had successfully sued Jean Rochet, the director of the French domestic security agency, the Direction de la Surveillance du Territoire, for defamation when the latter had accused Trepper of having collaborated with the enemy.

In November 1943, Moscow had alerted Guryevitch that Trepper was a traitor, but this warning may have been part of an increasingly complex **deception**. In a postwar study, the Central Intelligence Agency (CIA) was inclined to the opinion of investigator Willy Berg who wrote: "Trepper appeared neither surprised nor dismayed by his arrest. Instead he congratulated his captors on their skill and offered them his wholehearted collaboration." The CIA is emphatic that the evidence points to **Henri Robinson** having been "betrayed by Trepper" in December 1942, but Trepper gave an entirely different version of the events that led to the arrest at a routine rendezvous in a Paris street. He says Robinson, whom he called "Harry," had been under German surveillance for months, and certainly since August. He concedes that he was present at the scene, sitting in a **Gestapo** car in handcuffs: "I watched Harry's arrest without being able to do anything."

TRICYCLE. MI5 code name for **Dusan Popov**.

TRINIDAD. Located in the southern Caribbean, the British colony of Trinidad accommodated a British **defence security officer**, a **contraband control** officer, and a very large branch of **Imperial Censorship** that scrutinized all correspondence exchanged between South America and western Europe. All merchant shipping crossing the Atlantic was required to obtain a Navy Certificate before completing a voyage, and examination of the crew, passengers, cargo, and mails was a condition imposed by the British authorities. Information gleaned from these inspections proved exceptionally fruitful.

TRIPLEX (XXX). MI5 code name for intelligence derived from the illicit copying of the contents of diplomatic pouches dispatched from neutral diplomatic missions in London.

TURING, ALAN. A Cambridge-educated mathematician, Alan Turing played a key role in **Government Communications Headquarters'** cryptographic attack on the **Enigma** cipher machine and led the team that designed COLOSSUS, the world's first programmable analog computer, built to race through the permutations of the **Geheimschreiber**.

TURKISH INTELLIGENCE. At an important espionage crossroads in the Near East, the Turkish Sûreté maintained an ambiguous relationship with the British, Soviets, and Germans. It cooperated with the British **defence security officer** against the Germans, but collaborated with the Germans against the Russians. One of the most successful **double agents** run by **Security Intelligence Middle East**, DOLEFUL, was passed on to the organization by the Turks. All the major intelligence agencies maintained representatives in **Istanbul** and **Ankara** and mounted operations against each other.

TWENTY COMMITTEE. The interdepartmental committee created on 2 January 1941 to supervise the activity of **MI5**'s growing stable of **double agents**. Chaired by **John Masterman**, with John Marriott acting as its secretary, the committee took its name from the Roman numerals XX—essentially a pun for "**double cross**"—and met weekly until May 1945. Officially a subcommittee of the **Wireless Board**, the Twenty Committee included representatives from the Naval Intelligence Division, the director of military intelligence, the director of air intelligence, the **Security Executive**, the **Secret Intelligence Service**, the Home Forces, and the Air Ministry branch responsible for the construction of bogus airfields.

Similar structures were developed in other theaters, such as the 212 Committee, which supervised double agent operations in the 21st Army Group area at the **Supreme Headquarters Allied Expeditionary Force** headquarters. The **Thirty Committee** operated in **Cairo** from March 1943 and the **Forty Committee** supervised activities in **Algiers** with a representative from the French Deuxieme Bureau. In addition, a Fifty Committee worked briefly in Nairobi, and a Sixty Committee oversaw Allied activities in **Lisbon**.

– U –

U-33. After having been caught on the surface by HMS *Gleaner* off the Firth of Clyde in February 1940, Hans-Wilhelm von Griesky scuttled his U-33, but the following day Royal Navy divers returned to the wreck and recovered three of the submarine's eight **Enigma** rotors from the radio room. Interrogation of the crew revealed that some believed their captain could have evaded the surface vessels and should have attempted to escape. The dissent, skillfully exploited by Naval

Intelligence Division interrogators, revealed that the Kriegsmarine relied on three separate Enigma keys: the Home Waters cipher, known as *heimisch*, and code-named DOLPHIN by **Bletchley Park**; the Distant Waters key, *auserheimisch*, code-named PIKE, which would never be solved; and Neptun, the third, an officers-only key, code-named OYSTER, which would also resist the cryptographers.

U-110. On 9 May 1941, U-110, a Type IXB long-distance, oceangoing submarine, was forced to the surface in the Atlantic by HMS *Bulldog*. Korvetleutnant Julius Lemp ordered his crew into the water and then set the scuttling charges, but these failed to detonate, allowing Lt. David Balme to climb aboard and recover a four-rotor **Enigma** from the radio cubicle, together with a complete collection of rotors and the officers-only key, code-named OYSTER at **Bletchley Park**, together with various other valuable documents, including the DOLPHIN Home Waters keys for April and June. The U-110 was put under tow, but sank the following day.

U-BOAT INTELLIGENCE. On the outbreak of hostilities, the Kriegsmarine submarine (U-boat) fleet amounted to 57 boats, as allowed by the Treaty of Versailles, a number accurately estimated by the British Admiralty. By the end of December 1940 this figure had increased to 75, despite the loss of 24 to enemy action. During 1940, U-boats sank 375 ships, amounting to 1,804,494 tons. But when the naval **Enigma** keys succumbed to Allied cryptographic attack in May 1941, U-boat losses began to escalate dramatically, with the loss of merchantmen falling correspondingly. *See also* ATLANTIC, BATTLE OF THE; U-33; U-110.

ULTRA. The secrecy classification introduced in 1942 to protect the highest category of signals intelligence material derived from cryptographic attacks on the enemy's communications. ULTRA replaced its predecessor, **BONIFACE**, because the source had not been taken seriously by some of its recipients. Once the original traffic had been decrypted and translated at **Bletchley Park**, it was circulated in the form of a "flimsy" to approved analysts, who sanitized the source by preparing summaries for wider distribution. Depending on the urgency of the information, indicated by up to five *Z*'s on the signal, the

ULTRA text was transmitted in a **one-time pad** cipher on **Special Communications Unit (SCU)** channels from Whaddon Hall in Bedfordshire to SCU stations attached to individual military commands. There, a specially cleared officer would deliver it to the designated recipient and then ensure its destruction.

Very few people either had access to ULTRA or knew the true nature of the source, and that included Prime Minister **Winston Churchill**'s private secretaries John Martin, Leslie Rowse, and Jock Colville. Most **Secret Intelligence Service (MI6)** officers were not cleared for signals intelligence or its derivatives such as ISOS, PANDORA, or **BJ**, and the name of any candidate for a name to be added to what was known as the Prime Minister's List was submitted to MI6's **chief** and, with his approval, to **MI5** for vetting. *See also* MOST SECRET SOURCES.

UNITED STATES INTELLIGENCE. Prior to the establishment of the **Office of Strategic Services** in June 1942, the United States did not possess a unified intelligence collection and assessment organization. Instead, it was dependent on the competing activities of the **Office of Naval Intelligence** and the Military Intelligence Division, which, apart from a cryptographic bureau in Washington, D.C., concentrating on Japanese naval and diplomatic wireless traffic, was devolved down to individual commands, leaving Gen. Douglas MacArthur to organize his own intelligence branch under Col. Charles Willoughby.

UNNAMED FRIEND. **Federal Bureau of Investigation** code name for a member of RUDLOFF's network, a **notional agent** supposedly a friend of WASCH's who in 1945 was willing to make radio contact with the Japanese from the West Coast.

UREN, ORMOND. A senior **Special Operations Executive** officer and deputy head of the Hungarian Section, Capt. Ormond Uren was convicted in June 1943 of passing classified information to a **Communist Party of Great Britain** official, **Douglas Springhall**, and sentenced to seven years' imprisonment.

USTINOV, IONA. Formerly the press attaché at the German embassy in London, Iona "Klop" Ustinov became an agent handler for **MI5**

and recruited his successor, **Wolfgang zu Putlitz**, as an informant. Ustinov spent much of 1943 and 1944 in **Lisbon**, attempting to cultivate Nazi diplomats.

– V –

VASILEVSKY, LEV. The **NKVD** *rezident* in Mexico City during World War II, Lev Vasilevsky adopted the alias Lev Tarasov and participated in the murder of Leon Trotsky in August 1940, as well as subsequent attempts to enable his assassin, Ramon Mercader, to escape from prison. Code-named YURI, Vasilevsky had previously served in Paris and until his departure in December 1944 operated under first secretary cover at the embassy.

The assassination, code-named DUCK, had been masterminded by Leonid A. Eitingon, code-named TOM, the senior NKVD officer in Mexico, with his immediate subordinate being Pavel Pasternyak, of the Soviet consulate in New York, on temporary assignment at the Soviet embassy between November 1943 and May 1944 with the rank of second secretary. Vasilevsky was replaced as *rezident* in Mexico by **Grigori Kheifets**, formerly the *rezident* in San Francisco, whose principal task was to manage a network that had penetrated the **Manhattan Project** in Berkeley and Los Alamos.

VELASCO, ANGEL ALCAZAR DE. *See* ALCAZAR DE VELASCO, ANGEL.

VELOCIPIDE. Code name for an **MI5** agent.

VENLO. The small town in the Netherlands on the German border was the scene of a notorious abduction in November 1939 when two **Secret Intelligence Service** officers, Maj. **Richard Stevens** and Capt. **Sigismund Best**, were seized on Dutch territory while they waited to attend a rendezvous with a man purporting to be a senior anti-Nazi. A car carrying **Sicherheitsdienst** gunmen burst through the frontier, grabbed the two men and took them back to Germany, where they remained in captivity for the remainder of the war.

VENONA. The Anglo-American cryptographic source code-named VENONA, which consisted of 2,900 Soviet decrypts of messages exchanged between 1940 and 1948, provided proof of **NKVD, GRU**, and **Naval GRU** operations conducted across the globe and were especially revealing about wartime spy rings active in Great Britain and the United States. Among the many wartime spies compromised by VENONA were Klaus Fuchs, **Donald Maclean**, Harry Gold, and the physicist Ted Hall.

VERMEHREN, ERICH. A senior **Abwehr** officer based in **Istanbul**, Erich Vermehren and his wife Elizabeth, both devout Roman Catholics, were persuaded to **defect** to the British by the **Secret Intelligence Service**'s **Nicholas Elliott** in December 1943. The incident, which by agreement was intended to be presented as an abduction and not a defection until a leak wrecked the plan, proved to be the catalyst for the subsequent absorption of the Abwehr into the **Reichssicherheitshauptamt**. When news of the defection reached Berlin, having been accidentally publicized in **Cairo**, Vermehren's mother, Vera, the *Das Reich* correspondent in **Lisbon**, was arrested by the **Sicherheitsdienst** and incarcerated at the Oranienburg concentration camp, despite being related by marriage to the German ambassador in **Ankara**, Franz von Papen.

VICHY INTELLIGENCE. The French administration in the unoccupied zone of France headed by Marshal Henri Petain encompassed a large security and intelligence apparatus, although many of its personnel had divided loyalties. The Deuxieme Bureau was headed by Col. Louis Baril, who had from the outset established his credentials as an anti-Nazi with the U.S. embassy in Vichy and later made covert contact with the **Secret Intelligence Service (MI6)** station in Geneva. Foreign intelligence, collected by the **Service de Renseignements**, was directed by **Louis Rivet**, with a counterespionage section headed by **Paul Paillole**. Internal security was the responsibility of Commandant Rollin's Direction de la Surveillance du Territoire, with Col. Georges Groussard heading the Groupe de Protection. Groussard, code-named ERIC, was also in touch with MI6, but he was arrested while on a visit to **Algiers** in July 1941 and thereafter was obliged to run his organization on behalf of the Allies as a fugitive.

VICKERY, PHILIP. Director of the **Indian Political Intelligence Bureau** in London from 1926 to 1947. Born and educated in Ireland, Vickery joined the Indian police in 1909 and was knighted in 1948.

– W –

WALDBURG, JOSÉ. A 25-year-old German from Mainz, José Waldburg was landed by boat at Dungeness in September 1940 with **Sjord Pons**, but was arrested almost immediately. He was tried in November and hanged at Pentonville in December.

WÄLTI, WERNER. An **Abwehr** agent who landed at Portgordon in September 1940 from an amphibious aircraft, accompanied by **Karl Drücke** and **Vera von Schalburg**, Werner Wälti was executed in August 1941.

WASCH. Federal Bureau of Investigation code name for a member of RUDLOFF's network, a **notional agent** who was supposedly REP's brother and a civilian employee of the U.S. War Department in Washington, D.C.

WASHOUT. MI5 code name for a **B1(a) double agent**, **Ernesto Simoes**, a Portuguese with British parents, who was active between June and September 1942.

WATCHDOG. MI5 code name for **Waldemar Janowsky**, an **Abwehr** agent landed with a 40-watt radio transmitter near New Carlisle, Quebec, by a U-boat in November 1942 and run by **MI5**'s Cyril Mills while he was held in custody by the Royal Canadian Mounted Police. A former French Foreign Legionnaire, he had been instructed to carry out reconnaissance in **Canada** with a view to assisting six saboteurs who were to land in 1943. He was arrested wearing civilian clothes, but under interrogation revealed that he was in fact a lieutenant in the Wehrmacht and had buried a naval uniform upon landing. He also revealed he had been given a code within his code that would indicate to his German controllers if he had fallen under enemy control. If so, he was to insert three *U*'s into the fifth group of any message.

Janowsky had three cover addresses and proved entirely cooperative, producing identity documents taken from Canadian prisoners at Dieppe, altered to the name under which he was to live in Canada. He had previously lived in Canada between 1930 and 1933 and had married a Canadian woman still resident in Toronto. He carried $1,000 in U.S. gold pieces and $5,000 in Canadian notes. Janowsky was formerly in the Afrika Korps before being posted to Brussels to recruit agents for the **Abwehr**. Despite an indiscreet reference to his arrest by a member of the Quebec Parliament and a report in French-language papers in Canada, the WATCHDOG case was judged a success, and radio contact was established with the Germans in December, after some delays. However, when it was determined that no saboteurs were to be sent to Canada, Janowsky was transferred to **Camp 020** in England for the remainder of the war.

WEASEL. MI5 code name for a **B1(a) double agent**, a **Belgian** doctor active between May and December 1942.

WEISS, ERNEST. A **GRU** illegal, Ernest Weiss arrived in England in May 1932, but when he was interrogated by **MI5** after the war he claimed to have been inactive as a Soviet spy. According to his account, his network had been quite small. He had received scientific information from a German refugee named Hans Lubszynski, a former Telefunken radio engineer who had come to England in 1934. Lubszynski was in turn in contact with an unconscious source, a physicist from Berlin named Dr. Heinz Kallmann, then working as a researcher pioneering television technology for the firm EMI. However, Kallmann had moved to the United States in February 1939, thus reducing Lubszynski's usefulness. Weiss's other contacts included André Labarthe, a scientist who had worked for the French Ministry of Air until 1938; Prof. Marcel Prenant of the Sorbonne, a leading French biologist and prominent Communist; and Jacques Soustelle, another academic who was to rise high in Gen. Charles de Gaulle's intelligence service.

WELTZIEN, KUNO. One of the **Abwehr**'s representatives in **Lisbon**, operating under commercial cover as the local Krupp armaments agent, Kuno Weltzien worked for Uwa & Weltzien and mounted a skillful operation in January 1941 to persuade the **Secret Intelligence Service (MI6)** that several Britons, including Lt. **W. Haeburn Little**, were on his payroll, and then to entrap MI6 agents as they attempted to burgle his office. The fiasco proved a major embarrassment for MI6. Weltzien was eventually arrested by the **Polícia do Vigilância e Defesa do Estado (PVDE)** in March 1943, together with three of his subordinates, Kurt Foester, Ernst Schmidt, and Hans Grimm, following the conviction of **Rogeiro de Menezes** in London. Although Weltzien was released, pending his expulsion a month later, his network was broken up by the PVDE, which acquired documents from MI6 that suggested he had attempted to recruit sources inside the Portuguese War Ministry. They also implicated a cipher clerk in the Foreign Ministry named Cardozo and three radio operators. This evidence had incensed Antonio Salazar, who ordered the PVDE to put an end to German espionage in Lisbon.

WENDY. MI5 code name for a **double agent**.

WENZEL, JOHANN. A veteran member of the Kommunistische Partei Deutschlands from Danzig, Johann Wenzel was a **GRU** wireless operator for the **Rote Kapelle** who had been trained in Moscow and sent to work in **Belgium** illegally, having been expelled as an undesirable in October 1937. At that time, Wenzel had been studying engineering but early the following year he slipped back into Brussels. After his arrest by the **Abwehr** in July 1942, Wenzel refused to help his German interrogators in any way, but their study of the messages found beside his transmitter, which had been warm when the German investigators burst into his house, led them to a hitherto undiscovered branch of the Rote Kapelle based at the very heart of the Reich. After eight weeks of torture in Berlin, Wenzel was returned to Brussels and installed with a guard and his radio equipment in an apartment in the rue Aurore, where he cooperated fully until he eluded his German captors in November 1942 and sent a message to the Soviet embassy in London that **Konstantin Effremov** was in enemy hands and that his radio was operating under control. Wenzel reportedly ended the war in Holland, but was imprisoned in Moscow by an ungrateful **NKVD** after he had made his way to Moscow.

WHITE, DICK. An **MI5** officer since 1933 and the case officer for **Wolfgang zu Putlitz**, Dick White was appointed chief of counterintelligence in 1944 at **Supreme Headquarters Allied Expeditionary Force**.

WILFRED. Code name for a Flemish saboteur and **double agent** dropped by parachute near Malines in February 1945 with PIP and SQUEAK. All three were taken into custody and remained active until the end of hostilities.

WILLIAMS, GWILYM. Code-named **G.W.** by **MI5**, Gwilym Williams was a retired Swansea police inspector believed by the **Abwehr** to be a Welsh nationalist. Recruited by SNOW, Williams attended a meeting with his Abwehr controllers in Antwerp in October 1939 and received instructions to build a network in Wales. All his agents were entirely **notional**, and his plan to poison a reservoir providing water to the Midlands, code-named GUY FAWKES, was supervised by his MI5 case officer, **T. A. Robertson**. Even after SNOW had been terminated by MI5 in March 1941, G.W. remained active until the following February, having been given a contact at the Spanish embassy in London.

WIRELESS BOARD. The interdepartmental committee created in 1939 to supervise the activities of controlled enemy **double agents**. It was replaced in January 1941 by one of its subcommittees, the **Twenty Committee**.

WIRELESS EXPERIMENTAL STATION (WES). Bletchley Park's outpost in India operated under the cover of the Wireless Experimental Station at Anand Parbat, just outside Delhi, and was commanded by Peter Marr-Johnson, formerly of the **Far East Combined Bureau**. The WES consisted of five branches: A Section, administration; B Section, collation of intelligence; C Section, cryptography; D Section, traffic analysis; and E Section, interception and communications. The WES received its raw Japanese intercepts from two subordinate sites, located at Barrackpore, near Calcutta, and at Bangalore. In addition, a station at Abbottabad in the North-West Frontier, which had concentrated on Russian traffic, continued to intercept diplomatic signals for processing at Bletchley Park.

WITCH. Supreme Headquarters Allied Expeditionary Force code name for a French radio operator parachuted behind Allied lines near Verdun at the end of October 1944. His companion proved uncooperative, but under **Special Counter-Intelligence Unit** supervision, WITCH maintained radio contact with the **Abwehr** from St. Avoid until April 1945 and was awarded the Iron Cross.

WOHLBURG. Located on the outskirts of Hamburg, Wohlburg was the **Abwehr**'s regional radio station exchanging signals with agents in Great Britain.

WOLKOFF, ANNA. The daughter of Tsar Nicholas II's last Russian naval attaché in London, Anna Wolkoff was a Nazi sympathizer convicted in London in 1940 of breaches of the Defence of the Realm Act and sentenced to 10 years' imprisonment. Her coconspirator, **Tyler Kent**, was also convicted and received seven years' imprisonment.

Wolkoff had acted as a conduit for Kent, supplying information from him to others, among them Christabel Nicholson, the wife of Adm. Wilmot Nicholson, a retired former chief of the Royal Navy's submarine service, the Nicholsons also being members of the Right Club. She had been interested in Kent's telegrams concerning **Winston Churchill**'s negotiations for U.S. Navy destroyers, and the deal had been considered so secret that initially Mrs. Nicholson was detained, but not prosecuted; she was later tried, but acquitted, and was then served with another detention order.

MI5 feared that Wolkoff had passed the same information to another of her contacts, Col. Francesco Marigliano, the assistant naval attaché at the Italian embassy, but she was not charged with that offense. Nevertheless, there was evidence that at least one of her messages had reached the Germans, because she had requested the Nazi broadcaster William Joyce to mention "Carlisle" three times in one bulletin from Berlin as confirmation of safe receipt and that transmission was monitored by the BBC. As well as receiving documents from Kent, Wolkoff also tried to penetrate MI5, where some of her friends worked, and the Postal Censorship Department, which employed her parents.

WORM, THE. MI5 code name for a **B1(a) double agent**, a Yugoslav named **Stefan Zeis**, who was active from July 1943 to January 1944.

WORMWOOD SCRUBS. MI5's emergency headquarters in London, evacuated in 1940.

– X –

X-2. Designation of the counterintelligence branch of the **Office of Strategic Services**.

X GROUP. Soviet code name for a **GRU** spy ring active in London in 1940 and 1941 with a membership that included BARON, INTELLI-GENSIA, MINISTER, NOBILITY, and RESERVIST.

XX COMMITTEE. *See* TWENTY COMMITTEE.

XXX. *See* TRIPLEX.

XY. The Soviet designation of joint **NKVD/GRU** *rezidenturas* established in cities from which penetration of the **Manhattan Project** was managed. Introduced in late 1941, Moscow's objective in abandoning the conventional separation between the networks run by the two agencies was in recognition of the priority attached to the acquisition of atomic intelligence.

In New York, XY was headed by Leonid Kvasnikov, who was posted to the front company Amtorg between March 1943 and October 1945, ostensibly as an engineer, leaving **Lev Vasilevsky** in his place in Moscow in charge of all scientific and technical intelligence. Overall, ENORMOZ was supervised by the head of the Third Department of the NKVD's First Directorate, and later by the deputy head of intelligence, Gaik Ovakimyan. A staff intelligence officer, Maj. Yelena M. Potapova, was directly responsible for the processing and translation of all the material, assisted by André Graur, a Third Department officer who had fled London in June 1943 following the arrest of **Douglas Springhall**. In addition, Yelena Modrzhinskaya, Dmitri F. Ustinov, and an aide named Cohen were initiated into certain purely operational aspects of the case, and Ovakimyan reported on all operational questions and intelligence material received directly to the head of the First Directorate, Pavel Fitin. Either through him or the head of the NKVD, Vsevolod N. Merkulov, all the material reached **Lavrenti Beria**, who coordinated the entire project.

Outside the NKVD, only three civilians in Moscow knew about the collection of atomic intelligence: the deputy chairman of the Council of People's Commissars and people's commissar for the chemical industry, Mikhail G. Pervukhin; his personal secretary, A. I. Vasin; and the chief physicist, Igor Kurchatov. The concentration of the NKVD's efforts brought its first results in the beginning of 1943, when Vladimir Barkovsky established an XY *rezidentura* in London. He would later claim that he had been personally responsible for running between 15 and 18 different sources in London, among them ERIC, MOOR, and KELLY.

Having started the ENORMOZ project in the autumn of 1941 on the basis of **John Cairncross**'s reports, the London *rezidentura* remained Moscow's main source of Allied atomic secrets at least until the end of 1944, by which time Klaus Fuchs, formerly run by the GRU in England, had been transferred from Birmingham, England, to Los Alamos, New Mexico, and the XY *rezidentura* had begun to run networks headed by Harry Gold and Julius Rosenberg and to receive information from Ted Hall, Clarence Hiskey, and Zelmond Franklin.

Ultimately the combination of the GRU and NKVD networks, which probably increased the efficiency of XY collection and management, served to undermine internal security and allowed the **Federal Bureau of Investigation** to unravel ENORMOZ's many strands. XY's decision to recruit members of the **Communist Party of the United States of America** also helped compromise some of XY's sources, especially in San Francisco and New York.

– Y –

Y SERVICE. The term initially applied to the Royal Navy's worldwide network of shore wireless telegraphy establishments. Developed by Comdr. Humphrey Sandwith and responsible for monitoring wireless traffic to establish the location of individual ships, the Y Service expanded in wartime to include all stations engaged in direction-finding and interception operations. These included specially equipped Royal Air Force aircraft, the mobile Special Wireless Groups of the Royal Signals, and static bases at Sarafand, Heliopolis, and Anand Parbat managed by **Government Communications Headquarters**.

– Z –

ZABOTIN, NIKOLAI. Papers purloined from the Soviet embassy in Ottawa in September 1945 by a **GRU** cipher clerk, Igor Gouzenko, proved that his *rezident*, Nikolai Zabotin, had spent much of the war conducting espionage operations against the Canadians. Gouzenko, who had been posted to **Canada** with his wife in June 1943, feared the reception he would receive when he was recalled to Moscow and instead approached the Royal Canadian Mounted Police and **defected**. Col. Zabotin, code-named GRANT, had relied heavily on two principal subagents—Fred Rose, the former Communist Party organizer in Quebec and a member of Parliament for Montreal since August 1943, and Sam Carr, a longtime party activist—using a diplomat, Sergei Kudriavtsev, code-named LION, as their handler. Originally from the Ukraine and named Schmil Kogan, Carr had immigrated to Canada in 1924 at the age of 18 and then five years later had attended the Lenin School in Moscow. By 1937 he had been appointed organizing secretary of the Canadian Communist Party, which was later to become the Labour Progressive Party.

Zabotin was also a key figure in **ENORMOZ** and cultivated several sources with access to atomic research in Canada. Those implicated by Gouzenko's 109 stolen documents were a Canadian Army officer, Capt. D. Gordon Lunan, code-named BACK, who was in touch with a spy code-named BADEAU, a member of the National Research Council with access to "secret work" undertaken on "nuclear physics (the bombardment of radioactive substances to produce energy)." BADEAU assured Lunan that this research "is more hush-hush than radar and is being carried on at the University of Montreal and at McMaster University at Hamilton." BADEAU was identified as Durnford P. Smith, a member of the National Research Council apparently run by a member of Zabotin's *rezidentura*, Maj. Vasili Rogov. Among Gouzenko's papers was a request to Rogov to ask BADEAU to obtain a sample of uranium 235 and to acquire more information about a "radium-producing plant" recently purchased by the Canadian government.

Zabotin's other GRU scientific sources were Israel Halperin, code-named BACON, then attached to the Directorate of Artillery; Prof. Raymond Boyer of McGill University; Edward Mazerall, a radar expert code-named BAGLEY; and a rather reluctant Allan Nunn May, code-named ALEK, who had been transferred to Canada and was bullied by the GRU into continuing the cooperation he had given previously in England. As Zabotin reported after a meeting held in August 1945 (according to a Royal Commission report):

> The facts communicated by alek are as follows:
>
> 1. Test of the atomic bomb has been conducted in New Mexico. The bomb dropped on Japan was made from Uranium 235. The magnetic separating plant in Clinton is known to be producing 400 grams of uranium 235 a day. . . . It is planned to publish the research done in this field but minus the technical details. The Americans have already published a book on this.
> 2. Alek handed us a slide with 162 micrograms of uranium oxide on a thin film.

May's report and the sample were carried personally by the GRU's Col. Motinov to Moscow, where he was met at the airport by GRU chief Gen. Fedor Kuznetsov.

Zabotin was withdrawn to Moscow as a consequence of Gouzenko's defection and attended a Special Commission of Inquiry, set up by Josef Stalin under the chairmanship of Viktor Malenkov, consisting of **Lavrenti Beria**, Georgi Abakumov, Gen. Kuznetsov, Vsevolod Merkulov, and Beria's assistant Stepan S. Mamulov, which found him and his wife culpable. They were both imprisoned in the Gulag and not released until after Stalin's death.

ZEIS, STEFAN. A Yugoslav double agent, recruited by **Dusan Popov** and code-named THE WORM by **MI5**, who reached England in September 1943.

ZEPPELIN. The **Sicherheitsdienst** code name for an operation in 1942 intended to recruit Soviet prisoners of war for missions behind the Russian lines. ZEPPELIN, initially managed by **Walter Schellen-**

berg, was abandoned when it became evident that many of the agents were surrendering after they had been infiltrated into Russia. Schellenberg later boasted that two of his agents had even penetrated Marshal Rokossovsky's headquarters, whereas the NKVD revealed that 600 German spies equipped with radios had been captured, including ALEXANDER, head of the FLAMINGO network. All had been manipulated by the Soviets, who supplied them with occasionally authentic information to enhance their credibility. *See also* KURSK.

Z ORGANISATION. A European-based intelligence-gathering network assembled by **Claude Dansey** in 1936, the Z Organisation recruited agents already working under well-established, authentic expatriate business or journalistic covers with the intention that it would operate in parallel to, but in isolation from, sources managed by **passport control officers (PCO)**. Z agents were identified by numbers and reported to a commercial front headed by Kenneth Cohen and located at Bush House, Aldwych, which was then a large London office development filled with numerous anonymous suites. Dansey, a former PCO in Rome, exercised personal control over all Z agents, whom he recruited personally, but the structure was compromised when the two separate networks were combined on the outbreak of hostilities, and the main Z figure in Holland, **Sigismund Best**, was abducted at **Venlo** in November 1939.

ZUBILIN, VASILI M. Code-named MAXIM and working under the alias of Col. Zarubin, Vasili Zubilin was the **NKVD** *rezident* in New York from December 1941, and then from late 1943 in Washington, D.C., where he was assisted by a large staff that included his wife, Elizaveta Zubilina, also an experienced intelligence professional, until their withdrawal to Moscow in August 1944.

Zubilin had become a Chekist in 1920, and five years later he was operating undercover in **China**. In 1926 he was appointed *rezident* in **Finland**, and he then operated as the illegal *rezident* in Berlin, where he married Elizaveta Gorskaya. Between 1929 and 1933, they operated together in France, and then returned to Germany until 1937. Before his departure for New York in October 1941, as a *rezident* aged only 47 but with the personal authority of an audience with Josef Stalin, Zubilin had returned briefly to China to reestablish contact with one of his German agents, a man who had been appointed an adviser to Chiang Kai-shek.

Once in the United States, Zubilin took over from Pavel Pasternyak, alias Pavel Klarin, code-named LUKA, a 45-year-old former member of the NKVD Border Guards, and supervised a large network of agents, many of them members of, or on the fringes of, the **Communist Party of the United States of America (CPUSA)**. Rather than maintain direct contact with CPUSA cadres, Zubilin acted through intermediaries, such as Steve Nelson, but he would come under intensive surveillance by the **Federal Bureau of Investigation (FBI)**, which later employed a **double agent**, Boris Morros, to reconstruct forensically his espionage activities.

In August 1944 Zubilin was recalled to Moscow to face charges leveled against him by one of his disgruntled subordinates, Vasili Mironov, alias Col. Markov, who evidently hated Zubilin for whom he had acted as secretary. Mironov had written a long letter to Stalin accusing the *rezident* of being a spy for the Japanese, and in August 1943 had authored a similar denunciation to the FBI. After a lengthy inquiry in Moscow, Zubilin was cleared of the allegations, and Mironov was incarcerated in an insane asylum. Zubilin's replacement *rezident* in New York was MAY, Stepan Z. Apresyan, and when in March 1945 he was transferred to San Francisco under consular cover, he was succeeded by his deputy, Roland Abbiate, alias Vladimir S. Pravdin, who operated under TASS news agency cover. Zubilin's successor as *rezident* in Washington was **Anatoli Gorsky**.

Bibliography

CONTENTS

I. INTRODUCTION

Books written on the subject of World War II intelligence fall into three broad categories: official histories sponsored by participating governments; personal memoirs written by individual combatants; and other works compiled by outsiders, historians, researchers, and journalists.

The first group is small and is dominated by the titles prepared under the auspices of the British Cabinet Office. Most were drafted as departmental or unit histories commissioned from members of staff shortly before they were demobilized, with no immediate plan to release them outside Whitehall. Their purpose was to provide a lasting record of events so the appropriate lessons could be learned in the eventuality of a future conflict, with candor necessitating a very restricted circulation. Thus William Mackenzie, Jack Currie, Roger Hesketh, David Garnett, John Masterman, Tomas Harris, and Robin Stephens were invited to complete accounts of their organization's activities, and more than a dozen volumes were drafted to cover Government Communications Headquarters' various sections. However, under the terms of the Public Record Act, copies of these confidential documents were lodged in the Public Record Office under the stipulation that they should be closed to public scrutiny for a particular period, usually 50 years, to reflect their sensitivity.

Under normal circumstances, they would have remained unpublished for the term of the relevant closure recommended by the Lord Chancellor, but in 1999 a relaxation in the rules governing Crown copyright enabled the official histories of the Political Warfare Executive, Operation FORTITUDE, Special Operations Executive, and British Security Coordination to be released and published independently. In addition, the Polish and British governments collaborated to produce a study of wartime Anglo-Polish intelligence cooperation, a project that had its roots in disappointment in 1979 over the first volume of Harry Hinsley's magisterial *British Intelligence in the Second World War*. His team's account of the contribution made by the Biuro Szyfrow underestimated the impact of Col. Gwido Langer's Enigma research, and the error was rectified in a subsequent volume. Thereafter more attention was paid to the role played by Polish intelligence personnel who worked in parallel with their British counterparts, and the joint history, compiled by Tessa Stirling, Daria Natecz, and Tadeusz Dubicki, was eventually released in 2002. As well as these official publications, there is a subgroup, a veritable industry, indeed, of official reports published in facsimile form, such as Robin Stephens's *Camp 020* and Tomas Harris's *Garbo*.

Although the official histories serve to answer empirically most of the issues raised by previous historians who did not enjoy access to the original archives, a few mysteries remain, but most of these, upon examination, are not actually matters that really need to be resolved, for they turn out to be castles built on sand. Did Stewart Menzies ever hold a secret rendezvous with Adm. Canaris in Spain? Did Amy Pack steal the Italian naval attaché code that enabled the Royal Navy to triumph at the Battle of Cape Matapan? Was ULTRA shared with Josef Stalin? How did the Rote Drei acquire their information about future German plans?

When the literature surrounding these topics is studied, a pattern emerges. First, there are the memoirs written by the protagonists who relied on their memory, having been denied access to the relevant records. In Britain, because of the ferocity of the Official Secrets Acts, the numbers involved were few, and apart from Dudley Clarke, Dennis Wheatley, and David Mure, who wrote more broadly about strategic deception than what might be termed "sources and methods," almost no former officers ventured into this field. This is not surprising, for Col. Alexander Scotland had attracted considerable opprobrium when he first attempted to publish *The London Cage* in 1957, and the one MI6 officer who followed his example, Leslie Nicholson in 1966, did so from abroad, having adopted the pseudonym of John Whitwell. Two years later, one of his former Section V colleagues, Kim Philby, sheltered in Moscow while his representatives in Paris negotiated the distribution of an English edition of *My Silent War*.

Whitehall's reticence, of course, posed no obstacle for Harford Montgomery Hyde, a distinguished barrister before he joined MI6 in 1939 and later a member of Parliament. Having been Lord Londonderry's prewar private secretary before serving nine years in the House of Commons, Hyde certainly knew his way around the civil service mandarins and their lawyers, and in 1962 he published *The Quiet Canadian*, remarkable mainly because this was a book by a former MI6 officer, about another, Sir William Stephenson, who had been the organization's wartime representative in New York. Sir William, then resident in Bermuda, had long pockets and much goodwill in London, while the impecunious Hyde enjoyed his sponsorship and a fertile imagination. The book was hardly a threat to national security and had been given a reluctant approval by the authorities in London, who wisely acknowledged that the combination of Stephenson and Hyde would be a formidable adversary if a dispute arose. Accordingly none did, and word spread from Whitehall that the biography contained more fiction than fact, a verdict the author cheerfully accepted, before he went on to pen the rather more fanciful *Cynthia* in 1965, which required no special horse-trading in the corridors of power, even if his subject, Betty Pack, had used her charms for MI6 before and during the war.

While most of the immediate postwar titles were concerned with special operations and not intelligence, several of MI5's wartime double agents took up authorship, including Eddie Chapman (code-named ZIGZAG), Lily Sergueiev (TREASURE), Roman Garby-Czerniawski (BRUTUS), and later—after the 1972 watershed marked by the reluctant release of J. C. Masterman's *The Double Cross System of the War of 1939 to 1945*—Dusan Popov (TRICYCLE), John Moe (MUTT), and Juan Pujol (GARBO). Once these not always entirely accurate autobiographies had been circulated, it was possible to compare their content with the more authoritative analyses found in Roger Hesketh's *Operation FORTITUDE* and Sir Michael Howard's official history of deception, the last volume of the Hinsley series. Finally, both sources have been examined by members of the third group of authors to bring all the strands in truly comprehensive studies, as exemplified by Thaddeus Holt's *The Deceivers* and Richard Aldrich's *Intelligence and the War against Japan*.

A question arises as to why the intelligence history of World War II has developed in this way, and the inaccessibility of the original files is certainly one explanation, but it is not the whole picture. Part of the story lies in the tendency of some authors to at best embroider, and at worst fabricate. It may be that other periods of history have experienced the same problems, but the occurrence during the postwar era is marked, and the lasting influence of these writers is evident and in some cases has skewed perceptions. Take, for instance, the bizarre episode of Sir Humphrey Clarke's wife Constance who in 1956 wrote *I Looked Right* using the pseudonym Elizabeth Denham and gave a graphic account of her clandestine missions into Nazi-occupied France, during one of which in June 1943 she was arrested by the Germans and tortured, but managed to escape. As her embarrassed family knew perfectly well, Lady Clarke had never left England at any time during the war, on a covert assignment nor for any other reason, but this did not prevent a real participant in the secret war, Maurice Buckmaster, the wartime head of Special Operations Executive's (SOE) F Section, from being duped and referring with approval to her exploits in his 1958 memoirs, *They Fought Alone*. While this is an extreme example, but certainly not unique, others followed suit, with R. J. Minney inventing, in his biography of Violette Szabo *Carve Her Name with Pride*, a completely fictitious scene in which the SOE agent was tortured in Amiens prison. In fact, there was never any evidence that she had been maltreated by her captors, but several books in the same vein established some stereotypes that were all too easily accepted and even adopted by others equally lacking in scruples.

It was in this atmosphere of a certain laxity of attention to detail, and in a vacuum of official data, that a genre began to emerge, and two books in particular turned a large part of the intelligence history of the war into sheer myth. The first offender was Anthony Cave Brown's *Bodyguard of Lies*, which was later followed by an almost entirely fictitious *A Man Called Intrepid*. Both were written by newspapermen, and the Canadian author William Stephenson definitely had the edge over Cave Brown in sheer invention. At least the latter, who developed the theme that the midlands city of Coventry had been deliberately sacrificed to a massive Luftwaffe air raid to protect the ULTRA source, a myth mistakenly uttered by Fred Winterbotham in 1974 in *The Ultra Secret*, did not resort to actual fabrication, but he did resort to conjecture when he reported that Stewart Menzies had held a secret rendezvous with Wilhelm Canaris in Spain and that MI5's double agent TATE had been responsible for betraying the disastrous Bomber Command strike against Nuremberg, in which the Royal Air Force had suffered appalling losses.

With growing public awareness of clandestine warfare and an apparently insatiable appetite for speculation, at a time when embarrassing disclosures were being made about treachery committed from within the secret world by such traitors as Kim Philby, Anthony Blunt, Leo Long, and John Cairncross, more authors warmed to the view that the Allied wartime intelligence community had been inhabited largely by Soviet spies and ruthless incompetents. Anti-Nazi plotters in Germany had been undermined by Philby, claimed some, while others suggested that Blunt had been responsible for the tragic losses suffered by SOE's networks in Holland or that he had traveled to Germany to retrieve the Duke of Windsor's letters to Hitler, and that a Communist conspiracy had manipulated information about Yugoslavia so Tito's Partisans could triumph over Draza Mihailovich's Cetniks.

Did MI6 really send agents to their deaths deliberately to promote deception schemes? Was Claude Dansey responsible for waging a campaign against his rivals in SOE that led to wholesale betrayals to the Sicherheitsdienst? Who really assassinated Gen. Wladyslaw Sikorski? Why was the order to convoy PQ-17 to scatter an act of recklessness? Did the OSS plan Adm. Darlan's assassination? Was COBWEB responsible for jeopardizing merchantmen on the Arctic route to Murmansk by luring the *Scharnhorst* into open waters? How did Himmler really die? Was an agent decorated with the Victoria Cross after he sabotaged a Dutch submarine that stumbled across the Japanese carriers heading to Pearl Harbor? Did the Duke of Windsor compromise the Maginot Line by passing its secrets to the Nazi collaborator Charles Bedaux?

No scenario was too improbable or too dastardly to contemplate, but there were plenty eager to fill any historical lacunae with invention. One respected war correspondent wrote convincingly about a Canadian spy sent to France masquerading as a deaf mute; another revealed the existence of a Nazi agent in London code-named DRUID, while a third reported that the headquarters of the Afrika Korps had been penetrated by a British spy who had conveyed Rommel's plans to Monty. Other authors made some astonishing claims about their own supposed exploits behind enemy lines, all of which were entirely fictional, leaving some of the reading public rightly baffled about the integrity of those working in this arcane field. Several women invented secret missions for themselves and one, Josephine Butler, turned out to have been serving a prison sentence for fraud at the very time her book asserted she was bravely parachuting from a Lysander to aid the French resistance. A few insisted that their roles had been so highly classified that only Winston Churchill had known of their covert activities, and even a respected surgeon falsified a series of medical cases to support his tale of having altered the appearances of agents to fool the Gestapo.

These somewhat unreliable witnesses were able to perpetrate their mischief in part because so little authentic material had been made available from official sources. Even the vanquished made the task of discriminating between fact and fiction harder by sanitizing the German version of the clandestine war. The Abwehr's Erwin Lahousen refused to disclose his war diaries for years before he showed them to Gunter Peis, and Walter Schellenberg's memoirs, published with a foreword by Alan Bullock, bear little resemblance to the transcripts of his immediate postwar interrogation, now finally declassified and released. Indeed, Ladislas Farago, who uncovered several steel footlockers in the U.S. National Archives bearing the Hamburg *Abstelle*'s records, concluded that the files were virtually worthless because the best German spies, such as JONNY, FRITZCHEN, ALARIC, and IVAN had turned out to be the MI5 double agents Arthur Owens, Eddie Chapman, Juan Pujol, and Dusan Popov.

Inevitably, at the beginning of the 21st century, there are fewer original wartime memoirs available for publication, and the end of the Cold War and the passage of time have allowed more documents from official sources to undergo declassification. Many of these have had a significant impact on our understanding of what took place in the intelligence war and make the current *Historical Dictionary* series so attractive as a reliable resource, containing data drawn from the very latest releases.

II. REFERENCE WORKS

Blackstock, Paul, and Frank Schaf. *Intelligence, Espionage, Counterespionage and Covert Operations,* Detroit: Gale, 1978.

Constantinides, George. *Intelligence and Espionage: An Analytic Bibliography.* Boulder, Colo.: Westview Press, 1983.

Foot, M. R. D. *Secret Lives.* Oxford: Oxford University Press, 2002.

Kross, Peter. *The Encyclopedia of World War II Spies.* Fort Lee, Va.: Barricade, 2001.

Mahoney, M. H. *Women in Espionage: A Biographical Dictionary.* Santa Barbara, Calif.: ABC-Clio, 1993.

Minnick, Wendell L. *Spies and Provocateurs.* London: McFarland, 1992.

Newton, David E. *Encyclopedia of Cryptology.* Santa Barbara, Calif.: ABC-Clio, 1997.

O'Toole, G. L. A. *The Encyclopedia of American Intelligence and Espionage.* New York. Facts on File, 1988.

Parrish, Michael. *Soviet Security and Intelligence Organizations, 1917–1990.* Westport, Conn.: Greenwood, 1992.

Polmar, Norman, and Thomas Allen. *Spy Book.* New York: Random House, 1997.

Pringle, Robert W. *Historical Dictionary of Russian/Soviet Intelligence.* Lanham, Md.: Scarecrow Press, 2006.

Rocca, Raymon, and John Dziak. *Bibliography on Soviet Intelligence and Security Services.* Boulder, Colo.: Westview Press, 1985.

Turner, Michael A. *Historical Dictionary of United States Intelligence.* Lanham, Md.: Scarecrow Press, 2006.

West, Nigel. *Historical Dictionary of British Intelligence.* Lanham, Md.: Scarecrow Press, 2005.

——. *Historical Dictionary of International Intelligence.* Lanham, Md.: Scarecrow Press, 2006.

III. CANADA

Beeby, Dean. *Cargo of Lies*. Toronto: University of Toronto Press, 1996.

Bothwell, Robert, and J. J. Grantastein. *The Gouzenko Transcripts*. Toronto: Deaneau, 1982.

Bryden, John. *Best-Kept Secret: Canadian Secret Intelligence in the Second World War*. Toronto: Lester, 1993.

Sawatsky, John. *Gouzenko: The Untold Story*. Toronto: Macmillan, 1984.

IV. EUROPE

Bassett. Richard. *Hitler's Spy Chief*. London: Weidenfeld & Nicolson, 2005.

Bazna, Elyesa. *I Was Cicero*. London: André Deutsch, 1962.

Bertrand, Gustave. *Enigma*. Paris: Plon, 1976.

Best, Sigismund Payne. *The Venlo Incident*. London: Hutchinson, 1950.

Brissaud, André. *Canaris*. New York: Grosset & Dunlap, 1974.

Carter, Carolle. *The Shamrock and the Swastika*. Palo Alto, Calif.: Pacific Books, 1977.

Clough, Bryan. *State Secrets*. Hove, Sussex: Hideaway, 2005.

Colvin, Ian. *Chief of Intelligence*. London: Gollancz, 1951.

Cookridge, E. H. *Gehlen: Spy of the Century*. New York: Random House, 1971.

———. *Inside SOE*. London: Arthur Barker, 1966.

Davidson, *Special Operations Europe*. London: Gollancz, 1980.

Delatre, Lucas. *Betraying Hitler*. London: Atlantic Books, 2005.

Dodds-Parker, Douglas. *Setting Europe Ablaze*. London: Springwood, 1983.

Doerries, Reinhard. *Hitler's Last Chief of Foreign Intelligence*. London: Frank Cass, 2003.

Dourlein, Peter. *Inside North Pole*. London: William Kimber, 1953.

Duggan, John. *Herr Hempel at the German Legation in Dublin, 1937–1945*. Dublin: Irish Academic Press, 2003.

Farago, Ladislas. *Game of the Foxes*. New York: McKay, 1973.

Frischauer, Willi. *The Man Who Came Back*. London: Frederick Muller, 1958.

Garlinski, Josef. *Intercept*. London: Dent, 1980.

Gehlen, Reinhard. *The Service*. New York: World, 1972.

Gisevius, Hans Bernt. *To the Bitter End*. London: Jonathan Cape, 1948.

Giskes, Hermann. *London Calling North Pole*. London: William Kimber, 1953.

Höhne, Heinz. *Canaris: Hitler's Master Spy*. New York: Doubleday, 1979.

———. *Codeword Direktor*. London: Secker & Warburg, 1971.

Höhne, Heinz, and Hermann Zolling. *The General Was a Spy*. New York: Coward, McCann, & Geoghegan, 1972.

Hull, Mark M. *Irish Secrets*. Dublin: Irish Academic Press, 2003.

John, Otto. *Twice through the Lines*. New York: Harper & Row, 1972.

Johns, Philip. *Within Two Cloaks*. London: William Kimber, 1979.

Kahn, David. *Hitler's Spies*. New York: Macmillan, 1978.

Marenches, Alexander de. *The Third World War*. New York: Morrow, 1992.

McKay, C. G., and Bengt Beckman. *Swedish Signal Intelligence, 1900–1945*. London: Frank Cass, 2003.

Moravec, Frantisek. *Master of Spies*. London: Bodley Head, 1975.

Moyszich, Ludwig. *Operation Cicero*. London: Wingate, 1950.

O'Halpin, Eunan. *MI5 and Ireland, 1936–1945*. Dublin: Irish Academic Press, 2003.

Paine, Lauren. *The Abwehr*. London: Robert Hale, 1984.

Peis, Günter. *The Man Who Started the War*. London: Odham's Press, 1960.

———. *The Mirror of Deception*. London: Weidenfeld & Nicolson, 1976.

Pirie, Anthony. *Operation Bernhard*. New York: Morrow, 1961.

Porch, Douglas. *The French Secret Service*. New York: Farrar, Straus, & Giroux, 1995.

Putlitz, Wolfgang zu. *The zu Putlitz Dossier*. London: Allan Wingate, 1957.

Rado, Sándor. *Codename Dora*. London: Abelard-Schuman, 1977.

Schellenberg, Walter. *The Schellenberg Memoirs*. London: André Deutsch, 1956.

Stephan, Enno. *Spies in Ireland*. London: Macdonald, 1963.

Stirling, Tessa, Daria Natecz, and Tadeusz Dubicki. *Intelligence Cooperation between Poland and Great Britain during World War II*. London: Valentine Mitchell, 2002.

Valtin, Jan. *Out of the Night*. New York: Garden City, 1941.

Wighton, Charles, and Günter Peis. *Hitler's Spies and Saboteurs*. New York: Henry Holt, 1958.

V. THE FAR EAST

Aldrich, Richard. *Intelligence and the War against Japan*. Cambridge: Cambridge University Press, 2000.

Boyd, Carl. *Hitler's Japanese Confidant: General Oshima Hiroshi and MAGIC Intelligence, 1941–1945*. Lawrence: University Press of Kansas, 1993.

Clarke, Ronald. *The Man Who Broke Purple*. London: Weidenfeld & Nicolson, 1993.

Deakin, F. W., and G. R. Storry. *The Case of Richard Sorge*. London: Chatto & Windus, 1966.

Drea, Edward J. *MacArthur's Ultra*. Lawrence: University Press of Kansas, 1993.

Elphick, Peter. *Far Eastern File*. London: Hodder & Stoughton, 1997.

Elphick, Peter, and Michael Smith. *Odd Man Out*. London: Hodder & Stoughton, 1993.

Ind, Allison. *Allied Intelligence Bureau*. New York: David McKay, 1958.

Komatsu, Keiichiro. *Origins of the Pacific War and the Importance of "Magic."* New York: St. Martin's Press, 1999.

Matthews, Tony. *Shadows Dancing*. New York: St. Martin's Press, 1993.

Meissner, Hans-Otto. *The Man with Three Faces*. New York: Rinehart, 1955.

Mercado, Stephen. *The Shadow Warriors of Nakano*. Washington, D.C.: Brassey's, 2002.

Prados, John. *Combined Fleet Decoded*. New York: Random House, 1995.

Spector, Ronald. *Listening to the Enemy*. Wilmington, Del.: Scholarly Resources, 1988.

Stripp, Alan. *Codebreaker in the Far East*. London: Frank Cass, 1989.

U.S. Department of Defense. *The "Magic" Background to Pearl Harbor*. Washington, D.C.: GPO, 1977.

Whymant, Robert. *Stalin's Spy*. London: I. B. Tauris, 1996.

Willoughby, Charles. *Shanghai Conspiracy*. New York: E. P. Dutton, 1952.

VI. GREAT BRITAIN

Andrew, Christopher. *Secret Service*. London: Heinemann, 1985.

Babington-Smith, Constance. *Air Spy*. New York: Harper Brothers, 1957.

Bazna, Elyesa. *I Was Cicero*. London: André Deutsch, 1962.

Beesley, Partick. *Very Special Intelligence*. London: Greenhill, 2000.

Beevor, Jack. *SOE Reflections*. London: Bodley Head, 1981.

Bennett, Gill. *Churchill's Man of Mystery*. London: Routledge, 2006.

Best, Sigismund Payne. *The Venlo Incident*. London: Hutchinson, 1950.

Booth, Nicholas. *Zigzag*. London: Portrait Books, 2007.

Borovik, Genrihk. *The Philby Files*. London: Little, Brown, 1994.

Bower, Tom. *The Perfect English Spy*. London: Heinemann, 1995.

Bristow, Desmond. *A Game of Moles*. London: Little, Brown, 1993.

Cairncross, John. *The Enigma Spy*. London: Century, 1997.

Calvocoressi, Peter. *Top Secret Ultra*. London: Cassell, 1980.

Carter, Miranda. *Anthony Blunt: His Lives*. New York: Farrar, Straus, & Giroux, 2001.

Cave Brown, Anthony. *Bodyguard of Lies*. London: W. H. Allen, 1976.

——. *C: The Secret Servant*. London: Michael Joseph, 1998.

Cookridge, E. H. *Inside SOE*. London: Arthur Barker, 1966.

Costello, John. *Mask of Treachery*. London: Collins, 1988.

Davidson, Basil. *Special Operations Europe*. London: Gollancz, 1980.

Delmer, Sefton. *Counterfeit Spy*. London: Hutchinson, 1973.

Denniston, Robin. *Thirty Secret Years*. Clifton-upon-teme, Worcestershire, England: Polperro Heritage Trust, 2007.

Dodds-Parker, Douglas. *Setting Europe Ablaze*. London: Springwood, 1983.

Driberg, Tom. *Guy Burgess*. London: Weidenfeld & Nicolson, 1956.

Elliott, Geoffrey. *I Spy*. London: St. Ermin's, 1998.

Farago, Ladislas. *Game of the Foxes*. New York: McKay, 1973.

Foot, M. R. D. *SOE in France*. London: HMSO, 1966.

Frank, Charles. *Operation Epsilon: The Farm Hall Transcripts*. London: IOP, 1993.

Fuller, Jean Overton. *The Starr Affair*. London: Gollancz, 1954.

Garlinski, Josef. *Intercept*. London: Dent, 1980.

Hesketh, Roger. *Operation FORTITUDE*. London: St. Ermin's, 2000.

Hinsley, F. H. *British Intelligence in the Second World War*. London: HMSO, 1979.

Hodges, Andrew. *Alan Turing: The Enigma*. London: Burnett Books, 1983.

Howarth, Patrick. *The Shetland Bus*. London: Thomas Nelson, 1951.

Hyde, H. Montgomery. *Secret Intelligence Agent*. New York: St. Martin's Press, 1982.

Johns, Philip. *Within Two Cloaks*. London: William Kimber, 1979.

Kahn, David. *The Codebreakers*. London: Weidenfeld & Nicolson, 1967.

———. *Seizing the Enigma: The Race to Break the German U-Boat Codes, 1939–1943*. Boston: Houghton Mifflin, 1991.

Lewin, Ronald. *Ultra Goes to War*. New York: McGraw Hill, 1978.

Lovell, Mary S. *Cast No Shadow*. New York: Pantheon Books, 1992.

Macintyre, Ben. *Agent Zigzag*, London: Bloomsbury, 2007.

Mackenzie, William. *The Secret History of SOE*. London: St. Ermin's, 2000.

Masterman. J. C. *The Double Cross System of the War of 1939–1945*. New Haven, Conn.: Yale University Press, 1972.

Masters, Anthony. *The Man Who Was M*. Oxford: Basil Blackwell, 1984.

May, Ernest, ed. *Knowing One's Enemies*. Princeton, N.J.: Princeton University Press, 1984.

Moen, Jan. *John Moe: Double Agent*. Edinburgh: Mainstream, 1986.

Montagu, Ewen. *Beyond Top Secret U*. New York: Coward, McCann, & Geoghegan, 1978.

———. *The Man Who Never Was*. London: Evans Bros., 1955.

Moss, Norman. *Klaus Fuchs*. London: Grafton Books, 1987.

Moyszich, Ludwig. *Operation Cicero*. London: Wingate, 1950.

Nesbit, Ray Conyers. *Eyes of the RAF*. Stroud, England: Sutton, 1996.

O'Halpin, Eunan. *MI5 and Ireland, 1936–1945*. Dublin: Irish Academic Press, 2003.

Page, Bruce, Phillip Knightley, and David Leitch. *The Philby Conspiracy*. New York: Doubleday, 1968.

Peebles, Curtis. *Shadow Flights*. Santa Barbara, Calif.: Presidio, 2000.

Penrose, Barry, and Simon Freeman. *Conspiracy of Silence*. London: Grafton, 1986.

Philby, Eleanor. *The Spy I Loved*. London: Hamish Hamilton, 1967.

Philby, Kim. *My Silent War*. London: McGibbon & Kee, 1968.

Philby, Rufina. *The Private Life of Kim Philby*. London: St. Ermin's, 1999.

Popov, Dusko, *SpyCounterspy*. London: Weidenfeld & Nicolson, 1974.

Pujol, Juan, with Nigel West. *Garbo*. London: Weidenfeld, 1985.

Richards, Brooks. *Secret Flotillas*. London: HMSO, 2004.

Ring, Jim. *We Came Unseen*. London: John Murray, 2001.

Seale, Patrick, and Maureen McConville. *Philby: The Long Road to Moscow*. London: Hamish Hamilton, 1973.

Seaman, Mark. *Garbo: The Spy Who Saved D-Day*. London: Public Record Office, 2000.

Scotland, A. P. *The London Cage*. London: Evans Bros., 1957.

Smith, Michael. *Foley: The Spy Who Saved 10,000 Jews*. London: Hodder & Stoughton, 1999.

Stirling, Tessa, Daria Natecz, and Tadeusz Dubicki. *Intelligence Cooperation between Poland and Great Britain during World War II*. London: Valentine Mitchell, 2002.

Strong, Kenneth. *Men of Intelligence*. London: Cassell, 1970.

Sweet-Escott, Bickham. *Baker Street Irregular*. London: Methuen, 1965.

Wheatley, Dennis, *The Deception Planners*. London: Hutchinson, 1980.

Whitwell, John. *British Agent*. London: William Kimer, 1966.

Williams, Robert Chadwell. *Klaus Fuchs, Atom Spy*. Cambridge, Mass.: Harvard University Press, 1987.

Winterbotham, Frederick. *The Ultra Secret*. London: Weidenfeld & Nicolson, 1974.

Wright, Peter. *Spycatcher*. New York: Viking, 1987.

VII. LATIN AMERICA

Artuco, Hugo Fernandez. *The Nazi Underground in South America*. New York: Farrar & Reinhart, 1942.

Hilton, Stanley E. *Hitler's Secret War in South America, 1939–1945*. Baton Rouge: Louisiana State University Press, 1981.

Rout, Leslie B., and John F. Bratzel. *The Shadow War*. Frederick, Md.: University Press of America, 1986.

VIII. THE MIDDLE EAST

Clarke, Dudley. *Seven Assignments*. London: Cape, 1948.
Mure, David. *Practise to Deceive*. London: William Kimber, 1977.

IX. THE PACIFIC

Ballard, Geoffrey St. Vincent. *On Ultra Active Service*. Richmond, Victoria, Australia: Spectrum, 1991.
Bennett, J. W., W. A. Hobart, and J. B. Spitzer. *Intelligence and Cryptanalytic Activities of the Japanese during World War II*. Laguna Hills, Calif.: Aegean Park Press, 1986.
Bleakley, Jack. *The Eavesdroppers*. Melbourne, Australia: Brown Prior, 1992.
Davis, Burke. *Get Yamamoto*. New York: Random House, 1969.
Hansen, James H. *Japanese Intelligence: The Competitive Edge*. Washington, D.C.: National Intelligence Book Center, 1996.
Holmes, W. J. *Double-Edged Secrets*. Annapolis, Md.: Naval Institute Press, 1979.
Lewin, Ronald. *The Other Ultra*. London: Hutchinson, 1982.
Phillips, Claire, and Myron B. Goldsmith. *Manila Espionage*. Portland, Or.: Binfords & Mont, 1947.
Smith, Bradley. *The Ultra-Magic Deals*. Novato, Calif.: Presidio Press, 1993.
Smith, Michael. *The Emperor's Codes*. London: Transworld, 2000.
Zacharia, Ellis M. *Secret Missions*. New York: G. P. Putnam, 1946.

X. THE SOVIET UNION

Damaskin, Igor. *Kitty Harris: The Spy with Seventeen Names*. London: St. Ermin's, 2001.
Driberg, Tom. *Guy Burgess*. London: Weidenfeld & Nicolson, 1956.
Dziak, John. *Chekisty: A History of the KGB*. Lexington, Mass.: Lexington Books, 1988.
Feklisov, Alexander. *The Man behind the Rosenbergs*. New York: Enigma, 2001.

Foote, Alexander. *Handbook for Spies*. London: Museum Press, 1964.
Glantz, David. *Soviet Military Intelligence in War*. London: Fank Cass, 1990.
Kesaris, Paul, ed. *The Rote Kapelle*. Frederick, Md.: University Press of America, 1973.
Knight, Amy. *Beria: Stalin's First Lieutenant*. Princeton, N.J.: Princeton University Press, 1993.
Knightley, Philip. *Philby: KGB Masterspy*. London: Jonathan Cape, 1997.
Modin, Yuri. *My Five Cambridge Friends*. London: Headline, 1994.
Perrault, Gilles. *The Red Orchestra*. London: Arthur Barker, 1968.
Rado, Sándor. *Codename Dora*. London: Abelard-Schuman, 1977.
Seale, Patrick, and Maureen McConville. *Philby: The Long Road to Moscow*. London: Hamish Hamilton, 1973.
Sudoplatov, Pavel. *Special Tasks*. London: Little, Brown, 1994.
Werner, Ruth. *Sonia's Report*. London: Chatto & Windus, 1991.

XI. THE UNITED STATES

Albright, Joseph, and Marica Kunstel. *Bombshell*. New York: Random House, 1997.
Barron, Robert Louis, and Michael Warner, eds. *Venona: Soviet Espionage and the American Response, 1939–1957*. Washington, D.C.: National Security Agency/Central Intelligence Agency, 1996.
Bentley, Elizabeth. *Out of Bondage*. New York: Ivy Books, 1988.
Breindel, Eric, and Herbert Romerstein. *The Venona Secret*. New York: HarperCollins, 1999.
British Security Coordination. London: St. Ermin's, 1998.
Brook-Shepherd, Gordon. *The Storm Petrels*. London: Collins, 1977.
Cave Brown, Anthony. *The Last Hero*. New York: Time Books, 1982.
Chambers, Whittaker. *Witness*. New York: Random House, 1932.
Colby, William, and Peter Forbath. *Honorable Men*. New York: Simon & Schuster, 1978.
Dallin, David. *Soviet Espionage*. New Haven, Conn.: Yale University Press, 1955.
Dulles, Allen. *The Craft of Intelligence*. New York: Harper & Row, 1963.
Feklisov, Alexander. *The Man behind the Rosenbergs*. New York: Enigma Books, 2001.
Gazur, Edward. *Alexander Orlov: The FBI's KGB General*. London: St. Ermin's, 2002.
Granovsky, Anatoli. *I Was an NKVD Agent*. New York: Devlin Adair, 1962.
Halperin, Maurice. *Cold War Exile*. Columbia: University of Missouri Press, 1995.

Haynes, John Earl, and Harvey Klehr. *Venona: Decoding Soviet Espionage in America*. New Haven, Conn.: Yale University Press, 1999.

Hyde, H. Montgomery. *Room 3603*. New York: Farrar, Straus, 1962.

Karlow, Peter. *The OSS War Report*. New York: Walker, 1996.

Kern, Gary. *A Death in Washington*. New York: Enigma Books, 2004.

Kessler, Lauren. *Clever Girl*. New York: HarperCollins, 2003.

Klehr, Harvey, and John Haynes. *The Secret World of American Communism*. New Haven, Conn.: Yale University Press, 1995.

Krivitsky, Walter. *In Stalin's Secret Service*. New York: Harper Brothers, 1939.

Lewin, Ronald. *The American Magic*. New York: Farrar, Straus, & Giroux, 1982.

Massing, Hede. *This Deception*. London: Sloane & Pearce, 1951.

Morros, Boris. *My Ten Years as a Counterspy*. New York: Viking Press, 1959.

Olmsted, Kathryn. *Red Spy Queen*. Chapel Hill: University of North Carolina Press, 2002.

Orlov, Alexander. *Handbook of Intelligence and Guerrilla Warfare*. Ann Arbor: University of Michigan Press, 1965.

———. *The Secret History of Stalin's Crimes*. New York: Random House, 1953.

Persico, Joseph. *Piercing the Reich*. New York: Viking, 1979.

Rees, David. *Harry Dexter White: A Study in Paradox*. New York: Coward, McCann, & Geoghegan, 1973.

Roberts, Sam. *The Brother*. New York: Random House, 2001.

Roosevelt, Kermit. *The Overseas Targets*. New York: Walker, 1976.

Scrodes, James. *Allen Dulles: Master of Spies*. Washington, D.C.: Regnery, 1999.

Smith, R. Harris. *OSS*. Berkeley: University of California Press, 1972.

Troy, Thomas. *Donovan and the CIA*. Frederick, Md.: Alethia Books, 1981.

Turrou, Leon. *The Nazi Conspiracy in America*. London: George Harrap, 1939.

Weinstein, Allen, and Alexander Vassiliev. *The Haunted Wood*. New York: Random House, 1999.

Winks, Robin. *Cloak and Gown*. New York: Morrow, 1987.

Yardley, Herbert. *The American Black Chamber*. Indianapolis, Ind.: Bobbs-Merrill, 1931.

Index

Note: Entries in all capital letters refer to operations.

212 Committee, 244

A-3, 1
A-54, 52
Abakumov, Georgi, 266
Abakumov, Viktor S., 211, 228–29
Abbiate, Roland, 268
Abbott, G. W., 110
Abwehr, xvii, 1–2
ACCOST, 2
Acheson, Dean, 237
Action, 18
ADA, 104
Adams, Donald, 41
ADDICT, 2
Adlercreutz, Carlos, 244
Admiral Graf Spee, xv, 3–6
ADMIRALTY, 240
"A" Force, 6, 38
Agiraki, Anna, 92
AGNES, 201
Akhmedov, Ismael, 6
Alacazar de Velasco, Angel, 6, 14
Aladren, José Maria, 14
ALARIC, 6, 190
ALBERT, 94
ALBERTO, 36
Alblas, Aart, 163–64
ALEK, 266
ALERT, 51

ALEXANDER, 267
ALEXANDRE, 52
ALFREDO, 28, 184
Algiers, 6
ALLIANCE, 6–7, 221
Allied Intelligence Bureau (AIB), 7
Almanna Sakerhetstjantsen, 245
Almasy, Count Laszlo, 131
ALMURA, 190
ALTE, 206
Alto Estado Mayor (AEM), 234
Amé, Caesar, 224
AMICOL, 7
Amtorg, 263
ANDERSON, 7
ANDRIES, 95
Andringa, Leonard, 160
ANDROS, 7
ANGEL ONE, 7
Ankara, 7–8
ANNA, 49, 204
Anthell, Henry W., xv, 8
ANTHONY, xviii, 8
ANTONIO, 132
ANVIL, 8
Aosta, Duke of, 38
APOSTLE, 8
APPRENTICE, 8–9
Apresyan, Stepan Z., 157–58, 268
ARABEL, 9

283

BRUTUS, xvi, 35, 39
Bruyne, M. R. de, 67
Bryan, Dan, 91
Bryce, Ivar, 29
Buck, Herbert, 78
Budenz, Louis, 77
Buizer, Johannes, 161
Bukkens, Sjef, 162
BUNBURY, xvii
Bundespolizei (BUPO), xvii, xix,
    xvi, 36, 85, 86, 195, 201–3, 246
Burdeyron, Noel, 112–13
Bureau Centrale de Renseignements
    et d'Action (BCRA), 60
Bureau Inlichingen, 67
Burgess, Guy, 37
Burney, Christopher, 113
Büro Ha, 246
Büro Wagner, 82

C, 36
CAESARO, 4
Cairncross, John, xv, 27, 37, 96, 134,
    178, 264, 272
Cairo, 37–38
Calthrop, Edward, 18
Calvo, Luis, xvi
CAMILLA, 38
CAMOUFLAGE, 38
Camp 020, 39
Camp 020R, 39
Camp, Eric Gardiner, 38
Camp Z, 39
Campos, Arsenio Martinez de, 234
Canada, 40
Canaris, Erika, 41
Canaris, Wilhelm, xvii, xviii, xi, 1–2,
    40–41, 93, 121, 135, 201, 239,
    246, 270, 272
Canning, Albert, 34
Cape Matapan, Battle of, 41–42, 270
CAPRICORN, 42

Carboni, Giacomo, 225
CARBUNCLE, 42
Cardozo, 260
CARELESS, 42
Caroli, Gósta, 42–43, 214, 244
Carr, Fred, 264
Carré, Mathilde, xvii, 43–44, 109–12
CARROT, 44
CARVALHO, 189
CELERY, xv, 44
Central Bureau, 44–45
Central Intelligence Agency (CIA),
    237, 252
Central Intelligence Group (CIG), 237
Centrale Inlichtingendienst, 67
CEREUS, 60
Cervell, Frank, 123
CHARIOT, 112
CHARLIE, 45
CHARON, 157
CHEESE, 45
CHER BEBÉ, 45
Chichayev, Ivan, 157
Chidson, Monty, 8
Chief, 45
Chile, 45–47
China, 47
Chojnacki, Szczesny, 246
CHOPIN, 36
Christiansen, Niels Christian, 238
Churchill, Winston, 47
CICERO, xvii, 47
Ciezki, Maksymilian, 24
Circuit, 47
Clamorgan, Lt., xvi, 152
Clarke, Dudley, 6, 38, 84, 270
CLAYMORE, 47
Clayton, Illtyd, 37, 150
Clegg, Hugh, 76, 106
CLEVER GIRL, 20
COBWEB, 48
Codrington, John, 94

Godfrey, John, xvi, 34, 60, 96
Godot-la-Loi, Guy, 100
Goerdeler, Karl, 201
Goertz, Hermann, 40, 68, 91, 113–14
Gold, Harry, 257, 264
Goldschmidt, Helmut, 156, 176
Golikov, Filip I., 99
Gollnow, Herbert, 207
Golos, Jakob, 20, 126
GOOSE, 96
Gorskaya, Elizaveta, 267
Gorsky, Anatoli, 20, 21, 96, 157, 178, 268
Gouzenko, Igor, 100, 265, 266
Government Communications Headquarters (GCHQ), 96–97
Graf, Georges, 15, 39, 94, 97–98, 181
Grand, Laurence, 98
GRANT, 265
Graur, André, 96, 238, 236
Green, Oliver, 98, 100
Greene, Benjamin, 131, 147–48
Greenglass, David, 74
GREIF, 98
Griesky, Hans-Wilhelm von, 253
GRILLO, 30
Grimm, Hans, 260
Grosjean, Roger, 79
Grosse, Kurt, 96, 98
Grossvogel, Leon, 98–99, 142, 207, 208, 210, 251
Groupe de Protection, 257
Groussard, Georges, 257
Groves, Leslie, 143
GRU, 99
Gubbins, Colin, 57, 238
Gudgeon, USS, xvi, 100
Guehrle, Emil, 189
GUINEA, xvii, 100
GUN, 100

Guryevich, Viktor, 100–102
GUSTAVO, 102
Guthrie, Keith, 114
GUY FAWKES, xvi, 102
G.W., 102

Haas, Jan De, 160
Haberfield, Harold D., 88
Haines, Jasper, 155
Haldane, J. B. S., 103, 108
Hall, Robert, 126
Hall, Theodore ("Ted"), 257, 264
Hall, Virginia, 112
Hallamaa, Reino, 81–82
Halperin, Israel, 266
Hambro, Sir Charles, 238
Hamburger, Rudi, 133, 230
Hamburger, Willi, 55, 103, 114
Hamel, Olga, 203
HAMLET, 103
Hampshire, Stuart, 194
Hanako, Mikaya, 231
Hanau, Julius, 222
Hankey, Lord, xv
HANS, 103
Hansen, Georg, 2
Hardouin, Roger, 85
Harker, Jasper, 58, 60, 103, 146, 223
HARLEQUIN, 103
Harmel, Lodo van, 158
Harnisch, Hans Leo, 9–10
Harris, Arthur, 123
Harris, Kitty, 49, 103–4, 141
Harris, Tomas, 120, 189, 227, 269, 270
Hart, Herbert, 15, 104
Hart, Jenifer, 104
HATCHET, 104
Hattem, Johan van, 158
HAT TRICK, xvii, 104
Hatz, Ottto, 61

About the Author

Nigel West is a military historian specializing in intelligence and security issues. While still at university, he worked as a researcher for two authors: Ronald Seth, who had been parachuted into Silesia by Special Operations Executive, and Richard Deacon, a former wartime naval intelligence officer and later the foreign editor of *The Sunday Times*. He later joined BBC-TV's General Features department to work on the *Spy!* and *Escape* series.

West's first book, coauthored with Richard Deacon in 1980, was the book of the *Spy!* series and was followed by other nonfiction: *British Security Service Operations, 1909–1945* (1981); *A Matter of Trust: MI5, 1945–1972* (1982); *MI6: British Secret Intelligence Service Operations, 1909–1945* (1983); *The Branch: A History of the Metropolitan Police Special Branch* (1983); *Unreliable Witness: Espionage Myths of the Second World War* (1984); *Garbo* (coauthored with Juan Pujol, 1985); *GCHQ: The Secret Wireless War* (1986); *Molehunt* (1987); *The Friends: Britain's Postwar Secret Intelligence Operations* (1988); *Games of Intelligence* (1989); *Seven Spies Who Changed the World* (1991); *Secret War: The Story of SOE* (1992); *The Faber Book of Espionage* (1993); *The Illegals* (1993); *The Faber Book of Treachery* (1995); *The Secret War for the Falklands* (1997); *Counterfeit Spies* (1998); *Crown Jewels* (with Oleg Tsarev, 1998); *Venona: The Greatest Secret of the Cold War* (1999); *The Third Secret* (2000); *Mortal Crimes* (2004); *The Guy Liddell Diaries* (2005); *MASK* (2005); *Historical Dictionary of British Intelligence* (Scarecrow, 2005); *Historical Dictionary of International Intelligence* (Scarecrow, 2006); and *Historical Dictionary of Cold War Counterintelligence* (Scarecrow, 2007).

In 1989, West was voted the Experts' Expert by a panel of spy writers selected by the *Observer*. He is the European editor of the *International*

Journal of Intelligence and Counterintelligence and teaches the history of postwar intelligence at the Center for Counterintelligence and Security Studies in Alexandria, Virginia. In October 2003, he was awarded the U.S. Association of Former Intelligence Officers first Lifetime Literature Achievement Award.